In Other Words

What we say always consists of prior words, structures and meanings that are combined in new ways and re-used in new contexts for new listeners. In this book, Deborah Schiffrin looks at two important tasks of language – presenting 'who' we are talking about, (the referent) and 'what happened' to them (their actions and attributes) in a narrative – and explores how this presentation alters in relation to emergent forms and meanings. Drawing on examples from both face-to-face talk and public discourse, she analyses a variety of repairs, reformulations of referents, and retellings of narratives, ranging from word-level repairs within a single turn-at-talk, to life story narratives told years apart. Bringing together work from conversation analysis, interactional socio-linguistics, cognitive linguistics, semantics, pragmatics, and variation analysis, *In Other Words* will be invaluable for scholars wishing to understand the many different factors that underlie the shaping and reshaping of discourse over time, place and person.

DEBORAH SCHIFFRIN is Professor of Linguistics and Chair of the Department of Linguistics at Georgetown University. She has previously published *Discourse Markers* (Cambridge University Press, 1988), *Approaches to Discourse* (1994), *Meaning, Form and Use in Context* (1984), and *The Handbook of Discourse Analysis* (2001). She is on the advisory board of *Cambridge Approaches to Linguistics*, and on the editorial board of several journals, including *Language in Society*.

Uses "text" + "textual worlds"
with conversation. (see 209)
Schiffrin 1994a: C 10

Form Cont, p. 160 "story world"
164

Studies in Interactional Sociolinguistics

EDITORS
Paul Drew, Marjorie Harness Goodwin, John J. Gumperz,
Deborah Schiffrin

In Other Words

Variation in reference and narrative

DEBORAH SCHIFFRIN
Georgetown University

CAMBRIDGE
UNIVERSITY PRESS

CAMBRIDGE UNIVERSITY PRESS
Cambridge, New York, Melbourne, Madrid, Cape Town, Singapore, São Paulo

Cambridge University Press
The Edinburgh Building, Cambridge, CB2 2RU, UK

Published in the United States of America by Cambridge University Press, New York

www.cambridge.org
Information on this title: www.cambridge.org/9780521484749

© Deborah Schiffrin 2006

First published 2006

Printed in the United Kingdom at the University Press, Cambridge

A catalogue record for this book is available from the British Library

ISBN-13   978-0-521-48159-5 hardback
ISBN-10   0-521-48159-7 hardback
ISBN-13   978-0-521-48474-9 paperback
ISBN-10   0-521-48474-X paperback

For Laura

Contents

Figures

Tables

Preface

There is a sense in which each event in our life is new and unique, just as each sentence in our language is one of an infinite variety of possible sentences. Yet there is also another quite different sense in which both events and sentences are recurrences – reiterations, replays, reminders – of earlier instantiations of life and language. Not only can we speak of *déjà vu* experiences when we feel that we are reliving something that has happened before, for example, but our days are often organized by routines and schedules; we follow scripts; we learn how do things by repeating them. And although our sentences may be filled with different words, and their constituents differently arranged and combined, they all follow the implicit rules of our grammar.

These two perspectives on 'same' and 'different' bring to mind something that my husband Louis once casually mentioned to me several years ago as a way to characterize people. Although Louis cannot now remember where he heard (or read) it – just as I cannot remember exactly when, how, where or why he mentioned it to me – we both remember the gist of what he said. It was this: the world can be divided into two kinds of people, either lumpers (who focus on similarities) or splitters (who focus on differences). Louis could firmly characterize himself as a splitter, in both his everyday life and his work. But I immediately began to wonder which characterization described me and my work as a linguist. Do I focus on similarities? or differences?

Consider, for example, that what I said in my initial statement implies that I lump things together. My use of the term *just as* brought together two different kinds of entities: events in our lives and sentences in a language. But I also wonder whether this lumping together of action and knowledge is justified. Notice that the equivalence depends on the newness and uniqueness of events being similar to what seems to be the infinite reach of sentences. But is this enough to justify an overall lumping of events and sentences together?

Instead of focusing on the huge variety of both phenomena, I could just as easily highlight their differences. Consider, for example, the issue of boundaries: whereas events sometimes flow into other events with no formal boundaries separating them, sentences have beginnings and ends that firmly establish their structural integrity. Or take the material/concrete vs. mental/abstract foci. The uniqueness of each event plays out physically in a world in which 'what happens' is situated in different times, places, with different participants, with different co-occurring and adjacent events, and within different background contexts. But the infinite variety of sentences – at least as they are conceptualized by theoretical linguists – does not unfold in a material world of action and reaction: it remains a potential of our implicit knowledge of language. Do these differences obviate the importance of the similarities?

Deciding what is the same and what is different underlies a great deal of work in linguistics. *In other words* joins this discussion by focusing on how we redo references, to both entities and events, that are the same in some ways (they may evoke the same person or occurrence), but different in others: the word, phrase or sentence may shift, as may the text and interaction that provides (and creates) context. Also different is the amount of material that is redone, ranging from forms as brief as the indefinite article *a* to those as long as a narrative that is part of a life story. Not surprisingly, the time span separating an initial occurrence (of an article, a noun, a narrative) from subsequent occurrences also differs: whereas some nominal references are separated by a second, the retelling of a life story can be separated by years. And whereas contexts may remain pretty much the same for some redoings (e.g. repeating a noun that is being repaired), they may change drastically for others (e.g. retelling a narrative to a different audience ten years later).

Despite these differences, each chapter in *In other words* concerns the redoing of something that is, in some important sense, roughly the same. After describing how linguists (and others interested in language, text, and interaction) work with both implicit and explicit notions of sameness and difference (Chapter 1), we turn to repairs of problematic referrals that adjust either *what* entity is evoked, or *how* an entity is evoked using different words (Chapter 2), repetitions (or alterations) of the definite (*the*) or indefinite (*a*) article prior to a noun (Chapter 3), repackaging a referent from noun to clause or sequence to reset its information status for a recipient, and using a variety of linguistically different, but pragmatically similar, clauses to evoke referents (Chapter 4), reissuing mentions of 'who' in referring sequences in different genres (Chapter 5), reframing 'what' and 'where' in a narrative (Chapter 6), redoing the structure of a narrative (Chapter 7) and reusing referrals in recurrent narratives (Chapter 8). A summary is in Chapter 9. Although each chapter stands on its own – and can be read on its own – taken together, they highlight how speakers resolve tensions between continuity (saying the 'same thing') and change (adapting the 'same thing' to new circumstances) during both short term (moment by moment) and long term (year by year) processes of text and talk in interaction.

The data from which I draw in many of the studies of redoings and replays in this volume result from my involvement (as a graduate student) in William Labov's research project on linguistic change and variation in Philadelphia – a study completed by Labov and his students more than twenty years ago. I have continued to rely upon these data not so much as a source of data for my more recent work, but in my teaching of sociolinguistic field methods at Georgetown. Each time that I take a small section from an interview with those whose words I once knew so well – Henry, Zelda, Irene, Jack, Freda and their neighbors – I am astonished at how useful the data continue to be and how much I missed in my earlier studies!

A question of focus, certainly: we all have to pick certain phenomena to study and thereby exclude others. But it is not just focus. When I began my study of discourse markers for my 1982 dissertation, discourse analysis was still in its early stages of development. So much is now grist for the discourse analytic mill, that the words of the speakers whose voices quickly become familiar again each time I rehear them, are now telling me new things. Of course not all of them can be reported and analyzed here. Although the reader will find some excerpts from those whom I have studied before, there are still many phenomena that will be left untapped: the pervasive turn co-constructions of Jan and Ira, or overlaps of Jack and Freda, that construct two such different marital styles; the underlying logic of

Henry's or Jack's argumentation (so different, but each so eloquent); the ideology of child rearing (including the role of gender) that Zelda presents; the construction of friendship between Henry and Irene; the theories of race, ethnicity and religion that are tested out by the couples and among neighbors.

When my interests shifted from discourse markers to the study of grammar and interaction, I turned to additional interviews from Labov's Philadelphia data. I was fortunate enough to receive a National Science Foundation grant (BNS-8819845) to study topic-related variation: how 'what we are talking about' is reflected in (cf. constrains) the internal configuration of a sentence. My analytic goals focused on different levels of 'aboutness.' One level was at the entity level, typically encoded through nouns and often in subject position in a sentence. Another level was at the proposition level: what propositions could be taken as 'given' and whether that had an impact on clause order.

The former interest led me to explore the vast literature on reference and referring terms, partially summarized in Chapter 1 and the topic of several chapters. The latter interest – on givenness at the propositional level – was further nurtured during the time I spent at University of California, Berkeley (1991–1993) where I became familiar not only with the cognitive linguistic perspectives of George Lakoff and Eve Sweetser, but also with the work of Elizabeth Traugott (from Stanford) on grammaticalization, Robin Lakoff, who helped me incorporate a more broadly based view of social and cultural processes into my work, and Suzanne Fleischman, from whom I expanded my view of narrative. These frameworks have worked their way most explicitly into part of one chapter in this book on pragmatic prototypes (Chapter 5), but they also appear in my analysis of lists (in Chapter 4) and my attention to the subtle linguistic changes in narrative retellings (Chapters 6, 7).

The NSF grant noted above has contributed to the current volume in another important way: data. I added to my original corpus of sociolinguistic interviews with seven lower middle class Jewish Americans, an additional set of eleven interviews with working class Italian Americans and Irish Americans who had been interviewed by Anne Bower. Also added was a smaller set of two interviews with middle class suburbanites (interviewed by Arvilla Payne), whose ethnic identity was not a salient part of their everyday lives, identities and relationships. Although I did not "get to know" these people as well as the initial group that I had interviewed, their family discussions, stories of family and neighborhood life, moral dilemmas and means of co-participating in an interview have greatly enhanced my knowledge of ways of speaking.

The chapters on narrative in this book use different data and adapt somewhat different analytical approaches. My Georgetown colleague Ralph Fasold has pointed out that in addition to seeking different kinds of information about language, Linguistics also represents different modes of inquiry. He has characterized my work as using both a humanistic mode of inquiry (roughly akin to that used in literary work and recent anthropology) and a social scientific mode of inquiry (involving quantitative measurements). This makes sense to me. In fact, not just a humanistic approach, but the human side of language – how it helps people configure, manage and understand their lives – is one of the underlying attractions of the study of language for me. Yet I have also always been intrigued by the idea that there are systematic patterns (possibly quantifiable), of which we are unaware, at different levels of language (sound, form, meaning) that underlie what we say, what we mean and what we do in virtually all realms of our lives.

The effort to join the humanistic with the social scientific modes of inquiry underlies all of the articles in this book, but it is especially pertinent to those that focus more on narrative, especially narratives from oral histories of the Holocaust. I had grown up knowing about the Holocaust, and my sociolinguistic interviews with Jewish Americans often turned to topics of Jewish concern (intermarriage, anti-Semitism, Jewish history). When I learned about Holocaust oral history projects, I wondered what kind of discourse would be found there. My curiosity about this grew and I was lucky enough to be awarded a research fellowship at the Center for Advanced Holocaust Study at the United States Holocaust Memorial Museum in Fall 2000, assisted by a Senior Faculty Research Grant from Georgetown University. There I was immersed in a community of scholars (mostly historians and political scientists) whose reliance on a wide array of texts helped me put the 'telling of personal experience' into very different analytical and interpretive contexts.

Finally, I am fortunate to be part of the Georgetown community of linguists, whose ecumenical view of linguistics has for so long

incorporated sociolinguistics (including discourse analysis and variation studies, as well as cultural approaches to language and other
modalities of communication) into its canon. As usual, I am grateful for the support of Georgetown University for several Summer
Research Grants at different stages of this work, and to numerous
students who have helped with transcription, coding, organization
and editing: Marie Troy, Virgina Zavela, Zina Haj-Hasan, Winnie Or, Anne Schmidt, Aida Premilovac, Shanna Gonzales Estigoy,
Jennifer McFadden, Inge Stockburger and Margaret Toye. And of
course I am grateful (as always) for the support of my family (especially Louis and David) and friends, including those in San Francisco
and Washington D.C. An extra special thank you goes to my daughter Laura, who has brought immeasurable joy to all of us. I promised
her that this book would be dedicated to her, and so it is.

1

Variation

1.1 Introduction

Creativity and innovation appear in many different guises and on various levels of language, including sound, form, meaning and use. Instead of asking for *Cheerios* or *cereal* for breakfast, for example, my daughter blended them together and asked for *Cheerial*; when talking to some friends from a different region in the United States, my husband asked *y'all want to join us?* (rather than his own typical form *you want to join us?*); when describing a person who lived in our neighborhood, my son once coined the term *back door neighbor* to complement the term *next door neighbor*.

Linguistic creativity and innovation abound (even outside of my own immediate family!). For example, a speaker may know exactly about whom s/he is thinking when beginning a story about a specific person. But s/he may need to create a way to describe that person to an addressee that is more informative than the pronoun *she*, e.g. through a descriptive clause such as *she– y'know that woman that I met when I went with Laura, last weekend, to that festival at Glen Echo?* that actually tells a mini-story. And although we all have routine ways of asking for the salt (*Can you pass the salt?* or *Salt, please*), we may also vary our requests by saying *This food is really bland* or *Are we out of salt?* Likewise, the invitation *Care to dance?* – an utterance used as an access ritual (Goffman 1971a) that is part of the register of a particular social occasion – can be addressed to a woman (me) who accidentally bumped into a male stranger when she turned around too quickly in a checkout line at a busy shop in an international airport.

Public discourse also provides resources for creativity. Culturally familiar sentences (e.g. John F. Kennedy's *Ask not what your country can do for you, but what you can do for your country*) and lines from favorite books (Tolkien's *All who wander are not lost*) appear in high school term papers and college applications. And of course even single words travel to new public locations, as when the organization People for the Ethical Treatment of Animals protests the unethical treatment of animals by labeling a chicken dinner *Holocaust on a plate* on their web site and in print advertisements.

Despite the potential for wide ranging creativity in language, such creativity does not spread completely unfettered by restrictions. Numerous limitations arise simply because our sentences follow the implicit rules of our grammar. Although the sentence *She wants to do it herself* seems fine to speakers of standard American English, the sentence *Herself wants to do it* does not. And of course the innovative examples above actually follow regular linguistic patterns: *Cheerials* conforms to the syllable structure and stress pattern of *Cheerios*; it also reflects a semantic relationship of hyponymy ('Cheerios' are a type of cereal). Other restrictions are less formally grounded and may stem from our inability to clearly formulate the propositions that convey what we know (e.g. if we are trying to explain a complex equation), to state what we think (e.g. if we are trying to make a decision about something that we feel ambivalent about) or report what we feel (e.g. if we are still in emotional anguish forty years after a traumatic experience that we are recounting during an interview). Even if we may be perfectly able to access our knowledge, thoughts, and feelings, we may nevertheless find it difficult to verbalize them eloquently, in an appropriate manner or style, or in a way that fits the needs of our recipients or the demands of a situation. Although we are constantly speaking in innovative and creative ways, then, we are also limited as to what we are able to put into words, how we may do so, to whom, when, and where these new combinations and arrangements should appear.

The tension between innovation and restriction is partially reminiscent of, but also quite different from, two other oppositions inherent in our use of language to organize our thoughts, convey our intentions and manage our lives. Illustrated in Example 1.1 are dichotomies between same and different, new and old:

Example 1.1
(a)   There is another person whose name is Deborah Schiffrin.
(b)   Although she has the same name as me, she spells it
      differently.

The opposition between same and different is illustrated by the
content of line (a): the same name is used for two different people. What makes this linguistically relevant is that names are rigid
designators: they denote the same individual regardless of context.[1]
Names thus contrast with other ways of evoking people, such as
titles and common nouns. There can be more than one person
referred to as *the Dean*, and addressed as *Dean* even within a single
institution. At Georgetown University, for example, there is a Dean
of the College, the Graduate School of Arts and Sciences, Admis-
sions, School of Foreign Service (and so on) at any one time. Likewise, occupants of these offices change over time. Or take common
nouns. If I want to talk about 'a child,' I can either talk about a
generic child or specify only one 'child' of the many children in the
world.

The sentences in Example 1.1 also illustrate the opposition
between old and new. Once a referent has entered into the discourse,
its information status changes: it is no longer new and we can use
different words to evoke it. Thus, once 'another person whose name
is Deborah Schiffrin' has been introduced in Example 1.1, line (a), I
don't need to repeat it in all its detail in Example 1.1, line (b): instead,
I can use *she* to evoke the old referent. Word order also reflects information status. In Example 1.1 (a), 'someone shares my name' is new
information: it appears at the end of the sentence after the semantically weak predicate *there is*. The alternative information order is
awkward. *Another person whose name is Deborah Schiffrin exists*
seems appropriate only if I am announcing something (e.g. *Guess
what!*) or someone has questioned the issue (*Are you sure?*). Once
line (a) has been presented, however, the information about a second 'Deborah Schiffrin' is no longer new and can become a sentence
initial adverbial clause *Although she has the same name as me*, line
(b). And then what *is* new information – the spelling of the names –
can appear at the end of the sentence.

Not all of the oppositions – innovative/fixed, different/same,
new/old – that characterize our use of language have been studied by

linguists. One sort of difference that clearly matters for linguists is deciding whether a phonetic difference is associated with a different word meaning. If an unvoiced alveolar stop [t] is aspirated (ends with a puff of air) in Thai or Hindi, for example, it conveys a different word meaning than the same sequence of sounds with an *un*aspirated [t]. Not so in English: saying *Sit!* with an aspirated [t] would sound emphatic and perhaps angry, but still mean that I want my addressee (whether person or pet) to occupy a certain position in a chair or on the floor.

Of those oppositions that *are* pertinent to the systematic study of language, not all are equally interesting to the same linguists. Analyzing the role of repetitions, paraphrases and parallelisms in spoken discourse is interesting to linguists who study coherence (Becker 1984, Johnstone 1994, Tannen 1989) and intertextuality (Hamilton 1996), but perhaps less interesting to those who study reduplications, a form of morphological repetition common in pidgin and creole languages. Analyzing the organization of categories as prototypes (Rosch 1973, 1978, Taylor 1989) or radial categories (Lakoff 1987) might be interesting to cognitive linguists who study lexical meaning, but not to formal semanticists who study truth functional meaning. Other linguistic differences may be interesting to a variety of language researchers, but for quite different reasons. The analysis of speech errors, for example, interests psycholinguists because they can provide evidence for a particular model of language processing or production (e.g. Levelt 1983, 1999) or conversation analysts because of their role in the interactive construction of turns at talk (Fox and Jasperson 1995, Schegloff 1987).

One way that a subset of these oppositions – different ways of saying the 'same' thing – has been studied in Linguistics is through what sociolinguists have called variation analysis. After discussing this approach in Section 1.2, I turn to an overview of two aspects of language use on which this book will focus: *reference*, referrals to a person, place, or thing through a referring expression (Section 1.3); *narratives*, sequences of temporally ordered clauses that cluster together to report 'what happened' (Section 1.4). Each chapter (to be previewed in Section 1.5) addresses some aspect of variation that arises when the referral or the narrative recurs in a 'second position' in discourse.

CONTEXT
[referential]

CONTACT
[phatic]
social, interpersonal

ADDRESSOR   ADDRESSEE
[emotive]   [conative]
expressive   *recipient-design*

MESSAGE
[poetic]

CODE
[metalinguistic]

Figure 1.1 Speech functions

The situational component is in upper case; the function is bracketed; I italicize terms that I use interchangeably with Jakobson's terms.

1.2 Variation analysis: 'same' vs. 'different'

One of the main functions of language is to provide information: language is used to convey information about entities (e.g. people, objects), over time and across space, as well as their attributes, states and actions (when applicable), and relationships. The terms used to convey this function vary: denotational, representational, propositional, or ideational. Yet language clearly has more than a referential function. In figure 1.1 I have adapted Jakobson's (1960) framework, which includes not only a referential function, but also five other functions defined by the relationship between utterances and facets of the speech situation.

In addition to grounding the functions of language in the speech situation, Jakobson also makes another critical point: although an utterance may have a primary function, it is unlikely that it has only one function. *Do you know the time?*, for example, may have a phatic function (it opens contact), an emotive/expressive function (it conveys a need of the addressor), a conative/recipient-design function (it asks something of the addressee in a specific way), and a referential function (it makes reference to the world outside of language).

Despite the array of different functions that utterances serve, 'same' in Linguistics is usually understood as referential sameness:

sounds, morphemes, words, sentences, propositions, and texts are the 'same' if they contribute to a representation of the same thing in a world. Suppose I am telling a story about how 'my dog' took (and then hid) most of the Halloween candy, and refer to her as *Lizzy, she, a bad dog*, and *that clever girl*. These expressions can certainly refer to different entities in other contexts. And even in my Halloween story, the different expressions convey different attributes of the 'dog' and different attitudes of the 'speaker.' But they are all ways of referring to 'my dog' and the referent that they index would be the same throughout the story.

The referential function of language has always had a central role in the study of sound (phonology) and form (morphology, syntax). For many scholars interested in meaning, however, restricting semantics to the study of relatively stable referential meanings, especially those that can be formally mapped as the conditions under which a proposition would be true, ignores other sources and types of meaning. One way that semantics is thus supplemented is through the subfield of pragmatics and its concern with contextually dependent non-referential meanings.

The semantics/pragmatics distinction (at least in so far as we are thinking of truth-functional semantics) provides a paradigmatic example of the same–different dichotomy. In the perspective known as Gricean pragmatics, for example, referential (truth-functional) meaning can remain constant, but a speaker's adherence to, or manipulation of, the maxims of Quantity, Quality, Relation or Manner (grouped together as the Cooperative Principle (Grice 1975)) can add additional communicative meanings. Thus the conjunction *and* may very well maintain its truth-functional meaning ('if P is true, and Q is true, then it is also true that P & Q is true') each and every time it is used. In a sentence like Example 1.2, line (a), however, there may be an added inference of temporal order (stemming from a maxim of Quantity, Manner or Relation), but not necessarily in Example 1.2, line (b):

Example 1.2
(a) I got really busy on Sunday. I cleaned the closets and
     prepared things to give to charity.
(b) I got a lot of exercise on Sunday. I ran a mile and swam
     twenty laps.

To take another example, in Example 1.3 either line (a) or line (b) may be used to convey to a spouse a plan to get young children ice cream. But it is only line (b) that would implicate (because of a violation of Quantity, Manner or Relation) the speaker's intention of surprising the young children by the upcoming treat (Levinson 1983: Chapter 3):

Example 1.3
(a) Let's go get some ice cream.
(b) Let's go get some I-C-E-C-R-E-A-M.

Or consider the utterance *It's cold in here*, an example of an indirect speech act. Although the proposition conveyed in the sentence has the same referential meaning regardless of its context of utterance, a hearer would be remiss if – when hearing the utterance – he did not recognize its illocutionary force (Austin 1962, Searle 1969). Notice, however, that a variety of speech acts can be performed by *It's cold in here*: an assertion about the temperature, a directive to close the door, a request to get me a sweater, a complaint that the thermostat is too low. Because of its orientation toward action, and its contextual basis, the communicative meaning of an utterance cannot stem solely from referential meaning: it is now frequently considered in need of pragmatic analysis of how speakers (hearers) rely on context and inferential presumptions to convey (interpret) communicative intentions (Schiffrin 1994a: Chapter 6).[2]

Suggested thus far is that the referential function of language underlies phonology and syntax and helps to differentiate semantics from pragmatics. It has been less central to approaches to language that are more cognitively, socially, culturally or discourse based. In fact, it is in partial reaction to the emphasis on referential meaning and function that perspectives on language as varied as pragmatics, speech act theory, ethnography of communication, cognitive linguistics, functional grammar, interactional sociolinguistics, conversation analysis, critical discourse analysis and variation analysis have developed. Although the analyses in this book depend upon and draw from all of these perspectives, they will be brought together through a version of variation analysis (Schiffrin 1994a: Chapter 8) that alters and extends some of its traditional methodological and theoretical principles.

In an early statement describing the scope of variation analysis, Labov (1972a: 188) outlined the range of phenomena to be studied:

It is common for a language to have many alternate ways of saying 'the same' thing. Some words like *car* and *automobile* seem to have the same referents; others have two pronunciations, like *working* and *workin'*. There are syntactic options such as *Who is he talking to?* vs. *To whom is he talking?* or *It's easy for him to talk* vs. *For him to talk is easy.*

Despite the lexical, phonological, and syntactic examples above, most early research on sociolinguistic variation (from the late 1960s through the 1970s) sought to explain the variation that had been largely ignored by phonologists: the non-referential differences in pronunciation or 'free' variation.[3] Consider, for example, the alternation noted by Labov between *working* and *workin'*, more precisely, between the velar and apico-velar nasal. This alternation is constrained both linguistically and socially. The more frequent use of *in'* in progressives and participles than in gerunds, for example, reflects different patterns of historical development (Houston 1989). *In'* is also socially constrained by speaker identity and style: it is used more frequently by working class than middle class speakers and by men than women, i.e. all speakers use *in'* more than *ing* when they are speaking casually instead of carefully (Labov 1972a; Trudgill 1974). Thus variation in allophones (different phonetic realizations of a single underlying phoneme) can be explained by social factors.

Since variationists try to discover patterns in the distribution of alternative ways of saying the same thing, an initial step is to establish which forms alternate with one another and in which environments they can do so, i.e. what aspects of context might matter. Those contextual features that might be related to the alternation among forms are viewed as constraints that have a systematic impact on the appearance of one variant rather than another. Depending on the variable, constraints may range all the way from the physiology of articulation to social identity. The process of identifying, coding and counting alternative realizations of a variable, identifying their environments and coding the constraints within those environments sets up its own requirements. One has to define and identify all the possible realizations of an underlying type (i.e. a closed set), classify the factors in the environment with which those variants may be associated, and then compare the frequencies with which different variants co-occur with different factors/constraints.

Despite interest in lexical and syntactic variation (as noted in Labov's quote above), variation analysis requires that we first establish which forms are the same "by some criterion such as 'having the same truth value'" (Labov 1972a: 188). This requirement has made it challenging (and, for some, theoretically problematic) to extend the notion of variable to levels of analysis beyond the phonological.

For example, the conditions in which *David went to the store* is true are not the same as the conditions in which *David goes to the store* would be true. Yet a referential difference between the preterit and the present tense can disappear in narrative, when the present tense is interpreted as the historical present tense and has a 'present time' meaning. Switching between the preterit and the historical present in oral narratives has been explained in relation to speech activity (Wolfson 1978), episode organization (Wolfson 1979) and evaluative (cf. expressive) function (Schiffrin 1981). Although these explanations all support Hymes' (1985: 150) prediction that "the recognition of social function brings recognition of new structure, transcending conventional compartments," the new structures that are recognized are quite different, in part because of the role of meaning. Wolfson (1976, 1978) argues against any exploitation of a 'present time' meaning. Rather it is speaker/hearer solidarity and textual structure that account for tense switches. Schiffrin (1981), however, argues that 'present time' meaning underlies the evaluative function of the historical present, i.e. function has moved from a referential to expressive and interpersonal plane. Thus, both analyses agree that the historical present tense has social and textual functions; they disagree on whether tense retains and exploits semantic meaning, and if so, in what pragmatic realms it does so.

Suggested thus far is that morphological, lexical and syntactic forms convey meanings that may (or may not) be neutralized in different discourse environments (Sankoff 1988). Forms that are semantically distinctive in one environment may not seem so in another. However, it is difficult to say whether residues of those meanings remain with each occasion of use and whether they are exploited for textual and/or pragmatic purposes (Lavendera 1978).[4]

   The extension of variation analysis to discourse has taken two different directions, each of which has added further complications. The study of *discourse variation* attempts "to find patterns of language use that characterize the spoken language of a definable group in a specific setting" (Macaulay 2002: 284). As such, it encompasses a very broad view of discourse, variation and contextual factors (e.g. situation, participants). Studies grouped under this description could thus include analyses of all social and cultural differences in language use above and beyond the sentence: differences in conversational style by region (Tannen 1984) and gender (Tannen 1990), in contextualization cues by culture (Gumperz 1982), in narrative by gender (Johnstone 1980), race (Michaels and Collins 1984), or culture (Tannen 1980), in politeness strategies (Pan 2000) and dinner table conversations (Blum-Kulka 1997) by culture and situation. The list could clearly go on to include all studies of acting and speaking that are socially/culturally motivated and constructed.

   Variation of a sort, to be sure – but not the sort of variation easily conceptualized as 'same' at an underlying level of language structure with surface variants contingent upon linguistic and social factors. Thus it would be difficult to identify and categorize all the possible realizations of an underlying style, narrative, politeness strategy, or conversation, classify the contexts in which those variants might occur, and then compare the frequencies with which different variants co-occur with different factors. Nor would this necessarily be the best approach. Many aspects of discourse are locally negotiated and co-constructed: identifying them and understanding why they appear, and how they do so, requires close attention to minute details of emergent properties and sequential contingencies of multi-functional units in discourse that are notoriously difficult to identify, let alone count. Likewise, the idea that ongoing discourse "constrains" its constituent parts bypasses the ways that sentence and text can co-constitute one another and that situational meanings emerge from what is said and done. Because of these differences, analyses of social/cultural differences in ways of speaking often reject the logic underlying Labovian variation analysis and can better be characterized as part of pragmatics, interactional sociolinguistics, discourse analysis, linguistic anthropology and the ethnography of communication.

The second direction that extends variation analysis to discourse – *variation in discourse* – includes studies that focus specifically on language (e.g. the historical present tense, mentioned earlier) whose analysis is either at a discourse (textual) level or requires attention to discourse. Examples include comparisons between lists and narratives (Schiffrin 1994b), structural analyses of text-types (Horvath 1987), corpus comparisons of register that examine lexical, syntactic and textual differences (Biber 1998, Biber and Finegan 1994, Conrad and Biber 2001, Reaser 2003), the study of clause order (Schiffrin 1985, 1991, Ford 1993) and discourse markers (Schiffrin 1987, 2001a). Studies of grammar and interaction (Ochs, Schegloff and Thompson 1996) and functional approaches to syntax (DuBois 1987, Fox and Thompson 1990) can be also included in this group: they show that grammatical options emerge from interactional processes such as turn-taking and 'grounding' (but see Schiffrin 1994a: Chapter 7, 8 for comparisons).

Just as the 'discourse variation' direction can include areas of research more congruent with other subdisciplines, however, so too can the 'variation in discourse' direction. Studies of phonological (e.g. Bell 2001) and prosodic variation (Britain 1992), for example, reveal discourse (e.g. style, recipient design) constraints on linguistic variation, but do not deal with sequential processes of ongoing discourse construction. Likewise, even context-rich sociolinguistic studies of style (Eckert and Rickford 2001) do not always pay close attention to the emergent properties of talk in interaction.

To summarize the two directions: studies of discourse variation focus primarily on the details of language use in context so that ways of speaking and acting can be understood from "the inside out." By providing richly contextualized and detailed descriptions, these studies reveal "what I need to know in order to understand this person's (group's) way of using language (in this situation)." In contrast, studies of variation in discourse often focus primarily on a part of language (form, meaning or use) and aim to characterize what it is about that part of language that can vary and why. Answering the 'why' question usually requires analyzing the different variants specifically enough to be able to categorize, code, and count them in different contexts defined both narrowly (something in the text) or broadly (e.g. identity, situation, genre).

Studies of variation in discourse – the approach pursued here – inherit the problems of the search for morphological and syntactic variants. An additional problem stems from the status of discourse as a linguistic unit *per se*. Since texts do not have the same kind of internally constrained, externally bounded structure as sentences, it is difficult to define the theoretical status of discourse based variants. They are not alternative realizations of a single underlying form or representation (as one could argue for phonological, morphological, or syntactic variants); nor do they occupy a 'slot' (a phonological segment, a syntactic constituent) in a grammar or set of grammatical rules.

One solution to this problem is to analyze variation within a discourse unit whose structure is relatively easy to delineate, e.g. one can analyze alternative forms (e.g. preterit vs. historical present) that appear within specific slots (e.g. complicating action clauses) in a narrative structure. Another solution is to extrapolate from the functional diversity of utterances (recall Jakobson's model) to functional domains, e.g. ideational (cf. referential), action, exchange, information state and participation (Schiffrin 1987: Chapter 1). This approach has an additional advantage if the referential meaning of a variant varies along with domain, as is the case, for example, with discourse markers. Thus *but* can be understood as an interruption when its contrastive meaning (ideational domain) combines with 'overlap' in the exchange domain (Schiffrin 1986). And *then* can mark either a warranted inference in the information state ('I conclude this because . . .') or a warranted response in an action domain ('I do this because . . .') because of its temporal meaning in the ideational domain (Schiffrin 1990, 1992). Still another approach is to extend the domain of variation in discourse by arguing that interactional patterns (e.g. of encounter management) can constitute discourse variables (Coupland 1983).

To sum, we have been considering two main questions: What aspects of language are open to variation analysis? How can variation analysis be useful for discourse analysis? Each chapter in this book addresses these questions as part of an interest in the broad dichotomies introduced in Section 1.1: the balance between innovation (and fixity), old (and new), same (and different). They do so by focusing on two phenomena central to the study of language, text, interaction, and communication: *referrals*, the use of referring expressions to evoke a referent (Section 1.3); *narratives*, the use of event clauses to tell a story (Section 1.4). Since both phenomena are so broad, I narrow my focus to 'second position' referrals and narratives. The notion of second position is sequential and delimited by what occurs 'first,' e.g. an answer is in second position of a question/ answer adjacency pair. The sequences to be analyzed here arise when a speaker makes a referral and then redoes all (or part) of that referral, or tells a story and then replays all (or some) of that story. The recurrences in second position include repairing (Chapters 2, 3, 4, 8), repeating, paraphrasing and altering (Chapters 2, 3, 4, 5, 8), reframing (Chapter 6) and restructuring (Chapters 7, 8); the distance between first and second position varies, from the closeness of one constituent within one utterance to the distance of different times and situations. Before previewing the upcoming analyses (1.5), I provide a brief overview of what it is that will be redone: referrals; narratives.

1.3 Referrals

Referring to people, objects and other entities in the world is central to verbal communication: "the most crucial feature of each utterance, the feature which a listener must minimally grasp in order to begin to understand the utterance, is the expression used to identify what the speaker is talking about" (Brown 1995: 62). Given the centrality of reference to language and communication, it is not surprising that studies of reference are of interest to the disciplines of Philosophy, Linguistics and Psychology. Within Linguistics itself, such studies appear in the subfields of semantics, pragmatics, computational linguistics, discourse analysis (including in the latter, those interested in grammar and interaction, discourse processes, text structure and narrative) and variation analysis. And in keeping with its inter- and intra-disciplinary breadth, methodologies for studying reference include philosophical introspection and argumentation, the development of formal models and algorithms, corpus analysis, conversation analysis, and numerous approaches within both discourse analysis and pragmatics.

An important distinction in the linguistic study of reference is between *external* and *internal* perspectives: the former examines the "relation between symbols and the objects they represent;" the latter, the "relation of coreference between symbols" (Kronfeld 1990: 3). Although these perspectives are often separated in both principle and practice, they also intersect with one another. Before discussing the intersection, let us learn a bit more about each one independently.

The term 'reference' itself invokes the *external* perspective: a relation between language and something in the world.[5] Hence, in keeping with the view of semantics as the study of how signs are related to the objects to which they are applicable (Morris, 1938), the study of reference often falls to the linguistic subfield of semantics. But who is it that relates signs to objects and realizes their applicability? If we view the speaker – and not the linguistic signs themselves – as the critical conduit through which signs are related to objects, then the study of reference might belong more properly to pragmatics, defined in Morris' (1938) terms as the study of the process whereby people construct interpretations by taking account of the designata of sign vehicles.

Locating the analysis of reference in one linguistic subfield, however, assumes that those subfields are discretely bound areas of inquiry. Yet the boundaries between semantics and pragmatics are notoriously amorphous, depending to a large extent on what theory/ model is adapted in each: formal truth-conditional or cognitive semantics; the largely Anglo-American view of pragmatics as based on Grice's maxims or the more continental view of pragmatics as language use. Various aspects of meaning and use (e.g. presupposition) get caught up and differently allocated to each subdiscipline (Levinson 1983: Chapter 4); different relationships between the two are proposed, challenged and defended (Leech 1983).

Reference is one aspect of meaning that has been entangled in the semantics/pragmatics quagmire. Lyons (1977: 184), for example, states that "the fundamental problem for the linguist, as far as reference is concerned, is to elucidate and to describe the way in which we use language to draw attention to what we are talking about." Privileging the speaker within semantics is based on the belief that "it is the speaker who refers (by using some appropriate expression): he invests the expression with reference by the act of referring" (Lyons 1977: 177). A strikingly similar perspective is offered by Givón (1979: 175), but as part of pragmatics, rather than semantics:

Reference in a Universe of Discourse is already a *crypto pragmatic* affair. This is because every universe of discourse is *opened* ('established') – for whatever purpose – by a *speaker*. And that speaker then *intends* entities in that universe of discourse to either refer or not refer. And it seems that in human language it is that *referential intent* of the speaker that controls the grammar of reference. (emphasis in original)

Other areas of research that also assign speaker actions and intentions a necessary role in reference are quick to point out that it is the *hearer* who adds a sufficient condition for reference. The psycholinguists Clark and Wilkes-Gibbs (1992) speak of referring as a "collaborative process": they suggest that although a speaker can propose a referent, the identification of the referent needs to be seen as an outcome of speaker–hearer interaction.[6] Some types of reference are especially dependent on mutual knowledge. Clark and Marshall (1992), for example, argue that definite reference depends upon physical and/or linguistic co-presence and on each participant's ability to build (and then rely upon) models for one another that combine information analogous to both a general encyclopedia and an individual diary. From both a speaker's and a hearer's point of view, then, the process by which expressions refer to an entity can be seen as pragmatic: "the mechanism by which referring expressions enable an interpreter to infer an intended referent is not strictly semantic or truth-conditional, but involves the cooperative exploitation of supposed mutual knowledge" (Green 1989: 47).

Thus far we have started to shift from language to the world, including not just a world of objects to which we refer, but also the world of speaker and hearer (their knowledge and actions) who actively make referrals. To complicate matters further, it turns out that two kinds of referential relations – *denotation* and *connotation* – also straddle the language/speaker divide. Denotation is sometimes equivalent to *extension*: "the complete set of all things which could potentially (i.e. in any possible utterance) be the referent of a referring expression" (Hurford and Heasley 1983: 87). In the cognitive perspective summarized by Brown (1995: 59), however, even denotation is a speaker-centered construct: "the changing cluster of beliefs held by the individual about what is meant by the word . . . on the basis of the assorted experiences which each of us assembles from a variety of sources." Since denotation is mediated by speakers' beliefs and experiences, denotations end up varying not only from person to person, but also from one occasion to another depending on an individual's changing experiences. Even more variable is *connotation*: the "subjectively colored beliefs" (Brown 1995: 60) about what is meant by a word.

The sense of a word is also potentially variable among speakers. Since sense is based partially upon semantic connections among lexical items within a language, it is generally assumed that we share the sense of words through our knowledge of the semantic networks in which words are embedded and our membership in a speech community. Yet as Brown (1995) points out, our knowledge of the links between words and concepts depends not only on our conceptual knowledge, but also on how we intend to put that knowledge to use. Speakers may know on a rough taxonomic level, for example, that Brittany spaniels and Welsh Springer spaniels differ. But if they are required to use a set of combinatorial features to differentiate the two types (or tokens) of dogs, they may be unable to do so. Thus the link between words and concepts can be mediated by the goals of use and the contexts in which those goals arise.

Notice, also, that although sense is conceptually different from reference, they are also fundamentally related to one another: interrelationships among lexical meanings depend upon (and display) categorizations (perception and organization) of things in the world. Thus, the match between words and things can be altered. As we stretch or contract the range of entities a word can evoke (its reference), we are simultaneously expanding or shrinking the linguistic meaning of the word, and thus gradually altering its place in our network of sense relations. If the sense/reference relationship can exhibit the same variability and "orderly heterogeneity" of other form/meaning correspondences (Labov 1973), however, then a speaker-centered view of sense becomes as viable as a speaker-centered view of reference. What we know about the world, and how we subjectively orient toward it, can create variability within sense/reference not only across different speakers, but also over time and across contexts within a single speaker him/herself.

In contrast to the focus of the external perspective – mediation of the word-to-world relationship by speaker, hearer and context – is the focus of the *internal* perspective: word-to-word relationships in text. Here the criterion of success is not to establish a link between language and objects in the world, but to establish links within a text, i.e. the "right matching among symbols" (Kronfeld 1990: 4). With this shift in focus comes a shift toward discourse analysis. Since the link between an initial referring expression and the 'real world' has already been established in text, possible links between a subsequent referring expression, and the initial referring expression, are delimited by the characters, activities and scenes already evoked in the discourse.

The examples below (altered from Brown, 1995: 12) illustrate how discourse plays a role in resolving the internal problem of locating the textual antecedent, and thus the referent, of the pronoun *they*, first seen in Example 1.4 line (b):

Example 1.4
(a) As Mom and Dad drove up to the house, the boys had just started their cowboy game.
(b) Instead *they* ran out back to the car.

In Example 1.4, line (a), *Mom and Dad* are driving up to a house, inferable as their home, while *the boys* are engaged in *their cowboy game*. Within this textual world, we build upon our knowledge of how kin expressions lead to upcoming relational inferences to infer a domestic familial scene in which *the boys* are 'children of the parents.' This inferred relational connection allows other inferences: since children are usually eager to see their parents, *they* in Example 1.4, line (b) is co-referential with *the boys*.

Differences in referent and activity in Example 1.5, line (a) reconstruct the textual world in which an antecedent for *they* (in line (b)) is sought:

Example 1.5
(a) As the police drove up to the house, the boys had just started their robbery attempt.
(b) Instead *they* ran out back to the car.

In Example 1.5, line (a), the referent ('the police') and boys' activity ('robbery attempt') reconstruct the textual world as one in which *the boys* would not be running towards those driving *up to the house*. Thus the antecedent of *they* is less clear: we can imagine that it is either the police running towards (i.e. chasing) the boys, or the boys running away from (trying to escape) the police. Hence either *the police* or *the boys* can be running *out back to the car*.

Thus *they* in Examples 1.4, line (b) and 1.5, line (b) has different possible interpretations because of the different characters, activities and scenes in the textual worlds already established in the discourse.

In this section, we have seen that the external perspective on reference focuses on the link between a word and the world that is typically made in the first mention of a referent in a text; the internal perspective focuses on next links between a word and a referent, crucially, a link mediated through a prior word and its first link to the world, as well as the position already occupied by that referent in the textual world. By viewing the external/internal difference in terms of order of mention in a text, we can integrate them as different phases of one communicative goal: interlocutors seek to achieve general agreement about what referent is being evoked by both word-to-world and word-to-word connections.

We have also seen that the study of referrals – the relationship between referring expressions and referents – relies upon very similar constructs that have been instrumental in the development of more socially constituted views of language: speaker, hearer, context. Analyses of referrals can thus draw from approaches that have already helped us understand how we use language in everyday life: pragmatics, discourse analysis, and a broadly construed variation analysis that systematically analyzes what is 'same' and what is 'different' in specific sites of language use. What makes such analyses of referrals complex, however, is exactly why these socially constituted approaches to language can be so helpful. Sense vs. reference and external vs. internal perspectives on reference are not pairs of mutually exclusive dichotomous constructs. Like other aspects of language use, they are mediated by speaker and hearer who jointly manage and negotiate emergent realizations of what is said, meant and done.

1.4 Narratives

Narrative is a form of discourse through which we reconstruct and represent past experience both for ourselves and for others. Evidence of the pervasiveness of this genre abounds: we dream, reminisce, tell jokes and make plans in narrative; we use stories to apologize, request, plead, hint, persuade and argue.

Given the wide role of narrative in our lives, it should hardly be surprising that narrative is one of the most analyzed, and best understood, genres of spoken language. Scholars have investigated how and why narratives are told (e.g., Kirschenblatt-Gimblett 1974, Labov 1972b, Rosen 1988, Shuman 1986, Wortham 2001), how social and cultural characteristics of speakers bear on narrative form and interpretation (Blum-Kulka 1997, Gee 1989, Gee and Michaels 1989, Heath 1982, 1983, Michaels and Collins 1984), how stories are situated in different social contexts (Ferrera 1994, He 1996) and how stories are affected by modality (Tannen 1989) or tailored to specific interactional contingencies (Goodwin 1986, Jefferson 1972). Diachronic studies have addressed the development of story telling skills in children (Bamberg 1987, 1997, Nelson 1989) and how community narratives change over time (Johnstone 1980). In addition to contributing to linguistic discourse analysis, the study of oral narrative has also contributed to research on a wide variety of topics, including cognition (Britton and Pellegrini 1990, Chafe 1994), memory (DeConcini 1990), social interaction (Ochs and Capps 2001) and autobiography (Brockmeier and Carbaugh 2001, Bruner 1986, 1987, 1990, 2001, Linde 1993).

Like the study of variation, the sociolinguistic study of narratives also stems (at least in part) from the work of Labov. Oral narratives of personal experience provided a speech activity in which linguists found a relatively casual style of speech within a larger speech situation (the sociolinguistic interview) that could provide data in which to study the vernacular, especially (but not exclusively), the grammar of those whose linguistic competence had been publicly challenged (Labov 1972b).

Labov defines a narrative as a bounded unit in discourse in which the identities of constituent units are revealed through their syntactic and semantic qualities and their contribution to the overall narra- tive. Narratives are opened by an abstract, a clause that summarizes the experience and presents a general proposition that the narrative will expand. Orientation clauses (typically with stative predicates) follow the abstract: they describe background information such as time, place, and identity of characters. The main part of the narrative comprises complicating action clauses. Each complicating action clause describes an event – a bounded occurrence in time – that is understood to shift reference time: it follows the event immediately preceding it, and precedes the event immediately following it. Evaluation of what happened pervades the narrative: speakers can comment on events from outside of the story world, suspend the action through embedded orientation clauses, and report events that themselves indicate the significance of the experience. Speakers can also modify clause syntax as a way of revealing the point (cf. general proposition) of the story. Finally, the story is closed by a coda: a clause that shifts out of the past time frame of the story to the time frame of current talk.

Although narratives are discourse units that have been studied apart from their contexts, they are not independent of their personal, social and cultural meanings at both local and global levels. When we tell a story, we are always doing more than just reporting what has happened: we are recounting an experience, something that has happened to us and has significance for us, as well as a broader social and cultural significance that we assume (and hope) our listeners will recognize and appreciate. It is these crucial aspects of telling a story that are captured by evaluation: the way we make a 'point' about ourselves, our society, and/or our culture. Put still another way: the referential function is to report events and tell what happened; the evaluative function is to reveal the point of events for the speaker and his/her reasons for telling the story.[7]

This distinction between referential (what happened) and evaluative (why it matters) information harks back to some of the issues discussed in our general review of variation analysis (1.2) and our discussion of reference, referring expressions and referrals (1.3). Indeed, the distinction between the complicating action (the events) and the evaluation (their subjective value) is reminiscent of the distinction between referential and other functions of language as well as the difference between semantics (constant meaning) and pragmatics (contextual meaning).

Despite its heuristic usefulness, the degree to which the referential/evaluative distinction is actually realized during narrative production, or within a narrative text itself, is not always clear. The linguistic turn (urged by Rorty 1967), for example, immerses experience within language (and hence narrative): rather than report or transform a past experience, speakers construct 'what happened' (but see comments in Schiffrin 2003). Even Labov's notion of internal evaluation, in which evaluation is embedded within narrative clauses (and their syntax), obfuscates the presumably clear cut distinction between 'what happened' and the narrator's portrayal of 'what happened.'

Example 1.6 shows how the structural options through which we represent 'what happened' provide formal resources for conveying the expressive nuances and subtleties of evaluation. In Example 1.6 are four versions of an event from a narrative told during four different oral history interviews with one person about the Holocaust. (We learn more about this narrative in Chapters 6–7.) The speaker is talking about a plan that she and her family are undertaking (in 1944), to return from Hungary (where they had been fleeing Nazi persecution) to Slovakia, their homeland (where they expect to find refuge). The dates indicate when the stories were told.

Example 1.6

1982   And who for a certain amount they'll take a group of Jews back to Slovakia.

1984   And this would cost money,

1995a   (April) And for a fee uh they would take us back to Slovakia.

1995b   (May) Of course, it cost a lot of money and my father didn't have it.

In each of the lines above, the speaker is talking about a single facet of her experience: a requirement that her family pay money to participate in the planned escape. This requirement is differently referred to: *a certain amount* (1982), *money* (1984), *a fee* (1995a), *a lot of money* (1995b). It appears as an independent clause in two texts (1984, 1995b) and as a prepositional phrase in two texts: 1982, where it is also part of a relative clause, and 1995a.

Differences also appear in the role of the 'fee' and its integration into the story sequence and plot. The 'fee' gradually moves from being just another facet of the overall plan to an obstacle challenging the family's participation in the plan. This change from routine to obstacle is marked not only lexically (e.g. compare *a certain amount* (1982) to *a lot of money* (1995b)), but also by epistemic stance (*of course* (1995b)) and contrast (*it cost a lot of money and my father didn't have it* (1995b)). Once the 'fee' becomes an obstacle, its role in the story has become more overtly evaluative: the willingness of the family to consider actions that require sacrifice and risk reveals both their desperation and the perceived necessity of the plan for their safety and survival. Thus reporting and evaluating the 'fee' are intimately linked: the presentation of 'what happened' proceeds apace with the subjective integration of that event into the plot of the story.

[Thus far, we have been focusing primarily on the language through which narrative is told. We can think of this as a code-centered perspective. Scholars whose research is rooted in sociolinguistics, and (to a lesser extent) conversation analysis view narrative primarily as text and/or as a mode of language-based action and means of social interaction. Despite wide variation in methodology and assumptions about the co-construction of structure and meaning (compare Jefferson 1978 to Labov 1997; also see below), this perspective analytically privileges the language of stories, i.e. the code in which they are conveyed. Narratives are assumed to be

(1) relatively bound units of talk, whose beginnings, middles and ends are formally and functionally different from one another,

(2) composed of a set of smaller units (e.g. clauses, utterances, idea/intonation units) that are sequentially arranged in regular patterns, and

(3) tellable through the speech of one person, at one time, to one audience, in one setting.]

In contrast to the code-based perspective, a competence-centered approach analytically privileges the internal rules and logic through which we organize experience. Here the focus is less on the realization of narrative as 'text' and more on the potential of narrative as a cognitive means of organizing and constructing experience (e.g. Polkinghorne 1988). For psychologists, sociologists, and anthropologists who adopt this perspective, narrative is akin to a template that underlies a possible text. Within this template, people and their actions are

(1) organized into a structured representation of what is expected to happen and

(2) emplotted in a structured representation of what actually does happen.

The structured representations central to this perspective move fluidly from cognition to culture. Narrative templates serve as individual repositories for personal memory and experience, and, as cultural resources for knowledge and collective memories. Although one can investigate the *modus operandi* of individual consciousness (Chafe 1980b, 1994) and ways of thinking (Bruner 1986), such processes can also be conceptualized, and studied, at collective levels (Tonkin 1992, Wertsch 1998): they can operate as persistent and communal systems of knowledge, beliefs, and ideology.

Despite the usefulness of separating two perspectives on narrative in principle, they complement one another in practice: analyzing language provides information not only about how stories are told, but also about how our experience is organized. Code-based and competence-based perspectives on narrative thus come together in various ways. In addition to examining the stories that people tell as indices of how they conceptualize, store, and represent (reconstruct or construct) experience, one can examine how stories emerge from both knowledge and site of practice: how does a story actually reflect both our underlying narrative competence that lies in wait and the interactional contingencies in which talk is co-constructed? How is the underlying violation of a schema that underlies a story (Chafe 1980b) made accessible to, and available for appreciation by, hearers through narrative language (Tannen 1981)?

Also differentiating approaches to the study of narrative is the degree to which the narrative is treated as a process dependent upon audience design and co-construction. In the Labovian code-centered approach, the narrative is analyzed with no attention to how it is situated within, and molded to, the discourse in which it is told (often a sociolinguistic interview) In sharp contrast to what traditional variationists treat as benign neglect of context (apart from the relatively global and unexamined notion of situation in early work (Labov 1972a)), conversation and interaction analysts (Goodwin 1981, Jefferson 1978, Ochs and Capps 2002, Schiffrin 1996) argue (and demonstrate) that many important facets of narratives – their initiation, the entry and description of characters, the events, the point, the evaluation, the performance, the closure – are either designed for a recipient or explicitly co-constructed by the audience.

Questions of who tells what, how, when, why and where, and the extent to which these choices are recipient-designed and co-constructed, can also pertain to stories that are situated in more public and collective venues. Gaining the right to use one's own voice to tell one's own story in a plea for political asylum, for example, and have it received in the manner for which it was intended, may require legitimization that can be conferred only through the speaker's ability to use forms and formats acceptable to an institutional authority (e.g. Blommaert 2001). On more collective levels, negotiations over public memorials that represent communal or national experiences (e.g. of the Holocaust (Linenthal 1995), the Oklahoma City bombing (Linenthal 2001), or 9/11 (still in progress)) often require years of planning and negotiation among those with different relationships to, and interests in, both the experience being memorialized and the place of the memorial in contemporary social, cultural, and political milieus.

In sum, the study of narrative requires attention to many of the same details of language, text, and interaction as the study of referrals. Analysis of events (clustered together in narrative) and entities (people, places and things that also appear in narratives) both require attention to how speakers and hearers construct (and co-construct) versions of their worlds that make sense to one another both objectively ('this is what I am talking about') and subjectively ('this is my perspective in partial accommodation to your needs and interests'). The next section brings the study of referrals and narratives together by returning to the tensions between innovation/restriction, different/same and new/old in order to preview how analyses in this book will address these themes.

1.5 Preview: replaying and retelling

The study of variation in discourse can facilitate a comparison between what is innovative vs. fixed, new vs. old, and different vs. same in language, text and interaction. Such a study, of course, requires differentiating the innovative from the fixed, the new from the old, and the different from the same. It also requires finding sites in which we can compare the use of one option rather than another, assess which option is typical (cf. more frequent, less marked) and explain not only why one variant is preferred, but also why dispreferred options are sometimes used.

Although referrals and narratives are the general focus of the analyses to follow, my more particular focus is on how they both appear a second time or, to put it in sequential terms, in second position. A 'second time' implies repetition or paraphrase; 'second position' implies the next immediate slot in a sequence. As we noted earlier, however, these are just two possibilities: there are many other recurrences besides repetition and paraphrase that can count as a 'second time.' The recurrences in second position include repairing, repeating, paraphrasing, altering, reframing, replaying and restructuring; the distance between first and second position varies, from the closeness of one constituent within one utterance to the distance of different times and situations. Depending on the item that recurs, and the scope of the sequence in which that item recurs, even positions that are separated by person, time and place can count as 'second positions' (as posited by theories of intertextuality and interdiscursivity (Chapter 9)). Thus it is through analysis of recurrences in second positions that we will examine the tension between innovative and fixed, new and old, same and different. In other words, why redo a referral (or a narrative) in this particular way? Why here? Why now?

Chapters 2, 3, and 4 analyze recurrences of noun phrases (or parts thereof) that repair problematic referrals. Studies of linguistic repair (viewed as speech errors and disfluencies in psycholinguistics) typically focus on phonological, syntactic or semantic errors. Such studies reveal not only that there exist regular procedures by which to resolve troubles during ongoing talk, but also that what goes wrong – and how we make it right – is intricately tied to the underlying processes and strategies through which we produce language and use language to communicate.

The interactional importance of repairs has also been stressed by scholars. Schegloff, Jefferson and Sacks (1977) show that although either 'self' or 'other' may initiate or complete a repair, there is a preference for self-initiation and self-completion within a single turn (Moerman 1977, Schegloff 1987, 1992). Analyses of how self-repairs are situated in interaction show their sensitivity to the sentence/discourse boundary (Taylor 1985) or to shifts in audience (Goodwin 1986). Also shown is how specific repair forms and strategies are compatible with cultural parameters of participation frameworks (Ochs 1985), situated features of interchanges (Egbert 1996) and institutional configurations of situated activity systems (Goffman 1981b on radio talk). Indeed, so important is interaction that semantic meaning or syntactic well-formedness can be subordinated to interactional contingencies (Fox, Hayashi and Jasperson 1996, Schegloff 1979, 1987).

Mistakes and misunderstandings have also revealed subtle, but pervasive, relationships between many varied aspects of language and the principles that underlie mutual understanding (Gumperz 1982). Persistent misunderstandings can have harmful consequences for interpersonal relationships (Tannen 1984, 1990; cf. Hopper 1992). Even fleeting misunderstandings can have an interpretive cost. Referrals that do not enable a level of shared interpretation, for example, impact not only the ability of interlocutors to understand one another. They also hinder the creation of interpersonal involvement: we cannot be involved in, interested in, or appreciative of what the other is saying if (to put it simply) we don't know what they are talking about. Thus there is not only a referential cost, but also an interpersonal cost to referrals that go awry – a meta-message that whether or not you understand me really does not matter (Tannen, personal communication).

Chapter 2, *Problematic referrals*, begins the analysis of repair by identifying and analyzing four types of problems based on the fate of the referent and the referring expression. Both can be continued (Example 1.7, line (a)) or altered (line (b)); one can change, either the referring expression (line (c)) or the referent (line (d)). In Example 1.7 and the examples which follow, I use **bold** to indicate the site at which the repair is initiated; I use ***bold italics*** if the repaired referent remains the same at self-completion; if it differs I *italicize* (but do not bold) the repair. Multiple referrals that are part of the problem or solution are differentiated by subscript$_s$.

Example 1.7

 (a) Well I- *I* speak like doctors write.
 (b) **She-** *we-* I was supposed t' play elegy on the violin.
 (c) And they'd have **these eh** . . . they- *they read your tea leaves!*
 (d) I don't even think **they**$_1$ knew anymore what was- what **they-**$_{1/2}$? what was going on, **the Germans**$_2$.

After showing how the different problem types (and their resolutions) are integrated into ongoing discourse, Chapter 2 analyzes the location of the different problem types in sentences, text, and turns at talk.

Chapter 3, *Anticipating referrals*, turns to the self-interruption and self-continuation of articles, in examples such as those in Example 1.8:

Example 1.8

(a) H- How- how many in **the-** *the* crowd?
(b) Do people sit out on **the-** *their* porches and streets around here in the summertime?
(c) What I want t' do, now, is **the-** kind of *a* last thing on nationalities.

Since articles preview the information status of the referent about to be conveyed by the noun, their repair is puzzling: why delay the noun? After analyzing the differences between switched and repeated articles, Chapter 3 focuses on the repeated articles and compares noun, sentence, text, and interaction constraints.

Whereas Chapters 2 and 3 analyze problematic referrals in which self-initiation and self-completion of repair were confined primarily to the noun phrase, Chapter 4, *Reactive and proactive prototypes*, turns to problems for which a noun phrase is not the solution of choice. As illustrated in Example 1.9, some repairs of problematic referrals require a complex sentence for self-completion:

Example 1.9

I had **a viewer-** uh like you know *there was so many people up there like you might've thought Cassius Clay was fighting or somebody*, y'know.

After showing how referrals with faulty familiarity assumptions are repaired by anchoring the referent in familiar information, Chapter 4 shows that a fixed set of constructions are used for this anchoring work even when no repair has been self-initiated:

Example 1.10

(a) Now **there's** one block of brownstones
(b) **they had** their furnace rooms down there

Variants of this 'pragmatic prototype' provide sites for referrals that pre-empt the need for repair; they can also alternate with one another to help structure texts.

Chapter 5, *Referring sequences*, bridges the two foci of the analyses in the book – referring expressions and narratives – by

showing how topicality, distance, ambiguity and structural boundaries impact noun/pronoun variation in two different genres, lists
and narratives. The chapter also furthers a shift from referring
expressions to clause types, and from remedial to pre-emptive strategies (Chapter 4), by taking our level of analysis two steps higher (to
sequences and texts). Finally, by showing how the referring expression *concentration camps* caused a conflict (in sequences of public
Discourse) and how a mixed genre resolved the problem, Chapter
5 also presages the focus of the next two chapters: narratives of the
Holocaust.

Chapters 6 and 7 turn exclusively to retellings of narrative. The
limited scholarly attention to retellings creates a curious impasse in
the study of narrative. Story telling is part of an inherently dynamic
process: our memory of an earlier experience is activated and verbalized in ways that adapt to the contingencies of an ongoing interaction. Research on narrative has helped elucidate different parts
of this process and has hinted at intriguing links between how we
remember, think, speak, act and interact. Yet our analyses of narratives themselves remain relatively static[Despite cumulative knowledge about narrative form, meaning, use, and context-sensitivity,
then, we know little about how and why the forms and meanings so
critical to one person's initial telling of a story may be reshaped to
fit whatever changing circumstances frame the same person's subsequent telling of the same story.]

[Numerous studies have focused on how different speakers report
the same events at different times (Clancy 1980, Mushin 2001,
Tannen 1989).]The relatively few studies on retellings by the same
person about the same events assume, in line with Polanyi's (1981)
suggestion that the 'same story' comprises the same semantic core,
that we can separate a narrative core from its interactional contingencies.[Norrick (1997, 1998, 2000) and Sherzer (1981), for example, analyze how linguistic variation in events and evaluations is
tailored to specific interactional and situational contingencies (see
also Bauman 1986, Hymes 1985, Luborsky 1987 for variation in
elicited narratives). Tannen (1982) compares spoken and written
versions of stories from the same people with attention to involvement strategies. Other strands of research on retellings build from
the work of the British psychologist Frederic Bartlett (1932), whose
research on memory included analyses of "repeated reproduction"

of stories. Chafe's (1980a, 1986, 1994, 1998) ongoing research on language and consciousness likewise includes analysis of retellings. Chafe (1998), for example, begins with linguistic differences related to verbalization (finding that 'chunking' in intonation units is a more reliable indicator of consciousness than syntactic units) and continues to how language reflects narrative competence (e.g. memory, information processing, schemata).

Chapters 6 and 7 focus on one narrative that was told and retold during oral history interviews with a Holocaust survivor. The story is a small piece of an overall life story (we saw an excerpt from the story in Example 1.6 in Section 1.4). Yet like other retellings – perhaps even more so – they are mediated by a multitude of factors. In Chapter 6, *Reframing experience*, I analyze four tellings of the story (about a failed escape) in relation to its information sources. We see that experiences entering the speaker's life from very different sources (and at very different levels of initial familiarity) end up being leveled through successive retellings that incorporate the different sources of the experience. In Chapter 7, *Retelling a story*, I focus on the referential and evaluative changes in the same four versions of the story about the planned escape. We see that successive versions are not only more event-based and temporally ordered, but also reveal a more complex (and current) polyphony of voices.

Chapter 8, *Who did what (again)?* brings together analyses of referrals and narratives by analyzing the changing referrals in the story about the failed escape, along with a story (about a childhood prank) from a sociolinguistic interview in which the speaker tells the crucial part of the story twice. Analyzing how both stories use referring expressions to manage identity in both textual and social worlds, and construct events that both set up and dismantle expectations, provides a good opportunity to see how the two facets of language focused upon in earlier chapters can come together in 'second positions.'

In sum, each chapter in the book focuses on some part of language that appears more than once within a text that is being co-constructed by participants during a social interaction. Each recurrence is different in some way from the first, if only because it is the second 'doing' of something that has already appeared in discourse. Differences range in degree and distance. At the very lowest end of

'difference' is a word that is repeated immediately after its completion. In *I- I think so*, for example, we may rightfully say that this
is a small difference, defined only by the fact that the second occurrence of *I* follows a first occurrence of *I* with a glottal stop, whereas
the first token of *I* does not. At the highest end of 'difference' is a
life story narrative about a particular experience told more than ten
years apart.

Despite these differences, there are several themes running
throughout the different analyses. First, many of the same fifteen
people's voices will be appearing throughout Chapters 2–5.
Although the speakers have different ethnicities, religions, social
classes, and gender (but are all from Philadelphia), I do not focus
on social characteristics in discussion of individual examples. (I
say more about the speakers whose narratives are analyzed in
Chapters 6–8). Nor do I address how social identity through broad
categorical constructs may be related to trends in the data. There
may very well be social (as well as individual) differences in TYPE 2
repairs (Chapter 2), article switches (Chapter 3), pragmatic prototypes (Chapter 4) and full nouns for topical referents (Chapter 5).
But many of the phenomena to be examined are locally grounded
and sequentially based: grouping them together by speaker identity
would mean overlooking the many contingent particularities underlying each variant. Hopefully, however, the fine tuned analyses can
serve as precursors for further study of variation in the discourse of
larger and more controlled samples.

Second, each analysis addresses some aspect of variation in the
language used to represent entities (a person, place, or thing evoked
through a referring expression) or events (in sequences of temporally
ordered clauses that cluster together to report 'what happened') and
how that variation is situated in text and interaction. Everything
that is addressed can thus be defined as syntagmatic or sequential
variation: second position follows an initial occurrence of the 'same'
item. But once that second slot is opened, there is a variety of options
that range in terms of their innovativeness, newness and similarity
from the prior slot. Being in second position thus creates paradigmatic options, each of which can 'fit' with what precedes and what
will follow, albeit in ways that may alter interpretation of what came
before and set up very different frames of interpretation for what
will come next.

Third, the two analytic foci of the book – referrals, narratives – share three underlying concerns. ⌈Referrals and narratives both depend upon links between word and world;⌋ the building of textual and interactional sequences in which words themselves connect; an interplay among emergent (yet cumulative) referential, social and expressive meanings. Although these may be seen as three different axes, when a quality or feature along any one axis recurs in a second position referral or narrative, we need to examine all three axes to see what else changes (or stays the same).

⌈Finally, each chapter takes some facet of language and examines how and why it becomes something different upon re-use. It may seem obvious that we can represent the 'same' entity or event in *other* words as a resource for creativity, newness, and difference. But even re-use of the *same* words can create different meanings and functions – joining the realm of the innovative and new – simply because the redoing of word(s) always appears in a different text, i.e. at the very least in a next-position after a prior-position.⌋

Although each chapter can be read on its own, then, reading all the chapters will reveal recurrent concerns: how does the redoing and possible re-formulation of referential information both reflect (and create) text and interaction? how do alternative ways of saying the same thing (with differences in type and degree of what is 'the same') fit into emergent texts and interactions? Chapter 9, *Redoing and replaying*, helps pull the different analytical threads together. And although I have been describing my approach as a study of variation in discourse, Chapter 9 also reframes the overall discussion in relation to other areas of scholarly inquiry, all of which examine our efforts to balance innovation with restriction, new with old, and different with same.

Notes

1. That there is one consistently recognizable individual designated by a name is a powerful assumption. Although the other Deborah Schiffrin's voice sounds very different than mine, and her work differs (she is a producer for National Public Radio), confusions arise: not only have I been asked by people whether that was me on the radio, but I have also been congratulated at a faculty meeting by our Department Chair for my versatility in producing such an interesting piece on the radio. All this, because what is the 'same' about *Deborah Schiffrin* is the sequence of sounds and the assumption of constancy triggered by names.

2. Compare definitions in Fasold 1990, Leech 1983, Levinson 1983, and Mey 2001.

3. Other problems underlying the development of variation analysis were the progression of linguistic change and dialect differences (see Chambers et al. 2002). Since these issues are less pertinent to variation in discourse, I do not discuss them here (but see Brinton 2002 and Fitzmaurice 2004 on the development of discourse markers).

4. Further discussion can be found in Dines 1980, DuBois and Sankoff 2001, Labov 1978, Lavendera 1978, Lefebvre 1989, Macaulay 2002, Romaine 1981, Sankoff and Thibault 1981. See Myhill 1988 and Nicolle 1988 for illustrations of how to extend the notion of variables to morphology and semantics.

5. The world may be conceptualized as either the concrete world or a temporarily established discourse model. Within either, there may be material (and non-material) objects, attributes, relationships between them, and actions taken by (or upon) them. Although I will speak of 'referents' and 'world,' then, keep in mind that what I mean by the 'world' is actually a continuously evolving *model* of the world constructed by each participant as they exchange speaker/hearer roles.

6. See also Heeman and Hirst (1995) for a computational approach, Ford and Fox (1996) and Smith and Jucker (1998) for interactional analysis.

7. Compare Wortham's (2001) distinction between denotational and interactive meanings, Linde's (1993) discussion of the differences between narratives and chronicles, my own distinction between narratives and lists of events (Schiffrin 1994b).

2

Problematic referrals

2.1 Introduction

We noted in Chapter 1 that referring to people, objects and other entities in the world is central to verbal communication: "the most crucial feature of each utterance, the feature which a listener must minimally grasp in order to begin to understand the utterance, is the expression used to identify what the speaker is talking about" (Brown 1995: 62). Like other aspects of language production and comprehension, however, referring is sometimes problematic enough to warrant repair. And like most repairs, repairs of references are largely self-initiated and self-completed (Schegloff, Jefferson and Sacks 1977): we typically locate and remedy problems in our own speech on our own. Since we often talk our way through our repairs – pausing, interrupting words (phrases, clauses, sentences) in progress, restarting, replacing – the verbal details of our problematic referrals are audible to others and available for their inspection. Still, it is not always easy for us, as listeners or as analysts, to know why what another has said has become problematic in the first place or how it will (or will not) be resolved.

Consider the segments in Example 2.1, in which **bold** indicates the site at which the repair is initiated; if the repaired referent remains the same at self-completion, I use *bold italics*; if it differs, I *italicize* (but do not bold) the repair. Multiple referrals that are part of the problem or solution are differentiated by subscripts; a solution that becomes a problem is ***underlined bold italics***.

Example 2.1

SELF-INITIATED SELF-COMPLETED REPAIRS OF
REFERRALS

(a) And **they-** *they* came back down on her.

(b) Because there's maybe a- *a mi- mile long stretch.*

(c) And there happened to be- **it** was **a good pla-** it was-there-
there was *a whachacallthem* in there, y'know.

(d) And- but it was a barrack that was never finished, **no
window-** I mean there were windows cut out but *no- no- uh
glass* or anything in it.

(e) when **they-** when *we* were younger,

(f) They had the chairs which today they call ice cream parlor
chairs. Y'know, **the-** *thee uh metal*, the round, that twists
around.

(g) And they'd have **these eh** . . . *they- they read your tea leaves*!

(h) We used to come down on the trolley cars. And bring **the-**$_1$
like we$_2$ only had- like [*Ann*$_3$ *and I*]$_2$ *we-*$_2$ *my cousin, Ann*$_3$?
we-$_2$ like *she*$_3$ had Jesse$_4$ and *I* had my Kenny$_5$. And we$_2$ used
to bring *them two*$_1$ down on the trolley car.

The segments in Example 2.1 show that repairs can be self-initiated
either through interruptions known as "cut-offs" (the glottal stops
transcribed with a '-' in lines (a)–(g); see Jasperson (2003) for phonetic description), unfilled pauses (line (g)), filled pauses (*uh* lines
(d)–(f), *eh* (line (g)), the raising, fronting and diphthongization of
the unstressed vowel 'schwa' in *the* as [ie] often followed by *uh*
(line (f)), (see Arnold et al. 2003, Clark and Fox Tree 2002, Fox
Tree and Clark 1997, Jefferson 1974, Swerts 1998), and/or lexical
markers (e.g. *I mean*, line (d)). The material that is interrupted may
be prior to the noun (e.g. an article, line (a), (b), *the-* (lines (f), (h)), a
modifier (*a mi-* line (b)) and/or the noun itself (*they-* line (a), *window-*
(d), *they-* (e), *we* (h)). What is recycled are different parts of an interrupted unit: a partial word (*mi- mile* (b)), a word (*they- they* (a), *no-
no-* (d)), *the- them two* (h)), a dependent clause (*when they- when we*
(e)). Self-completion is through repetition (*they- they* (a)), addition
(*a- a mi- mile long stretch* (b)), replacement by the same constituent
(a noun (lines (a), (d), (e), (h)), including a dummy noun phrase
(*a whachacallthem* in (c), Clark and Wilkes-Gibbs 1992: 112)) or a
different constituent (noun → clause (g)), article → noun (h)).

Also illustrated in Example 2.1 is that the distance between self-initiation and self-completion of the repair varies. Whereas most of the self-completions are relatively close to the self-initiations, the repairs of *it* (line (c)) and *window* (d) proceed by way of existential *there* sentences (Chapters 4). The self-completion of the problematic *the-* in line (h) requires not only clausal support (i.e. *we had* and *I had [NP]* clauses), but also textual support since what first served as solutions then became problems, e.g. *we* was repaired by *Ann and I*; *Ann* was repaired as *my cousin, Ann?* The eventual replacement in line (h) of the definite noun phrase initiated by *the*, with the pronoun *them two*, thus depended upon a sequential organization of a cumulative set of referents that set up a textual world in which an initially problematic referral could be recognized (Schiffrin, in press).

With so many possible problems, and so many possible solutions, how can we approach problematic referrals in a systematic way? In Section 2.2, I begin with a brief review of previous studies that have focused on identifying the error (the site of self-initiation) and/or the repair (the site of self-completion). After discussing some methodological issues facing the analysis of problematic referrals in Section 2.3, I differentiate four types of problematic referrals (all illustrated in Example 2.1) and discuss the trajectories of the problems and their solutions, as well as where they occur and why (Section 2.4). My conclusion compares the locations of the problem types in order to address general implications of problematic referrals (Section 2.5).

2.2   Problematic referrals

Referring is a multi-faceted process based on interactive coordination between speaker production and hearer interpretation. Both depend upon general pragmatic principles (of quantity and relevance) that work along with information accrued during prior text/context and developed within emergent interactional sequences. Although facets of the overall process of using and interpreting referring expressions can be conceptualized independently and as somewhat different from one another, I assume that they are integrated in practice: what a speaker produces is intended to be interpreted by another person within a discourse that is cumulatively and jointly constructed during an ongoing interaction.

Referrals are communicative attempts by a speaker to evoke a referent (the idea a speaker has of something in the world) through a referring expression (a linguistic expression that can represent and evoke an entity). Referrals can be first- or next-mentions in a discourse. As first-mentions, we can think of the speaker as "accessing" the referent; as next-mentions, as "maintaining" the referent. The success of a referral depends on coordination between speaker and hearer. In an ideal world, a speaker intends to evoke a particular entity and uses a referring expression that captures that intention, e.g. a lexical noun that appropriately evokes a referent (a world-to-word connection), a pronoun that can be interpreted (through a word-to-word connection) as indexing a referent. The referring expression used by the speaker would then (again, ideally) allow a hearer to recognize the speaker's intention: to identify a referent sufficiently similar to what the speaker intends so that each can then say (and understand) something about that referent.

Psycholinguists have suggested that the referring process comprises different stages, including conceptual preparation, selecting a semantically and syntactically specified word form (sometimes called a "lemma") from a mental lexicon, retrieving word forms from the mental lexicon for morphological and phonological encoding, and rapid syllabification and articulation (Levelt 1999). Although various models differ in detail, there seems to be general agreement that information flows back and forth (e.g. from phonology to semantics) through "spreading activation or interactive activation . . . in which an initial impetus progressively fans out and activates more words as it spreads along the various connections" (Aitchson 1973; see also Butterworth 1981, Dell and Reich 1981, Levelt 1999, Levelt et al. 1999).

One of the ways that linguists have learned about speech production is through the study of repair. The early seminal studies of Fromkin (1973, 1980) argued that a variety of speech errors (neologisms, word substitutions, blends, misordered constituents) demonstrated the psychological reality of phonological, morphological and syntactic rules and provided evidence for ordered phases in speech production. Such studies have also suggested that although speakers have little or no overt access to their own speech processes, they are able to continuously monitor their own speech, and if they detect a problem, to then self-interrupt, hesitate and/or use editing terms, and then make the repair (Levelt 1983).

Psychologists and psycholinguists interested in the source of errors (and their repercussions for speech production models) often rely on experimental studies that manipulate stimuli to induce (or inhibit) errors or measure picture naming latencies to test models of reaction times in word production. Levelt (1983), for example, constructed a controlled elicitation task (for Dutch speakers examining a set of visual patterns) and then classified the spontaneous self-repairs that occurred during that task. The repairs were divided into three main categories:

appropriateness (Do I want to say it this way? (30%));
lexical, phonetic, and syntactic errors (Am I making a mistake? (42%));
covert repair (repetitions and unfilled interruptions that offered no clue as to their cause (25%)).

Other researchers (both psychologists and linguists) have taken advantage of large already existent corpora to classify problem types and compare their frequency. Garnham et al. (1981) used the London-Lund corpus to identify the putative target of errors and to gloss their types, e.g. vowel reduction, anticipation, omission, pronoun substitution. Nearly half of the errors (99/191 (42%)) were substitutions, which included phonological, semantic and pronominal substitutions. Other corpus studies have addressed a subset of repair types to question 'why this repair now?' Bredart (1991), for example, found support (in a corpus of French) for Levelt's finding that self-initiation of an interruption *within* a word is more frequent for erroneous (rather than merely inappropriate) words.

The most diverse classification of repairs involving reference appears in Geluykens (1994): repairs are differentiated by their conversational trajectories (e.g. other/self initiated/completed), turn locations, prosodic contours, anaphor vs. full noun repairs, and within the latter group, by further factors, including distance and specificity (e.g. violation of an Economy or Clarity Principle). Geluykens' multi-faceted and multi-dimensional approach allows him to identify a repair strategy at the nexus of syntax and turn-taking: 'right dislocations,' in which a subject pronoun is specified by a full noun at the end of the sentence, that are intonationally segmented and interactionally positioned at transition relevance places.

The category of 'appropriateness' (noted by both Levelt and Bredart) brings to mind Jefferson's (1974) finding that inappropriateness can be based on interactional factors, such as recipient, style, or register. Not surprisingly, the interactional side of repairs has been addressed primarily by conversation analysts. In addition to showing a preference for self-initiation and self-completion within a single turn (Schegloff, Jefferson and Sacks 1977), further studies show that repairs are oriented toward the organization of turn-taking, as evinced through their distribution across turn-transition places (Schegloff 1979) or their occurrence in turn beginnings (Schegloff 1987).

Psycholinguistic studies of how we reformulate referrals, however, also have come to embrace the idea that referrals are an interactional process. For example, Levelt (1983) suggests an interruption rule (interrupt when the word is complete) and a well-formedness rule (maintain the syntax of the interrupted utterance as much as possible), both of which suggest an orientation toward interaction, i.e. an underlying attentiveness to the listener's need for comprehension. Whereas conversation-analytic studies of repair location suggest that speaker's repairs are designed to maintain the turn and provide the listener with the information within an open floor, then Levelt's rules are geared more toward facilitating the listener's incorporation of the referent into his/her discourse model. Clark and Marshall's (1992) comparison between horizontal and vertical repairs shows how different sources of information can facilitate hearer comprehension and thus compensate for speaker disfluencies (see also Brennan and Schober, 2001, and Clark and Schoeder 1992). Whereas horizontal repairs add information within the reference without changing the basis for mutual knowledge, vertical repairs strengthen mutual knowledge by moving to a stronger basis for such knowledge, e.g. from community membership to linguistic co-presence to physical co-presence. The success of vertical repairs suggests that additional information does not in and of itself increase the success of a referral: chances of success are better if the additional information builds upon a more accessible base of mutual knowledge.

Although my brief review of speech errors and repairs has barely scratched the surface of the range of phenomena that may be studied and the frameworks for doing so, two questions have emerged. Where and why are repairs self-initiated? How do repairs self-complete? My approach to these questions in this chapter will begin by locating repairs that occur within the noun phrase as indicated by a hyphen in the transcript, a signal of a 'cut-off' or self-interruption either within or at the end of a word (Section 2.3). Based upon my view of referrals (as outlined in Chapter 1), I then suggest a systematic classification of repairs that takes into account a process of speech production that differentiates a referent (presumably a selection at a conceptual level) from a referring expression (presumably a selection at the lexical level). In addition to discussing how the problem types are situated in texts and interactions (Section 2.4), I compare various features of the repairs, including their location in syntactic and interactional units (Section 2.5).

2.3 Finding problems

One of the difficulties in studying problematic referrals is that we (as speakers) are not always aware that we have chosen the 'wrong' word; nor do we always discover that our hearers' knowledge is not sufficient for the successful resolution of a pronoun. The problems for us as listeners are different: we may not realize that we have interpreted the 'wrong' referent until it seems too late to backtrack and too awkward to begin the appropriate adjustments. Luckily problematic referrals are often self-initiated relatively quickly through false starts, cut-offs, unfilled pauses, *uh* and *um*, restarts, and/or repetitions that are followed (although sometimes after a delay) by another referral. As we see in this section, however, these mechanical cues are neither necessary (problems are displayed in other ways) nor sufficient: instead of indicating a problematic referral, the same features may index other kinds of reformulations or be part of a potential turn transition space.

Consider, first, that in addition to the disfluencies illustrated in Example 2.1, also indicative of repair is phonological variation in *the* and *a*, sometimes conditioned by *uh* and *um*. In a corpus-based study of the effects of disfluencies on the pronunciation of function words, Bell et al. (2003) found that high frequency monosyllabic function words – including *the* – were likely to have longer vowels not only near disfluencies (such as *uh* and *um*), but also when the next word is less predictable in context.

Variants of *the* and *a* are illustrated in Examples 2.2 and 2.3. In Example 2.2, Rick is telling Arvilla (a sociolinguist) about their church, suggesting that it might be a good church for her to join (zig-zag **Z** shows no perceptible inter-turn pause):

Example 2.2

Rick: (a)   Well, they have a-

                                    Z

Lucy: (b)   Yeh.

Rick: (c)   They have [ey] **uh** seven thirty service at night.[1]

Arvilla: (d)   Well, that's good.

Rick: (e)   And there's **a** parking lot right across the street.

Rick's description illustrates two variants of *a* pronunciation: unstressed schwa (in lines (a) and (e)), and 'long a' (in line (c)). The tokens of *a* in lines (a) and (c) both indicate repair: *a* in line (a) is cut-off (the segment is truncated by a glottal stop); [ey] in line (c) is followed by *uh*, a marker of an upcoming resolution for a solution to a possibly complex problem (Clark and Fox Tree 2002 and Fox Tree and Clark 1997).

Comparable variants of *the* are in Example 2.3, where Dot is describing the chairs in an old fashioned oyster bar:

Example 2.3

Dot: (a)   And they-

          (b)   in **thee** oyster saloon they had **the** chairs

          (c)   which today they call ice cream parlor chairs.[2]

Anne: (d)   Yeh.

Dot: (e)   Y'know, **the- thee uh** metal, the round,

                that twisted around.

Thee appears in lines (b) and (e). In line (b), *thee* is phonologically conditioned by the next segment, a vowel in the noun. In line (e), *thee* is likewise conditioned by the following segment, also a vowel. The phonological segment being anticipated in the pronunciation of *thee* in line (e), however, is the vowel in *uh*, not the initial consonant in *metal*. In *the- thee uh metal* (line (e)), then, we find three micro-phases of the repair. Dot's cut-off *the* self-initiates the repair. Dot's restart, and use of *thee*, projects upcoming trouble with the noun, e.g. Dot cannot access a way of describing the 'chair.' Dot's *uh* delays the self-completion of the repair (a delay that has comprehension benefits for hearers (Arnold et al. 2003, Clark and Schober 1992)) as she gains time to access the right word for the object in mind.

Not all self-interruptions or delays of a referring expression, however, indicate a problem in identifying a referent or verbalizing a referral. Although *thee uh* can indicate cognitive processing and planning as in Example 2.3, for example, it can also indicate a switch to a referring expression that is interactionally (rather than referentially) preferred (Jefferson 1974): *thee uh policeman*, for example, can show the speaker's switch in register from the more vernacular term "cop" to the more formal term "policeman" (cf. what Levelt 1983 would call an "appropriateness repair").

The next three examples show that an interruption within a referring expression need not indicate a problem with the referral itself.

Example 2.4
(a) My father took me out in a rowboat in the bay **in the-** *down the shore*
(b) It's- *it's a- it* was a big section.
(c) and we used to take **our s-** *get on our sleds.*

In Example 2.4, a referral is interrupted (at the article in lines (a), (b)) or at the phonological onset of the noun (line (c)). But as the repair is self-completed, we see that the problem for each was actually at an earlier point within the larger phrase: *in* ➔ *down* in the prepositional phrase (a); present to past tense *('s* ➔ *was)* in the verb phrase (b); *take* ➔ *get on* in the verb phrase (c).

Finally, just as disfluencies do not always indicate problematic referrals, so too, problematic referrals are not always overtly displayed by disfluencies. Prior to Example 2.5, Zelda (a middle aged woman) and I had been talking about our recent weekends at the beach. Whereas Zelda had been babysitting for her twin toddler grandsons, I had been with my parents, my older brother and his wife, and their infant son. Zelda had been describing the thrill she felt when her grandsons first started calling her "Grandmom."

Example 2.5
Zelda: (a) I think Grandmom's nice.
Debby: (b) I think it's nice too.
Zelda: (c) I like it.
Debby: (d) Yeh. I [call my-
Zelda: (e)   [Does **your baby** talk?
Debby: (f) Uh: he doesn't t- [say my name yet. =
Zelda: (g)   [Oh.
Debby: (f) Um . . . he: makes a lot of noises!

After a series of topic closures through repeated and shared assessments (lines (a) to (c)), Zelda and I both propose stepwise topic transitions. I draw upon my own family status as a grandchild to begin to mention what *I call my* grandmother (line (d)). Whereas my statement places me in a position lateral to Zelda's grandchildren, Zelda's question *does your baby talk* (e), positions me as lateral to the adult member of the generation (i.e. to her). But it does so in a way that was confusing to me: because Zelda says *your baby*, I am afraid that Zelda has mislabeled the *baby* who is my nephew, as my son. Notice that the referent is partially the same: we are still talking about 'the infant with whom I was on the beach last weekend.' But it is also different in a fundamental way: since I had no baby son, there was nothing to refer to; any propositions about 'my baby' would have been false.[3] Rather than other-initiate an other-completed repair (e.g. "Oh it's not my baby, it's my brother's"), I later present information that clarifies the infant's family status: I mention that 'he' has a deep voice, so does my brother, and that 'he' knows the word 'mama.'

In this section, we have seen that not all self-interruptions during, or adjacent to, the referring expression indicate problems with the referring process *per se*. In order to identify problematic referrals, I searched in my corpus of sociolinguistic interviews for noun phrases (or their parts) that were cut off (by -). I then identified the problem type and coded broadly for different factors that I thought might be relevant to their distribution: type of noun, location in sentence and turn, material included in self-completion of the repair. Section 2.4 discusses my classification of problem types and illustrates these.

2.4 Problem types

In this section, I propose four different types of problematic referrals that arise as the speaker identifies the referent (what is being denoted) and/or formulates the referring expression (the lexical item used to evoke the referent for the hearer). The four problem types are differentiated by separating what happens to the referent from what happens to the referring expression. The four possibilities are the following:

TYPE 1 – CONTINUE REFERRING EXPRESSION AND CONTINUE REFERENT (e.g. *he* → *he*)

TYPE 2 – CHANGE REFERRING EXPRESSION AND
CHANGE REFERENT (e.g. *he* ➔ *they*)

TYPE 3 – CHANGE REFERRING EXPRESSION BUT CON-
TINUE REFERENT (e.g. *he* ➔ *Bob*)

TYPE 4 – CONTINUE REFERRING EXPRESSION BUT
CHANGE REFERENT (e.g. *they* (= 'friends') ➔ *they* (=
'cousins')

Each problem type is illustrated through an examination of whatever factors – linguistic form, prior and posterior text and speaker/hearer interaction – contribute to the problem and its solution. In each example, I **bold** the problematic referral. If the repaired referent remains the same, I *italicize* (and **bold**) the next-mention. When the referent changes, I *italicize* (but do not bold) the next referring expression. If there are several active referrals in the text that bear on the problematic referral, I differentiate them with numerical indices at each mention.

2.4.1 TYPE 1 *Continue referring expression and continue referent*

In the first type of repair, TYPE 1, the speaker continues to use the same referring expression to evoke the same referent. Because this creates a disfluency – but gives no overt indication of the problem in production – these are sometimes called covert repairs (Levelt 1983).

In the simplest case, the speaker merely restarts and repeats the referring expression, as in Example 2.6:

Example 2.6
And she was puttin' this stack of dishes away.
And **they-** *they* came back down on her.

In Example 2.6, *they* is anaphoric to *this stack of dishes*; the speaker repeats *they*, with no change in form or meaning.

Other repetitions are the basis for increments that build a more specific referent onto preliminary material, often just the indefinite or definite article. In Example 2.7, for example, the speaker begins with an article (*a-*), repeats the article but adds a partial modifier (*a mi-*), and then completes the referral with the modifier and noun (*mile long stretch*).

Example 2.7
(a) Because there's maybe a- *a mi- mile long stretch.*
(b) And they used to run along there.

Likewise, in Example 2.8, the speaker begins with an article (*the-*), repeats the article with an incipient noun (*the s-*) and then repeats the noun (*scoop*):

Example 2.8
(a) Rita, you had your turn.
(b) I've got to get to **the-** *the s- scoop* from these guys.

Notice that we cannot be absolutely sure that the same referent *is* intended by the speaker in Examples 2.7 and 2.8. In Example 2.7, for example, perhaps the intended referent was *a mile*, then extended to *a mile long stretch*. In Example 2.8, it could be that the speaker's initial *the-* and/or *the s-*, was intended to preface *the story* rather than *scoop*. The question of whether the potential referent is continued for the *hearer* takes us in still more complex directions. Although the hearer may have anticipated a completion of *s-* in Example 2.8, the truncated beginnings provide so little specific information that the hearer may very well have put her inference of any referent 'on hold.'

Other self-initiations and self-completions of TYPE 1 repairs open a textual space for the insertion of material between first- and next-mentions of the referent (cf. Polanyi (1978) on "not so false starts" and Hayashi (2004) on "discourse within a sentence"). I will call these long distance TYPE 1 repairs. As we see in the next three examples, these self-interruptions seem due not to problems with the referent itself, but to the placement of the referent in a discourse.

In Example 2.9, Anne and Sue are talking about the misbehavior of young girls in Sue's neighborhood. *They* is cut-off twice:

Example 2.9

Sue: (a) But **they-**
      (b) yet *they* were probably smokin' and drinkin' beer like when they were ten or eleven.
      (c) Like sneaky things.
      (d) And [*they-*]
Anne: (e) [Like] what, for instance?
      (f) Can you think of anything in particular?
Sue: (g) Yeh, like *they* would sleep over each other's houses.

Sue self-interrupts *they* (line (a)), but then substitutes the concessive marker *yet* (line (b)) for the contrastive marker *but*. *They* reappears in the restarted utterance in (line (b)). Sue's next self-interrupted *they-* (line (d)) relinquishes her turn to Anne's overlapping request for a specific example (*like what?* (in line (e)) that builds upon Sue's *like sneaky things* (line (c)). Sue provides a specific example *Yeh, like they would sleep over each other's houses* (line (g)) that recycles her own recurrent use of *they* (from lines (b) and (d)). So although there are two cut-offs of *they-* in Example 2.9, neither reveals an overt problem.

In Example 2.10, Dot has been talking about the problems facing the elderly poor in her city. She gives an example of one particular person whose landlords (*they*) were evicting her.

Example 2.10
(a)   And for some reason, **they-**
(b)   whether or not she owed rent or something like that,
(c)   **they** were putting her out

Dot begins a clause with *they* and then self-interrupts (line (a)) to insert a qualification that intensifies the injustice about to be reported (line (b)): people should not be evicted from their apartments if they are not behind in their payments of rent. Dot then returns to the same referent and referring expression (line (c)).

Example 2.11 illustrates that repeated items can bracket another person's turn. Arvilla and Rick have been talking about cultural differences within the United States:

Example 2.11
Arvilla: (a)   I bet there's more of a- =
Rick: (b)   I do, too.
Arvilla: (c)   = of a- *a* barrier between uh when you come here
                         than when you're in Europe.

Arvilla withholds her self-completed referral to *a barrier* until after Rick has agreed with her projected assertion. Again, this is a referral marked as problematic that is not a problem with the referent itself.

Examples 2.9 to 2.11 have illustrated how material inserted between self-initiation and completion of a problematic referral can be relevant to its anticipated use in upcoming discourse and alter the textual world into which the referral is then integrated. But the repair itself is minimally disruptive to the ongoing flow of talk: the speaker returns to the prior text and syntax of the interrupted sentence. The completion of a long distance TYPE 1 repair thus retroactively defines the inserted material as a temporary frame break (cf. Goffman's (1974) negative transfix) in which a temporary activity delays, but does not diminish, the completion of prior talk.

2.4.2 Type 2 Change referring expression and change referent

Rather than continue referring expression and referent, speakers may abandon referring expression and referent. These TYPE 2 problems often involve shifts in textual and/or deictic world (i.e. temporal, spatial and personal parameters of the speech event).

In Example 2.12, Rick and his wife Lucy have been answering questions that Arvilla has been asking about dating restrictions when they were younger:

Example 2.12

```
Rick:   (a)   But after high school I'm-
        (b)   like I said there was no really limit [to our- =
Lucy:   (c)                                         [No restriction. No.
Rick:   (d)   = I know they- my mother-
        (e)   my father died when I was young and
              uh . . . =
                     Z
Lucy:   (f)            umhmm
Rick:   (g)   = and my mother didn't care for me to stay out all
              hours.
```

Rick's self-interruption of his first referral *they* (line (d)) to *my mother* is a switch from a plural pronoun to a noun whose referent could have been included within its referential scope. The only problem is that the 'they' in which his mother could have been included is no longer part of a 'they' during the time period of which he is speaking. As Rick explains, his mother was his only parent (*my father died when I was young* (line (e))) during the period of time about which he was speaking (*after high school*, line (a)). Thus Rick's repair is based on a mismatch between words and world. (Note, also, that Rick's repetition of *my mother* (g) is a long-distance TYPE 1 repair).

Similar to Rick's *they* ➔ *my mother* repair is a switch from a collective *they* to component parts of *they* in Example 2.13. Anne is checking some demographic information about Gary's parents, when she recalls what Gary's wife Donna had already told her:

Example 2.13
(a)   So- they-
(b)   well, I remember Donna said that *your mom* was born at Third and Diamond,
(c)   and *your dad* was at Second and Diamond.

Anne's query begins with *they* (line (a)) anaphoric to the recent antecedent *parents* (not included here) and then shifts to each parent separately. The separation of *they* into two referents: *your mom* (line (b)); *your dad* (line (c)) alters the referent 'parents' by individuating the two members of the group. This change in referent from collective to each individual member is consistent with what is being predicated (where each person was born) and the branching structure of that information. The two subparts of the referent are textually united through syntactic parallelism and ellipsis of *born* in the second conjunct (a structure consistent with the list-like text (Chapter 5)).

Like Rick's switch from *they* to *my mother* in Example 2.12, Anne's switch from *they* to *your mom* and *your dad* in Example 2.13 reflects the particular textual world in which the entities have gained relevance. Thus if Rick had been talking about his parents when he was an infant, and if Anne had been talking about the more general neighborhood in which Gary's parents had been born, then *they* would have matched the representation of the world at that time and in that place. Thus both repairs reflect not only a mismatch between words and world, but also a shift back to an earlier reference time in which either two parents were alive (for Rick) or Anne did not know (or had not realized) that Gary's wife Donna had already told her where his parents had been born.

In Example 2.14, a repair stems from a shift in deictic center, i.e. the (usually) egocentric location in a speech event to which person, time and place is oriented. Ceil and Anne are driving around Philadelphia so that Ceil can give Anne a visual tour of different neighborhoods. Their change in location facilitates recurring changes in deictic center.

Example 2.14

Ceil: (a) This is where a lot of your Kensingtonians$_1$ moved to.
Anne: (b) Okay.
Ceil: (c) Was up here.
Anne: (d) How come they$_1$ moved up there, Ceil?
Ceil: (e) Well, **they$_1$**-
         (f) *the coloreds$_2$* started to come in.
Anne: (g) Yeh.
Ceil: (h) See?
         (i) That's- so they$_1$ moved up.

Two referring expressions, serving as two different referents, appear in Example 2.14: *a lot of your Kensingtonians* ((a), people from Ceil's neighborhood); *the coloreds* ((f), a term for African Americans in 1970s Philadelphia).

The first referent, *a lot of your Kensingtonians* (a) is pronominalized in Anne's question *How come they moved up there* (line (d)), which continues both subject and predicate from Ceil's *moved to* (line (a)). Ceil begins to answer Anne's question by continuing the thematic position of this referent in subject position (*well they$_1$* (line (e)). But she then self-interrupts *they*- and switches to *the coloreds* (line (f)). One possible reading of this switch is that *they* and *the coloreds* evoke the same referent through different referring expressions (TYPE 3 (Section 2.4.3)): *coloreds* might be specifying who is being evoked by the vague and multi-indexical *they*. But both deixis and text show that rather than continuing the same referent evoked by the referring expression *they* (TYPE 1), *the coloreds* is actually a new referent.

As Ceil and Anne enter different neighborhoods in the city, their spatial deictics (both adverbials and verbs of motion) shift. Ceil's proximal deictics *this* (line (a)) and *here* (line (c)) index the neighborhood that the two women have just entered. However, Anne's distal deictic *there* in her question *how come they moved up there* (line (d)) switches the deictic center back to the textual world of Kensington, the neighborhood *from* which (not *to* which) *the Kensingtonians* moved. Ceil's verb 'come' in *the coloreds started to come in* (line (f)) retains Kensington as the deictic center from the perspective of the location into which *the coloreds* entered. Thus *there* and *come* show that it is *the coloreds* who *started to come in*, a switch in reference from the *Kensingtonians*, who were the *they* who *moved up there* (line (d)) out of the neighborhood.

After her brief explanation of shifting populations, Ceil returns to *they*$_1$ ('the Kensingtonians' (line (i)) to repeat (from *up here* (line (c)) and *up there* (line (d)) who moved *up* to the neighborhood in which Ceil and Anne are driving. By repeating Anne's predicate 'move up,' as well as the referring expression *they*$_1$, Ceil reaffirms the gist of her answer to Anne's question. Thus Ceil's repair of *they-* (line (e)) to *the coloreds* (line (f)) switches referent and referring expression due to the shift in deictic center. Ceil's repetition of *they*$_1$ (line (i)) also shows that *they-* (line (e)) was simultaneously the opening of a long distance TYPE 1 repair.

Still another example in which *they* becomes part of a repair in which both referring expression and referent are abandoned is Example 2.15. After asking Bess if she had a lot of responsibilities as a kid, Anne asks about her sisters' responsibilities:

Example 2.15
Anne: (a)   How about your older sisters?
          (b)   What'd they do?
Bess: (c)   We- *they- we all* did it.

Anne's referring expressions reflect a sequential dependency of the second part of her question on the first (cf. Fox 1987): after *your older sisters* (line (a)) establishes a first-mention of a referent, Anne asks about that referent through the next-mention pronoun *they*. Bess' answer begins with an inclusive referring expression *we*, switches to the exclusive *they*, and then uses the most inclusive *we all*. Each switch from *we* to *they* and back to *we* is a brief abandonment of a referring expression and a referent.

Switching between referents of *they* and *we* is not always as simple as we saw with Bess' change. *They* and *we* typically evoke mutually exclusive entities whose identities depend upon boundaries between 'self' (*we*) and 'other' (*they*) collectives. Despite the referential variability always associated with these "shifters" (Jakobson 1957), the entities in the external world to which *they* and *we* point are thus unlikely to be the same, at least within whatever referential world is evoked through a single utterance. In Example 2.16, however, Gary's switch from *they* to *we* is a change in referent, but it is difficult to identity the referent to which he has switched:

Example 2.16

Anne: (a)   Were a lot of the guys that hung, um, on your
                    corner in school with you, too?
Gary: (b)   Well, most of us g- went to grade school,
           (c)   Catholic school together.
Anne: (d)   Oh, so you were all-
Gary: (e)   Then there was a few went to public school
           (f)   when *they*- when *we* were younger, growin' up,
           (g)   the ones that went to Catholic school,
           (h)   we hh *we* used to fight *them* all the time.

The segment begins with Anne asking whether *a lot of the guys* from
the neighborhood went to the same school (line (a)). Gary opens his
answer by reiterating the partitive construction *a lot of the guys* (line
(a)) in Anne's referral in his response *most of us g-* (line (b)). Notice,
however, that he resets the quantity from *a lot* to *most* and then cuts
off the noun at what seems like an incipient repetition of *guys* (*g-* in
line (b)). Gary then modifies another part of Anne's question. Anne
has asked whether the guys were *in school* with Gary. Gary replies
by specifying the level of school (*grade school*) and a subtype of
that school (*Catholic school* (lines (b), (c)) that *most of us* attended
(line (b)).

   Thus far Gary has modified the size of the group and the type of
school without overtly correcting Anne's presumptions about either
the group or the school. Subtle modification of both referents continues as Gary uses the list introducer *then there was* (Chapter 5) to
introduce *a few* (line (e)) as the complement to *most* (line (b)) who
went to *public school* ((e) the other subtype of grade school). Thus
even though Gary refines the partitioning of the group ('who'), the
type of school ('where'), and their relationships (who went where),
the referrals through which he does so do not themselves become
problematic.

   What does become openly problematic are the first and third
person plural pronouns *we* and *they* in *when **they**- when we were
younger, growin' up* (line (f)). But who is the referent of *they*? And of
we? Since adjacent text often provides antecedents for pronouns, we
can search in the text for our answers. The referent for *they* is easy to
find: *they* is anaphoric with the more informative noun *a few* in *then
there was a few went to public school* (line (e)) simply because it is a

syntactically bound anaphor whose textual antecedent is identifiable through the syntactic constraint known as c-command.

We is more difficult. Although we know that *we* includes Gary, we cannot be sure in which collective Gary includes himself. Although *we* (line (f)) might very well encompass the entire group (all those who *were younger, growin' up* (f)), it could also be the narrower subgroup: those who *went to Catholic school* (line (g)) and *used to fight* (line (h)) the others. The referent of *we* depends on how we group together intonationally differentiated units (Chafe 1991) into syntactic units, and thus to a certain degree, on the prosodic features of the utterances. The following arrangements of the text highlight the differences:

Example 2.17
  (a) Then there was a few went to public school when *they-*
       when *we* were younger, growin' up, the ones that went to
       Catholic school, we hh *we* used to fight *them* all the time.
  (b) Then there was a few went to public school
       when *they-* when *we* were younger, growin' up,
       the ones that went to Catholic school, we hh *we* used to fight
       them all the time

In Example 2.17 part (a), *we* looks like part of a right disloca-tion repair (argued by Geluykens (1994) to be a typical form of self repair for underspecified or interactionally insufficient first-mentions). With this structure, we would have a narrow reading. But in Example 2.17 part (b), *we* is a replacement for *they* and includes all of those *growin' up* together irrespective of their different schools.

2.4.3 TYPE 3 *Change referring expression but continue referent*

In contrast to the two problem types discussed thus far – in which referring expression and referent share the same fate – speakers may treat the word and world differently. In the type to be discussed here (TYPE 3), speakers abandon a referring expression, but continue the referent previously evoked by that term. As we see through some of the examples in this group, however, it is not always easy to say that a referent has been continued or whether it is continued in the same way for both speaker and hearer.

I begin with an example in which it is relatively clear that the referent *is* continued. In Example 2.18, Gary is telling a story about an accident that happened to a childhood teacher: a *stack of dishes* (line (a)) fell on her. Although the accident is the turning point in the story plot, it also has a second, more subordinate role in the story: the accident is what led the usually strict teacher to be more lenient with her students (who were being punished for misbehavior) that day.

Example 2.18
(a)   So, we had to sit in the back of the cafeteria
(b)   and right at the back they had the kitchen where the nuns ate.
(c)   And she was puttin' this stack of dishes away.
(d)   And they- they came back down on her.
(e)   And she cut her hand up.
(f)   But when **the-**
(g)   we heard *them* fall and somebody yelled her name,
(h)   so we ran in to see if she was all right.

The story follows a canonical narrative syntax in most of the clauses in Example 2.18. Gary introduces a referent 'stack of dishes' (line (c)) while describing the activity of his teacher (*And she was puttin' this stack of dishes away*) in a simple narrative clause. He focuses upon the dishes in the next clause *they came back down on her* (line (d)), showing its information status through a pronominal reference *they* and by making it the subject of the clause. Gary then switches back to the main character 'teacher' as the pronominal subject (*she*) to describe the outcome of the accident for the teacher: *And she cut her hand up* (line (e)).

In *But when the-* (line (f)), Gary seems about to return to the 'dishes' referent through *the-*. Although breaks from temporal sequence – such as the simultaneity conveyed by *but when* in (line (f)) – often indicate internal evaluation, Gary then switches to a different means of evaluation. *We heard them fall and somebody yelled her name* (line (g)) returns to a more canonical narrative syntax to backtrack into the temporal flow of the accident itself in order to provide more detail about the turning point in the story. Notice that once Gary returns to the scene of the accident, and describes it from his point of view (*we heard* (line (g)) the temporal/epistemic starting point (Chapter 7)), the referent 'stack of dishes' (line (c)) reappears as *them*. Thus, the repair from *the-* to *them* – a change in referring expression, but continuation of the referent 'stack of dishes' – is related to the way the referent is temporally and evaluatively re-embedded within the narrative sequence.

In Example 2.18 just discussed, a speaker abandoned a referring expression but continued a referent by substituting one referring noun for another. In the next two examples, speakers abandon nominals altogether and find other ways of evoking referents. In these cases, we cannot be sure that the same referent is actually continued. Describing an identity through a typical activity (in a clause), rather than labeling the identity (in a noun), might mean that speakers are representing and evoking somewhat different concepts. Despite this possibility, I have considered these as continuations of the referent: they contrast with those repairs in which speakers clearly abandon a referent, because a concept (however fuzzy) that the speaker had in mind does continue to be salient in the discourse.

In Example 2.19, the speaker abandons a referring expression, here initiated as a definite *the*, for a phrasal representation of the salient idea.

Example 2.19
(a) Especially some mornings when you wake up you have **the-**
(b) *can't sit up for a day.*

Prior to Example 2.19, the speaker had been discussing drinking (alcohol). But instead of using a nominal to convey the morning-after effects of drinking (e.g. *the worst hangover*), the speaker captures the idea as an event *can't sit up for a day* (b).

In Example 2.20, the speaker begins an indefinite referring expression *a* in (b) that would nominalize a description of his father (*he isn't like a-*). But he self interrupts, uses *uh-*, and then rephrases the idea that a type-identifiable indefinite NP (Gundel et al. 1993) could have captured.

Example 2.20
(a) I think my grandmother and grandfather knew a little bit German, of German.
(b) And my father knows words but he isn't like **a- [ey] uh-**
(c) *I wouldn't say he speaks German.*

Based on what the speaker says about his father – *my father knows words but* line (b), *I wouldn't say he speaks German* (line (c)) – we might guess that a nominal like *a bilingual* or *a native speaker* could have provided a type-identifiable referent in line (b). Instead, the speaker captures the idea of not speaking a language through the clause *I wouldn't say he speaks German* (line (c)).

Although I have been discussing the continuation of referents in this section, we have also seen that we can not be completely sure that a referent actually is being continued. Both analysts and hearers rely largely on referring expressions to identify referents. Thus, when a speaker abandons part (or all) of a referring expression, we cannot always know whether the same referent is intended. This problem is especially acute for the problematic referral illustrated next: word searches; misnamings.

First, word searches. Sometimes we are thinking or talking about someone and thus have a very specific referent in mind (e.g. 'the person I knew in graduate school who finished her dissertation in one year'), but we cannot remember a term (e.g. a name) that displays our degree of familiarity with that referent. We may try different referring expressions only to abandon them – even while the referent remains the same in our mind. But until we find the 'right' word, different referents may be evoked for our hearers – or even no referent at all.

Example 2.21 illustrates a word search (we saw part of this in Example 2.1c). Charlie is telling a story about almost falling off a ladder while painting a house.

Example 2.21
   (a)   And somehow or other I- I managed to grab the edge of the roof.
   (b)   And there happened to be-
   (c)   it was a **good pla- it** was-
   (d)   there- there was *a whachacallthem* in there, y'know?
   (e)   And I could hold on to it.

Charlie first locates a site (*the edge of the roof* (line (a)) and then begins to predicate the presence of something else on the roof with *there happened to be-* line (b). Even though a referring expression was not initiated in line (b), *there* sentences are often used to introduce new or less familiar referents (see Chapter 4). *There* in line (b), however, is ambiguous between its existential reading and its locative meaning: *there* could be spatially anaphoric to *the edge of the roof*.

Without yet specifying the place, Charlie abandons his previous format to begin to say something about the place: *it was a good pla- it was-* (line (c)). But Charlie then abandons *it* and returns to a sentence in which *there* appears twice, with the two different meanings that had been ambiguous in line (b): existential *there* in line (d) predicates existence of the place *on the edge of the roof* as a *whachacallthem*; locative *there* in line (d) anaphorically conveys its location.

Notice that the dummy noun phrase (Clark and Wilkes-Gibbs 1992) in Example 2.21 does not really tell us the source of the problem: it may display either a general inability to find a conventional term through which to evoke the specific place (a referring expression problem) or a lack of information about what the place actually is (a denotation problem). But regardless of the source of Charlie's problem, he can then rely upon the dummy noun phrase to continue his story: in *and I could hold on to it* (line (e)), Charlie uses the pronoun (*it*) as a referral that assumes familiarity with the place just mentioned. Notice that Charlie may still have no idea of what to call the place (or what the place is) – the ledge? gutter? drainpipe? – just as the hearer may still not know exactly what place Charlie was able to *hold on to*. Nevertheless, some place with qualities relevant to the story has been evoked and can thus have a role in the story. Charlie is thus able to use the referent to continue his story, even though he has given up on the presumably prior goal of identifying the referent.

Misnamings also illustrate the continuation of a referent but change in the referring expression. Misnamings can appear in terms of address (which can also be used as terms of reference) as when Jack addressed me, and referred to me as Barbara when speaking to Freda. Similar phonological and semantic interference can lead not only to misnaming people, but to erroneous words. While I was taking my daughter Laura to tennis camp, for example, I asked whether she had her *backpack*, changed it rapidly to *lunch pack* and then finally got it right with *lunchbox*. Laura herself asked if we had *the tennis-* and then self corrected to *the ten dollars* needed for the day.

In such cases, it is hard to be sure of what referent is actually activated in the speaker's mind and even more difficult to know what is being evoked for the other. And we do not often ask. For example, when Laura and I were talking about how cold the weather had been this past spring, Laura said that the *hedgehog* must have made a mistake back in February when he saw his shadow (an outcome that forecasts an early spring). I knew exactly what she meant about the weather, and the general practice that she was talking about, even though I also knew that the right animal was 'groundhog' and even though I *didn't* know what animal she actually had 'in mind.' Rather than overtly correct her, I just answered by saying "yeh, what makes the groundhog an expert anyway . . ." We kept talking about the weather and Laura then mentioned the 'groundhog' without remarking on any of the terminological (or other) changes she might have noticed.

2.4.4 TYPE 4 *Continue referring expression but change referent*

In the final problem type, TYPE 4, the same referring expression is used for a different referent. Referring expressions – especially pronouns – are often used repeatedly in discourse even when they are intended to evoke different referents within that discourse. If the referring expressions are embedded in a text that facilitates their intended recognition as different referents, they need not become sites of repair In Example 2.22, for example, we can identify four different referents of *they*:

Example 2.22

Ceil: (a)   *They$_1$* said **this bank$_2$** got robbed yesterday.
          (b)   I don't know whether *they$_2$* did or not.
Anne: (c)   What? Really?
Ceil: (d)   Yeh.
Anne: (e)   Wow.
Ceil: (f)   But *they$_3$* caught them the minute *they$_4$* walked out the door.
          (g)   That's what *they$_1$* claim.

The only *they* in Example 2.22 that has a clear textual antecedent is *they$_2$* (line (b)) for the prior *this bank$_2$*. The referent of two other instances is inferable through the predicates: *they$_3$* in *they caught* is an authority ('police' or 'guards'); *they$_4$* in *they walked out the door* is the thieves themselves. Although *they$_1$* (in lines (a), (g)) is vague, it seems to be the source of information (e.g. newspapers, radio, TV). And what *is* clear is that *they*₁ in lines (a) and (g) are the same and are not the referents of the other uses of *they*.

Example 2.23 comes not from the sociolinguistic interview data, but from the corpus of Holocaust oral histories that I have been studying (see Chapters 6–7). Ilse Kahane is recounting her arrival at the concentration camp Bergen Belsen. The scene there is one of devastation and death. Just prior to the fragment here, Ilse had been describing the job that she is required to do (move bodies). She begins in lines (a) to (c) to describe the dead and dying inmates whom she is required to move. The problematic referral is the repeated use of the same referring expression *they*. *They* is used in lines (b) to (d) for the inmates₁ and for the Germans₂ line (j):

Example 2.23

(a) **Some of them**₁ were just so skinny, and-
     and just dropped down, y'know.
(b) I mean **they**₁ would have-
(c) if **they**₁ weren't dead at that moment,
(d) **they**₁ would have been dead most probably twenty-four
     hours later.
(e) That was my job.
(f) But then- . . .
(g) It was a chaos in this place.
(h) I don't even think **they**₁? knew anymore
(i) what was- what **they**- ₁→₂ what was going on,
(j) *the Germans*₂.
(k) Except "Let's kill them or, let's get rid of them, or let them
     die."

The uses of *they* in lines (b) to (d) are referentially clear: *they* refers to the inmates. The referring problem arises in line (h) when *they* is used again. Ilse first self-interrupts at *what was-* (line (i)) to recycle back to the complement of *knew* (line (h)). After beginning to replace *what was-* (line (h)) with *what they-* (line (i)), she completes the complement clause as *what was going on*, adding *the Germans* in a right-dislocation repair (Geluykens 1994). Notice that the content of lines (h) and (i) had allowed an interpretation of *they* as the inmates: perhaps the inmates were the ones who no longer *knew . . . what was going on* (line (i)). It is not until the clause final noun *the Germans* (line (j)) that we learn that the Germans were the intended referent. This is confirmed by the reported speech that then represents the Germans' plans (*"Let's kill them or, let's get rid of them, or let them die"* (line (j))) whose outcome had just been described.

2.4.5 Summary

In this section, we have categorized problematic referrals by two different criteria: whether the referring expression continues or changes; whether the referent continues or changes. This classification assumed that we could separate different phases of the referential process: the speaker's identification of a referent; the speaker's encoding of the referent through language that would allow the hearer to infer the speaker's referential intention. In the next section, I briefly consider how the four problem types are distributed in discourse and then discuss the consequences of my approach for the understanding of referrals.

2.5 Problem types: what, where and why?

My taxonomy of problem types has treated each combination as equally possible and equally distributed throughout discourse. But this is far from the case. After briefly reviewing the frequency of each problem type and suggesting some reasons for the problems, I profile the general characteristics of each type along different dimensions, with special attention to syntactic and turn-taking positions of the repair. Different features and/or distributions of the problem types might suggest that the problem types reflect different aspects of speech production or glitches in the referential process.

We begin by comparing frequency and overall distribution of the problem types in Table 2.1. The problem types are labeled and listed according to the order in which they were presented in Section 2.4. Thus TYPE 1 is CONTINUE REFERRING EXPRESSION AND CONTINUE REFERENT (Section (2.4.1)), excluding long distance TYPE 1 repairs. TYPE 2 is CHANGE REFERRING EXPRESSION AND CHANGE REFERENT (Section (2.4.2)). TYPE 3 is CHANGE REFERRING EXPRESSION BUT CONTINUE REFERENT (Section (2.4.3)), excluding noun → clause repairs, word searches and misnamings because I could not identify, code and count them in the

Table 2.1 *Distribution of problem types.*

	FREQUENCY	MORE INFO?	PRONOUN?	SUBJECT?	TURN INITIAL?
TYPE 1	70% (95/135)	14% (95)	64% (95)	64% (95)	49% (95)
TYPE 2	19% (26/135)	11% (26)	69% (26)	84% (26)	19% (26)
TYPE 3	10% (14/135)	21% (14)	43% (14)	71% (14)	14% (14)
TYPE 4	1% (2/135)				

same way. TYPE 4, CONTINUE REFERRING EXPRESSION BUT CHANGE REFERENT (Section (2.4.4)), is excluded from distributional analysis since there were only 2 examples from the sociolinguistic interview data.

After a general discussion of frequency, I turn to each feature.

The most frequent problem type (70%, 95 examples) was TYPE 1, CONTINUE REFERRING EXPRESSION AND CONTINUE REFERENT. Levelt (1983: 44–45) calls these covert repairs:

> If no morphemes are changed, added, or deleted, one has to do with what will be called a *covert repair*. The most minimal form . . . is the case where after the interruption and editing phase, the utterance is continued where it broke off (i.e. zero alteration) . . . Quite common are covert repairs where the same word is repeated without change.

Although the target of covert repairs is unclear (p. 55) since there is no change in the form or meaning, perhaps these brief restarts provide needed planning time: they might be intuitively characterized as 'buying time.' We will explore this idea when discussing the distribution of TYPE 1 repairs in sentences and turns below.

Next most common, with 26 occurrences (19%), was TYPE 2, CHANGE REFERRING EXPRESSION AND CHANGE REFERENT (similar to Levelt's 'error' group). Since these repairs involved two changes, they might reflect a fusion of external and internal problems (to draw upon Kronfeld's 1990 distinction, see Chapter 1): inserting the 'right' word-to-world match within the word-to-word constraints of the text. This would account, for example, for the problems incurred with referring expressions that do not match the time, space and/or information state of the current text.

Next in frequency (with 14 cases, 10% of the total) was TYPE 3, CHANGE REFERRING EXPRESSION BUT CONTINUE

REFERENT.[4] Notice that TYPE 3 problems reflect two separate questions implicitly faced by a speaker when formulating a referral. The first question is: "Do I want to say it this way?" (Levelt 1983: 51). Standards against which this question is addressed when formulating a referral are so broad that they are grouped together by Levelt as "appropriateness," which includes "potential ambiguity given the context, the use of appropriate level terminology, and coherence with previously used terms or expressions" (Levelt 1983: 52). The second question is: "Am I making an error?" (Levelt 1983: 53). Levelt (p. 54) suggests that lexical errors are the result of the "right input message, but . . . the wrong lexical item(s) got activated and phonetically realized as output."

The least frequent problem type was TYPE 4, CONTINUE REFERRING EXPRESSION BUT CHANGE REFERENT. Since there were no examples of this type in the sociolinguistic interviews, I used the example from the corpus of Holocaust narratives for illustration; I found one other example in that corpus, also of *they*. It is important to also note, however, that I found ample uses of multiple *they*s in discourse that were not problematic. Example 2.22, in which *they* was used for three or four referents disambiguated by textual information (see also Chapter 5), was not unique. Since TYPE 4 repairs were so rare, I could not include them in further comparisons.

Let us now return to the other factors in Table 2.1, starting with the MORE and PRO columns. The MORE column shows whether self-completions of the repair were confined only to the noun, or included other material prior to the noun. MORE includes self-completions prefaced by new material (Example 2.24) as well as repeated material; the others had no new material, just repeated material (Example 2.25). Underlining shows the position and the content of the additions (Example 2.24) and repetitions (Example 2.25).

Example 2.24
    ADDED MATERIAL IN REPAIR-COMPLETION
(a)   And they want to go out and play ball.
       But _   they-
       like, *they* come down here,

(b) ___ **That-**
    <u>well</u>, ***that*** whole section up there is Mayfair.

Example 2.25
NO ADDED MATERIAL IN REPAIR-COMPLETION
(a) I mean they had thousands of people. This was <u>like</u> **Johns-**
                                                   <u>like</u> *Stetsons*
(b) I mean, and you have pride, <u>you can keep</u> **a home-**
                                            <u>you can keep</u> *the neighborhood* up.

Although the examples above show TYPE 1 repairs (Example 2.24 (a) and (b)) with the addition of new material (which turned out to be mostly discourse markers) and TYPE 2 repairs (Examples 2.25 (a) and (b)) with no added material, neither problem type was likely to add material prior to self-completion (only 14% and 11% of the cases respectively); TYPE 3 included slightly more (21%). The general tendency to redo only the repairable, without adding more material, conforms to the findings of other scholars: the speaker self-initiates a repair at the point of the problem; the repair maintains the syntactic category of the problematic word; the repair is inserted into the original utterance (Bredart 1991, Levelt 1983, Nooteboom 1980). Since the repairs here began with cut-off parts of a noun phrase (NP), what was likely to be repaired was the NP with no extra material appended to it.

The PRONOUN column in Table 2.1 shows the frequency with which a pronoun was the site of self-initiation. In TYPE 1 repairs, in which both referent and referring expression continued, if the initiation was a pronoun, so was the completion. The other problem types could begin as pronouns, but end as either pronouns or full nouns. Over half of TYPE 1 (64%) and TYPE 2 (69%) repairs (and close to half of TYPE 3 (43%) repairs) included pronouns – not surprising, given the frequency of pronouns in discourse due to their common use in next-mentions (Chapter 5). This is consistent with Garnham et al.'s (1981) findings that 57% of the noun substitutions involved at least one pronoun.

We turn now to two different positions in which problematic referrals occurred: the first, defined syntactically as SUBJECT; the second, defined interactionally as TURN INITIAL. Although sentences and texts both emerge in interaction, sentences also have grammatical and structural characteristics that impinge upon their eventual form. Turns, on the other hand, are *prima facie* units of interaction. Although they mold – and are partially molded by – sentences and texts, they are realizations of the exchange system that underlies interaction. I discuss each separately and then consider the intersection between syntactic role and turn-position.

We noted several times in this book that "the most crucial feature of each utterance, the feature which a listener must minimally grasp in order to begin to understand the utterance, is the expression used to identify what the speaker is talking about" (Brown 1995: 62). The canonical order of English sentences is subject-verb-object. If it is crucial for listeners to grasp the entity about which the speaker will say something, then we might expect the verbalization of this entity in the subject position to be a source of extra attention and potential trouble.

In order to see whether sentence role was related to problem type, I differentiated problematic referrals broadly into four different syntactic roles. However, I ended up separating subject from others because subjects begin the sentence; the others were more varied in their position.[5] Examples of each problem type in several different positions (noted broadly as SUBJ or OTHER) are below: TYPE 1 in Example 2.26; TYPE 2 in Example 2.27; TYPE 3 in Example 2.28:

Example 2.26
(a) SUBJ **This-** *this* is at Front and Ontario.
(b) OTHER Maybe I'm getting **my-** *my* cross street wrong.

Example 2.27
(a) SUBJ Well, when I was going to school **my-** *they* just, frowned on

  OTHER going out on **weekend-** *week nights* period.
(b) OTHER This is the **Ac-** *one of the Acmes.*

Example 2.28
(a) SUBJ As a matter of fact my aunt lived in one of these. And **one of her-** *our- my cousin Jane* was born in one.
(b) OTHER One of my girlfriends went steady with Tony, with **her-** with *Sally's husband.*

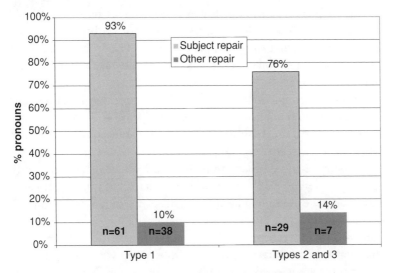

Figure 2.1 Pronouns, subjects and problem types

Table 2.1 shows that regardless of problem type, the subject is the primary position of a majority of the problematic referrals: 64% of TYPE 1 problems were subjects, 84% of TYPE 2, and 71% of TYPE 3. This consistency suggests that repairs of the first referral in the sentence are not used *just* to 'buy time' to plan the rest of the sentence, as might be the case if it were only TYPE 1 repairs (continue both referring expression and referent) in subject position. Rather, given that the highest cluster of problems in subject role (84%) was actually TYPE 2, CHANGE REFERRING EXPRESSIONS AND CHANGE REFERENTS, it seems that the subject may be less pre-planned and less ready to serve as a starting point than might otherwise be expected.

Also important to note is that subjects were overwhelmingly pronouns (cf. Prince 1992) as we see in Figure 2.1. The preference of pronouns in subject position reflects Chafe's (1996: 4; see also 1994: 90–91) light subject constraint: "subjects express referents that are usually given, occasionally accessible, but only rarely new." As we see in later Chapters (3, 4), 'heavy' and relatively new information clusters near the end of sentences: thus the nouns at the 'other' location are not surprising either. The relevance for our discussion here is that when the three problem types (especially TYPE 1) appear in subject position, it is not because the referent itself – available through a word-to-world connection – has not yet been evoked for the hearer or is still in limbo in the discourse. The problematic referrals in subject position are more likely to already be familiar entities in the discourse.

Although sentences are certainly units in which a focal referent appears – a referent about which something will be said – turns are the interactional units within which (and for some scholars *through* which) sentences emerge. We cannot hope to have our listener hear what we have to say about something unless our listener not only 'gets' the referent that we intend, but perhaps even more basically, hears what we are saying because he/she is not him/herself talking.[6] The fact that transitions between turns depend on so many different factors (intonational, syntactic, semantic, pragmatic, cultural, etc.) that make them so frequently negotiable (when will a next-speaker become a current-speaker?) also makes turn beginnings prime environments for repair (Schegloff 1987). Not only are turn beginnings often dependent on another's ending (with overlaps either permitted or not), but placing one's own contribution next-in-the-sequence cannot automatically guarantee that the listener grasps continuity between the new contribution and a prior turn (e.g. through proposition, topic, or action). Yet eventually (despite varying gap and overlap), one speaker is likely to hold the floor for a given duration until the exchange process begins again.

As we discuss in a moment, however, turn-initiation is a prime location for only one type of problematic referral. I will consider turn-initiation to be the first intonation unit in a speaker's turn. Included are turns that overlap with another speaker (unless the 'other' unit is a turn continuer (back channel)) and intonation units with initial discourse markers that may themselves be intonationally separated. Examples are below:

Example 2.29
(a) Anne: They really [keep up the building nice, don't they?
    Ceil: [But **this**- *this* was here when I was a kid.
(b) Arvilla: They look at people as people and not as [a- a situation.
    Lucy: [Mmhm mmhm.
    Rick: Right, well, **I**- [*I* still don't./
    Lucy: [But **it** *it* takes a- y'know, like these
             people say they're non conformists.

Returning to the distribution in Table 2.1, we saw that more TYPE 1 repairs (CONTINUE REFERRING EXPRESSION AND CONTINUE REFERENT) repairs were in turn-initial utterances (47%), than either TYPE 2, CHANGE REFERRING EXPRESSION AND CHANGE REFERENTS (19%) or TYPE 3, CHANGE REFERRING EXPRESSION BUT CONTINUE REFERENTS (14%). We can explain this preference in terms of the onset of talk: the speaker is activating (or re-activating) a referent that will be a central part of the utterance. Thus perhaps repeating one's referral in the turn initial utterance provides a launching point for the speaker much as playing scales on the piano 'warms up' one's fingers for a sonata, or doing stretches 'warms up' one's legs for a run. And like the use of *um* and *uh* (Arnold et al. 2003), perhaps TYPE 1 repairs also alert the recipient to the focus of speaker attention.

The data thus far suggests that TYPE 1 repairs may have less to do with linking referring expressions to referents than the other problem types. Consider, for example, that 15% (14/95) of TYPE I repairs are *I- I* repairs. Although this might seem relatively low, the frequency is lower for TYPES 2 and 3: *I* appears in 7% (3/40) of the TYPES 2 and 3 repairs. Since the referent of *I* is undisputable, accessible to the speaker and identifiable by the hearer, *I- I* cannot reflect problematic links between word and world (cf. Chapter 6 on footing). What is predicated of *I* offers an explanation: 71% (10/14) of the *I- I* repairs precede verbs that convey internal states (cognition, emotion, sensation) rather than action. If internal states are more difficult to articulate, then perhaps the problematic *I* (always in subject position) reflects a starting up process that buys time to prepare what comes next.

If activation and preparation for a referent do underlie TYPE 1 repairs, then we might expect to find the strongest preference for TYPE 1 repairs when *two* starting points coalesce. This is exactly what we see when we compare the syntactic role and turn location of TYPE 1 repairs to the other problem types in Figure 2.2.

As we see in Figure 2.2, 55% of TYPE 1 subject repairs (including, but not limited to, the 14 *I- I* repairs) are turn initial, compared to 25% of TYPE 1 repairs of referrals in other syntactic roles. This pattern is strikingly different for the other problem types. Although we saw a majority of TYPES 2 and 3 repairs occupying subject roles (Table 2.1), a minority of these are in turn-initial position. Not only are fewer TYPES 2 and 3 subject repairs turn initial (16%),

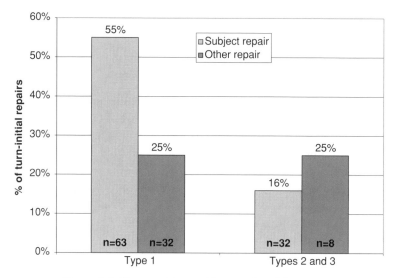

Figure 2.2 Turn position, subjects and problem types

but slightly more of the TYPES 2 and 3 in other parts of the sentence are turn initial (25%). Thus the difference between TYPE 1 repairs (in which referring expression and referent both continue) and other problem types shows up most strikingly when we combine two beginning points – sentence and turn – at which grammar and interaction come together. Recall, finally, that most of the subjects are pronouns: thus TYPE 1 repairs involve familiar information at the onset of syntactic and interactional units. Using a premium location from sentence grammar and the turn exchange system for relatively familiar referents maximizes the opportunity – however brief it may be – to implant the rest of the utterance in an ongoing interaction in which the 'other' can attend to what is being said.

To summarize: in this chapter, we have examined problem types through both broad and narrow lenses. We began by isolating problematic referrals with one type of mechanical problem: a glottalized 'cut-off' during a referral. We then separated two different components of the referral: the referring expression and the referent. Having made this separation, we then proposed two different outcomes for each: continue (referring expression or referent) or change (referring expression or referent). We were then able to locate examples

of each of the four resulting types within discourse, using whatever features of discourse helped explain the source of the problem
and/or its solution.

The quantitative comparison in this section allowed us to compare the frequency of each problem type, general properties of the
noun, and location in different units (sentence, turn).[This comparison showed, first, that pronouns were involved in repairs more than
nouns, thus suggesting that internal relations in the text cause more
problems than external matching between word and world.]Fur-
ther analysis would separate repairs in which both the problem and
the source are pronominal, from those in which one is a full noun
(cf. discussion of noun/pronoun variation in Chapter 5). Also interesting about this finding is that pronoun repairs were more likely to
be subjects regardless of their problem type: pronouns were problematic when speakers continued referring expression and referent
(TYPE 1) or changed one or both (TYPES 2, 3).[The problems with
pronouns, then, might be with the speaker's assessment of what a
hearer will be able to identify – and/or be familiar with – in a position
associated with old information.]

The quantitative comparison also showed that TYPE 1 repairs
(a subtype of Levelt's covert repairs) appeared more often than
TYPES 2 and 3 in turn-initial utterances.[Consistent with Schegloff's
(1987) observation that restarts in turn initial position have a turn-
constructional function, I suggested that TYPE 1 repairs at the coa-
lescence of grammar (sentence) and interaction (turn) provide planning time for the rest of the utterance.]The different distribution of
TYPE 1 repairs vs. TYPE 2 and TYPE 3 repairs also suggests that
TYPE 1 repairs may indicate that a delay at the articulatory phase
of production for an initial noun can give the speaker time to recycle
back in the production process to conceptual or lexical preparation
for the remaining constituents in the sentence/utterance.

To close, we have examined small differences in form, and subtle
differences in meaning, in the redoing of referrals. Each combination
of same or different, new or old, was part of an ongoing discourse
and was attuned to the contingencies of that discourse. In the next
chapter, we turn to problems that arise within one part of a referral –
the article *the* or *a* – again, examining both changes and recurrences
of the articles in order to identify not only how they project information status of the referring expression, but also how they may be

associated with properties of the referent, location in the sentence, and appearance in the text.

Notes

1. I use *a* in transcripts to indicate either short 'a' (as in the word 'apple') or the unstressed vowel known as schwa (as in the word 'but'). Either of these are pronunciations of the indefinite article *a*. I use [ey] to show pronunciations that sound like the vowel in 'take.'
2. I use *the* in transcripts to indicate an instance of 'the' in which the vowel is the unstressed vowel known as schwa (as in the word 'but'). I use *thee* to indicate a long [i] or diphthongized [iy]. Either of these are pronunciations of the definite article *the*. Notice that because I focus exclusively on *the/a* repairs in Chapter 3, they are not included in this analysis.
3. The question of whether a definite noun phrase that evokes a non-existent entity makes a sentence false, or meaningless, has been an important philosophical and linguistic problem. See review in Levinson 1983: Chapter 4.
4. Although the overall repair type includes word-to-world problems (switching from an incipient lexical item to a clausal description, using dummy noun phrases, misnaming due to phonetic and/or semantic similarities), these are not included in Table 2.1.
5. I separated existential sentences (i.e. *There is an* X) and predicate nominatives (i.e. *It is a* X) from other post-verbal object positions: although *there* and *it* share properties with subjects, neither is a referring expression (see Chapter 4). Since these sentences often contain a great deal of referential information in post-copular position, it is this position in which I counted the problem types. Finally, I excluded prepositional phrases (e.g. *in the classroom*) whose sentence position can vary.
6. Of course not all overlaps are considered interruptions and what is an unwelcome intrusion for some is enthusiastically embraced by others.

3

Anticipating referrals

3.1 Introduction

The linguistic form through which we refer – convey a person, place, or thing about which we will say something – is the noun phrase, either a full lexical noun (e.g. *the boy, a new family on the block, my high school friends, her house*) or a pronoun (e.g. *he, they, we, it*). Earlier chapters have explored some underlying processes of referrals (Chapter 1) and the types of problems that can arise (Chapter 2). In this chapter, I focus on repairs of what may seem like a preliminary and very small part of a referral: the articles (definite *the*, indefinite *a*) that preface a lexical noun. I identified article repairs by locating *the-* and *a-* in my corpus of sociolinguistic interviews. Analyzing the self-initiation and self-completion of article repairs helps us address both external (word-to-world) and internal (word-to-word) problems that arise as speakers and hearers work together to manage referrals.

After reviewing the functions of *the* and *a*, I present the three possible outcomes of article repairs in Section 3.2: dropping the article and noun; shifting to a different article; repeating the same article. Since the first outcome has already been noted (Chapter 2) and will be further elaborated (Chapter 4) this chapter focuses on shifting and repeating articles. Whereas article shifts reflect a variety of problems (Section 3.3), article repetitions reflect word-to-world problems that impinge on activation of a referent – local problems (Section 3.4.1) rather than sentence (Section 3.4.2), text (Section 3.4.3) or turn-taking problems (Section 3.4.4). My conclusion addresses general implications of the analysis for our understanding of the principles that have been proposed as accounts for the orderliness and predictability of the referring process (Section 3.5).

3.2 Background: articles and their repair outcomes

The article *the*, along with pronouns, proper nouns (names, titles) and possessives, is a formal indicator of definiteness. The article *a*, along with quantifiers and numerals, is a formal indicator of indefiniteness. But what does it mean to call a reference definite or indefinite? And are all definites or indefinites alike? Although we can formally identify definite and indefinite nouns through the forms above, it is not easy to describe the meanings and functions of those forms.

Here I will suggest that the articles *the* and *a* establish a presumption of intersubjectivity that underlies how a referent is conceptualized by the speaker in his/her own mental model and how it is verbalized in a way that eases its representation in the hearer's mental model. Within this approach, articles indicate the *epistemic status* of an entity for the speaker: the level of specific knowledge about, and hence ability to uniquely identify, an entity. But articles also allow the hearer to anticipate something about an upcoming referent and delimit its general parameters (including its epistemic status for the speaker). Thus articles also convey *information status*: the degree to which an upcoming referent is assumed (by the speaker) to be recognizable to a recipient.

Although *the* and *a* both convey information status, the type of status indexed is very different. *The* indicates the speaker's intention to refer to an entity that the speaker assumes can be specifically identified and recognized by the hearer based on whatever prior clues (textual, contextual) or knowledge (situational, cultural) are already available (Clark and Marshall 1992, Hawkins 1978). The potential link between *the* prefaced nouns and prior text/context suggests a level of anaphoricity not shared by *a* prefaced nouns: *a* occurs when an entity "is being introduced into the discourse for the first time – and without any *speaker's presumption of hearer's familiarity*" (Givón 1989: 179, emphasis in original). The indefinite article *a* may also convey "that the epistemic status of the referent is not (or may not be) well-grounded for both participants" (Brown 1995: 70–71).[1]

The difference in information status between *the* and *a* can be illustrated in Example 3.1 by comparing Joe's several references to 'explosion' and 'granary:'

Example 3.1

Joe:	(a)	They had **the explosion** out at uh **the granary,** remember?
Meg:	(b)	Yeh.
Joe:	(c)	When I was going to school at Drexel,
	(b)	they had a- **a granary explosion.**
	(c)	The ceilings fell in in the school and, uh,
	(d)	they had school-
	(e)	I was home sick,
	(f)	and I get a call from somebody,
	(g)	"Hey, you're lucky, you're home."
	(h)	And I'm, "No, I'm dyin'. I'm sick."
	(i)	"There was **an explosion.**"

Joe initially mentions *the explosion* in *the granary* with *the* prefacing both nouns (line (a)). This is hardly surprising: a level of familiarity with the incident is presumed by the reminder tag *remember?* and affirmed by Meg's *yeh*. Rather than continue to next-mention definites (either *the* NP or pronoun (Chapter 5)), however, Joe's *they had a- a granary explosion* (line(d)) retreats to a weaker assumption of familiarity (with the pragmatic prototype *they had* (Chapter 4)), in which *they* is anaphoric to *Drexel* (line (c)). This retreat is part of the narrative that Joe has opened, in which temporal displacement (*when I was going to school at Drexel*, line (c)) from the world of speaking creates a textual world prior to the speaking world. To put this another way: the narrative shifts the deictic center of the discourse back to an earlier time – and a prior information state – during which the explosion cannot be presumed familiar simply because it hasn't yet occurred.

Although Joe then begins to describe the physical outcome of the explosion (*The ceilings fell in in the school*, line (e)), he self-interrupts in the next clause (*and, uh, they had school-* line (f)) to retract to a still earlier time frame during which he will re-enact his own discovery of the calamity through a friend's phone call (lines (g), (h)). The chain of constructed dialogue through which he does so allows an even more retroactive information shift – in which Joe retracts to an earlier epistemic status about 'explosion.' In the direct quote *"There was an explosion"* (line (i)), Joe positions himself as the recipient of *somebody* from whom he got *a call*. It is within this passive role that Joe voices *somebody* telling him the news (*"There was an explosion"* in line (i)) in which the new entity 'explosion' is presented not only an indefinite NP, but also in an existential clause (Chapter 4).

Notice, also, the discourse history of the term *granary*. As Joe recalls what happened, the granary is part of the reminder: the explosion was *out uh at the granary* (line (a)). As Joe retreats to narrative time (*when I was going to school* (line (c)), the 'granary' becomes syntactically incorporated with the 'explosion' as modification of the type of explosion being introduced as an indefinite (*a granary explosion*). Finally, when Joe retreats further into the sequence of events in which he learns of the explosion, the level of familiarity of that time and circumstance obviates the need for specificity of location altogether: the granary is not mentioned at all in the announcement of *an explosion* (line (i)).

Shifts in information status are by no means limited to referents in narratives in which speakers' knowledge base is deictically shifted backwards so as to accommodate the anterior narrative world. Such shifts occur when we switch not only to a different time, but to a different person. We routinely bring into conversation referents about which our own familiarity (the epistemic status of entities) exceeds the familiarity level that can be presumed by our hearers at the time of an incipient referral (the information status). Thus we are always making tacit judgments about the intersubjective conditions underlying referents.

Scholars have used different terms to capture the idea that speakers' choices of referring terms are attuned to assumptions about their hearers' familiarity with potential referents. Whereas Gundel et al. (1993) speak of cognitive status, for example, Ariel (1990) speaks of accessibility, Prince (1981) of assumed familiarity and Chafe (1994) of active, inactive, and peripheral consciousness. Although these different terms represent somewhat different constructs, and are intricately related to different assumptions and theories about language, cognition, and interaction, they all differentiate sharply between indefinite and definite noun phrases.

Indefinite NPs do not appear on all scales of information status: some scales begin with accessible entities (Ariel 1990), or some minimal level of familiarity (Prince 1981). Gundel et al. (1993: fn. 2), however, differentiate between two possible uses of *a*. A specific referential reading of *a* lets the hearer know that the speaker is referring to a specific entity, 'perfect person' e.g. *I want to marry a perfect person that I met yesterday*. With a weaker 'type-identifiable' reading, *a* displays the speaker's assumption that the hearer can access a representation of the type of entity 'perfect person' about to be described, e.g. *I want to marry a perfect person if I can find one*, even though that entity may not even exist. These two readings of *a* are similar to referential and attributive uses of *the* (Donnellan 1966, Roberts 1993), i.e. one could substitute *the perfect person* for *a perfect person* in the two sentences above without altering the meanings of the sentences. Gundel's cognitive status scale places type-identifiable indefinites at the lowest end. Inclusion of *a* on the scale thus implies that the speaker assumes the following: even though there may be no specific upcoming referent that the speaker might have in mind, the hearer can still recognize what it would take – what conditions would have to hold in the real world – if such an entity were to exist.

Definite nouns do appear on all scales of information status. Although the definite article *the* conveys low accessiblity (in Ariel's 1990 model), it can appear as a first-mention if the speaker expects the hearer to know enough (through world knowledge or context) to recognize an entity similar to the one intended by the speaker. In (1), for example, the two definite NPs *the explosion* and *the granary* were first marked as familiar entities that co-occurred during an experience already presumed to be known to one of the addresses (recall the *remember?* tag). *The* NP can also appear as a next-mention if accessibility is based on prior text. Since *the* often presumes the prior establishment (and/or relevance) of common ground, *the* may also sometimes be seen not only as cataphoric, but also as anaphoric (Cornish 1999).

Thus far, I have suggested that the articles *the* and *a* mark the epistemic status of a noun for the speaker herself, and the information status of that referent for a hearer (as assumed by the speaker) as a characterization of presumed recipient knowledge. What happens, then, when that marker is self-interrupted? How is that self-initiated repair self-completed?

One means of self-completing a cut-off article is to repeat the article:

Example 3.2

(a)   Now they have **a-** *a* visitors' information bureau right there.

(b)   H- How- how many in **the-** *the* crowd?

Whereas article repetitions allow us to assume that both referring term and referent remain the same (TYPE 1 repairs, Chapter 2), this is not the case with the second outcome, switching to another article:

Example 3.3

(a)   Do people sit out on **the-** *their* porches and streets around here in the summertime?

(b)   What I want t' do, now, is **the-** *kind of a* last thing on nationalities.

Included in this group are articles that switch to an article with the same definiteness (or indefiniteness), as in Example 3.2, as well as those that switch definiteness (as in Example 3.3).

The third outcome is even more radical for our interpretation of referent continuity, when articles (with or without the nouns) are dropped:

Example 3.4

(a)   we had **a-** *we weren't allowed to come up in this way.*

In Example 3.4 line (a), Ceil is talking about a neighborhood that was off limits to her as a child. We can thus interpret the clause after *a-* as conveying a limit, a rule or a restriction. In Example 3.4 line (b), however, we are less sure that the clause does convey content that could have been encoded through the incipient referent of the cut-off article. Zelda has been describing how her toddler grandson was playing on the beach.

Example 3.4

(b)   He didn't know how to make **the:** *eh y'know dump the bucket up.*

In Example 3.4 line (b), the phrase *dump the bucket up* is difficult to paraphrase as a referral for several reasons: children usually turn a bucket with moist sand upside down (not *up*) to make a molded shape in the sand; what is made is the product of the action purportedly described. Whereas the fate of the incipient referent

Table 3.1 *Self completions of cut-off articles.*[2]

	What happens to *a*	What happens to *the*	Total
Repeat	57	48	105
Switch	8	16	24
Drop out	39	26	65
Total	104	90	194

in Example 3.4 line (b) is thus uncertain, the incipient referent in Example 3.4 line (c) actually drops out of discourse. In line (c), Sue is describing a mishap with her son when he fell out of what must have been some sort of vehicle for wheeling babies.

Example 3.4

  (c)   and he slips out of **the**- three of- we're all there and he drops
        and falls, onto the street, y'know?

The incipient referent in Example 3.4 line (c) is never developed. Rather than mention exactly what her son slipped *out of*, Sue's story develops the ironic presence of several women near her son's fall, none of whom moved quickly enough to prevent what happened.

   An overview of the distribution of article repairs with these three outcomes appears in Table 3.1.

   Repeating the cut-off article (cf. TYPE 1 repairs, Chapter 2) is the most frequent outcome of the three possibilities: 54% (57) of the 104 *a*- tokens self-complete the repair as *a*; 53% (48) of the 90 *the*- tokens self-complete the repair as *the*.[3] Next most frequent is a retreat from a nominal reference (cf. TYPE 3 repair, Chapter 2). I call this 'drop out' since the article disappears: 37% (39/104) of the *a*- tokens; 29% (26/90) of the *the*- tokens. We have already seen examples of these in which the referent was recoverable (Example 3.4 line (a)), uncertain (line (b)) or lost (line (c)): we discuss a subtype of these repairs in Chapter 4. Least frequent is when articles switch (cf. TYPE 2 repairs, Chapter 2). My focus here is self-completions with a repeated or switched article that precedes a noun.

   Now that I have reviewed the functions of *the* and *a*, presented an example of their differences in information status and an overview of repair completions, I turn to analysis of the cut-off articles

Table 3.2 *Switching articles.*

	To same definiteness	. . . To different	Total
From *a*	6	2	8
From *the*	6	10	16
Total	12	12	24

themselves. I begin with article repairs in which the article switches (Section 3.3) and then concentrate on those in which the article is repeated (Section 3.4).

3.3 Switching articles

In this section, we analyze the repairs of cut-off articles in which speakers switch to a different article. Although this was the least frequent means of self-completing a cut-off article, the article shifts show that the placement of *the* and *a* prefaced nouns is sensitive not only to temporal displacements in epistemic status, but also to the link between the referent and the world (an external problem), and the position of the referral in sentence and text (an internal problem) and interaction.

I begin by noting that article switches can either maintain (as illustrated in Example 3.5 line (a)), or alter (as in Example 3.5 line (b)), definiteness:

Example 3.5
(a)   Do people sit out on **the-** *their* porches and streets around here in the summertime?
(b)   What I want t' do, now, is **the-** *kind of a* last thing on nationalities.

Table 3.2 shows that maintaining and altering definiteness were equally frequent.

The column totals in Table 3.2 show that just as many articles switched, as maintained, definiteness: 12/24 (50%) for both *a-* and *the-*. But *the-* and *a-* differed: whereas only 25% (2/8) of the *a-*repairs switched to definites (i.e. to stronger assumptions of recipient familiarity), 63% (10/16) of the self-completions of *the-* repairs switched to indefinites (i.e. to weaker assumptions of recipient familiarity).

Let us begin with the switches that alter definiteness. The relatively small group of indefinite ➜ definite switches arise from deictic re-centering. Example 3.6 illustrates a switch from *a* to *that* that in which information status is re-centered by the re-framing of time (cf. *the* ➜ *an explosion* in Example 3.1) and source of experience (see discussion in Chapter 6). I have just asked Henry how much education he thinks is necessary nowadays:

Example 3.6

Henry:	(a)	I saw a guy workin' on the beach with a PhD!
	(b)	Couldn't get a job!
Debby:	(c)	Ohhh what was he getting his degree in?
Henry:	(d)	Oh I wasn't talkin' to him,
	(e)	a woman was tellin' me.
	(f)	"See a- see *that guy*, he's a: uh- lookin' at the badges on the beach."

Henry's answer in lines (a) and (b) to my prior question about education illustrates the futility of advanced degrees, an answer to which I respond in line (c) with nervousness about my own future (since I was working on my PhD at the time). Henry then re-frames what I had assumed to be first-hand experience (*I saw a guy* (line (a)) as second-hand experience: *Oh I wasn't talkin' to him, a woman was tellin' me* (lines (d), (e)). However, Henry begins quoting the woman without making the necessary deictic shifts back to the story world and the reported speech: he first replays his own first-mention *I saw a guy* (line (a)) as *see a-* (line (e)), a referral that does not shift back to the woman's first-sighting of the person. Switching *a* to *that* achieves this shift: *that* is a demonstrative used when recognition of a referent can be achieved through joint visual attention. (Notice that the next description of the referent reflects the discourse presence of 'guy' through a next-mention *he*, but drops the subsequent *a: uh* for a clausal description of his job.)

Switches in the opposite direction – from *the* ➜ *a* can also reflect deictic re-centering. In Example 3.7, we see a deictic shift stemming not from the source of the experience (as in Example 3.6), but from its time. I have just asked Zelda and Henry how they found their doctor:

Example 3.7

Zelda: (a)   He's **the family d-** he's *a doctor around here*

         (b)   and when-   we just star- y- =

                    Z

Henry: (c)   neighborhood doctor.

Zelda: (d)   = everybody used t' go t'him.

         (e)   And so we did too.

Debby: (f)   Yeh. Do you go to *the same doctor* Irene?

         (g)   *The neighborhood doctor?*

Irene: (h)   Yeh I use **a neighborhood doctor,**

         (i)   but it's not *the same doctor.*

Zelda's switch from *the family d-* to *a doctor around here* is a descriptive switch: both NPs (as predicate nominals) characterize the same specific person already evoked as *he* in subject position, but in different ways. The articles play a role in this shift: they alter the referral from a uniquely identifiable individual to a type-identifiable referent. This change reflects (and indexes) Zelda's backtracking to an earlier epistemic state and earlier time: before her family had actually chosen their specific doctor from the pool of candidates for that position. The clear difference between these two referents appears in my later question to Irene, in which I specify *the same doctor* (line (f)) and then assume that I can safely move to *the* to show that there is one specific individual (*the neighborhood doctor* (line (g)) who is being discussed. Irene's response clarifies that there is more than one member in the general type *a neighborhood doctor* (line (h)).

As we saw in Table 3.2, 63% (10/16) of the switches from *the-* shift to indefinite articles: deictic re-centering does not exhaustively account for all of these shifts. In addition to retreating to and marking an earlier information state, *the* → *a* shifts reflect three changes in projected entities: from narrow to broad scope (or *vice versa*), from core to peripheral status, from specific (referential) to general (attributive). I discuss each below.

First, a switch from definite to indefinite can clarify the referential inclusiveness of a referent by altering its scope. Much as *we* can range in inclusiveness – bringing together a collective as wide ranging as all living creatures or as narrow as two co-present individuals – so too, can *the* NP. We see this in a question in Example 3.8 in which I shift from *the-* to *all- all the men.* I had been asking

Henry and Zelda about their friends and activities (as part of my interest in social networks in their neighborhood). Henry had been describing some friends with whom he had weekly card games, and after answering my question about where these friends live, he continues to describe their activities. Note his repeated use of *we* (in lines (a)–(f)) and then Zelda's specification of 'we' as *men only* (in lines (g) and (h)):

Example 3.8

Henry: (a) And we save twenty dollars a m- a week.
       (b) We save eighty dollars a month.
       (c) And out of that money now we get four, five, six
            hundred dollars,
       (d) out of that money we'll go out to a race track,
       (e) we'll have dinner,
       (f) and we'll em:

                              Z
Zelda: (g)   Men only.
                                       Z
Henry: (h)   Men only.
       (i) Ah: we cut the women out. Only strange
            women. =
Zelda: (j) hhhhhh
Henry: (k) = And we'll bet on the horses . . .
       (l) Which is very good.
Debby: (m) So y'do that once a year?
       (n) With the- [*all- all the* men?
Henry: (o)   [Oh. No maybe a couple times a year!

Henry lists the group's activities through the repeated subject NP *we* in lines (a) to (f). When Henry pauses in line (f) with *em*: (perhaps about to preface what he later reports in line (k), the somewhat socially stigmatized activity of betting *on the horses*), Zelda adds *men only*. (As Zelda tells me later, the wives' role at the card games is to prepare and serve snacks.) After repeating *men only*, Henry mentions *strange women*. This is an apparent joke that I do not get, but seems to be appreciated by Zelda.[4]

After Henry concludes his list with a positive evaluation of betting on horses (note the continued referrals through *we*), I ask two questions. The first is about frequency *So y'do that once a year?* (line (m)); the second is about participants: *With the- all- all the men?* (line (n)). Since I had just been told by both Zelda and Henry that it is *men only*, my switch from *the* → *all the* NP takes into account their prior mention that the collective is *men only*: it acts as a self-initiated and self-completed repair of my understanding of their intended referent. After correcting my calculation of the frequency of their outings, Henry resumes his list of the men's activities, again continuing his referrals with *we*.

The next type of switch from *the* → indefinite is when the referral is projected as a peripheral, rather than core, member of a referential category (Rosch 1973). Although addition of peripheral members of a category broadens the scope of membership, it does so by adding vagueness (or fuzziness) to its boundaries. Not surprisingly, then, such switches are accompanied by hedges. In Example 3.9, for example, I use *kind of a* to preface a change from questions about ethnic groups to a paper and pencil task about ethnic groups.

Example 3.9
(a)   What I want t'do, now, is **the-** *kind of a last thing* on nationalities.

Since the task continues the ethnic group topic, but transforms its medium from vocal to written, it is not exactly the last thing in a uniform set. This is exactly what we find in the article switch: although the article prefacing *last thing* switches from *the*, it is to *kind of a* rather than *a* alone. Likewise, in Example 3.9 line (b), Dot's description of Philadelphia, Broad Street is neither an official nor a rigid border between ethnic groups, but a street that acts like a border.

Example 3.9
(b)   And the Italians came west up Broad.
      Broad Street used to be **the-** *sort of a dividing line.*
      East of Broad, the Italian families, west of Broad were the Irish.

Note that both of these 'hedging' switches appear in discourse that implies a greater ethnic or racial divide than the speaker might want to project. Enlarging the referential scope of a projected entity about an 'other' can help to mitigate its potential divisiveness.

The final kind of switch from *the* → *a* occurs due to a functional convergence between indefinites and definites (Roberts 1993: Chapters 4 and 5). We noted earlier two possible uses of *a* (Gundel et al. 1993). A specific referential reading of *a* lets the hearer know that the speaker intends to refer to a specific entity. With a weaker type-identifiable reading, *a* displays the speaker's assumption that the hearer can access a representation of the type of entity about to be described even though that entity may not even exist.

Example 3.10 without a *the-* → *a* repair illustrates that both *the* and *a* can be used for non-specific (attributive) mentions of an entity. Betty is talking about promiscuity among men and women. Her position is that although it is good for neither men nor women (line (c)), it is worse for women (lines (f) and (g)). Here we focus on the word *woman*:

Example 3.10
Betty:
(a)   Well, I don't think it's good for the man in a-
(b)   y'know, **the- *the woman*** shouldn't do it but the man could.
(c)   I don't think either party should do it,
(d)   but, **the woman,** when you think of-
(e)   to me, anyway.
(f)   when I think **of a woman** doin' it, like it- that's pretty bad.

Betty frames her statements as opinions: *I don't think* (lines (a) and (c), *you think* (line (d)), *I think* (line (f)). Opinions are speech acts in which people can maintain a belief in a state of affairs without having to claim responsibility for its veracity (Schiffrin 1990). Linguistic philosophers and semanticists point out that this stance creates an opaque context in which the possibility of referential truth is suspended: a consequence is that the existence of a referent cannot be guaranteed. The opaque context facilitates the interpretation of both *the woman* (lines (b) and (d)) and *a woman* (line (f)) as mentions of a non-specific entity with characteristics attributable to those of 'woman': the entity is recognizable, even if it lacks a specific instantiation or concrete presence. Thus both evocations of 'woman' can be interpreted as type-identifiables.

A *the-* → *a* repair of this type appears in Example 3.11. Dot is clarifying a government policy that provides financial benefits for women, based on what she had read in the newspaper:

Example 3.11
(a)   The answer I think is in tonight's paper or last night.
(b)   If she had been employed,
(c)   and hers would bring in more money,

(d)   when **the-** that- when *a woman* reaches-
(e)   as a widow can start collecting at sixty.

The situation that Dot is describing is hypothetical (note the conditional *if* (line (b)) and thus (like the opinions in Example 3.10) creates an opaque context. Given the possibility of employment (line (b)) and a higher salary than her husband (line (c)), women can collect benefits when they turn sixty. Notice that the first-mention of the hypothetical 'woman' begins with *the-*. As Dot specifies the hypothetical financial situation, both the 'woman' and the more specific 'widow' remains non-specific through *a*.

A comparable switch appears in Example 3.12, in which Henry switches from *the- d to a dentist* (line (b)) in his coda to a story about doctors' fallibility:

Example 3.12
Henry:
(a)   They are not God.
(b)   **The d-** *a dentist* can make a mistake as well as a plumber can make a mistake.

Since Henry's story had been about the mistakes of two particular doctors, *the d-* could potentially be a next-mention of one of the specific doctors whose mistakes had been recounted. Switching to *a dentist* clarifies the general applicability of his statement.[5]

In Example 3.13, we see a more complicated trajectory of a *the* ➔ *a* switch. First, a referential use of *the* is abandoned for a *thee: um* that conveys a lexical search (Arnold et al. 2003). Next, *thee um* disappears as Arvilla switches to a question about the existence of a possible referent with *a* (line (j)). Example 3.13 begins as Arvilla asks Rick and Lucy where they met:

Example 3.13
Arvilla: (a)   Did you meet at a dance or-
Rick: (b)   No, you were playing cards.
Arvilla: (c)   What kind of cards?
Lucy: (d)   Poker.
                          Z
Rick: (e)   Rummy, I think it was. =
                                  Z
Lucy: (f)   Rummy.

Rick: (g)   = If I remember correctly.
Lucy: (h)   I don't have a- hhhh.
Arvilla: (i)   Was this like in **the- thee um-**
           (j)   was there like *a big center which you could go to for-*
Rick: (k)   No, it was around the swimming pool.

Notice, first, the progression from *the-* to *thee um*, with *thee* indicating an upcoming search and *um* indicating a possibly long and
complex search (line (i)). Arvilla then backs away from the incipient
nominal to ask an existential question (*was there*) about a referent
initiated by *a* (line (j)). The switch to *a* is not surprising given the use
of existential *there* (see Chapter 4). Also predictable is the retreat
to a type-identifiable *a*, a meaning that is entailed by definite *the*
(Gundel et al 1993: footnote 2).

Two further points also bear on the *the* → *a* switch. First, Arvilla
still needs to describe the referent in a way that facilitates identification. She uses *like* to indicate a general 'type of' place, the general
noun *center*, and initiates a relative clause to present a vague goal
(*go to for*). This description is enough for Rick to realize that it is
an inappropriate match for where he and Lucy met – *around the
swimming pool* (line (k)). The second point is that questioning the
existence of *a big center* makes explicit that the incipient definite
noun might have been a suitable candidate for a referential use, but
must now be interpreted as attributive. Since attributive uses of definites are functionally parallel to non-specific indefinites – precisely
what *a big center* is – the switch from *the-* to *a-* is, again, a formal
switch that maintains function.

Whereas self-completions of cut-off articles that alter definiteness
reflect either deictic shifts, fluctuations in the property of a referent, or functional convergence between *the* and *a*, self-completions
that maintain general information status (either in definiteness or
indefiniteness), reflect recipient-designed efforts to increase referent
accessibility by re-locating the referent within sentence, text and/or
interaction.

The *a–* shifts that maintain indefiniteness are shifts to quantifiers
(e.g. *a* NP → *one of the* NP; *a* → *a lot of NPs*) or to nonspecific
nouns that evoke type-identifiable entities. These shifts suggest a
convergence of speaker-based accessibility problems with a referent
and interactional problems with the placement of a referral in an

ongoing sentence and/or sequence. In Example 3.14, for example, Lucy has just been describing her involvement with the church choir. Arvilla then asks about previous activities at the church:

Example 3.14

Arvilla: (a)   What were some of the things you used to do?
Lucy: (b)   Well, um, that- it- was the main thing, um, choir.
          (c)   We had a- yeh, that's fine.
                                              Z
Arvilla: (d)   [Hhhh
Lucy: (e)   [We had *[ey] uh plays and
          things and concerts and, y'know, all that sort of thing,
          that kept us   quite busy.
                         Z
Arvilla: (f)   Mmhmm

Although activities other than the choir are conveyed as peripheral (line (b)), Lucy nevertheless begins to provide the information requested by Arvilla in a pragmatic prototype (Chapter 4, *we had a* (line (c)) that places the new information in sentence-final position. This information is interrupted when Lucy breaks frame to respond to some other ongoing activity with *yeh, that's fine* (line (c)). The frame break occurs within a long distance TYPE 1 (continue expression and continue referent referring) repair (Chapter 2) as "discourse within a sentence" (Hayashi 2004): an interactional side sequence is inserted into a sentence that is resumed after the side sequence closes and recedes from the dominant involvement. Thus Lucy restarts her answer to Arvilla by repeating both *we had* and the indefinite article in line (e), the latter with a lengthened and raised [ey] and *uh* both indicating ongoing revision in the referral. What is then revised is the level of specificity in the referent: rather than mention one specific activity (conveyable through *a* NP), Lucy lists types of general activities, not just general *plays* and *concerts*, but also *things* and *all that sort of thing*.

The *the-* shifts that maintain definiteness are also relatively minimal adjustments in information status, e.g. *the* NP → *their* NP; *that/those* NP(s) → *they*. As we see in Chapter 5, shifts involving full nouns and pronouns suggest re-calculations of thematicity, distance, and/or ambiguity of earlier referrals. Here we focus on how *the-* shifts that maintain definiteness suggest a convergence of speaker-based accessibility problems with a referent and text-ual/interactional contingencies.

Example 3.15 is a straightforward example of a shift from *the* ➔ proper noun, in which the antecedent of *the* NP (recall that *the* can be anaphoric) could have been one of two 'Fathers.' After establishing *Father Gallagher* as recognizable (a), Ceil brings up *Father Gormley* (b):

Example 3.15
(a) Father Gall-allagher, right?
(b) And they sent Father Gormley there.
(c) Do you know what **the-** *Father Gallagher* said about Father Gormley?

As Ceil begins to report on what one of the priests said about the other, she self-interrupts to more explicitly evoke 'Father Gallagher' who had become not only less recent, but also could not be unam-biguously evoked through *the* NP.

Example 3.16 shows a move from *the* ➔ *that* NP. Henry and Zelda have been telling me about the restaurants where they enjoy dinners with their extended family. Henry's list of the family mem-bers who join them for dinner is intertwined with Zelda's list of restaurants. Zelda's referral to a specific restaurant *Seafood Shanty* shifts from *the* ➔ *that*:

Example 3.16
Henry: (a) The cousins come down and eh . . .
        (b) and they says, "Look,"
        (c) and then- and my brother, [and the kids eh: y'know . . .
        (d)   [We eat at **the-** we ate at
Zelda: *thee* [eh that Shanty? Seafood Shanty?
                                 Z
Debby: (e)   [Yeh.   Oh yeh,
        (f) I've heard that's good.

Zelda's initial introduction of the Seafood Shanty (line (d)) overlaps with Henry's list (line (c)). Her first try at prefacing the referral to the restaurant locates it at the end of a brief clause reporting a habitual activity *we eat at the* (line (d)). As Henry's list winds down (note his *eh: y'know* . . . in line (c)), Zelda's second try shifts to a past tense clause (perhaps a more reportable event that may also help Zelda retrieve the name of the restaurant). Prefacing the referral, still in final position, with *thee eh* gains more turn space and 'thinking time.' Indeed, right after my *yeh* (line (e)), oriented toward Henry's list), Zelda prefaces the name of the restaurant with *that* in a try marker intonation as *that Shanty?* (line (d)). Since *that* is a demonstrative whose 'pointing' function is inherited from its use as a distal deictic, *that* indexes a higher level of accessibility than *the* (Ariel 1990). Reifying that assumption of heightened familiarity is Zelda's use of a proper noun *Seafood Shanty* (giving the full name of the restaurant without an article) in its own intonation unit and its own turn space.

We have seen in this section that shifts between the articles reflect a variety of problems with the article, the referring term, or the referent. The relatively small group of *a* ➔ *the* shifts were deictic shifts in information state. The larger group of *the* ➔ *a* shifts was more varied. Some were shifts to an earlier factual world in which a type-identifiable entity had not yet become a specific recognizable entity. Others introduced entities whose epistemic changes had different sources: a lack of individuation due to an emphasis on generally shared attributes; porous levels of inclusiveness; an entity whose peripheral status prohibited its core membership in a larger set of entities. Still other shifts reflected functional convergence between *the* and *a*. In contrast, the article shifts that maintained (in)definiteness reflected the re-placement of a referral in an ongoing sentence and/or sequence.

3.4 Repeating articles

Repetitions of cut-off articles have the same surface appearance as the covert repairs (Levelt 1983) analyzed in Chapter 2, in which speakers continued referent and referring term (TYPE 1). In comparison to other problematic referrals, TYPE 1 repairs of nouns (both lexical nouns and pronouns) clustered at the starting point of a sentence and/or turn. The preference for initial position suggested that speakers may need time to plan and prepare the remainder of their sentences and turns at talk. Despite surface similarity – both noun and article repairs repeat the form and maintain the meaning – repetition of articles might not stem from the same trouble source as repetition of nouns, simply because of the functional and structural differences between the two parts of a noun phrase.

On the functional side, the noun (lexical nouns, pronouns) provides information that helps the hearer make a word-to-world or a word-to-word connection. In contrast, articles cue the hearer on the information status of the referent to be evoked by the noun. On the structural side, if we think of sentences as hierarchical tree-like representations, then sentence (S) is the top node. A noun phrase (NP) node branches into an article (also called determiner) node and a noun node. Forms that fill the determiner slot (including articles) are thus the first branch of the NP node; the noun is the second and final branch of the NP constituent.

If we combine Levelt's (1983) self-initiation principle (initiate a repair at the site of the problem), with his observation that a speaker is better at detecting a problem toward the end of a constituent, we are led to different predictions about the source of trouble for noun and article repetitions. For example, it might make sense for problems with the noun to appear – and its repair to be completed – as the NP constituent nears completion and makes way for the rest of the sentence. But since articles structurally precede only nouns – not the rest of the sentence – they might be oriented more toward completion of the noun than completion of the sentence (the largest constituent). Whereas noun problems are attuned to the upcoming sentence (as we saw in Chapter 2), then, article problems might be attuned to the upcoming noun.

In this section, we examine the different levels of linguistic structure to which covert repairs of *the* and *a* (*the- the, a- a*) might be attuned. We do so by examining cut-off repeated articles in relation to upcoming noun (Section 3.4.1), sentence (Section 3.4.2), and sequence of mentions in a text (Section 3.4.3). We also examine cut-off repeated articles in relation to a more interactional unit, the turn at talk (Section 3.4.4).

3.4.1 *The noun: verbalizing the referent*

Since the articles are near completion when they are cut-off, right before the onset of the noun, the problem might be located in the short interval between the article and the noun, i.e. in anticipation of the noun. What goes wrong in that interval might be the concept or entity itself: "who is that person? what object or place do I have in mind?" But it may also be the word: "I know who I'm thinking of, but I can't remember his name." Whether at the conceptual or lexical level, the coordination of intersubjectivity about the upcoming referent cannot go very far if the speaker does not know what entity is 'in mind' or what to call it.

The analysis of repeated articles in this section begins by exploring these suggestions. As we see in the first few examples, a speaker may project information status through an article without knowing what to call the entity for which that information status is assumed. We then explore a possible consequence of this finding: if information status can be projected without lexical access, is it also possible that repeated articles extend the projection of information status so as to give the speaker more time to access and/or verbalize a referent?

Consider, first, that information status can proceed without a referring term to guide the recipient toward recognition of a referent. In Chapter 2, we saw an example in which Charlie was telling a story about almost falling off a ladder while painting a house:

Example 3.17
(a)   And somehow or other I- I managed to grab the edge of the roof.
(b)   And there happened to be-
(c)   it was a good pla- it was-
(d)   there- there was **a whachacall**it in there, y'know?
(e)   And I could hold on to *it*.

Earlier discussion noted that we could not really identify the source of Charlie's referring problem. It could have been either a conceptual problem (a lack of information about what the place actually was) or a referring expression problem (inability to find a conventional term through which to evoke the place). In either case, Charlie gives up on his presumable goal of formulating a lexically informative referral. A *whatchamacallit*, however, allows him to say more about this unspecified entity, enough, in fact, to continue and finish his story: because he *could hold on to it* (line (e)) – whatever 'it' was – Charlie managed to avoid a nasty fall on the ground as his ladder began to slip off the roof.

Notice, now, that like Charlie's appropriate use of the next-mention *it* after the first-mention *a whatchamacallit*, the information status of the NPs in Example 3.17 also follows a standard pattern. What Charlie grabs is *the edge of the roof*, a definite NP and thus a specific identifiable place. The definite articles here (*the edge*, *the roof*) are not surprising: we already know from Charlie's story that he is standing on a ladder that is leaning on a roof; we also know that all roofs have edges. Likewise, the indefiniteness of *a whachacallthem* is not surprising. Even before Charlie gets to this dummy NP, an assumption of low familiarity with that entity is indicated through *there happened to be* (line (b)). The predicate 'happen to be' conveys that one cannot assume existence of the to-be-focused upon entity on all roofs: rather, it is a matter of chance or luck. Despite difficulty in finding the right words, then, Charlie can still convey the information status of an unnamed 'something.'

The separation of information status from lexical choice suggests that a speaker can have an entity in mind, and assume that hearers will either be familiar or unfamiliar with that entity, even if the speaker does not know how to verbalize it. In the next two examples, the repetition of cut-off articles shows that information status of an incipient referral remains stable despite recurrent lapses in the process whereby an entity is verbalized as a referent.

In Example 3.18, an elderly couple, Gina and Jim, are trying to remember what they called the item used by Gina's parents to punish her brothers when they were mischievous many decades earlier:

Example 3.18

Gina:	(a)	They all got hit.
	(b)	They went to bed.
Anne:	(c)	Did she hit 'em with **the broom**? [Or with **the** . . .]
Gina:	(d)	[No, no.]
	(e)	She had **the l-** *the-*
Jim:	(f)	She had *the macaroni spoon.*

Z

Gina:	(g)	*The macaroni uh* . . .
Jim:	(h)	Hey what do you call it, *thee uh* . . .
Gina:	(i)	*the one that you uh:*

Z

| Jim: | (j) | *the rollin' pin.* |

Z

| Gina: | (k) | *the rollin' pin.* |

The search for a referent starts with Anne's question (line (c)) about what the brothers were hit with: Anne offers an option (*the broom*) and opens alternatives (*or with the . . .*). The quick onset of Gina's *no, no* (line (d)) shows that the broom is not the correct referent. *The* recycles in several locations: after the item initiated in line (e) is abandoned (*the l- the-*); with each candidate referral (*the macaroni spoon* (lines (f) and (g)) and *the rollin' pin* (lines (j) and (k)) including the vague *the one that you uh:* (line (i)). Notice, also, the use of *uh:* (lines (g) and (h) and the long [iy] in *thee:* (line (h)): both index local and upcoming (Clark and Fox Tree 2001, Jefferson 1974, Schegloff 1979: 273–274) problems in the next syntactic slot (i.e. the noun). Even Gina's attempt to find a descriptive clause to replace the nominal referent (cf. Chapter 2, Section 2.4.3) maintains the information status of the incipient referral: the replacement noun (Clark and Wilkes-Gibbs 1992) serving as head of the relative clause (*the one that you uh:* (line (i); note also *uh:*)) is the definite NP *the one*. Throughout the search for the correct referent (lines (e) to (k)), then, the repetition of *the* shows the stability of the assumptions that a specific item existed, was used to hit the brothers, and that it is familiar enough to be recognized by the hearer.

In Example 3.19, we see that lexical gaps can persist despite the stable marking of information status through *a*, as well as *the*. (The Philadelphia hockey team The Flyers had just won the Stanley cup, the top prize in national hockey competitions.)

Example 3.19

Meg: (a)   Y'know I saw **a-** *what's a name*,
         (b)   *a- a replica of the cup the kids made.*
         (c)   They were hauling [it outside with- =
Carol: (d)   [Oh, yeh, I saw it, yeh.
Meg: (e)   = with **thee** uh, uh what do you call it,
         (f)   *the foil?* Is it the foil?

Meg conveys the information status of two items whose name she cannot recall. These referential gaps are made explicit after the initial articles: *a- what's a name* (a); *thee uh, uh what do you call it* (line (e)). Both *what's a name* and *what do you call it* could have served as dummy NPs and completed the referrals (as in Example 3.5)). Instead, Meg continues to propose more informative referrals that maintain the information status marked through the initial articles:

Table 3.3. *Animacy of referent with a- a and the- the NPs.*

	Inanimate	Animate	Total
a- a NPs	35	22	57
the- the NPs	31	17	48
Total	66	39	105

a- a replica (line (b); *the foil* (line (f)). Assumptions about familiarity persevere with (and without) the words.

We have seen thus far that cut-off repeated articles delay referrals when words fail to appear at their proper juncture between referent and referring expression. Another way to explore this juncture is to classify the NPs in terms of the type of referent represented. Analysis of the distribution of cut-off repeated articles with different referent types might show that some referents are delayed more than others.

I begin with a straightforward distinction between animate ('living') vs. inanimate ('not living') referents. Table 3.3 shows that cut-off repeated articles preface inanimate referents slightly more than animate referents.

More inanimate referents (63% (66/105)) were prefaced by cut-off repeated articles than animate referents (37% (39/105)). Both *a- a* NPs (61% (35/57)) and *the- the* NPs (65% (31/48)) contributed to the presence of inanimate NPs with repeated articles.

At first glance, we might think that the slight skewing toward inanimates is because they include abstract constructs (e.g. 'ideas,' 'facts') that might be difficult to formulate as well as concrete physical objects (e.g. 'chair,' 'cup' (but see Labov 1973)) that are easy to label. To check this, I differentiated concrete and abstract referents. This distinction works somewhat differently for inanimate and animate referents.

Concrete inanimate referents are items that exist in a material sense (e.g. 'a porch', 'the wall', 'a lamp', 'a knife'). Abstract inanimate referents are items with no material presence in the world (e.g. 'a fact', 'perspectives', 'the sex angle'). Between these two extremes are entities with some physical manifestation in the world (e.g. 'the temperature', 'summertime', 'a religious service') but no tangible material presence apart from transient indicators that allow us to sense or embody them: these will be considered as abstract. The

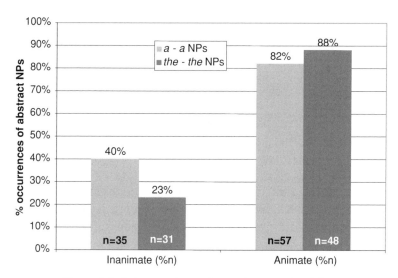

Figure 3.1 Animacy, abstraction and repeated articles

concrete/abstract distinction works differently for animate referents. Concrete animate referents are members of a specific membership category (e.g. 'the policeman', 'a mother,' 'my son'). Abstract animate referents appear *only* within an undifferentiated group (e.g. 'a new' 'bunch of girlfriends,' 'the crowd') including those that do not specify social membership (e.g. 'a type of person that can control this'). If these NPs have an attributive reading, it is this quality that accounts for their abstractness. But even with a referential reading, it is the emergent and unspecified aspect of collectivities (e.g. crowds fluctuate in membership over time and space) that I take as a basis for abstractness.

Figure 3.1 shows that animate and inanimate referents are sharply differentiated by the concrete/abstract distinction. Figure 3.1 shows a sharp difference between *a- a/the- the* nouns by abstractness/ concreteness and animacy: more abstract animate nouns are delayed by cut-off article repetitions (82%, 88%) than abstract inanimate nouns (40%, 23%).

That *a- a/the- the* delays a reference to an abstract set of animate referents that has been (or is being) grouped together is surprising. Here I can only offer a partial answer that suggests that the problem lies at the conceptual level of the referring process. Formulating an animate abstract referent such as 'the police,' 'a White gang,' or 'a new group of friends' combines three steps:

(1) ignoring some differences among individuals,
(2) highlighting some similarities among individuals,
(3) collecting individuals whose similarities matter (i.e. are relevant) for the topic at hand.

We can think of these steps as working together to produce a relatively abstract category of social membership, in which the referral evokes a general category 'name' that underlies a potential collection of people (cf. the highest node of a list (Chapter 5)).

   In sum, we have seen in this section that one particular phase of the referring process – turning an entity into a referring expression that can evoke a referent – can be delayed by cut-off repeated articles. Repeating an article reserves a slot in discourse in which information status is already marked for the hearer. Although the speaker may still be searching for the 'right' entity, its 'right' linguistic formulation, or grouping together and labeling entities into a set, the hearer already has been told what level of familiarity will characterize whatever referral will soon appear.

3.4.2 The sentence: weight and position

We suggested earlier that, since articles are part of a noun phrase, they might be more oriented toward completion of the noun phrase than other larger structural units. In this section, we examine whether *the- the* and *a- a* repairs are also attuned to sentence position.

   Before beginning, however, it is important to note that the underlying logic and interpretation of the sentence analysis in this section, and the text analysis in (Section 3.4.3), is somewhat different from that of the noun (and turn analysis (Section 3.4.4)). All assume that the linguistic environment of the referent impinges upon its means of expression. However, the type of potential trouble differs, as does the participant (speaker or hearer) for whom the trouble is consequential. The analysis of repeated articles in relation to nouns (animate/inanimate; abstract/concrete) assumed that qualities of a referent could pose speaker-based problems (conceptualizing, accessing or verbalizing the entity). The analysis of the same referents in sentences (are they in initial or final position?) and in texts (are they first-mentions or next-mentions? (Section 3.4.3)), however, assumes that sentence or text position could pose not just production problems for speakers, but also interpretation problems for hearers.

The logic and interpretation of the quantitative analyses of article repetitions in sentence and text incorporate insights from both markedness theory (Fleischman 1990) and conversation analysis (Bilmes 1988, Pomerantz 1984). Despite their very different starting points, both perspectives depend upon implicit assumptions about the pairing of forms with meanings and/or contexts. Markedness theory assumes that formal deviations from a linguistic paradigm or pattern are structurally marked: for example, use of the present tense (to convey a prior event) in a narrative about the past with mostly preterit verbs. Conversation analysis assumes that exceptions to an interactional norm are structurally dispreferred: for example, prefacing non-compliance to another's request with *well* mitigates the face-threat of not complying with another's request.

Repetitions of self-initiated cut-offs of articles (*the- the, a- a*) maintain the information status of the upcoming referent. Why, then, does the speaker delay presentation of the referent? Is it because the referent is misplaced (marked or dispreferred) in some way either in the sentence or text? Since analyses of what is atypical presuppose knowledge of what is typical, the first step in each analysis is to review the unmarked (or preferred) typical environments of non-problematic *the* NPs and *a* NPs. We then examine whether *a- a* and *the- the* referents mark deviations from the norm in sentence (Section 3.4.2) or text (Section 3.4.3)

Let us begin by noting that since sentence-initial position traditionally serves as a site for 'topic' or familiar information, we might expect to find definite nouns as sentential subjects (Chafe 1976). Likewise, since sentence-final position is traditionally associated with new information, we would expect to find indefinite nouns as sentential objects (Prince 1992). If *a- a* and *the- the* delay a referent because of a mismatch between information status and sentence position, however, then we would expect to find *a- a* nouns where indefinites do *not* typically appear (i.e. initial position). Since definite nouns vary more in their information status, we might expect the positions of *the- the* nouns within sentences to show a more equitable distribution.

Table 3.4 *Sentence position of a- a and the- the NPs.*

	Initial Subject	Final object	Existential	Pred Noms	Total
a- a NPs	2	10	19	21	52
the- the NPs	19	7	1	2	29
Total	21	17	20	23	81

In order to examine the location of *the- the* and *a- a* NPs in sentences, I differentiated sentence-initial subjects (Example 3.20 line (a)) from a range of sentence-final objects, including objects of active verbs (Example 3.20 line (b)), objects of stative verbs including the copula in expletive *there* sentences (line (c)) or other variants of pragmatic prototypes ((Example 3.20 line (d)); see Chapter 4) and objects of the copula in predicate nominatives (Example 3.20 line (e), (f)).[6]

Example 3.20
(a) Well, **the-** *thee* only thing that's saving that part of the city is the students.
(b) Well, I read **a-** *a* clipping about a man last week
(c) Y'know, like uh if there is **a-** *an* upset in the family
(d) They used to have **uh: the-** *the* wagons and the ponies for the hucksters.
(e) I think the Irish guys for the most part, eh:, are **the-** are *the* toughest guys.
(f) He was **a-** *a* real diehard, I mean, when it came- the Democrats could do no wrong.

Table 3.4 shows a sharp differentiation between the positions of *a- a* NPs and *the- the* NPs within sentences.[7] A- *a* NPs appear more frequently as we move from sentence-initial to sentence-final positions: 4% (2/52) in sentence-initial subject position, to 96% (50/52) in the (combined) sentence-final positions. *The- the* NPs show the opposite pattern: from 66% (19/29) in sentence-initial subject position to 34% (10/29) in the (combined) sentence-final positions. The sentence positions of *a- a* and *the- the* nouns are thus consistent with the traditional distribution of indefinite and definite nouns: even nouns for which repair is initiated in the very first indicator of information status follow this old → new trajectory

Table 3.5 'Weight' of a- a and the- the NPs.[8]

	Light bare NP	Mid modifier + NP	Heavy (mod) NP + 1 or more	Total
a- a NPs	11	16	30	57
the- the NPs	27	11	10	48
Total	38	27	40	105

in sentence structure. Thus it does not look as if a- a and the- the delay their referents because of a mismatch between information status of the referent and position in the sentence.

We will see in a moment that another site of variation – the weight of a noun – intersects with sentence position. We can operationalize weight as a combination of length, complexity and informativity, as in Figure 3.2.

Predicted by various approaches to information status is a correlation with noun weight: the more familiarity can be presumed about a referent, the less needs to be said about it. Thus accessibility scales position light vs. heavy nouns differently (e.g. Ariel 1990); both conversation analysts (Sacks and Schegloff 1979), and neo-Gricean analyses of minimization (Levinson 2000), use light nouns to illustrate recognizables (see also Arnold et al. 2000). Indeed zero anaphora – the lightest noun of all, conveying no lexical information – is always associated with greatest accessibility, familiarity, predictability and activation of a referent in consciousness.

Table 3.5 shows that there is a relationship between weight and definiteness. In Table 3.5, I have grouped the six points on the light → heavy continuum into three major types: bare nouns, nouns whose modifiers (adjectives and intensifiers such as 'very, really') precede them; nouns with modifier (e.g. relative clauses, temporal and locative phrases/clauses) following them; these could also have adjectives preceding the nouns.

Table 3.5 shows a striking difference in the 'weight' of the a- a and the- the nouns. The heavier the noun, the more indefinites: 29% (11/38) of the light nouns were indefinites, moving to 59% (16/27) of the mid-weight nouns, and 75% (30/40) of the heavy nouns. Reciprocally, the lighter the noun, the more definites: 71% (27/38) of the light nouns were definites, 41% (11/27) of the mid-weight nouns, and 25% (10/40) of the heavy nouns.

LIGHT				HEAVY	
noun	modifier + noun	noun + 1 modifying phrase or clause	modifier + noun + 1 modifying phrase or clause	noun + >1 modifying phrase or clause	1 modifier + noun + >1 modifying phrase or clause
a dog	*big dog*	*dog with/* *that had no tail*	*big dog with/* *that had no tail*	*dog with/* *that had no tail* *that it could wag*	*big dog with/* *that had no tail* *that it could wag*

Figure 3.2 Weight of nouns

Although we might consider weight to be a property of the noun (Section 3.3), Chafe (1994: 90–91) proposes a light subject constraint that suggests a relationship with sentence position: "subjects express referents that are usually given, occasionally accessible, but only rarely new."[9] Compare Example 3.21 line (a) and (b):

Example 3.21
(a)   So then **thee the war** came along
(b)   They have a- they own a **whole half of a house over on Forty fifth Street in Baltimore, which is where I used to live.**

In Example 3.21 line (a), the NP in subject position is light: a single lexical item *war*, not even specified as which war (it is World War II). In line (b), the NP, the sentence-final object of the verb *own* is heavy: it is long, complex (a modifier before the noun, two prepositional phrases and a relative clause) and informative (portion of house, location of street and city, relation to speaker's prior place of residence).

If *a- a* and *the- the* nouns follow the light subject constraint, we would expect to find more light *a- a* nouns in sentence-initial, than in sentence-final, position. We might also expect the light *the- the* nouns to be less sensitive to sentence position, simply because their information status is more varied.

Figure 3.3 shows that *a- a* NPs and *the- the* NPs conform to what the light subject constraint predicts in terms of sentence-position: the distribution roughly conforms to the information status associated with indefinite and definite nouns. In keeping with the status of indefinites as relatively new, we find more light *a- a* nouns in initial (50%) position – the preferred position for relatively new information – than final (16%) position. And in keeping with the status of definites as more easily identifiable through familiarity, we find roughly the same relative frequency of light *the- the* nouns in initial (68%) and final (60%) positions. Thus it does not look as if the delay created by article repetition is due to a mismatch between the information status conveyed by the articles and the combined effect of noun weight and sentence position.

To summarize: the NPs delayed by *a- a* and *the- the* occur in the same general locations as unproblematic indefinites and definites, i.e. in general conformity with the light subject constraint. The analysis

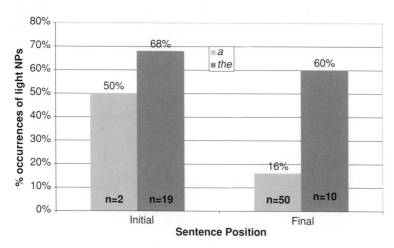

Figure 3.3 Sentence position, 'weight' of NPs and repeated articles

thus suggests that references are not delayed because of a mismatch between information status and sentence position of the referent.

3.4.3 The text: first- or second-mention

The information status of definite and indefinite articles predicts their use in different sequential positions in text. Definite articles can preface a noun that provides either a first- or next-mention of an entity. With definite first-mentions, it is background knowledge that allows a speaker to presume hearer familiarity with a referent; with definite next-mentions, it is prior text. Indefinite articles typically preface a noun that is the first-mention of an entity, i.e. a referent that is neither inferable by prior text nor assumed to be accessible through world knowledge. Markedness and preference approaches suggest that a noun might be delayed – through cut-off and repeated articles – if the information status anticipated by the article is inappropriate to its place in the text.

Table 3.6 shows the distribution of *the- the* NPs and *a- a* NPs in two general positions within a referring sequence in text, first-mention and next-mention. Table 3.6 shows that the distribution of *a- a* and *the- the* nouns follow the general distribution of *a* and *the*. Since both definites and indefinites can be appropriate as first-mentions, they are evenly distributed in this position: 50% (31/62)

Table 3.6 *Text position of a- a and the- the NPs.*[10]

	First-mention	Next-mention	Total
a- a NPs	31	5	36
the- the NPs	31	17	48
Total	62	22	84

of first-mentions are *a- a* NPs; likewise for *the- the* NPs. The distribution of the problematic articles in the next-mentions is more skewed: 23% (5/22) of the next-mentions (the dispreferred environment) are *a- a* NPs, with the remaining 77% (17/22) *the- the* NPs.

The skewed distribution of *the- the* and *a- a* with next-mentions reflects the typical distribution of definites and indefinites with next-mentions. Indeed when we examine the *a- a* nouns with next-mentions, we find that this repetition is not contingent on sequential position of the referent in text. In Example 3.22, three of the five next-mention *a- a* NPs are in requests for clarification that Anne directs to Gary, who has been talking about a neighborhood fight (Example 3.22 line (a)) and childhood ball games (line (b)):

Example 3.22

(a) I mean, how- how do you get into- into **a- a fight** like that?

(b) Oh, so you- you- he wouldn't throw **a- a half ball**.
     He'd throw just **a- a whole pimple ball**.

The next-mention *a- a* NPs are not specific referents, but type-identifiable entities whose specific 'type' was either provided in prior talk (*a- a fight like that* (Example 3.22 line (a)), or embedded in a clarification sequence (line (b)). Indicators of other-initiated repair abound in both. In Example 3.22 line (a), *I mean* marks a redoing of a prior understanding; both *how* and *into* are cut-off and repeated. In Example 3.22 line (b), Anne follows a common 'not X (*half ball*), but Y (*whole pimple ball*)' repair format; *oh* indicates receipt of new information; pronouns change from the indefinite *you* to the definite *he* to pinpoint the specificity of the repair. Thus although *a- a* NPs are in a dispreferred next-mention slot, they are also enmeshed in broader clarification activities about the 'type' of entity being evoked.

In contrast to the next-mention *a- a* nouns, the next-mention *the-the* nouns are embedded within the paradigmatic choices that arise from constraints (distance, ambiguity, topicality, structural boundaries (Chapter 5)) within referring sequences themselves. We see some examples of the sequential complications that arise when we discuss how article repairs are located in turns (Section 3.4.4).

We have seen in this section that *a- a* and *the- the* NPs are sequentially located in texts in ways that conformed with the distribution of indefinites as first-mentions and definites as either first- or next-mentions. Maintenance of this preference structure suggests that *a- a* and *the- the* delays in references do not reflect an overall mismatch between the information status of the referent and its sequential position in text.

3.4.4 The turn: initial or medial position

Turns-at-talk are the interactional units within which (and for some scholars *through* which) sentences emerge. Transitions between turns depend on so many different factors that the precise location at which a current-speaker ends, and a next-speaker begins, is typically managed (and frequently negotiated) on a turn-by-turn basis. The uncertainty of turn-initiation suggests that it might be a prime location for problematic referrals – and indeed, it was for TYPE 1 problematic referrals (continuation of referent and referring expression). In this section, we examine whether turn-initiation is also a prime location for problematic referrals involving cut-off repeated articles. (In keeping with the practice of Chapter 2, I consider turn-initiation to be the first intonation unit in a speaker's turn, including turns that overlap with another speaker (unless the 'other' unit is a turn continuer) and intonation units with initial discourse markers that may themselves be intonationally separated.

Table 3.7 shows that *the- the* and *a- a* repairs are not overwhelmingly common in turn-initial position. Table 3.7 shows that *a- a* repairs are turn-initial in 28% (16/57) of the turns; *the- the* repairs are turn-initial in 33% (16/48) of the turns. Thus the article repetitions (both *a- a* and *the- the*) are less frequent than TYPE 1 repairs (48%) in which referent and referral remain the same (Chapter 2).

Although these results clearly deserve finer analysis, the examples below suggest that articles might be cut-off and repeated in

Table 3.7 *Turn position of a- a and the- the NPs.*

	Turn-initial	Turn-medial	Total
a- a NPs	16	41	57
the- the NPs	16	32	48
Total	42	73	105

turn-initial position when the referent is important in the content of upcoming talk and when the turn itself is helping to alter the floor. The term 'floor' differs from 'turn': it evokes a larger interactional arena within which turns may be differently distributed or allocated (Edelsky 1981). Thus the 'floor' of a classroom lecture allocates speaking rights and privileges primarily to a teacher, a 'floor' of joking rounds alternates among speakers, and a shared 'floor' occupied by close friends out to lunch may involve rapid exchange of turns as well as overlapping turns.

Examples 3.23 and 3.24 show turn-initial article repairs when the turn is a prelude to an extended share of the floor. In Example 3.23, Ginny's initial (and only) utterance in her turn serves as a 'ticket' for an upcoming story, in which the referent 'the cookies' has an important role in the story:

Example 3.23
Ginny: (a)   Heard about my mom baked **the-** *the- the coo- the*
                 cookies?
Joe: (b)   Yeh, tell 'em about it.

Introduction of 'the cookies' in line (a) is treated by Joe as Ginny's bid to tell a story – a bid that Joe endorses, such that Ginny then occupies the floor for the duration of her story.

The referent evoked by *the synagogue* in Example 3.24 is also part of a bid for a single-person floor in which the referent is part of the point of a story. Prior to this segment, Henry has been talking about the pros and cons of living year round in a small town on the New Jersey shore whose summer population swells with vacationers. At the time of the conversation, my parents had been planning to move to this town after they retired. Henry and his extended family share ownership of a cottage in a nearby town that they use for summer vacations. Henry would like to retire in his cottage; Zelda is not so sure because *it seems so lonely there in the winter* (line (a)).

Henry begins a turn (*Well see*) that is about to augment Zelda's hypothetical solution: (*if you know people* . . . (line (c)) by arguing that membership in the synagogue provides social contact. Henry begins with a sentence-initial light definite *the- the sy-* (i.e. synagogue). Because 'synagogue' is a first-mention, however, it conflicts with the light subject constraint and is interrupted mid-word (an atypical interruption site):

Example 3.24

Zelda: (a) It seems so lonely there in the winter, =

                                                                Z

Debby: (b)   yeh
Zelda: (c) = but I guess if you know people . . .
Henry: (d) Well see [the- the syn-₁ =
Debby: (e)   [Well you'd make =
Henry: (f) = [**the- the only way you go down there t'live there₂,**
Debby: (g) = [friends.
Henry: (h) = y-y-y-y'have t'join **the synagogue₁**.

              (h) Y'must. Because there they have social activities.

Although Henry begins with a definite reference to 'the synagogue' (a first-mention) in sentence-initial position (line (d)), he then switches to a complex NP *the only way you go down there t'live there* (line (f)). Like 'synagogue,' this is also a first-mention. But unlike 'synagogue' (line (d)), it is so long, complex and informative that it takes up the entire intonation/idea unit (line (f)). Structural possibilities do exist for Henry to continue this first-mention heavy noun within a single equative sentence, e.g. 'the only way you go down there t'live there is to join the synagogue.'[11] Instead, Henry moves *the synagogue* to a new intonation/idea unit that comprises its own clause with *the synagogue* in sentence-final position: *y-y-y-y'have t'join the synagogue* (line (h)).

Following introduction of 'the synagogue,' Henry immediately begins a story about a man he met who lives in the community that we have been discussing. Although the man is not Jewish, he belongs to both the synagogue and the local church, the former, purely for social reasons. Thus the turn-initial position of *the synagogue* previews its major role in upcoming discourse – a role that is facilitated by a longer 'one person' floor in which to portray why that referent is crucial to the point of a story.

It is not only turn-initial article repairs that reflect management, and possible alteration of the floor, but also turn-medial article repairs. In Example 3.25, we see a turn-medial article repair that has a role in altering the overall distribution of turns within the floor. Henry, Zelda and I have been discussing the 1967 war in the Middle East. In order to understand the *eh: the: eh the Israelis* repair (line (o)), we need to backtrack to the use of *they*, first in a pragmatic prototype (lines (b), (h)) and then as a referral to Israelis (line (k)). (*He* in line (a) is Henry and Zelda's son.)

Example 3.25

Henry:	(a)	He got up eh: one morning
	(b)	when **they** had the war in 1967, this one {points to picture}
	(c)	he says, "[Dad I'm goin' to Israel to [fight."
Debby:	(d)	[Umm [yeh.
	(e)	I felt the same way. I really did.
		Z Z
Zelda:	(f)	Yeh:: Well I had said that too that had I been young, in my twenties, =
		Z
Henry:	(g)	She would.
Zelda:	(h)	= I would've, [too, when **they**, =
Debby:	(i)	[Yeh. I bet you would have.
Zelda:	(j)	= y'know [had the war.
Henry:	(k)	[**They**'re havin' a hard time. Y'know how it is.
Debby:	(l)	Oh it's:- it makes me sick, really. I really worry =
		Z
Zelda:	(m)	Yeh:
	(n)	= about it. But **they** just accept it!
	(o)	**eh: thee eh thee Israelis** accept it.
Debby:	(p)	That's the thing, yeh,
	(q)	**they**- **they** accept it as part of- =
		Z
Zelda:	(r)	of living.
Debby:	(s)	= the- the risks of living there. That's what my uncle says.

There are two uses of 'they' in Example 3.25. First is *they* as part of a pragmatic prototype (Chapter 4) in Henry's *they had the war in 1967* (line (b)) and Zelda's *they, y'know had the war* (lines (h) and (j)). Second is *they* as an anaphoric next-mention of 'the Israelis': *they're havin' a hard time* (line (k)) and *but they just accept it* (lines (m) and (n)). It is the latter *they* (n) that switches to *the- the* full noun (line (o)).

We can understand the sequential mechanics of *eh: thee eh thee Israelis* (line (o)) by moving back to Zelda's prior *but they just accept it* (line (n)). Here Zelda is providing a contrast to my own statement *I really worry about it* (line (n)) by juxtaposing the difficulty of the Israelis' current existence with a quality we had previously been noting – their ability to put up with hardship. In her next presentation of this claim, Zelda's switch to the more informative *the Israelis* (line (o)) can be seen as a more explicit assertion of the group's continuing endurance as a national characteristic (Chapter 5 on referring sequences).

When we look more carefully at the progressive organization of turns, however, we see that Zelda's rhetorical move is also interactionally contingent. Until line (n), Zelda, Henry and I had been overlapping and latching onto each others' turns, thus portraying participant involvement through joint engagement with the topic in a shared floor. The upshot of this shared floor is that potential turn-transition spaces had been filled with next-speaker's new turns that latched onto, or overlapped with, current-speaker's continuing turns. As Zelda completes her first assertion of acceptance *But they just accept it!* (line (n)), however, the turn-transition space remains open: neither Henry nor I pursue the opportunity to become next-speaker. Thus a turn space is still available to Zelda: she can continue rather than cede her turn.

By opening her utterance with *eh: thee* (line (o)), Zelda pivots between turn-transition (giving me or Henry a chance to speak) and turn-maintenance (continuing to speak). Notice that this strategic ambiguity is provided by both the lack of lexical meaning in *eh:*, and its placement following an intonationally and propositionally complete unit (*But they just accept it!*). When Henry and I both remain silent, Zelda moves further toward a renewal of her turn. Rather than repeat the next-mention *they* of her prior turn, Zelda restates her claim with a full NP *thee eh the Israelis accept it*. Thus, the renewal of Zelda's turn space – and its repositioning of her as the sole manager of a 'one person' floor – is matched by the renewal of the referent through a definite NP.[12] The article repair in turn-medial position is attuned to a shift in ownership of the floor.

In sum, article repetitions pattern differently in turns than noun repetitions. Their role in turn-taking seems more attuned to the presentation of referents that will have an important role in upcoming discourse. Depending on the type of floor in which turns had been allocated, entering an important referent into discourse can require alteration of the floor – regardless of whether that referent was in turn-initial or turn-medial position.

3.5 Conclusion

In this chapter, we analyzed problematic uses of articles by focusing on what happens to two forms – definite *the*, indefinite *a* – when a speaker self-initiates and self-completes repair on a member of that set. Analysis of article switches suggests that although some switches reflect a functional convergence between *the* and *a*, others reflect deictic shifts in information state, epistemic changes, porous levels of inclusiveness, or the peripheral (vs. core) status of a referent within a category. Article shifts that maintained (in)definiteness reflected the re-placement of a referral in an ongoing sentence, text and/or interaction. Thus, article switches seemed to reflect not just miscalculations of information status, but also trouble finding the 'fit' between word and world that would also fit comfortably within a text.

Analysis of article repetitions did not (in general) reveal problematic placement in sentence or text: distributions of both *a- a* and *the- the* nouns generally conformed to the typical occurrence of indefinites and definites in sentence position, in noun weight (in relation to position) and in text. What the article repetitions seemed to reflect, instead, was the very local problem of verbalizing a noun, especially animate abstract nouns that evoked collections of people or social roles. This makes sense in relation to Levelt's (1983) suggestion that the speaker interrupts when self-monitoring identifies the problem only if what is identified is a problem with the upcoming noun. Since articles are forward looking – projecting aspects of information status of an upcoming referent – interrupting them prior to the noun might offer preparation time to conceptualize the referent, access the noun, or articulate the referring expression, just as TYPE 1 repairs (the continuation of referent and referring expression) might offer preparation time for the sentence and turn.

The local nature of the problem indicated by repeated articles is thus not surprising. The cut-off and repeated articles, and the nouns that they preface, are already appropriately placed within their sentences (in initial or final positions) and texts (as first or next-mentions). Thus coordination among information status, sentence and text can proceed even prior to choice of a noun that will activate for the hearer recognition of the speaker's referential intention to connect a word with an entity from the world.

In sum, *a* and *the* work in tandem with methods of placing information so that it can be felicitously received and interpreted by a recipient. Speakers choose an article in ways consistent with their positioning of the referral in a sentence and text – sometimes before they are sure what noun they will use for the referral. Thus even if the speaker has to briefly delay a referral, the hearer is able to anticipate the appropriate familiarity level of the upcoming referent.

Delimiting the options for an upcoming referral might offer exactly the kind of benefits assumed to underlie pragmatic principles for producing and interpreting referents. It is often noted that we use referring expressions that provide the least amount of information needed for recognition by another (Sacks and Schegloff 1979): if we can count on our hearers to understand who we mean if we say *he*, rather than a more informative noun phrase like *the man who sold me coffee this morning*, we will do so. Recent research on 'minimization' in pragmatics builds upon the idea that we can 'mean more' by 'saying less' (Blackwell 2003, Huang 1994, Levinson 2000). Since the articles *the* and *a* delimit the information status of an upcoming referent, they help to streamline hearers' effort to set initial parameters around an upcoming referent. Hence, problematic referrals involving articles can help us understand not only the processes underlying this small phase of the referring process, but also the entire process through which we design our referrals for others. In the next chapter, we turn to what happens when minimization fails, sometimes right at the point of the article.

Notes

1. Because they relate a lack of familiarity to a lack of specificity, many traditional accounts of reference conclude that *a* prefaced nouns are non-referential and do not evoke referents. As observed by Donnellan (1966/1978), however, even supposedly non-referential uses of indefinite expressions can be the antecedent of anaphors (e.g. '*I want to marry a perfect person, even though he might not exist*'). And once a pronoun is indexed to a nominal expression (as *he* is indexed to *a perfect person* above), that nominal becomes a referring expression regardless of its initial indefiniteness (see Cornish 1999: 153–159 and Kartunnen 1976 for this argument in relation to a mental 'discourse model.')

2. Two points. First, the quantitative comparisons will not allow us to compare the overall frequency of *a*- repairs to the overall frequency of *the*-repairs. To do this, we would need to identify all the *non*-repaired referrals with *a* and *the*. The comparisons that we will make are between *a*-*a* and *the*- *the* repairs in particular environments. Second, the quantitative analyses will have different totals (between 81 and 105) because the specific parameters to be examined can end up excluding some forms. For example, although predicate nominals, and referents within prepositional clauses, are included in Table 3.1, they will not always be included in subsequent quantitative comparisons (for reasons to be explained when relevant). I note for each table or figure what is excluded.

3. Recall that these were not included as TYPE 1 repairs in Chapter 2.

4. It is possible that *strange women* evokes one of the wives who has not been an eager participant in the 'hostess' role typical of the wives of the card-player friends. A brief story about her appears later in the interview, as does a story about an argument among the friends.

5. Two points. First, the incipient *the d*- in Henry's coda could have been interpreted as a next-mention for a specific doctor mentioned in the narrative. But what Henry was reporting was not an action undertaken by a particular character. Rather, Henry was creating an equivalence between two abstract social types in order to present a general evaluative conclusion: professionals can make mistakes as readily as plumbers (his own occupation). Thus Henry's switch from an incipient definite NP *the d*- to the indefinite *a dentist* was a switch from what could have indexed a higher level of familiarity than the type-identifiable entity appropriate for his narrative coda.

   Second, the term 'dentist' is a mistake in reference, but it is not a completely random category confusion. Henry knew that my father was a dentist, and elsewhere we had talked about the status that this occupation conferred in relation to a doctor's ability to give misinformation to a patient. Given that we are here talking about doctors' mistakes, it is not all that surprising that Henry mistakenly brings 'dentist' into the story – an echoing of the earlier role of my father 'the dentist' who was a patient in an earlier story about doctor's confusions.

6. Because the NPs here are descriptive rather than referential, I did not include them in earlier quantitative comparisons. All the predicate nominals in my data add descriptive information about an already existent referent; they do not assert a (symmetrical) equative relationship between two referents (Lyons 1977: 185). In example 3.20 line (e), *the Irish guys* is the referent; the site of repair (*the toughest guys*) adds descriptive information about that referent (cf. *are tough*, a predicate adjective) that modifies the hearer's identification of the referent (e.g. from *Irish guys* to *tough Irish guys*).

7. The totals differ in Table 3.4 (and Table 3.6) differ from other tables. This is because I have not included referrals in prepositional phrases (e.g. *at the corner store, in my mother's bedroom*) because they can be either sentence initial or final. It was surprising, however, that roughly half of the *the- the* referrals were in prepositional phrases – mostly sentence-final provisions of locational information.

8. Since Table 3.5 is not examining sentence position, it includes both predicate nominals and prepositional phrases.

9. Chafe actually uses the term "light" to reflect something like processing cost: if a referent is already activated in consciousness, it requires little effort – or imposes a 'light' burden – on the hearer. I am using 'light' here more as a physical metaphor, i.e. the weight of a noun through quantity of information and amount of constituents. So my statement of the light subject constraint concerns a relationship between 'given' and weight.

10. A few points. First, next-mentions include not just paraphrases of the 'exact' referent evoked by a first-mention, but also entities inferable through schema knowledge, and contained/containing set relationships (Prince 1981). Second, excluded from Table 3.6 are NPs appearing in predicate nominatives. Although the structure and function of these can seem comparable to existentials (cf. the use of *it's a supermarket down the block* for *there's a supermarket down the block* in African American Vernacular English and some Southern dialects), their use in Standard American English is not the same: whereas existentials (and their variants (Chapter 4) can introduce new referrals (e.g. *There's a guy with two Mercedes on my block*), predicate nominatives provide attributes of, and modify, an already familiar referent who is in subject position (e.g. Who lives there? Oh *he's a/the guy with two Mercedes*).

11. Compare the following, from a conversation between Gary and Anne about the neighborhood that Anne lives in which is near the university and inhabited by both poor African Americans and students: *Well, the- thee only thing that's saving that part of the city is the students.* Here Gary uses an equative sentence in which the heavy initial definites provides a frame of interpretation for *the students* (cf. Wh-clefts).

12. This switch to a full noun across turn boundaries is comparable to the use of next-mention full nouns across adjacency pair boundaries (Fox 1987 on adjacency pairs) or structural boundaries in lists (Schiffrin 1994a: Chapter 9).

4

Reactive and proactive prototypes

4.1 Introduction

The process of referring to an entity about which we want to say something can be derailed by a variety of problems that can be remedied by a variety of solutions. In Chapter 2 on problematic referrals, we analyzed repairs in which referent and/or referring terms continued and/or were abandoned. We saw that speakers could interrupt and restart a noun phrase (e.g. in TYPE 1 repairs, *we-we*), substitute one noun phrase for another (e.g. in TYPE 2 repairs, *we → they*), or replace an incipient noun phrase with a descriptive clause (e.g. in TYPE 3 repairs *a- I wouldn't say he speaks German*). In Chapter 3, repairs of cut-off switched articles (*the → all of the*, *a → the*) revealed different word-to-world connections; repairs of cut-off repeated articles (*a- a*, *the- the*) revealed lexical and/or conceptual uncertainty despite stable assumptions of hearer familiarity with an upcoming referent and felicitous placement in sentence and text.

The problematic referrals analyzed in this chapter differ in both problem and solution. The problem is the failure of the familiarity assumption: the speaker begins a referral by assuming a level of familiarity that then appears to be unwarranted. The solution draws together syntactic, semantic and discursive features as a single *pragmatic prototype* that can both remedy and pre-empt familiarity problems. Chapters 2 and 3 previewed important pieces of this solution: abandoning nominals for descriptive clauses; the sentence-initial presentation of familiar 'light' information and the sentence-final presentation of less familiar 'heavy' information. Here we will see how these features can combine in a single recurrent strategy.

The analysis begins by examining the remedial redistribution of information from a noun to less densely packed sentences and text (Section 4.2). After presenting reasons for viewing this strategy as a pragmatic prototype, we see that this same strategy brings information into text in ways that attempt to prevent potential interpretive problems by tying information to prior text and differentiating among potential foci of attention (Section 4.3). My conclusion (Section 4.4) addresses the benefits of the syntactically simple presentation of 'one piece of information at a time' in one turn-unit at a time.

4.2   Reactive strategies

In this section, we examine problematic referrals in which a recurrent problem (speaker assumes too much recipient familiarity with a referent) is repaired by decreasing the density of the referral through the redistribution of information within sentence and text, and the anchoring of the information to already available information. Before beginning, however, it is helpful to have a quick overview of where the problematic referring terms fall on scales of assumed familiarity (Section 4.2.1). I then go on to describe each problem and its solution (Section 4.2.2). I summarize in Section 4.2.3.

4.2.1   Overview of trouble sources

Various scholars have observed that referring expressions form a rank order scale in which expressions at either end of the scale convey speaker assumptions of low (or high) hearer familiarity with a referent. Expressions between the two poles of the scale are then ordered according to intermediate levels of familiarity; they may also be seen as forming a scalar implicature (Gundel et al. 1993).

Scholars speak of the scale in different terms: whereas Prince speaks of assumed *familiarity* (1981), the term used by Ariel (1990) is accessibility, Chafe (1994) speaks of degrees of activation of consciousness, Clark and Haviland (1977) of given/new, Clark et al. (1992) of common ground, Gundel et al. (1993) of cognitive status of a referent, and Halliday (1967) of theme/rheme. Although the choice of terminology does reflect different assumptions about referring processes (e.g. whose perspective is central, speaker or hearer? is information status encoded in language? within speaker's consciousness?), the order of terms within the scales is overwhelmingly similar.

The scale in Figure 4.1 incorporates features from several scales. The forms are on a rough continuum from low to high assumed familiarity; under the forms are comments on referential potential, whether referrals are indefinite or definite, and whether the link between 'word' is with the 'world' or inferable to 'world' through text or context.

Speakers sometimes choose a referring expression that assumes more recipient familiarity than is warranted, i.e. a form that is too 'mimimal.' As I illustrate in this section, such problems can develop not just from the referring expression itself, but also from the way expressions are embedded in ongoing talk. And such problems can be repaired by a strategy in which syntax, semantics and pragmatics provide a familiar 'location' in which the referent can be accessed, identified, and recognized.

4.2.2   From problematic noun to remedial text

I begin with an example of an other-initiated, self-completed repair (Section 4.2.2.1) and continue with the more typical self-initiated, self-completed repairs (Section 4.2.2.2). We will see comparable strategies of self-completion regardless of other- or self-initiation: each problem is resolved by reducing the density of information in the problematic noun and redistributing it to sentence and/or text in which it is anchored to familiar information.

4.2.2.1   Other-initiated and self-completed repair

In this section, I discuss one example of an other-initiated, self-completed repair of an assumed familiarity problem. In Example 4.1, Meg has been explaining how she used to play hide and seek; she mentions two places where she and her friends used to hide (line (c)).

ASSUMED FAMILIARITY

Low   High

a NP	*quantifier/numeral (NP)*	*this NP*	*the NP*	*pronoun*	*zero*
non-specific referent	may be containing inferable	false definite	referential	referential	
or type identifiable		or def demonstrative	or attributive		
indefinite	indefinite	definite? indefinite?	definite	definite	definite
'word-to-world'	text inferable or context inferable	text inferable ---------------------------text inferable			

Figure 4.1 A scale of information status

Example 4.1

Meg: (a)   How'd we play it?

Anne: (b)   Yeh.

Meg: (c)   We'd hide in the alley or with **the storekeepers' bread-
              boxes**. Hhhh.

Anne: (d)   The storekeepers' breadboxes?

Meg: (e)   *Yeh, they had breadboxes on the wall.*

       (f)   And we climbed up and got in there.

As Meg describes hide and seek, she says that one hiding place was
with the storekeepers' breadboxes (line (c)). Anne's repetition of the
entire NP with rising intonation (line (d), an echo question) suggests
that Meg's use of a definite NP was inappropriate because it did not
evoke a referent that Anne could identify.[1]

Meg's response *Yeh, they had breadboxes on the wall* (line (e))
self-completes Anne's other-initiated repair in several different ways.
First, Meg confirms Anne's hearing of the phrase with *yeh* (i.e. "that
is what I said"). Next, and more relevant for analysis of the referring process itself, Meg alters the complex nominal used to evoke
the referent 'store-keepers' breadboxes.' Rather than again bury the
possession of breadboxes by storekeepers in a 'NP's NP' structure
(the prototypical form of possessives in English), Meg predicates
possession through *they had* in a clause. Notice that Meg's use of
pronominal *they*, anaphoric to 'storekeepers,' suggests that the referent 'storekeepers' is not a problem and can safely be assumed to
be old information. But her switch from *storekeepers'* to *they had*
suggests that the possession of breadboxes cannot (and should not)
be assumed familiar to Anne.

In his work on language and consciousness, Chafe (1994) suggests that speakers verbalize one new idea at a time, such that one
new piece of information is typically presented as one intonation
unit and in one clause. The syntactic change from 'NP's NP' to *they
had* NP – a switch from an NP to a clause that comprises an entire
intonation unit – suggests that Meg is now treating the idea that
storekeepers have breadboxes as new to Anne.

Notice, also, that *storekeepers' breadboxes* is itself comprised of
two compound nouns, both of which encode complex relationships
(people keep stores, boxes contain bread) that need to be understood to access the referent. Meg's change to *they had breadboxes*

dissects the complex referent not only by predicating possession of 'breadboxes' by 'storekeepers,' but also by placing *breadboxes* in post-verbal position (i.e. *they had breadboxes* rather than *breadboxes were on the wall*). The placement of a noun that presents new and/or referentially complex information in final position is not surprising: final position is often reserved for information that may be more difficult to process. The processing benefit for new, complex material is amplified here through its contrast to what is in initial position: a predicate (*they had*) that is both semantically simple and tied (through *they*) to prior discourse. Thus, Meg's switch from *storekeepers' breadboxes* to *they had breadboxes* shows how information is packaged not just for the speaker herself, but also (or alternatively) with a particular audience in mind: what counts as a new idea is assessed in relation to another's knowledge and presented in a position designed to be received by the hearer.

The syntactic shift just described is not the only way that Meg's *They had breadboxes on the wall* adapts her referral to her altered assumption about Anne's knowledge. Meg also shifts away from her earlier definite expression (*the . . . breadboxes*) to a type identifiable indefinite *breadboxes*, thus again retreating from her earlier assumption that Anne was familiar with storekeepers' breadboxes. And in addition to using anaphoric *they* to explicitly anchor 'breadboxes' to 'storekeepers,' Meg's *on the wall* (line (f)) also anchors 'breadboxes' to prior text as a contained inferable: storekeepers 'keep' a store and one part of a store is its walls.

What Meg says next – *And we climbed up and got in there* (line (f)) – suggests that she now assumes Anne's familiarity with the referent 'storekeepers' breadboxes'. Notice, first, that Meg returns to her description of hide and seek: her use of *and* (line (f), Schiffrin 1987) continues her prior description and retroactively defines *Yeh, they had breadboxes on the wall* (line (e)) as an embedded side sequence that is now closed. More revealing in relation to the referring process itself is Meg's next-mention of the referent. Instead of using the full NP *breadboxes* as the destination of *got in*, Meg uses the spatial pronoun *there* – a form displaying an assumption of higher familiarity via its anaphoric relationship with the prior NP *breadboxes*. Thus, after repairing a definite reference (*the storekeepers' breadboxes*) by anchoring (*had*) an indefinite form (*breadboxes*) to a familiar entity (*they*), Meg returned not only to a definite form, but to a pro-form (*there*).

Whereas Example 4.1 illustrated an other-initiated, self-completed repair, the next examples conform with the overall preference for speakers to both initiate and complete their own repairables (Schegloff et al. 1977). Despite the difference in repair initiation, we see the same strategies of repair-completion.

4.2.2.2 *Self-initiated and self-completed repairs*

We see in this section that speakers self-complete the repairs that they themselves initiate in ways that are surprisingly consistent with completion of other-initiated repairs: a term high in assumed familiarity is rephrased as a term lower on the scale, placed in its own clause in a relatively prominent position, and anchored to an entity that can be assumed familiar to the hearer. We start with an example in which a speaker interrupts the definite article *the*. As discussed in Chapter 3, *the* NPs assume familiarity based on prior text or world knowledge: the speaker expects hearers to have the knowledge enabling them to identify an entity similar to one that has been specifically identified by the speaker (Epstein 2001).

In Example 4.2 Bob is describing his plans (to see an ice hockey game) for the evening to Joe (a friend) and Anne (a sociolinguistic interviewer):

Example 4.2

Bob:	(a)	Yeh, I think I'm goin' down- downtown tonight and see **the-**
	(b)	y'know, **the- the-**
	(c)	*there is such a team in Philadelphia as the Flyers.*
Fred:	(d)	How're you gonna get in, [Bob?
Anne:	(e)	[I've heard of the Flyers.
Fred:	(f)	= That's gonna cost you ninety dollars a seat.

After opening his repair with *y'know* (line (b), marking a change in shared information state, Schiffrin 1987: 267–294), Bob cuts off and repeats *the* (line (b)), thus suggesting a problem with formulating the upcoming referent. Bob then replaces the definite *the* with an indefinite *such a team in Philadelphia as the Flyers* in a 'there' sentence (line (c)).

The use of *there is* in Bob's repair recalls Meg's use of a semantically weak predicate (*they had*) to highlight the self-completion of her repair in sentence final position. Also like Meg's repair, Bob anchors the repairable referent to more familiar ground. The phrase 'such a NP as the NP' presents an unfamiliar referent as a member of a familiar set whose members are related to the set through hyponomy. Thus we might mention an unfamiliar breed of dog by locating it in a larger, more familiar class of items, e.g. *There is such an animal/dog/sheepdog as the Briard*. Notice that once the general class of items is introduced as a type-identifiable indefinite, we can then evoke a specific item with a definite expression: the familiarity of that item can be assumed through its membership in the prior mentioned class (i.e. it is a contained inferable).

'Such a NP as the NP' seems especially well suited for the introduction of names. Names do not themselves have membership in semantic fields because they are less conventionally associated with classes of items than other nouns. Names of ice hockey teams, for example, do not form a natural class. Rather, the lexical items used for team names draw from a variety of semantic fields whose properties may capture different desired qualities of the sport (e.g. *Flyers* with speed, *Sharks* with viciousness, *Bruins* with strength), but are not themselves closely related semantically. Likewise, the name *Flyers* could be used to designate not an ice hockey team, but a model airplane club, a rock band, or a group of bird watchers. Bob thus uses an expression well suited to introducing the name of a team. 'Such a NP as the NP' introduces *the Flyers* as an inferable contained in a familiar (type-identifiable) referent (*a team*) in a shared location (*in Philadelphia*). Bob thus repaired his truncated definite *the-* with an expression that not only required less familiarity than a definite term, but actually built an identity in relation to membership in a familiar set.[2]

The next example illustrates a problematic use of the pronoun *they*, another type of definite noun. Example 4.3 begins as Gary (a high school graduate) is answering a question about whether having a college education helps one get a better job. In defense of his answer that college education makes little difference, he points out that many of his co-workers have college degrees: *The same guys I'm workin' with are all college guys* (line (b)).

Example 4.3

(a) Well, y'know, it is.
(b) The same guys I'm workin' with are all college guys.
(c) I work-
(d) **they-**
(e) I had *two guys that work with me.*
(f) They're both from uh LaSalle College.

After introducing the people with whom he works (*the same guys I'm workin' with*) and saying something about them (they *are all college guys*, line (b)), Gary begins to repeat *I work* (line (c)), but changes to *they*. He then self-interrupts *they-* to use *I had* to anchor the indefinite *two guys that work with me* (line (e)) to a familiar entity (himself) in post-verbal position. In *They're both from LaSalle College* (line (f)), the pronoun *they* is anaphoric with the prior *two guys* (line (e)).

The problematic referral in Example 4.3 is *they* (line (d)). Like other pronouns, *they* assumes familiarity. Because pronouns convey little semantic information other than gender, number, animacy and case, they are often used when a referent is recent and topical in the text (Chapter 5). Since the antecedents of pronouns are textually given, however, locating the referent (through the word-to-word internal link (Chapter 1)) may also require parsing of, and inferencing from, the prior text. This is exactly where Gary's problems with *they* begin.

The likely antecedent of Gary's self-interrupted *they* is the recent, semantically compatible noun phrase *the same guys I'm workin' with*. A problem arises, however, because of what Gary has just said about *the same guys I'm workin' with*. Notice that Gary had used a predicate nominative ('X is Y') form to describe an attribute (*all college guys* (Y)) of a referent (*the same guys I'm workin' with* (X)). The problem is the quantifier *all*. What *all* conveys is twofold: X is co-extensive with Y; both X and Y have more than two members. Thus, if the antecedent of *they* is indeed *The same guys I'm workin' with*, then *they* is a group of more than two co-workers. What Gary says next, however, is inconsistent with this group size: *two guys* (e) and *both* (f) explicitly convey two people. Thus, *they* (line (c)) is a problem because the referent evoked by its most likely antecedent conflicts with the referent to be used in upcoming discourse.[3]

Although the problematic *they* in Example 4.3 is embedded in text differently than the repaired referrals of earlier examples, the problem raised by its use is surprisingly similar. Like the full NPs in Examples 4.1 and 4.2, the definite pronoun *they* in Example 4.3 assumes more familiarity than warranted. *They* displays an assumption of high familiarity with a referent that is, moreover, assumed to be "in focus" because of its recent mention. Gary's text, however, does not provide the appropriate interpretive site for *they*: *they* is not warranted if referents are assumed familiar *only* through contained inferability, i.e. the inferential relationship whereby $X_{1,2 \ldots n}$ are interpreted as members of a set X.[4]

Gary's self-completed repair of *they* follows a pattern similar to those in earlier examples. I repeat the key sentences below, in a more schematic form:

SUBJECT NP	VERB	OBJECT	
The same guys I'm workin' with	are	all college guys	(b)
I	had	two guys that work with me	(e)
They	are	both from LaSalle	(f)

First, Gary expands the number of syntactic and/or intonational units in which information is presented. In line (b), a college identity (*all college guys*) was predicated of *the same guys I'm workin' with* in only one sentence. The same proposition occupies two units in lines (e) and (f): a college identity (*from uh LaSalle College*) is predicated of *two guys that work with me* in two syntactic/intonation units. Second, Gary shifts the position of the referral within the sentence. In line (b), *the same guys I'm workin' with* was in sentence-initial subject position. In line (e), however, *two guys that work with me* is in post-verbal position (after *I had*) in line (e). Thus, like earlier examples, Gary repackages information by expanding the units in which that information is presented and reserving sentence-final position for the repackaged information.

Just as important to the repair-completion as Gary's changes is what he keeps the same. Two features remain constant. One is the form used for the referral: NP [relative clause] for both *the same guys* rel [*I'm workin' with*] and *two guys* rel [*that work with me*]. The inclusion of the relative clause in both referrals suggests that the information in the relative clause (*I'm workin' with, work with me*) is an integral part of the referral. The second constant in Gary's repair-completion is the structure of the sentences establishing the identity of Gary's co-workers: 'X are Y' in both *The same guys I'm workin' with* (X) *are all college guys* (Y) and *They* (X) *are both from LaSalle* (Y). Like the repeated NP [relative clause], the repeated 'X is Y' format suggests the importance of the information being verbalized – the descriptive equivalence between X and Y.

Both the constants in Gary's repair (the form of the referral, the form of the sentence) and the changes (repackaging, shifts in position) serve referential and expressive functions in Gary's answer to the question about college education. By repeating the NP with the relative clause – but in a more focal position, after *I had* – Gary provides an informative and unambiguous antecedent for the upcoming *they* (f). In other words, Gary creates a site that takes full advantage of textual recency (Chapter 5): the sentence-initial *they* in line (f) can be unambiguously tied to its antecedent *two guys that work with me* in line (e).

Note, finally, that an expressive function is served by repeating the equivalence between himself and college graduates in the same syntactic frame ('X is Y'), but in two units rather than one. The repetition allows Gary to use and re-use his own experience as evidence that there is no difference in job performance between high school graduates (like himself) and college graduates. Like the repetition, the repackaging of his experience in two units devotes more time to the equivalence. Thus, the format of Gary's repair creates an expanded textual world in which parallel forms can serve as an iconic reflection of parallels and equality in the real world in which Gary and *all college guys* work.

In sum, the repair of the problematic referral *they* in Example 4.3 reveals some of the same reasons – and solutions – for referring problems seen in earlier examples. Here we have also seen, however, that information is packaged not just in relation to its newness for the speaker and/or hearer, but also in relation to how that information fits into a text and how it contributes to the speaker's interactional and social positioning (see Chapter 7).

In contrast to the definite referring terms in examples thus far, the problematic referral in (4) is *this*. Although *this* can be used as a demonstrative because of its deictic basis, when it is used as a determiner, its status wavers between definite and indefinite – hence, the term "false" definite. Gundel et al. (1993) locate this term higher on their scale than indefinite *a* for the following reason. The article *a* can receive either a referential reading (speakers intend to refer to a specific entity) or a type-identifiable reading (the speaker assumes that the hearer can access a representation of the type of object described by the expression). But because *this* is used only referentially, *this* is higher on the scale.

In Example 4.4, Ceil has been describing some past experiences and is about to tell a story about one particular experience.

Example 4.4

Ceil: (a) We used to sit on the steps, across from **this-**
       (b) *there was a Catholic school across from us.*
Anne: (c) Mhm.
Ceil: (d) And the priest was a real dud.

The problem in Example 4.4 is the assumption indexed by *this-* about the cognitive status of the 'Catholic school.' Although Ceil continues to use an indefinite *a* in her repaired referral, this is a switch to a lower end of Gundel's cognitive status/assumed familiarity scale than *this*. A second difference in the solution is the means by which the replacement clause *there was a Catholic school across from us* accomplishes the repair. Like the earlier examples in this section, Ceil uses a new syntactic and intonation unit that locates a referent in sentence final position, precedes it with semantically weak information, and anchors the referent to something familiar (a location *across from us*). After Anne's receipt of this information (*mhm*), Ceil can thus assume that 'Catholic school' is sufficiently familiar as a referent to use as a "container" in which to locate the inferable 'the priest' as a definite NP.

The next example shows that what serves as a repair for one referral can cause a problem for another. In Example 4.3, Bob had repaired the problematic referent 'the Flyers' by introducing it as a contained inferable of 'a team in Philadelphia.' We will see in Example 4.5 that trying to rely upon a relationship of contained inferability between two referents can cause problems if the identity of the 'container' is not straightforward.

In Example 4.5, Alice begins a story (in line (c)) to provide a specific illustration of Betty's general point that *people have . . . some weird things that they get kicks out of* (line (a)). Alice's story tells about *white kids* (line (j)) who mistreat an elderly woman by trying to force her to drink a can of paint. Although it is relatively easy to introduce the *white kids* in lines (i) to (k) as a subset of *people* (line (a)), introducing the victim of their abuse is more challenging (lines (c) to (g)).[5]

Example 4.5

Dot: (a) People have some things that they, y'know- some
                weird things that they get kicks out of.
Anne: (b) Oh, I was just destroyed by that.
Alice: (c) Y'know, well, **one of the old-**
              (d) *one of my-*
              (e) I told you what had happened to *the old ladies down
                my mother's.*
              (f) *There was one of the women that owned the house.*
              (g) They had taken her house and put her in the projects?
Dot: (h) Yeh.
Alice: (i) And these weren't black kids,
              (j) these were white kids [I'm] talking about, [remember?
Dot: (k)   [Oh,]   [yeh.]

After prefacing her story with *y'know, well,* Alice begins her orientation by introducing the story protagonist with *one of the old-* (line (c)). Although indefinite *one* assumes little hearer familiarity with a referent, *of the old* begins to anchor *one* into a group assumed to be familiar (re: *the*). When Alice self-interrupts *the old* and recycles the phrase as *one of my* (d), however, the singularity conveyed by *one* is re-anchored into a group that is brought closer (through the shift to *my*) to a familiar entity (herself).

Notice, crucially, that Alice's two referring attempts thus far – *one of the old-*, *one of my* – combine a member of the group (*one of*) and a characteristic of the group (either age (*the old*) or relation to self (*my*)). However, her next attempt at reference – *the old ladies down my mother's* (line (e)) – utilizes a "reminder" (*I told you what had happened*) to separate the different tasks of (line (a)) describing the age of the group and (b) singling out one member of that group.

Reminders differ from the weak and uninformative predicates *they had, I had,* and *there is* of our earlier examples: they mark a presumption of familiarity with information by invoking a prior speech situation and/or a prior text. Such information may be important for different reasons, ranging from the information itself serving an immediate action-oriented goal (I may remind you to take your medicine) or as background for a more distant goal (I may remind you to stop at the drugstore, but not mention that it is because you need to pick up your medicine). Reminders that are information-oriented – like *I told you what had happened* – have sequential effects opposite to those of pre-announcements like *Guess what happened?* Pre-announcements preface information that the speaker assumes is both new to the hearer and worthy of sharing (i.e. news); they open an interactional space in which that information can be foregrounded. But as suggested above, reminders can open an interactional space for information that need not be relevant in and of itself, but may instead serve as background to something else.

Alice's reminder *I told you what had happened to the old ladies down my mother's* (in line (e)) provides background for a problematic referrals by assuming three pieces of given information: age (*old*), gender (*ladies*), location (*down my mother's*), and a personal relationship (*down my mother's* anchors the referent to self). Temporarily abandoned is the effort to single out a member of the group.

After using the reminder to define a set ('the old women who lived near my mother'), Alice locates *one of the women* (line (f)) as a contained inferable. Note, also, that the referral is syntactically relocated from clause-initial (*one of the old* in lines (c), (d)) to clause-final position (*There was one of the women that owned the house* in line (f)) – a position whose import has already been noted in previous examples. Alice then builds upon the textual givenness of the referent to use pronouns, i.e. indefinite general *they* and *her* (*they had taken her house and put her in the projects?* in line (g)) to complete the reminder. As reflected by its final rising intonation (line (g)) and Dot's affirmative *Yeh* (line (h)), these events are included in the information about which Alice had been reminding Dot. Alice then continues her narrative orientation by introducing the remaining characters in the story.

In sum, Alice's referral began by combining a group referent and a single member of the group: *one of the old, one of my*. After abandoning her initial description (*old*, line (c)) by anchoring it to herself (*my*, line (d)), she separates the task into two components and elaborates a group referral *the old ladies down my mother's* (line (e) as the focus of a reminder clause *I told you what had happened*. The individual referral – a contained inferable *one of the women that owned the house* (line (f)) – is re-introduced in the syntactically focal position of a *there* sentence, and then treated as textually given (*her* in line (g)). Thus, as we have seen in earlier examples, a referring problem is repaired by repackaging complex information into separate clauses, moving information to focal positions, and anchoring information in familiar domains.

The final example contains two repairs: from *all the neighbors* to *a viewer*, and then, to *so many people*. Prior to Example 4.6, Rita had been talking about her neighborhood and describing how her Aunt Bess sometimes intervened in neighborhood feuds. Example 4.6 is in the evaluative climax of Rita's story about a fight that she initiated to defend her mother who had been insulted:

Example 4.6

(a) With that I went up the playground and **all the neighbors-**
(b) I had **a viewer-**
(c) uh like you know *there was so many people up there like you might've thought Cassius Clay was fighting or somebody, y'know.*
(d) And uh, my Aunt Bess came up and got me.
(e) She wouldn't let me fight.

It is while reporting a pivotal action – going to the playground after the insult – that Rita first introduces the referent *all the neighbors* (line (a)) as the subject of an upcoming clause conjoined to the critical action *With that I went up the playground*. Since she has previously been talking about her neighborhood (and more generally, since it is part of our common knowledge that people have neighbors), it is easy to identify the referent of *all the neighbors* as a large group of Rita's neighbors. Why, then, does Rita self-initiate and complete a repair?

Notice that Rita's use of the quantifier *all* is evaluative. Rather than literally evoke her entire set of neighbors, *all the neighbors* intensifies the significance of the group of neighbors who will witness what is about to happen. The way Rita introduces the neighbors, however, is not positioned for a maximally evaluative effect. Rather than suspend the narrative action prior to the climax (Labov and

Waletsky 1967), Rita has begun to provide more information about the neighbors in a temporally sequential clause conjoined to a prior action clause. Rita's first repair – *I had a viewer* (line (b)) – increases the evaluative potential of 'the neighbors': the switch to an independent clause with a stative verb (*I had*) suspends the narrative action, anchors the referent to herself, and begins to specify the evaluative role of 'the neighbors' with a descriptive noun (*a viewer*) that conveys their significance in the narrative action.

The problem with *a viewer*, however, is not its indefiniteness, but the word-to-world connection. Because the referent 'viewer' is not commonly known, the listener can identify neither a referent nor a type-identifiable that can be indexed by indefinite *a*. Rita then shifts to a strategy similar to what we have seen in earlier examples. She uses a *there* sentence to introduce a long and complex referring expression in a focal position; she anchors the referent to a familiar entity (the antecedent of through *up there* (line (c)) is the prior *up the playground* (in line (a)).

Rita also fits her repair to the expressive goals of her narrative: *there were so many people up there . . .* recaptures the intensification of her first referral *all the neighbors*. Two evaluative devices are used. First is placement in narrative. Whereas the evaluating audience *all the neighbors* was buried in a narrative clause, *there were so many people up there . . .* suspends the narrative action, thus drawing attention to itself and building dramatic tension.

The second means of evaluation is the 'so X that Y' format. As illustrated in the hypothetical sentences in Example 4.7, '*so* + adjective' works together with a complement *that* clause to intensify the quality conveyed through the adjective:

Example 4.7

	Proposition 1	Proposition 2
(a)	I felt so angry that	I slapped her across the face.
(b)	I felt so angry that	I could have slapped her!

'So + adjective' works together with a complement *that* clause to intensify the adjective (e.g. *angry* in Proposition 1) such that an action (e.g. *I slapped her across the face*) in the *that* clause in Proposition 2 is interpreted as a consequence of the state in Proposition 1. As line (b) illustrates, the action (*I could have slapped her!* in Proposition 2) can even be a counterfactual outcome (not possible with

so, i.e. **I was angry so I could have pounded her*) whose intensity
to the point of impossibility actually intensifies the adjective *hungry*
and thus strengthens Proposition 1.

Rita's use of the 'so X that Y' format is slightly different because
of the comparator *like*. Rita's *so many people up there like you
might've thought Cassius Clay was fighting or somebody, y'know*
intensified the quantity of people who were watching her fight by
setting up a parallel between the *many people up there* and what
one *might have thought* if *Cassius Clay was fighting*. Notice that
the mention of Cassius Clay (a celebrity prize winning fighter, later
known as Muhammed Ali) has two effects. Since Cassius Clay
drew huge audiences to his fights, Rita intensifies the neighborhood
impact of her fight (an evaluative effect) and leads hearers to infer
the denotation of the problematic term *viewer* (a referential effect).

We noted above that it was relatively easy to identify the referent
of Rita's initial mention of *all the neighbors*. What was problematic about this referral, then, was not the referent *per se*, but its
placement in the narrative to whose evaluation it was supposed
to contribute. The next problem was the unfamiliarity of the lexical
item *viewer*. Rita combined a strategy seen throughout this section –
a *there* sentence with a referent anchored to a familiar entity – with
strategies specific to the textual location and evaluative meaning of
the referent in the narrative.

4.2.3   From problem to solution

In this section, I analyzed six examples of problematic referrals stemming from a speaker's miscalculation of a hearer's familiarity with
a referent. We saw that speakers self-complete both other-initiated
and self-initiated repairs of referring terms from various places along
the assumed familiarity scale. Repairs moved down the scale, shifting to terms assuming less familiarity. We also saw two indications of
interdependence between reference and text. Just as text contributed
to problems in referent recognition, so too, it facilitated successful
referrrals when it provided textual cues that guided hearers toward
an adequate interpretation of a referent.

Also observed was regularity in the self-completions of repair, as
summarized in Figure 4.2.

In addition to weakening the level of assumed familiarity associated with the noun phrase, speakers made syntactic and semantic

PROBLEMATIC REFERRAL	REPAIR		
NOUN HIGHER IN FAMILIARITY	SEM WEAK NOUN VERB	NOUN LOWER IN FML	FAMILIARITY ANCHOR
the storekeepers' breadboxes	they had	breadboxes	on the wall
the Flyers	there is	such a team...	in Philadelphia
they	I had	two guys	that work with me
this	there was	a Catholic school	across from us
one of the old	'reminder'	the old ladies	down my mothers
all the neighbors/a viewer	there was	so many people	up there

Figure 4.2 Repair strategies

changes at the clause level. Each new referral was placed in its own clause in a relatively prominent position (sentence-final, following a weak predicate with a potential to evoke familiarity) and anchored to an entity accessible to the hearer, thus redistributing information from a problematic noun to less densely packed sentences and text.

Anchoring a referent to easily accessible information is consistent with insights from several lines of research, for example Clark and Marshall (1992) on the success of vertical repairs that strengthen mutual knowledge, Firbas' (1964) views on communicative dynamism, Chafe's analysis of information flow (1987) and proposal that speakers linguistically package one new piece of information at a time (1994), and Lambrecht's (1994) Separation of Reference and Role Principle, i.e. 'do not introduce a referent and talk about it in the same clause.' Because this remedial strategy presented very little new information other than the referent itself, then, it was an efficient way to provide information about an entity about which hearers might not have had prior knowledge, without also forcing them to immediately make use of that entity in a more elaborated way.

4.3 A proactive strategy: pragmatic prototype

In this section, I suggest that the anchoring strategy just discussed can be viewed as a schema that instantiates a *pragmatic prototype*. My view of prototype combines two constructs: an event schema that "summarizes important attributes abstracted from a large number of related events, and . . . has to do with stereotyped situations that we are constantly confronted with" (Heine 1997: 46) and a prototype that is "a schematic representation of the conceptual core of a category" (Taylor 1989: 59) in which entities can be core (central) or peripheral instantiations of the category. Prototype theory has been applied to lexical semantics, morphology, syntax, phonology and intonation (for examples, see Lakoff 1987, and Taylor 1989, 1996). I view the group of features revealed in the repairs in (Section 4.2) as different instantiations of a construction in which a pronoun (often referentially vague) and a copular ('be') or possessive ('have,' 'got') verb preface a noun phrase (of varying length) to provide a context-sensitive strategy through which a speaker cooperatively exploits mutual knowledge to remedy and pre-empt familiarity problems in referrals. I will suggest that the existential *there* sentence THERE IS X, in which *there* provides a link to a potential 'place' reference in the text, is the central member; the *they have* sentence THEY HAVE X, in which *they* provides a potential link to a 'person' reference, is less central.

After discussing the conceptual and linguistic relationships among existence, location and possession (Section 4.3.1), I show how both THERE IS and THEY HAVE constructions establish familiarity (Section 4.3.2), and how variants of the pragmatic prototype help separate competing foci (Section 4.3).

4.3.1 Location, existence and possession

The conceptual links among existence, location and possession – and their reflection in language – are well established. Lyons (1967: 390) observes that "in many, and perhaps in all, languages existential and possessive constructions derive (both synchronically and diachronically) from locatives." Here I suggest that location and existence mutually entail one another: an entity cannot be 'there' unless it exists; an entity cannot exist unless it is somewhere.[6] Possession entails existence: one cannot possess something unless it exists. Finally, the possessor/possessee relationship conveys (through metaphor) either a physical or symbolic location in which to begin and/or continue that relationship.[7]

Linguistic relationships among these three conceptual realms are well attested diachronically, developmentally and cross-linguistically. Heine (1997), for example, traces the origins of sentential structures of possession back to lexical items originally used to convey 'grasping' or 'taking hold of' objects, a movement that bring objects closer to one's location. He suggests that a process of grammaticalization over time led to the more abstract idea of 'possession' in which lexical verbs express possession even without explicit indicators of co-presence between possessor and possessee.

Other indications of the conceptual relationships among existence, location and possession can be found in languages in which the three concepts are differently distributed among linguistic forms. In modern Hebrew, for example, possessive constructions are formed with the morpheme *yaesh* (roughly translatable as 'exist') and the preposition *le-* (to) preceding the possessor (Example 4.8 line (a)).[8]

Example 4.8

(a) Le-Anat   yaesh et   ha-sefer   ha-ze.
     To-Anat   exist *acc*   the-book   the
     Anat has the book.

The same morpheme is used without a possessor to convey only existence in Example 4.8 line (b).

(b) Yaesh   sefer   ba bet ha-sefer.
     Exist   book   in the school.
     There is a book in the school.

Rather than use *yaesh* for location, however, there is a separate lexical item 'sham' that provides an adverb of location, as in Example 4.8 line (c).

(c) Ofer tzarich lalechet le bet ha-sefer. Hu shachach sefer sham.
     Ofer has   to go   to school.   He left   a book there
     Ofer has to go to school.   *He left a book there.*

Another type of relationship between location, existence and possession appears in the Akan cluster of Twi languages (spoken in Ghana). The possessive relationship in Twi falls within the scope of meaning conveyed by distinct verbs that express different types of relationships (e.g. existence, predication, attribution), all of which are possible meanings of the English copula 'be'. One of those

verbs – *wõà* – is also used for conveying both location and possession (Ellis and Boadi 1969). Thus, as Heine points out, the verbs
'be' and 'have' are closely related in many languages: "both receive
the same, or at least an etymologically related expression in many
languages" (Heine 1997: 43).

In sum, I suggest that existence, location and possession are the
basis for a pragmatic prototype that focuses information, as represented in Figure 4.3.

I will suggest in discussion of the *there is* and *they have* variants
that the distal properties of 'there' (as a place deictic) and 'they' (as a
person deictic) contribute to the prototype. *There is* moves an entity
from physical distance (*there* is not *here*) to discourse presence; *they
have* moves an entity from physical exclusion (*they* excludes *we*) to
discourse inclusion.

Let us turn now to the first variant of the prototype: *there is* sentences. 'There' in English has been identified as several different
forms that are used in different constructions, as Examples 4.9 to
4.11 briefly illustrate. In Example 4.9 a speaker is identifying some
women (line (b)) that he has just greeted (line (a)). His addressee (in
line (b)) is not the women themselves, but Anne, the sociolinguistic
interviewer with whom he had been talking:

Example 4.9
Charlie: (a)   Hello there.[9]
          (b)   **There's** the old ladies from the home.

There in line (b) is a spatial deictic, contrasting with *here* to indicate
distance from the speaker's current location (cf. 'I worked there'
would indicate that 'there' is not the speaker's current location
or current workplace). Thus, the referent ('the old ladies from the
home') to which *there* "points" can be physically present, but not
immediately close to (or moving closer to) the speaker (i.e. he did
not say *Here's the old ladies from the home*).

There in Example 4.10 also has a locational meaning. But because
it situates referents within a textual world, rather than the here and
now of the physical world, it is not deictic. Example 4.10 is from
a story in which Gina is telling about how her brother (as a child)
had discovered some treats that their mother had hidden from the
children.

CONCEPT	SCHEMA	LINGUISTIC FORM			SEMANTIC INTERPRETATION
		Distal pro+ stative vb + obj			
existence	X [be]	*there*	*is*	X	X = entity$_1$
location	X [be [there]]	*there*	*is*	X	X = entity$_1$ in place
possession	X [be [there] [with Y]]]	*they*	*have*	X	X = entity$_2$ (possessee) of entity$_1$ (possessor)

Figure 4.3 A pragmatic prototype

Example 4.10

(a)   So, my mother went out,

(b)   and my brother$_1$ says, "I gotta search around here."

(c)   So he$_1$ went upstairs in the bedroom

(d)   and **there** he$_1$ found them hid.

(e)   You know, she had hid them.

(f)   And **there was** him$_2$- my brother$_2$ and the dog$_3$, Prince.

(g)   They$_{2/3}$ had got on the bed

(h)   and he$_2$ was goin' to the dog$_3$, "One for me and one for you."

Two brothers are referents in the segment in Example 4.10. Brother$_1$'s search for the treats begins in line (c) as he travels *upstairs in the bedroom*; this location is marked by a fronted locative *there* in line (d), in what Lakoff (1987) calls a presentational deictic. *There* in line (f) – the case of interest – also marks location, indicating where (again, *upstairs in the bedroom*) brother$_1$ discovered brother$_2$ and the dog. Thus, both cases of *there* in Example 4.10 convey the location of an event: in line (d), the event is an action ('find'); in line (f), it is a state ('be').

Example 4.11 illustrates the use of *there* that has been said to differ most from *there* with deictic or locational meaning.

Example 4.11

Debby: (a)   Yeh. Well some people before they go to the doctor, they'll talk to a friend, or a neighbor.

           (b)   Is there anybody that uh . . .

Zelda: (c)   Well: well I guess-

Henry: (d)   Sometimes it works.

           (e)   Because **there's** this guy Louie Gelman,

           (f)   he went to a big specialist,

           (g)   and the guy . . . analyzed it wrong.

My initial question in Example 4.11 continues a series of questions in which I had been asking Henry and Zelda about communication in their neighborhood. My specific intent in lines (a) and (b) is to see if there is anyone in the neighborhood who serves as an informal source of medical advice. Rather than give me the information I had been hoping for – who Henry would talk to before seeing a doctor – Henry tells a story about a friend who talked to people about a medical problem before going to a doctor.[10] The friend, who is the central character (topical referent, Chapter 5) in the story, is introduced with an existential *there* in line (e).

There in Example 4.11 is not called a locative or a deictic, but an expletive (Fillmore 1968), pronominal (Erdmann 1976), presentative (Hannay 1985) or existential (Lakoff 1987, Milsark 1977). When used with a copula, 'there + be + NP' is said to assert the existence of an entity (e.g. *There's this guy Louie Gelman*) with or without an event (e.g. *There was this guy Louie Gelman who went to three doctors*). Important to the identification of what I call existential *there* is that the post-copular NP is an indefinite noun phrase.

The existential *there* construction has been studied by linguists interested in syntax (how is the sentence derived? what is its formal representation? (Aniya 1992, Freeze 1992, Milsark 1977), semantics (what is the meaning of the sentence? is it similar to other forms and uses of *there*?) and pragmatics (what are its contexts of use? what allows the use of definite nouns in post-verbal position?) Often the three foci are related to one another, especially in discussion of the 'definiteness' problem (i.e. the use of existential *there is* with *the* NP, as in lists or reminders (e.g. Abbott 1993, Rando and Napoli 1978, Ward and Birner 1995), and less so across social groups (Meechan and Foley 1994.)

As illustrated below, *there* appears to be more nominal (and more subject-like) with its existential use than its deictic use. The sentences in Examples 4.12 lines (a) and (c) show that subject noun phrases can invert with verb auxiliaries in yes-no questions (a) and Wh questions (c). Examples 4.12 lines (b) and (d) show that existential *there* also inverts. Example 4.12 line (e) shows that the deictic *here* (and by extension the deictic *there*) cannot be inverted.

Example 4.12
       Subject-auxiliary inversion
(a)   Is a doctor in the house?
(b)   Is *there* a doctor in the house?
(c)   Why is a doctor in the house?
(d)   Why is *there* a doctor in the house?
(e)   *Why is here a doctor in the house?

The comparisons in Example 4.13 show the same difference between existential and deictic *there*:

Example 4.13

Tag question

(a) A dog is in the yard, isn't it?
(b) *There* is a dog in the yard, isn't *there*?
(c) *Here is a dog in the yard, isn't here?
(d) **There* is a dog in the yard, isn't it?

Tag questions copy the subject NP, reverse polarity, and invert subject and auxiliary. As we see in Example 4.13 line (b), *there* behaves just like the subject NP *a dog* in line (a), but deictic *here* (in line (c)) does not – and neither would deictic *there* (line (d)).

Although the syntactic differences between deictic *there* and existential *there* have typically been explained in structural terms (e.g. Milsark 1977), Lakoff (1987) proposes that a cognitively based grammar can relate them semantically and conceptually as prototypes. I will adopt a view similar to Lakoff's (1987: 541) in which existential *there* is semantically and pragmatically similar to deictic *there*, but nevertheless remains distinct with "intermediate types of deictic *there* that are closer to existential *there*." In Lakoff's framework, the deictic/existential relationship is accounted for by grouping together numerous deictic *there* constructions whose individual properties distinguish them from a central deictic construction (p. 482; pp. 579 – 581).

Like existentials, possessives have also been said to have a prototypical form: 'NP$_1$'s NP$_2$' in which NP$_1$ is a noun (with *'s*) or possessive pronoun. The prototypical possessor/possessee relationship involves ownership (but see Heine 1997 and Taylor 1996 for discussion of conceptual extensions). The *they have* construction differs from the prototypical possessive (Taylor 1996: 341–343). Rather than present the possessor/possessee relationship within a single NP, THEY HAVE asserts the relationship in a short clause with a subject pronoun *they* and a transitive verb *have* that conveys the possessor/possessee relationship between the subject NP *they* and the object NP. That relationship deviates from what Taylor (1996: 340) calls the possession gestalt, i.e. the possessor in *they have* need not be a specific human being; the possessee is not necessarily an object of value.

Whereas most scholarly attention to THERE IS has focused on *there* rather than the copula 'be,' attention to THEY HAVE has focused mostly on the verb 'have.' In responding to research on expansion patterns of 'have' (Brugman 1988), Heine (1997: 191–192) observes an extensive process of grammaticalization:

It is widely held that both 'have' constructions and perfects in many Indo-European languages are part of a more general semantic evolution involving the following stages in particular: 'Take, take hold of, receive'>'hold, keep'> 'own, occupy'> 'have' (transitive verb)> 'have' auxiliary.

In addition to the linguistic process of grammaticalization, Webb (1977) suggests that cultural preconditions – the presence of a property-based or state-level economy – may be a necessary (but not sufficient) condition for the development of a possessive transitive verb such as 'have.'

As noted above, there has not been much attention paid to *they* in THEY HAVE. Yet like *there*, *they* is a distal deictic with both pure deictic uses (to index non co-present people) and anaphoric uses (as a pronoun to index textual entities). Both *there* and *they* have a broad range of indexical possibilities, perhaps because distance from the deicitc center (typically the speaker) can be perceived as extending indefinitely into time and space through an 'open field' deictic orientation. Recall, also, what was noted in earlier chapters: *they* as next-mentions of different first-mention nouns can co-exist within a single text, as long as the referents are separable by their predicate. This point is illustrated again in Example 4.14:

Example 4.14
Anne: (a) Well, I always wondered, how **older people**$_1$ managed to
            live on   the very small, Social Security.
                      Z   Z
Alice: (b)   Well,   every now
            and then you read it in the paper.
       (c) It's pretty sad.
       (d) Not too long ago **they had** a write up in the paper
       (e) that *they*$_2$- y'know, *they*$_1$ eat canned dog food.

Clearly the referent 'older people' in line (a) is not the same referent as *they* (in line (d)) who *had* a write up in the paper. The first appearance of *they* in line (e) is unclear: it could be a continuation of the inferable 'people' associated with the newspaper or an incipient next-mention of 'older people.' Once the predicate (*eat canned dog food*) is completed in line (e), the relationship between the second *they* in line (e) and 'older people' is clarified.

There are two more points pertinent to the use of *they* in THEY HAVE. First, *they* may actually lack a textual antecedent, as seen in Example 4.5 earlier in this chapter:

Example 4.5

    (e) I told you what had happened to the old ladies down my mother's.

    (f) There was one of the women that owned the house.

→ (g) **They** had taken her house and put her in the projects?

They in line (g) is not co-referential with either *the old ladies* or *the women*. Its vagueness and lack of specificity suggests indefiniteness, rather than definiteness: we return to this possibility when discussing antecedents for *there* and *they* below. Second, *they* is the most common pronoun used in the THEY HAVE construction (77% of the 107 examples analyzed here). Although we can't use the proximal deictic *here* with existential 'be' (as we saw in Examples 4.12 and 4.13), we can use the proximal first, or the second, person pronouns with *have* (or *got*), as in Gary's *I got two guys that work with me* (in Example 4.3). Now that I have outlined the basis for a pragmatic prototype that includes *there is* and *they have*, let us turn to how it works in discourse.

4.3.2 The prototype as a familiarity anchor

The conceptual and linguistic relationship among existence, location and possession provides a basis for a pragmatic prototype that pre-empts problematic referrals in discourse. After showing how THERE IS and THEY HAVE alternate in close sequence in discourse (Section 4.3.2.1), we see that both *there* and *they* are grounded in text (Section 4.3.2.2), as are the post-verbal nouns that they preface (Section 4.3.2.3).

4.3.2.1 Variants in text

Observe, first, alternations between THERE IS and THEY HAVE in discourse across different speakers (Examples 4.15 and 4.16) and within same-speaker speech (Example 4.17). I have bolded the constructions of interest and italicized 'place' references.

Example 4.15
Anne: (a) **Were there** like chaperones *at the canteen*, too?
Carol: (b) Oh, yeh.
       (c) Oh yeh, **they had** chaperones walking *all around*.

Example 4.16
Joe: (a) It's a little too far up, Eve.
     (b) **There's** nothing *in there*.
     (c) *It's* only factories in- that's *in there*, right?
Eve: (d) No:, not any more.
     (e) **They have** that Franklin uh Village.

Examples 4.15 and 4.16 both show that a respondent (Carol in the former, Eve in the latter) can respond to another's THERE IS with THEY HAVE. Example 4.15 also shows that a respondent's *they* can be interpreted metonymically in relation to a locational mention from the prior speaker: Anne's *canteen* is then re-evoked in Carol's *all around*, thus repeating the inferred locational source of possessor in the same clause as *they*. In Example 4.16, Joe and Eve had been talking about a neighborhood, pronominalized in *in there* (line (b)). Thus Eve's *they* might also be related (but very indirectly) to that location (we discuss this more below).

Alternations between THERE IS and THEY HAVE in same speaker's speech are similar to those across speakers:

Example 4.17
Val: (a) D'you think this would be a safer *neighborhood* with policemen around?
Freda: (b) *Every neighborhood* would be safer if **there were** policemen,
       (c) and I feel that *every neighborhood* would be safer if **they had** some foot patrols.

In Example 4.17, Freda's *there* can be anaphorically linked to her own mention of *every neighborhood*. Freda's *they* (line (c)) can be metonymically related to people living in the neighborhood or more directly to *policemen* (see below). Example 4.18 illustrates a same speaker repair between THERE IS X and THEY HAVE X:

Example 4.18
Charlie: (a) Yeh, Giant Steps with uh . . .
          (b) Like you had- **they**- **there was** one guy
          (c) and you have to ask him, "May I take two giant
               steps."

Charlie's self-interrupted *they* and its replacement by *there was* illustrates the alternation between THERE IS and THEY HAVE.

In addition to showing the ability of THERE IS X and THEY HAVE to alternate in discourse, the examples above have also shown that *there* and *they* can be anaphorically connected to prior text. Recall that the remedial referrals (Section 4.2) had locational reference within the anchoring clauses themselves: *on the wall* (Example 4.1), *in Philadelphia* (Example 4.2), *down my mothers* (Example 4.5), *up there* (Example 4.6), and the location presumed through *work with me* (Example 4.3). Below we examine whether *there* in THERE IS and *they* in THEY HAVE link the post-verbal noun to an explicit location (or third person plural entity) not only in the same clause, but also in prior text, and even in both clause and prior text. Such links would suggest that location and/or third person plural entity help to ground a referent not only in abstract cognitive and/or perceptual space, but also in concrete textual representations of places and people.

In the subsections to follow, I focus on how *there is* and *they have* anchor referrals in discourse. I include only *there* constructions whose post-verbal NPs can be possible referrals (thus excluding postcopular summarizing constructions, negatives, meta-linguistic phrases and so on (Collins 2001, Ziv 1982)). I begin with analysis of how THERE IS and THEY HAVE fit into discourse through anaphoric/cataphoric place and person mentions and then continue with the information status of post-verbal NPs.

4.3.2.2 There/they and location/person in discourse
In this section, we explore the possibility that *there* and *they* establish concrete links within the text, thus providing a means of cohesion to what has been (or will be) said that will help integrate the post-verbal nominal into discourse. In order to do so we first need to identify possible sites for location-mentions (Figure 4.4) and person-mentions (Figure 4.5) in nearby text.

PRIOR TEXT + CLAUSE	On one side is the *Naval Home*.
	There's a wall *there*.
PRIOR TEXT (EXPLICIT)	And in the summertime, in *our back kitchen*,
	there was a stove that we burned wood in.
PRIOR TEXT (INFERABLE)	As your friends *came in*,
	there was someone to take them upstairs and give them a
	shot.
CURRENT CLAUSE	Or else if uh if **there's** a couple boys *in the neighborhood* you
	did talk to, you bring them in.
NO ANTECEDENT	**There***'s* this guy Louie Gelman.

Figure 4.4 Possible sites for location of *there*

The possible sites for person-mentions (Figure 4.5) differ from those for *there*-mentions. First, although we found explicit place-mentions in *there* clauses, I found no explicit person-mentions in the THEY HAVE clauses.[11] However, it is possible to include in the same clause a location or event from which one can infer the presence of people (e.g. in *they have music at the party*, we can infer from 'party' the existence of people). Second, since *they* is a plural pronoun, arguing that *they* is metonymic to the location (e.g. *at the party*, *at Saint Monica's*) requires an assumption of multiple entities present at the place. Third, although we distinguish explicit from inferable locations in Figure 4.4 – and in Figure 4.5 – we will also add the possibility of no 'person' mentions for *they* if *they* is not referential (as illustrated in Example 4.14).

Figure 4.6 shows whether 'location' or 'third person plural entity' is presented anywhere within, or prior to, the THERE IS and THEY HAVE clause respectively. Arranged on the X axis is my approximation of the accessibility levels of possible antecedents in text: most accessible in text *and* clause; then in clause; through explicit mention in prior text; inferable through prior text; no accessibility.

Figure 4.6 shows two major differences between *there is* and *they have* in relation to the accessibility of 'place' and 'person' antecedents. First is the low relative frequency of 'person' in *they have* clauses themselves. As noted earlier, there are few opportunities for antecedents of *they* in the post-verbal portion of the clause: all that could be included in the same clause would be a location or event that could allow an inference of people. Second is the wide gap between *they have* and *there is* in 'text: inferable.' There are two

PRIOR TEXT AND CLAUSE (INFERABLE)

Delaware's beautiful.

Y'know, uh, there's *a place* you can play and all.

They have *a place*, like a little playground like.

PRIOR TEXT (EXPLICIT)   -Like I- I knew that was true for *drunks*,

say I've seen walkin' around.

They have just big brown paper bags full of things.

-There's one block of *brownstones* between Twentieth

and Twenty first on Walnut now. *Big three story houses.*

[text left out, see Example 4.23] Did you notice that **they have** an

outside entrance that goes down into the basement?[12]

PRIOR TEXT (INFERABLE)

  INFERABLE FROM *'people' of the parish*

Here at *Saint Monica's* which is downtown,

they have a commercial course.

CURRENT CLAUSE (INFERABLE)

What kind of mills did **they** have around *here, in*

South Philly?

NO ANTECEDENT   And uh, every once in a while we'd stop and get a soda,

y'know, or something like that.

And then- **they- they** always had these little ice cream parlors

around, which **they** don't have today

Figure 4.5 Possible 'person' sites of *they*

reasons for this: inferences about 'location' for *there* appear only
through verbs of motion; inferences about 'person' appear through
metonymy, i.e. people could be inferred through their presence at
a place (recall the 'text: inferable' example in Figure 4.5). Thus the
frequent grounding of *they* in prior text is actually due partially
to prior physical locations (e.g. cities, houses, restaurants) that are
assumed to be occupied by people.

The partial anchoring of *they* in prior locations has important
consequences. First, the same noun that can provide a textual
'place' antecedent for *there* can also provide an inferential 'person' antecedent for *they*. Second, since both *there* and *they* can
be anchored to a location, an upcoming referral can find not only
an abstract perceptual space (as suggested for existential *there* by
Bolinger (1977) and Lakoff (1987)), but also a concrete location
that has already been, or is about to become, salient in a textual
world. What is provided, then, is not only a background against

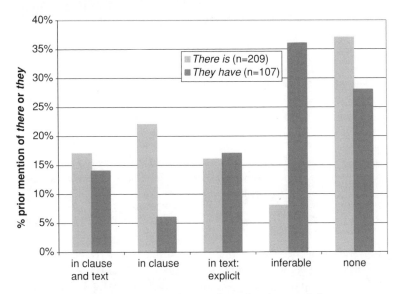

Figure 4.6 Location of antecedents for *there* and *they*

which other information may be foregrounded, but also a link to locations already (and/or about to be) included in a textual world. Whereas Lakoff (p. 541) suggests that the *there* of "perceptual and discourse subconstructions do not refer to a concrete location in space, but rather to abstract locations in perception and discourse," then, it seems that *there* (and sometimes *they*) can make concrete connections to physical locations in the textual world.

Finally, when we turn to the last set of comparisons (no antecedent), we see that not being anchored at all is less frequent than being anchored: 37% of the THERE IS sentences, and 28% of the *they have* sentences, lack textual anchors of 'place' or (inferable) 'person.' The presence of place anchors for 63% of the existential *there* cases suggests that "in many cases it is hard to decide whether an adverbial with demonstrative force or a pronominal *there* with deictic elements is intended" (Erdman 1976: 83). Likewise, the presence of anchors for 72% of the *they have* sentences suggests that 'they' still maintains a possessor role in the prototype.

Thus far, we have found alternations between *they have* and *there is* in both one and two party discourse, as well as anaphoric and/or cataphoric relationships between *there* and prior 'place,' and *situation*   There's one of you and two of them.

textually given

    repetition/paraphrase Now **Jewish people**, I lived in the neighborhood where there
                              were *Jews.*

    contained inferable   Question: When did **the Polish people** start moving in?
                              Answer: There used to be *a lot of them.*

     inferrable   Question: Do you think there's **more crime** now?
                              Answer : There's *too many people that've been hurt and*
                              mugged.

    new   -The sailors used to hang around there, from the navy yard and,
                         of course we used to sneak down because they had *a swimming*
                         pool and *nice big park.*

Figure 4.7 Assumed familiarity of post-verbal NPs

they and prior 'person' or 'place.' In our earlier analysis of reactive
strategies that repaired problematic referrals (Section 4.2), we saw
that post-copular information also helped to establish familiarity.
Let us turn, then, to the information status of post-verbal nouns.

4.3.2.3 Information status of post-verbal nouns
In this section, we examine the information status of post-verbal
nouns in order to see what kind of information is introduced by *there
is* and *they have*. I differentiate levels of familiarity in Figure 4.7.

    Figure 4.8 shows the information status of the post-verbal nouns
in both *there is* and *they have* constructions. Arranged along the X
axis are the sources of information according to the location and
strength of a textual anchor (cf. Clark and Marshall's 1992 co-
presence heuristic).

    Figure 4.8 shows that the post-verbal NPs after *they have* are rel-
atively evenly distributed among the textual anchors for post-verbal
NPs. The distribution after *there is* differs: the largest group (52%)
of these post-verbal NPs are anchored through inferences in prior
text, i.e. through prior information that provides background information in relation to which a referent can be inferred. Notice, also,
that post-verbal nouns in both *there is* and *they have* are rarely completely new (about 20% for each). Although a common assumption
is that existential *there* sentences introduce new discourse referents,
the finding that some level of familiarity has already been established
parallels Collins' finding (2001) that *there* sentences often highlight
information already present (sometimes implicitly) in the prior text.

Table 4.1 *There is, they have and 'animacy' of NPs.*

	There is	*They have*	Total
Animate	123 (59%)	17 (16%)	140
Inanimate	86	90	176
Total	209	107	316

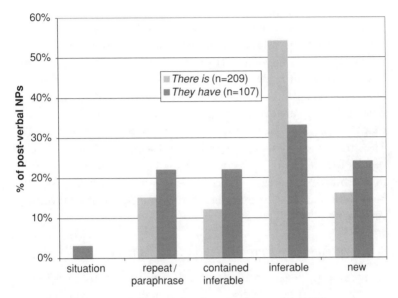

Figure 4.8   *There is, they have* and post-verbal NPs

Rather than provide a site in which to open a discourse space, then, the post-verbal nouns are more likely to select or develop a focus from prior talk.

The finding that a majority of post-verbal NPs in THERE IS and THEY HAVE are familiar, however, does not mean that the two constructions preface the same kinds of entities. Table 4.1 shows an overwhelming preference for animate referents in THERE IS.

Table 4.1 shows that 59% of THERE IS post-verbal nouns are animate, compared to 16% of those after THEY HAVE. The markedness of *they have* post-verbal animate nouns reflects the possessive meaning (however bleached) of *have* in these constructions: animate possessees are peripheral, rather than core, members of the prototypical possession schema (Heine 1997, Taylor 1996). Only a small range of animate nouns can occupy the possessee role, e.g. pets, family members, friends, employees. This semantic/pragmatic dispreference is reflected in the *they have* data: the 17 post-verbal animate nouns were type-identifiable referrals to social roles (cf. Sacks' (1992) membership categories), e.g. *visitors, guys, guides, a lot of patients*.

4.3.2.4 Summary

In this section, we have examined the similarities and differences between the two variants of the pragmatic prototype in a set of texts. We have seen that THERE IS and THEY HAVE alternate in discourse, that both constructions are tied to discourse through anaphoric/cataphoric relationships with 'place' and 'person,' that post-verbal NPs are overwhelmingly already somewhat familiar, and that THERE IS prefaces more animate referents than THEY HAVE. Thus the same syntactic, semantic and discourse features found in repairs to familiarity problems (Section 4.2) are clustered together in a pro-active strategy for bringing referents into discourse. The next section explores some reasons for using both variants within a single text.

4.3.3 Variants of the prototype together in discourse

Analysis thus far has focused on how two variants of a pragmatic prototype are situated in discourse, but not on how or why speakers might use both variants in a single text. In this section, we see that using both variants can differentiate potential foci in a text either evaluatively or referentially.

I start with the difference between *there* and *they* as anaphoric to prior place or person. We saw in Section 4.3.2.2 that it was possible for both *there* and *they* to have a locational antecedent. Whereas *there* could convey an explicit 'place' connection, *they* could connect through the implicit assumption of 'people' at that 'place.' Example 4.19 illustrates this difference.

Example 4.19

Baltimore has been changing.
(a)   There are more parks now.
(b)   They have more parks now.

Although the referential meanings of Example 4.19 lines (a) and (b) are the same, it could be that *there* and *they* focus on different aspects of the place: either its identity as a physical space or as a location in which people live, work, and so on.[13]

Focusing on place or person can be either referentially or evaluatively motivated. Although space prevents presentation of the full segment, the difference between Henry's *they have* (Example 4.20 line (a)) and Zelda's *there are* (Example 4.20 line (b)) shows a striking correlation with the content of their statements, I had just asked them if they thought there was life on other planets.

Example 4.20

(a) Henry: Why not? I think it's hhI think we're made out of gas! And I think as long as *they have* gas on other planetshhh? Really! {*omission*} If *they got* moon-*they got* dust on the moon, why can't *they have* it someplace else?!

(b) Zelda: Eh: I don't know. Well they're beginning to think like *there's* certain gasses up there that eh: . . . eh are registering like in a uhs . . .

The relationship between *they* and prior text in Example 4.20 line (a) is unclear: *they* could either be non-referential or a metonymic referral to the presumed occupants of *other planets* and *the moon*. Thus *they have* could provide a subtle indicator of Henry's belief about human life elsewhere. And Zelda's *there is* in line (b) could index her lack of commitment to the belief just stated by Henry.

In addition to creating evaluative focus, *they have/there is* alternation can also be used to differentiate referentially based parts of text, as illustrated in the next three examples. In Example 4.21 (seen earlier in Chapter 3 as Example 3.24) we see that *there* is used pronominally to evoke two places (the community$_1$ and the synagogue$_2$) with *they* focusing more on the people.

Example 4.21

Zelda: (a) It seems so lonely **there**$_1$ in the winter, =

                                                                    Z

Debby: (b)   yeh

Zelda: (c) = but I guess if you know people . . .

Henry: (d) Well see [the- the sy-$_2$ =
Debby: (e)   [Well you'd make =
Henry: (f) = [the- the only way you go down **there**$_1$ t'live **there**$_1$,
Debby: (g) = [friends.
Henry: (h) = y-y-y-y'have t'join the synagogue$_2$.
        (i) Y'must. Because **there**$_2$ they have social activities.

The uses of *there* in Example 4.21 are pronominal: two different places are indexed by repeated uses of *there*. By the time Henry is describing the benefits of joining the synagogue (place$_2$) in (line (i)), he has a choice between saying 'There$_2$ there are social activities' or 'There they have social activities.' We noted in Chapter 3 that 'the synagogue' is an important referent: it is what makes the community less lonely. Using THEY HAVE after pronominal *there* thus allows the referent 'the synagogue' to be emphasized as an important place because people at the synagogue, and the activities that *they have*, helps make the community less lonely in the winter.

Examples 4.22 and 4.23 illustrate how variants of the prototype differentiate referentially based segments of discourse: questions in a series (Example 4.22); parts of a list (Example 4.23). Example 4.22 is from a library reference interview, in which a patron (P) is asking the librarian (L) for information.

Example 4.22

P: (a)   Yes.
                           Can you tell me where I might   QUESTION 1
                           find a numismatic catalog
                           and if it can be taken from the library QUESTION 2
                           for a couple of days?
L: (b) Is numismatics coins?
P: (c) Yeah.
L: (d) Yes *there-*   ANSWER 2
         we do have some circulating books.   ANSWER 1
    (e) It would be on the second floor
    (f) and the call number for the coin books is 737.
    (g) *There's* a stairway to the left of the front door
    (h) and *there's* someone up there who can help you find . . .
P: (i) Thank you.
L: (j) You're welcome.

In line (a), P asks two questions, one about the location of a numismatic catalog and the other, about whether it can be checked out of the library. After checking the definition of *numismatics* (line (b)), L begins to answer the question with a *there* construction, but switches to *we do have* to mention *some circulating books* that answers P's second question about whether numismatic material can be taken from the library. L then returns to P's first question (a location question *where*) to describe on what *floor* (e) and by what *call numbers* (line (f)) the books can be found. Directions to the books (through *a stairway*) and to another source of help (*someone up there*) are provided by *there is* constructions. Thus L separates her answers to P's two questions by using two variants of the pragmatic prototype, thereby organizing not only the adjacency pairs [Q1[Q2 A2] A1]], but also the informational content of the answers.

In Example 4.23, several variants of the pragmatic prototype separate different levels of a complex list whose structure mimics the three floors (and sets of people) in a large house. THERE IS and THEY HAVE constructions are underlined, as is another variant of the prototype YOU HAVE. First-mentions of referrals that may also serve as antecedents for *there* and *they* are **bolded** and indexed. Next-mentions of referrals are *italicized* and indexed. Subparts of 'the houses' (the topical referent, Chapter 5) are connected through subscripts, as are different types of people working in the houses.

Example 4.23

Dot:　(a)　Now there's one block of brownstones between Twentieth and Twenty first on Walnut now.

　　　　(b)　**Big three story houses$_1$**.

Anne:　(c)　Y'know, I have a friend that had an apartment in one of those.

Dot:　(d)　Yeh.

Anne:　(e)　His address was twenty oh eight. I've seen [them

Dot:　(f)　　　　　　　　　　　　　　　　　　　　　　　[South, yeh-
on the south side, right.

　　　　(g)　Well, *they$_1$* were-

　　　　(h)　and uh, like, do you ever notice outside?

Anne:　(i)　Hm.

Dot:　(j)　Can you go d- did you notice that they$_1$ have *an outside entrance$_{1a}$* that goes down into **the basement$_{1b}$**?

(k) Well, **the help- a lot of the help**$_2$ lived *down there*$_{1b}$.

(l) And <u>they$_{1/2}$ had</u> their **furnace rooms**$_{1c}$ *down there*$_{1b}$.

(m) And their **kitchens**$_{1d}$ a lot of them in *the basement*$_{1b}$.

(n) Then <u>they$_{1/2}$? had</u> **dumbwaiters**$_{1e}$ that went upstairs to the **dining room**$_{1f}$

(o) and then **the maid**$_{2a}$-

(p) <u>they- they$_1$ had</u> **full**$_2$ uh,

(q) <u>you had</u> a **housekeeper**$_{2b}$,

Anne: (r) Mhm.

Dot: (s) <u>you had</u> a **cook**$_{2c}$,

(t) <u>you had</u> a **maid**$_{2a}$, =

Anne: (u) *They*$_2$ [all lived *downstairs*$_{1b}$.

Dot: (v) =   [<u>you had</u> a **butler**$_{2d}$.

(w) <u>They$_1$ had</u> **a full, raft of servants**$_2$.

Anne: (x) Isn't that something?

After introducing the houses (*one block of brownstones* in line (a)) with THERE IS, Dot uses THEY HAVE to list the following attributes of *big three story houses* (line (b)): *an outside entrance* (line (j), *furnace rooms* (line (l), *dumbwaiters* (line (n), *a full, raft of servants* (line (w)) earlier mentioned but abandoned as *full uh* (line (p)).

But a structuring problem arises for two reasons. First, *they* is used not only for *the houses* (lines (j), (l) and (m)) but also for the *help* (lines (p) and (w)). The referent is sometimes clarified by the object NP, e.g. *they* evokes 'houses' if the object NP is a part of the house, e.g. *an outside entrance* (line (j)). The second problem develops in lines (k) through (m) after 'the help' is introduced in line (k):

(k) Well, **the help- a lot of the help**$_2$ lived *down there*$_{1b}$

(l) And *they$_{1/2}$ had* their **furnace rooms**$_{1c}$ *down there*$_{1b}$.

(m) And their **kitchens**$_{1d}$ a lot of them in *the basement*$_{1b}$.

(n) Then *they$_{1/2}$? had* **dumbwaiters**$_{1e}$ that went upstairs to the **dining room**$_{1f}$

When *they* is used in the (l) – *And they$_{1/2}$ had their furnace rooms$_{1c}$ down there$_{1b}$* – right after introduction of *the help*, a recency effect (Chapter 5) allows the just-introduced 'the help' to be inferred as the possessor of *furnace rooms* (l), *kitchens* (m) and *dumbwaiters* (n): these places could 'belong' either to 'the houses' or to the people who manage the functions (shoveling coal, cooking) performed in those rooms and facilitated by the devices (e.g. *dumbwaiters* (n) moving food from the downstairs kitchen to the upstairs dining room).

The problem worsens when Dot introduces a type of worker (*the maid*) who is likely to be the person using the *dumbwaiters*:

> (o)   and then **the maid**$_{2a}$-
> (p)   *they- they*$_1$ *had* **full**$_2$ uh,
> (q)   *you had* **a housekeeper**$_{2b}$,

Dot's interruption of *the maid-* and her use of *they had* as a remedial strategy suggests that Dot had assumed a higher level of familiarity for 'the maid' than was warranted (Section 4.2), perhaps through an inference of her presence (note the use of the definite article *the*) in relation to the *dumbwaiters*.

Dot begins to remedy this problem by using *they had* to introduce the larger set in which *the maid* was a member (line (p)). Here we infer that *they* (in *they*$_1$ *had* **full**$_2$ uh line (p)) is either a next-mention of 'the houses' (a switch to the topical referent in the list, see Chapter 5) or with a more human emphasis, the owners of the houses.

Different facets of the problem are resolved by Dot's switch to *you had* (line (q)) for the servants, who are then listed with repeated *you had* (peripheral) variants of the prototype (lines (q), (s), (t) and (v)).[14] This subordinate part of the list establishes a subset in which the prematurely mentioned maid now has a slot. As the list proceeds, Anne can then use *they* (*They*$_2$ *all lived downstairs*$_{1b}$ (line (u)) as a clear referral to the servants (in line with recency (Chapter 5) and clarified by the verb *lived*). As the list ends, Dot's *They*$_1$ *had a full, raft of servants*$_2$ (w) can then return to the unambiguous use of *they* for the houses (and here, by inference, their owners) and provide the set to which *the maid* and the others belong.

In sum, this section has suggested that the variants of the pragmatic prototype can be strategically deployed in texts for evaluative and/or referential functions: to highlight qualities of 'person' rather than 'place'; to differentiate among competing foci in interactive discourse (e.g. to answer two questions) or in more monologic genres like lists (e.g. to separate levels of referents and clarify potential ambiguity; see Chapter 5). Thus what serves as a remedial strategy for problematic referrals is also a pre-emptive strategy for focusing entities in discourse and a textual resource for selecting and organizing entities and their relationships in discourse.

4.4 Conclusion

In this chapter, we began by analyzing a self-initiated self-completed familiarity problem in which a referent was reframed from noun to sentence and text. After describing the changes, I suggested that what served as a reactive strategy for resolving problems could also serve as a proactive strategy for referrals. We then examined *there is* and *they have* as variants of this strategy, grouped together as a pragmatic prototype based upon conceptual and linguistic connections among existence, location and possession. We saw how two parts of the prototype – *there*, *they*; the post copular NP – could anchor the referent into a knowledge base presumably shared by both speaker and hearer.

The basic features (form, content) of both reactive and proactive uses of the prototype establish what Clark and Marshall (1992) called vertical repairs. Whereas horizontal repairs add information about the referent without changing the basis for mutual knowledge, vertical repairs strengthen mutual knowledge by moving to a stronger basis for such knowledge, e.g. from community membership to linguistic co-presence to physical co-presence. The success of vertical repairs suggests that it is not additional information itself that increases the success of a referral, but additional information that builds upon a more accessible base of mutual knowledge. Since the pragmatic prototype anchors a referent in a text, it achieves linguistic co-presence. But the linguistic connections between *there/they* and prior 'place'/'person' also suggest something stronger: the symbolic incorporation of physical co-presence within a textual world.

The analysis also harks back to the distinction between what is a 'new' referent and what is an 'old' referent, and what (in sequential terms) is a first-mention or a next-mention. We already know that few referents are ever 'brand new' (Prince 1981). We have seen here that reactive and proactive familiarity strategies ground referents (that can themselves range in newness) into ongoing constructions of textual worlds in which symbolic representations of people and places provide anchors for those upcoming referents.

Finally, the comparison of different variants of a pragmatic prototype shifted questions concerning 'same' and 'different' from the analytical domain of referrals and nouns to a domain of nouns, verbs, clauses and texts. And by grouping together two semantically different clauses – *there is, they have* – as part of a pragmatic prototype, we have been allowing the locus of variability to expand in ways that have implied a fluid boundary between semantic and pragmatic meaning. In the next chapter, we shift the analysis of variability in still another direction: we consider referrals in two different genres that establish strikingly different textual worlds. By focusing on different genres – in which information is gathered together and represented for very different purposes – we will also be examining how the properties of a textual world impact the referrals that speakers offer to their interlocutors as hints about how to construct their continuously evolving mental models of discourse.

Notes

1. Analyses by both Brown (1995) and Clark (*inter alia* 1992) find that hearers ask questions about a referent, including questions about how they are to use the referent (see the listeners' interpretive intentions noted above). Such questions lead speakers to reformulate a referral until receiving evidence of their hearers' adequate interpretation. Overhearers who listen to – but do not contribute to – such interchanges fare much worse on referent recognition than hearers who are actually initiating such questions (Clark and Schoeder 1992).

2. Notice that the responses from Bob's interlocutors show that Bob's self-initiated repair is directed not to Joe, an old friend known to be familiar with the Flyers, but to Anne, a sociolinguistic interviewer not native to Philadelphia and not known to be a hockey fan. Whereas Anne's *I've heard of the Flyers* (f) acknowledges some familiarity with the Flyers after Bob's repair, Fred's overlapping response attends neither to the repair nor the referent, but to Bob's plans: in *That's gonna cost you ninety dollars a seat* (g), *that* is anaphorically tied to Bob's statement of his plans (in (a)).

3. I proposed *The same guys I'm workin' with* as the antecedent because it is the syntactic subject (a position more likely to be thematically continued in next-discourse, Walker, Joshi and Prince 1988). But the problem of incompatibility between prior and upcoming referents is the same even if we take *all college guys* as the antecedent to *they*.

4. The following hypothetical example with *they* shows that *they* assumes more familiarity than other referring terms, such as *two* or *two of them*, Suppose we are cooking a recipe that I'm familiar with, I want you to beat two eggs, and I say this:

 (a) There's a dozen eggs in the refrigerator.
 (b) They have to be beaten.

 Since the antecedent of *they* is *a dozen eggs*, my directive doesn't specify that I want you to beat two eggs (X1, X2), a subset of the dozen eggs (X). Thus, you might think that I wanted you to beat all the eggs (X). But if I say, "Beat two/two of them," you would be more likely to open the box and take out two eggs. This is exactly how Fred errs. A recency principle (Chapter 4) leads his hearer to infer *they* as co-referential with the most recent semantically compatible NP *(the same guys*, inferable as equivalent to *all college guys)* even though he intends to use only a part *(two guys)* of that set.

5. Notice that the antecedent of *these* is interpretable not through a recency principle (i.e. the women that owned the house (f)) but through topicality (Chapter 4). The main character – and agents – in the story are *the people* (a): the story is told to provide an example of this kind of person.

6. Two points. First, clauses that assert only existence are rare and require dispute or comparison, as in the following quote from a New York Times magazine article (8/15/04, p. 32) in which Ariel Sharon (Israel's Prime Minister) is talking about the history of Israel " *It's an unbeliev-able story*,' he said, '*Because I think all of <u>those old nations that were</u> then, disappeared. Don't exist anymore. <u>The Jews exist</u>'*." Neither of the two underlined sections include *there*; each predicates no more than existence, either through the verb to 'be' or 'exist.' Second, there is a minimum set of clauses (and clause types) that focus only on existence: either imperatives (e.g. *Let it be, Be that way*) or exclamatives (*So be it*) that convey the impossibility of, or futility of hoping for, change.

7. There are certainly other ways of viewing the relationship. Compare Clark (1978) who suggests that possessive constructions are locational constructions and Lyons (1977) for whom possessive constructions are a subtype of locational constructions.

8. I thank the Kimchi family for insights into Hebrew *yaesh* and *sham*. They also point out that Hebrew *yaesh* can be used in contexts of dramatic and unexpected change, as when soccer fans cheer with *Yaesh!* (comparable, perhaps to English *Got it!*, *Yay!* or *Hooray!*).

9. The use of *Hello there* can seem insulting. My father, for example, always complained about a relative who would greet him that way, rather than as "Uncle Len." The source of the insult may be a subjective extension of distal spatial deixis as social distance in an opening of an encounter (an important place for the affirmation and re-establishment of social relationships (Schiffrin 1977)).

10. I discuss reasons for Henry and Zelda's alternative interpretations of my question in Schiffrin 1997).

11. However, one could include a noun in a prepositional phrase, e.g. *They have lots of cookies with them* or *They have lots of good ideas between the two of them*. Notice, however, that the prepositional phrases imply a location that strengthens the implication of possessor (via co-presence).

12. Two points. First, notice that the difference between explicit and inferable may depend on whether the antecedent is singular or plural. If the antecedent is singular (e.g. *Delaware, the city*) *they* must be inferred from the presence of people (plural) in that place. But if the antecedent is plural (as in *big three story houses*), then *they* can be explicitly linked through plurality to 'houses.' Second, when there were when two possible antecedents, I counted the most recent.

13. The preference for *there is* or *they have* may be related to where the post-verbal nouns fall on a continuum of 'relationship to people.' Compare *there is* and *they have* with a range of referents from the closest to furthest 'relationship to people', e.g. 'beautiful homes', 'a lot of crime', 'new skyscrapers', 'humidity'.

14. Space prevents exploration of more peripheral members of the pragmatic prototype, including not only the use of different pronouns (*he, she, I, you*) and verbs (e.g. *got*), and the use of the dialectal variant of *it* expletives (Kaltenbock, 2003), but also an appeal to knowledge rather than possession, existence or location, i.e. the use of *y'know X* as part of the prototype (cf. Schiffrin 1987: Chapter 7).

5

Referring sequences

5.1 Introduction

Despite the complexities involved in formulating referrals and situating referring expressions (Chapters 2, 3, 4), once speakers initiate a referral (a first-mention), their next referrals (next-mentions) continue in ways that are fairly predictable. A first-mention typically begins with an indefinite (or definite) noun phrase (e.g. *a/the* NP, Chapter 3) in which the work of the article and the noun complement one another: the article conveys a level of assumed familiarity and specificity of the referent; the noun provides information that helps the hearer interpret the speaker's referential intention and identify a person, place or thing in the world. The next-mention is a definite noun. The next-mention can be *the* NP, in which the noun repeats the first-mention or evokes the same referent through other nouns. Another alternative is the demonstrative *this* or *that* (with optional NP) that conveys proximity to, or distance from, the first-mention. But more typical than any of these forms are next-mention pronouns that provide grammatical case, number, animacy, and gender, but no lexical information.

Analyzing how referrals continue to be evoked over time situates us firmly in the internal perspective to reference (Chapter 2) and the study of word-to-world relationships within discourse. Instead of focusing on how we achieve speaker/hearer identification of a word-to-world relationship in a single referral (Chapters 2, 3), or the clauses that help achieve the familiarity so helpful to recipient identification of a referent (Chapter 4), the discourse approach in this chapter will focus on how we build a sequence of referrals within a textual world in which referents reside: how do we continuously evoke people, places and things as they acquire attributes and relate to one another over time and space?

Although the NOUN FIRST/PRONOUN NEXT sequence is already well attested in discourse (e.g. Ariel 1990, Clancy 1980, DuBois 1980, Fretheim and Gundel 1996, Givón 1983), what has not been much studied is its appearance in the different genres through which textual worlds may be created.[1] The two genres of interest in this chapter are narratives and lists. In a narrative, a human referent takes action, interacts with others and (often) encounters something unexpected, faces a dilemma or solves a problem. In a list, a referent (sometimes human, sometimes not) is grouped together with other referents that share some qualities, but differ by others. Whereas a narrative tells us about referents by recounting an experience, then, a list tells us about referents by providing information about a collection in which they are members.

Analyzing referring sequences in different genres will not only allow us to see whether the constraints on next-mentions operate in similar ways across the two genres, but will also address a more subtle theme running throughout the different analyses in this book: the discursive value of marked, atypical or dispreferred forms. We have repeatedly examined specific forms in what may loosely be called their 'contexts' or more accurately their 'text' or 'co-text.'[2] This approach has allowed us to ask the following questions: where does a referring expression, article, and/or clause occur in relation to specific features of co-text? how might features of co-text (e.g. meaning, form, function) be related to the variants of referring expressions, articles and/or clauses?

Using quantitative data to answer these questions has helped us identify overall patterns of language use: which variant occurs more often than others; where (in what environment); why (what favors or inhibits selection among the options). But this is only part of the analytical task. Consider some familiar sociolinguistic findings: the use of title + name (instead of first name) as a term of address with an intimate friend (Fasold 1990); a direct order rather than an indirect request to an employer (Ervin-Tripp 1976); saying *gonna* instead of *going to* in a public speech (as (the first) President Bush often did). All of these can be viewed as strategies that are attuned to aspects of context that quantitative analyses did not (and in some cases, could not) codify and count: participants' definitions (or

re-definitions) of the situation, interlocutors' goals and/or alignments, interpersonal relationships, and so on. To put this more
generally, understanding the marked (rather than the unmarked),
the dispreferred (rather than the preferred), or the atypical (rather
than the typical) requires reaching into the rich and varied array of
personal, social and cultural meanings that are critical to a socially
constituted Linguistics (Hymes 1985).

In previous chapters, I have consistently sought to explain not
only co-occurrences between linguistic variants and co-text that
show up in the data as unmarked, preferred and typical, but also co-
occurrences whose lower frequencies suggest that they are marked,
dispreferred and atypical. By combining quantitative data with close
attention to sequences of discourse, I have not only tried to explain
frequent patterns and trends, but also to deconstruct situated, emergent, and negotiated meanings that can help us explain both the
general patterns and their specific modifications.

In this chapter, I use three interrelated analyses to address the
strategic balance between expected and unexpected referrals. I begin
by introducing four constraints on referring sequences and showing
in detail how they impact next-mentions in one narrative and one
list (Section 5.2). Next is a quantitative comparison of the relationship between the constraints and the next-mentions in a set of
narratives and lists, accompanied by analyses of referring sequences
that exemplify either the normative use or the deployment of the
less common option (Section 5.3). The third analysis (adapted from
Schiffrin 2001b) uses the tools and findings from the two prior analyses to analyze a place referral (*concentration camps*) that became
problematic in public D/discourse (over time and across users) and
was resolved in a text that combined features of narrative and list
(Section 5.4). In Section 5.5, I summarize how the sequential choice
to continue an earlier form, or switch to a different form, is sensitive
to many different levels of meaning.

5.2   Genre constraints on referring sequences

Narratives and lists are forms of discourse whose differences provide
a good basis for comparing referring sequences across genres. The
modus operandi of the genres differ: narratives recount events within
a linear temporal structure; lists enumerate items in a hierarchical

descriptive structure. The two genres also have different expressive and social functions. Although either telling a story or listing pieces of evidence can help us make a point in an argument, for example, it is through stories that we build solidarity with our friends and teach our children moral lessons. Lists, on the other hand, are often used as reminders that help us plan future actions (as when we list our own (or others') chores) or help make decisions either for ourselves (where to go on vacation) or for others (as when we recount our employment history to potential employers). And although both narratives and lists are relatively monologic – both can be told in a single turn at talk – narratives are more interactively contingent and their layers of evaluation more complex than lists.

In this section, I define and illustrate four constraints on next-mentions within a sample narrative and a sample list. The constraints are:

> *Recency*: a next-mention whose first-mention is no further back than two clauses within the speech of the same person[3]
> *Potential ambiguity*: the textual presence of more than one semantically compatible full noun within the two clauses prior to a next-mention
> *Topicality*: the entity that the text 'is about;' main character in a narrative; top node in a list (cf. Grosz 1986)
> *Boundaries*: functionally and/or structurally differentiated segments within the genre ('inner') as well as between the genre and surrounding discourse ('outer')

In the remainder of this section, we illustrate the constraints and begin to examine their consequences.

5.2.1   *Referring constraints in narratives: an example*

In telling a story, a speaker constructs a story world in which a limited number of characters act and interact with one another in specific locations and for a temporary period of time. Although stories are situated within conversations or other interactions, then, a story world can be somewhat independent of those worlds and can create distinct time, space and person shifts away from those worlds as the speaker regresses to an earlier epistemic state and possible assumption of decreased hearer familiarity (Chapters 3, 7). This means that referents are introduced and made relevant to domains that may not already be active in the interaction *per se*.[4] Stories thus offer the opportunity to find referring sequences in which new referents are introduced and continually used in a particular domain – a story world – in which they are relevant.

In Example 5.1, Zelda is telling a story in response to my question about seeking medical advice. Her story explains why she no longer trusts her neighborhood doctor, and hence, why she has difficulty answering my question. The nouns and pronouns that refer to the main character are in **bold**; other referents within the story world are underlined; a new referent after the story has closed is in *italics*. The labels on the right indicate different parts of the narrative, i.e. its inner boundaries. The slash between two labels (e.g. ANSWER 1A /ABSTRACT) indicates two simultaneous boundaries between two different segment types (question/answer adjacency pair; informational sections within a narrative). Boundaries more pertinent to the interaction are in SMALL CAPITALS; boundaries within the narrative are underlined in SMALL CAPITALS. CA is complicating action, the sequence of temporally ordered event clauses that reports 'what happened.' Segments continue until another one appears in the right margin.

Example 5.1

Debby:	(a)	Who would you go to wi- uh for medical advice, if you just didn't feel well, and you . . . wanted . . . to ask someone how-	QUESTION 1
Henry:	(b)	That's a hard situation.	
Zelda:	(c)	Well we have **a doctor in** **the neigh-**	ANSWER 1
	(d)	I have **a neighborhood doctor who we use,**	
	(e)	and I consider **him** . . . my family doctor.	
	(f)	But I really don't have that much confidence in **him.**	
Debby:	(g)	Hmm. [What happened?	QUESTION 1A
Zelda:	(h)	[But I u:-	
	(i)	Well . . . at one time **he** was a very fine doctor.	ANSWER 1A / ABSTRACT
	(j)	And **he** had two terrible tragedies. =	
Henry:	(k)	Terrible.	
Zelda:	(l)	= One year **he** lost <u>a young daughter</u>	

(m)   and the next year **he** lost <u>a son</u> through accidents.

(n)   **His** <u>daughter</u> was twenty,   CA: EPISODE 1
      or twenty one

(o)   <u>she</u> went t'California.

(p)   And <u>she</u> was in an automobile accident

(q)   and <u>she</u> was killed.

(r)   The following year, **his**   CA: EPISODE 2
      <u>son</u>, who ha-
      was eighteen years old just graduating high school.

(s)   [0] Was walking through thee em . . . the fountain,
      Logan Square Library?

(t)   y'know that fountain?   bare footed, =

                                Z

Debby: (u)   Yeh.

Zelda: (v)   = and [0] stepped on a- a- a [bare wire. =

Henry: (w)   [live wire.

Zelda: (x)   = And [0] was electro[cuted.

Debby: (y)   [My God!

Zelda: (z)   [0] Lived for a year in a coma.

         (aa) And **he** was an excellent   CODA/ANSWER 1A
               internist.

         (bb) After that happened I
               think **he** took in *a young
               doctor*,

         (cc) who I like,

         (dd) but I feel I don't have the con-

         (ee) I'd go to *him* for sore   ANSWER   1
               throats,
               and . . . y'know, minor stuff.

         (ff) But, God forbid if we had a- a major problem, I think
               we would look for someone else.

The main character in Zelda's story is 'the doctor' (in **bold**), who is described as convenient (*a neighborhood doctor*, line (d)), familiar (*our family doctor*, line (e)) and well qualified (*a very fine doctor*, line (i), *an excellent internist*, line (aa)). Despite these qualities Zelda doesn't *have that much confidence in him* (line (d)). When I ask her why (*What happened?* line (g)), Zelda tells a story that recasts the doctor as a father (*he lost a young daughter*, line (l), *he lost a son*, line (m)) whose tragedies are implicitly blamed (*after that happened* in line (bb)) for her loss of confidence in his professional ability.

Since what the story recounts is why Zelda lost her confidence in 'the doctor,' which is based on what happened to 'the doctor', I consider 'the doctor' to be the entity that the story is about, i.e. the referent that remains topical throughout the story. There is ample linguistic evidence of this status. First, Zelda introduces 'the doctor' through a pragmatic prototype (Chapter 4), *Well we have a doctor in the neigh-* (line (c)), *I have a neighborhood doctor who we use* (line (d)) that highlights information that will have a major role in an upcoming text. Second, the two tragedies are first framed as the doctor's tragedies (*And he had two terrible tragedies*, line (j)) and they are then specified in relation to his life: *he lost a young daughter* (line (l)), *he lost a son* (line (m)). Third, the two children are next-mentioned in relation to 'the doctor': *his daughter* (line (n)), *his son* (line (r)).

Although 'the doctor' remains a constant topic throughout the story, even when he is not mentioned, his recency changes as the story progresses and other referents accrue. In keeping with the two clause measure, 'the doctor' is recent only when evoked through *he* in lines (e) to (n). Non-recent mentions are possessive *his* (line (r)) and *he* in *he was an excellent internist* (line (aa)). Since the non-recent referral to *he* (line (aa)) is preceded by referrals to 'the son' that match both the gender (male) and number (singular) of 'the doctor,' *he* (line (aa)) is also potentially ambiguous. Notice, however, that several features of the discourse clearly establish that *he* (line (aa)) is a next-mention of 'the doctor.' First, what is predicated of the subject pronoun – *was an excellent internist* (line (aa)) – clearly applies to the doctor, not the son. In fact, we are already familiar with this information from the earlier syntactically and semantically parallel clause *he was a very fine doctor* (line (i)). Also disambiguating *he* (line (aa)) is a textual contrast between referrals for the two male referents. Zelda consistently used 'zero' anaphora for each next-mention of 'the son' in lines (s) through (z): [0] *was walking*, [0] *stepped*, [0] *was electrocuted*, [0] *lived*. Not only does the succession of zero pronouns link these events together in a single episode, but they also presume the highest level of accessibility for 'the son' (Ariel 1990) and establish a focus space for 'the son' that clearly separates referrals to 'the son' from referrals to 'the doctor.' When Zelda closes the episode, exits the focus space, and is about to end the narrative, she returns to the use of *he* for 'the doctor.' Thus ambiguity of *he* is avoided through what was predicated of *he* (medical ability), the repetition of the ability of 'the doctor' from earlier text, textual contrast between *he* and zero, and the use of zero in an episode bound in time and space within the story world.

In addition to reflecting topicality, recency and potential ambiguity, next-mentions also reflect structural boundaries. Within Zelda's story world, inner boundaries are between ABSTRACT (m) and COMPLICATING ACTION (n), and between the two episodes (line (q), cf. Abu-Akel (1993)) that nevertheless provide parallel information of time, character, and outcome. The opening (outer) boundary in Example 5.1 is between Zelda's self-interrupted part of her ANSWER 1 (*But I u*: line (h)) and her ANSWER 1A, *Well . . . at one time he was a very fine doctor* (line (i)) to QUESTION 1A, *What happened* (line (g)) that also serves as an abstract for her story. Zelda's story then tells what happened to sap the doctor of his ability: *well . . .* in her abstract suggests a long and non-straightforward answer that will contrast the doctor's ability (*at one time he was a very fine doctor*, line (i)) with a foreshadowed outcome of *two terrible tragedies* (line (j)).

The closing (outer) boundary of Zelda's story is more complex. Zelda's restatement of part of the abstract *he was a very fine doctor* (line (i)) in *and he was an excellent internist* (line (aa)) opens the closing boundary of her story. After this bridge between the story world and the current world, the outer boundary is firmly established through *After that happened I think he took in a young doctor* (line (bb)): the consequences of the past tragedies will be brought up to the present moment of Zelda's life-world problem (finding a doctor) and back to a problem situated in the interaction (how to answer my initial question about seeking medical help). Zelda then reinforces this return to the interactional world by replaying a couplet from her ANSWER 1 to my QUESTION 1 about who she would go to for medical advice, repeated below:

PRE-STORY VERSION OF ANSWER 1	POST-STORY VERSION OF ANSWER 1
(f) But I really don't have that much confidence in him.	(dd) but I feel I don't have the con-
(h) But I u:-	(ee) I'd go to him for sore throats, and . . . y'know minor stuff.

Recall that, in the pre-story version of ANSWER 1 to Question 1, Zelda introduced a doctor (*Well we have a doctor in the neigh- I have a neighborhood doctor who we use* (lines (c) – (d))), but then qualified her description of him with doubts about her confidence in him (line (f) above). As I was asking my narrative-prompting question (*what happened?* (g)), Zelda had begun to state *But I u:-* (line (h)) which appeared to be the circumstances under which she uses the doctor regardless of her doubts. These two qualifications about 'the doctor' comprise a pre-story couplet whose semantic content reappears after Zelda finishes her story as the post-story version of ANSWER 1.

Although Zelda's replay of the couplet helps to establish the story as ANSWER 1 to QUESTION 1, it also faces a referential problem. Prior to the replayed couplet, Zelda had introduced a new referent 'a young doctor' in *I think he took in a young doctor* (line (bb)), who is grounded not in the story world of tragedy, but in the interactional world of question and answer. This semantically compatible referral creates a problem for the interpretation of *him* in *I'd go to him for sore throats, and . . . y'know minor stuff* (line (ee)). Although the antecedent for *him* could certainly be 'a young doctor,' it could also be the topical referent 'the doctor.' Unlike the predicate *he was an excellent internist* (line (aa)) that could apply only to 'the doctor' and not 'the son,' the predicate in line (ee) could apply to either 'doctor.' Thus *him* (line (ee)) is potentially ambiguous because of a clash of constraints: recency favors 'a young doctor' and topicality favors 'the doctor.'

In this section, we have seen how four constraints impact next-mentions in narrative. Two constraints were defined and operationalized in general terms irrespective of genre: recency, potential ambiguity. Two other constraints were more sensitive to the genre: the topical referent was the main character in the story; boundaries were between story sections (inner) or between story and interactional sequence (outer). We focused primarily on the topical referent 'the doctor,' but also observed features of 'the daughter,' 'the son,' and 'a young doctor.' Next-mentions of the topical referent 'the doctor' within the story world were pronominal despite non-recency and potential ambiguity (with 'the son'). The two other story world referents – both children of 'the doctor' – were introduced in relation to 'the doctor.' Each was then evoked through a series of next-mention pronouns (*she*, 'zero') within their episodes in the story. Once Zelda ended her story and returned to the outer question/answer frame in which a new referent 'a young doctor' was introduced, the pronoun *him* was potentially ambiguous because of a clash between recency (favoring 'a young doctor') and topicality (favoring 'the doctor'). We will see in the next section that lists also create bounded discourse units, but rather than group together referents whose actions are mutually consequential within an organized sequence, lists group together entities whose relationship is based on co-membership in a conceptual category.

5.2.2 Referring constraints in lists: an example

When making a list, a speaker brings together in one text a collection of items that can be classified as the same by some criteria, but different by others. The sameness of the items in a list justifies their inclusion in a single group (i.e. as a category (Rosch 1978)) and the differences between them separate them into subgroups (i.e. as subcategories). Although lists can present a set of taxonomic categories in which each entity is an example of the class through which it is known, they can also present more *ad hoc* collections (Barsalou 1983) or schematic knowledge in which each entity is known through its participation or place in a collection (Mandler 1984). The variety of entities that can be listed reflects the fact that "events or entities can be known in various formats . . . a particular tiger can be known as a member of the feline category, as part of the scene viewed, and as a character in a book about the jungle" (Polkinghorne 1991: 139). Thus the entity 'tiger' may appear in a list of felines (e.g. tiger, lion, house cat), items seen in a picture of a jungle (e.g. tiger, pond, grasses) or characters in a children's story book (e.g. tiger, cheetah, snake).

The list in Example 5.2 will illustrate how the four constraints already discussed in a narrative are realized in a list. Like the narrative in Example 5.1, the list has outer boundaries: a comment about *your family* from Anne (line (a)) and a return to the general *other ones in the family* (u). Also like the narrative in Example 5.1, the topical referent (in bold) in the list in line (2) is family-based, here, 'my mother' (Jane's mother). Mary is Jane's niece; Anne is the interviewer.

Example 5.2

Anne:	(a)	That's right, I'm- slowly getting your family straight here [hh. It's-
Jane:	(b)	[hhhOh, when **my mother** died, they u-
	(c)	this is funny,
	(d)	**she** had forty five great grand- forty five grandchildren, and over: twenty five great grandchildren.
Anne:	(e)	Holy [Mackeral.]
Mary:	(f)	[Now it's] more than doubled.
Jane:	(g)	Oh, it's doubled since **she** died,
	(h)	I think **she's** must had about fifteen more born since **she** died.
Mary:	(i)	More than that.
Anne:	(j)	What, in ten years?
Mary:	(k)	Su:re.
Anne:	(l)	Wow[hhh.
Jane:	(m)	[Well, I know I'm losing track myself.
		Z
Mary:	(n)	[I had two, I had two,
	(o)	Susie had two,
	(p)	Peggy had two,
	(q)	Cathy had one,
	(r)	Theresa had three,
	(s)	Patsy had two more since **she** died. Three [more.
Jane:	(t)	[Three.
Mary:	(u)	And then there's a lot of other ones in the family.

Just as the topical referent in a narrative is the central figure in the complicating action, so too, the topical referent in a list is the one main item to which all members of a collection are related. As noted above, the topical referent is 'my mother' (since it is 'my mother' who connects the descendants) first-mentioned as *my mother* (line (b)). Other referents are mentioned only once and in ways that either presume their unique identifiability through proper names (e.g. *Susie*, line (o), *Peggy*, line (p)) or anchor them to the just-mentioned unique referent (e.g. *had two*, lines (o) and (p)).

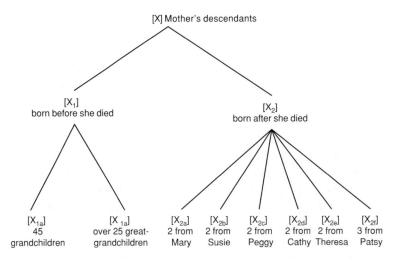

Figure 5.1 List of descendants

Since the hierarchical structure of a list involves branching relationships, we can represent it as a tree, as in Figure 5.1. [X] in Figure
5.1 is MOTHER'S DESCENDANTS. The descendants are first differentiated according to their time of birth in relation to the life of
'mother': DESCENDANTS BORN BEFORE MOTHER DIED [X1]
(*forty five grandchildren, and over: twenty five great grandchildren,*
line (d)); DESCENDANTS BORN AFTER MOTHER DIED [X2]
(*it's doubled,* line (g), *about fifteen more born,* line (h)). After the
general estimate of the number of DESCENDANTS BORN AFTER
MOTHER DIED [X2] is an expansion of [X2]: members of the family who are the mothers of the *fifteen more born since she died* (line
(h)). Each family member is mentioned only once and is connected to
the others through parallel structures ('name had numeral'). Other
than Mary herself, who self-refers as *I* (line (n)), the mothers of
DESCENDANTS BORN AFTER MOTHER DIED [X2] are listed
by name ((o) to (s)).[5] The only next-mention of a referent – and
only use of the pronoun *she* – is MOTHER [X] herself.

We can operationalize recency and ambiguity in lists exactly as
we did in narratives. Notice, then, that *she* in *Oh, it's doubled since
she died* (line (g)) counts as recent since *my mother* (line (d)) is two
clauses back. However, what about *she* in *Patsy had two more since
she died* (line (s))? Structural constraints within this sentence dictate

that the pronoun *she* would be co-referential with the noun *Patsy*. The problem with this interpretation, however, is that co-reference between *she* and the most recent noun *Patsy* would create a semantic anomaly: Patsy's children would be born after Patsy died.

Genre specific topicality and boundary constraints explain why *Patsy had two more since she died* (line (s)) can violate the structural constraint *without* being semantically anomalous. We have already noted that the topical referent in a list is at the top of the hierarchy, i.e. 'my mother.' The inner boundaries of the list are also defined in relation to hierarchical structure: whereas some boundaries are lateral (going from [X2] to [X3] or [X2A] to [X2B]), other boundaries are hierarchical (either going down, e.g. from [X2] to [X2A], or going up, e.g. from [X2a] to [X2]).

In the list about MY MOTHER'S DESCENDANTS, [X] provides the superordinate category *my mother* that dominates other list members. Two branches are established from this top node. One branch (opened by Jane in line (b)) is DESCENDANTS BORN BEFORE MOTHER DIED [X1] (line (d)). The other branch (introduced by Mary in line (f)) and restated by Jane (lines (g) and (h)) is DESCENDANTS BORN AFTER MOTHER DIED [X2]. The basis for the subdivision of [X] into [X2] – AFTER MOTHER DIED – appears at three crucial points in the list: the inception of [X2] *Oh, it's doubled since she died* (line (g)); right before the expansion of [X2] (*Oh, I think she's must had about fifteen more born since she died* (line (h)); at the closure of [X2] *Patsy had two more since she died* (line (s)). Thus next-mentions of 'mother' as *she* establish and re-establish a major branch of the list: the adverbial *since she died* opens, expands and closes the second branch in the list DESCENDANTS BORN AFTER MOTHER DIED [X2]. Once we view the next-mention *she* as part of the list, we no longer have to worry about syntactic ill-formedness or semantic anomaly. We interpret *she* in *Patsy had two more since she died* (line (s)) in relation to its place in the list structure, more specifically, as a next-mention of the topical referent in the list that crosses a lateral boundary between [X1] and [X2] within the list.

In this section, we have illustrated how four constraints are reflected in (and constrain) referring sequences in a list. We have not seen many effects of recency or ambiguity because there were few next-mentions. We did see, however, that a topical referent in a list – just like the topical referent in a narrative – can be next-mentioned with a pronoun despite (a) a lack of recency in the text, (b) other referrals whose semantic compatibility makes them candidate antecedents, and (c) when a lateral (rather than hierarchical) boundary is crossed. Although topicality and boundary constraints were operationalized in ways specific to list structure, then, their effect on next-mentions seemed similar to their effect in narrative.

5.2.3 Summary of constraints

Our discussion of constraints on next-mentions has been grounded in two different genres. To reiterate the constraints: recency is a prior mention (from the same speaker) no more than two clauses back from the current mention; potential ambiguity is the textual presence of more than one semantically compatible full noun within the two clauses prior to a next-mention; topicality is the main referent in the text, what it is 'about;' boundaries appear both within the text (between major segments within a narrative or between categories in a list) and at the outer edges of the text (between the openings/closings of a narrative or list and ongoing talk). In addition to illustrating the constraints in two genres, we saw some possible relationships among the constraints, e.g. possible ambiguities were resolved through topicality or boundaries, along with a pronoun whose referent could not be definitively established. In the next section, we turn from detailed discussion of referring sequences in two texts to quantitative comparison of the constraints within a larger set of texts.

5.3 Next-mention variation in narratives and lists

In this section, we combine the insights gained from close attention to a few texts with quantitative comparisons across multiple texts. This two-pronged approach will help us assess normative patterns within numerous narratives and lists, as well as specific contingencies in individual narratives and lists. In keeping with our interest in both typical and atypical uses, the quantitative comparisons – and discussion of particular cases – will follow the same logic underlying the analysis of *a- a* and *the- the* repairs in sentences and texts (Chapter 3): what pattern of nouns and pronouns is preferred (unmarked)? where and why do the dispreferred (marked) patterns appear?

Table 5.1 *Next-mentions in narratives and lists*

	Narratives	Lists	Total
Pronoun	137 (86%)	57 (81%)	194
Noun	22	13	35
Total	159	70	229

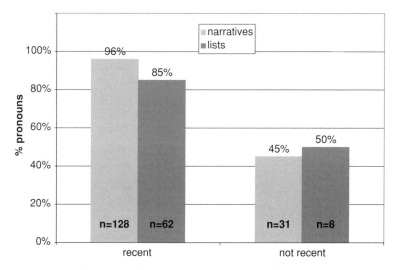

Figure 5.2   Recency and next-mentions by genre

We begin with an overview of the distribution of nouns and pronouns as next-mentions in narratives and lists.

Table 5.1 shows the frequency of next-mention pronouns is relatively high in both genres. The next sections examine differences
in referring sequences across the two genres. In each table, the constraint that would *favor* pronouns appears in the first pair of bars
in the charts.

5.3.1   Recency

Figure 5.2 shows that next-mention pronouns are more frequent
when their antecedent is recent than when their antecedent is distant.

The clear effect of recency on next-mention pronouns can be
explained through numerous constructs including salience based on

continued activation in consciousness (Chafe 1994), the centering of referents from prior text (Grosz, Joshi and Weinstein 1995, Walker, Joshi and Prince 1988), local topic continuity (Givón 1983b), or operation of the minimization principle (Levinson 2000). Why, then, use a full noun in a narrative or a list when its antecedent is recent?

The examples below suggest that nouns are used as next-mentions when the explicit identity of the referent is important to understanding the point of a narrative (Example 5.3) or a list (Examples 5.4 and 5.5). The excerpt in Example 5.3 follows a story that Agnes has just finished telling about her own premonition of her grandmother's impending death. Here she is starting a second story in (line (a)) about her father's premonition of his own death.

Example 5.3
(a)   And then **my father**- ohh!
(b)   **He** knew. **He** knew.
(c)   **My father** had a premonition he was gonna ABSTRACT
       die.
(d)   **He**- uh when we were kids we used to go to ORIENTATION
       Chez Vous
(e)   it was a skating ring, every Sunday, y'know.
(f)   And I had- I was at the age where I wanted a birthday party.
(g)   And I had says to **him**, "Dad, can I have a   CA
       birthday party?"
(h)   **He** says, "Well, y'know that basement isn't done," y'know.
(i)   So **he** says, "But I'll get the basement done for you," y'know.
(j)   And that Sunday morning **he** woke up.
(k)   And **my father** did not believe in workin'   EVALUATION
       on a Su-
       Sunday was his day.
(l)   **He** wanted to relax or take us out or . . .
(m) That Sunday morning **he** got up,   CA
(n)   **he** says to me, "Here," **he** says, "Here's money for you and your
       girlfriends"
       which were two other girls.
(o)   **He** says, "You go skatin' today and you have a good time."

Agnes introduces the story with explicit mention of the new topical referent *my father* (line (a)), switches to pronominal next-mentions (line (b)), and then back to *my father* in the more explicit abstract (line (c)). The next four referrals (not counting the interrupted *he-*, line (d)) in the orientation and the CA are pronominal despite the inner boundary switch from ORIENTATION to CA. In fact, Agnes uses *he* in 24 of the 26 referrals to 'father'(2 are zero pronouns) in the 41 clause narrative (not all included here).

The one recurrence of *my father* is in a habitual clause (*And my father did not believe in workin' on a Su- Sunday was his day*, line (k)) that evaluates the narrative action by establishing a contrast (Labov 1972b): waking up early on a Sunday is not the father's typical behavior. This break from expectation is important to the central claim and point of the narrative: Agnes' father had a premonition of his own death. If Agnes had not shared information about her father's routine with Anne (who may not have known the routine), neither she nor we would have been able to recognize that his decision to work on Sunday marked so significant a departure from what was typical that it provided evidence of his ability to forecast his own death. It was by showing her father's departure from routine in ways that showed a settling of commitments and relationships that Agnes shows her father's awareness of his impending death.[6] Thus in Example 5.3, the next-mention-noun in line (k) not only accompanies the crossing of an inner boundary (complicating action to evaluation): it also appears when it is crucial to know that it is 'the father' – no one else – who is breaking his own routine.

Example 5.4 illustrates how a next-mention-noun can also help establish the point of a list, that *progress is ba:d* (line (j)):

Example 5.4

Dot: (a)   But- see, years ago, every neighborhood had its own
                 little, uh stores,
          (b)   y'know, corner stores and everything,
          (c)   which the supermarkets knocked out of [commission.
Anne: (d)   [No kidding.
                 That's right.
Dot: (e)   And there were **little restaurants,**
          (f)   that you don't find today.
Anne: (g)   Well, like-
Dot: (h)   See, Horn and Hardarts come in and knocked all the
                 little restaurants out of business.
Anne: (i)   Well, that's really a shame.
Dot: (j)   Yeh. Right. Progress is ba:d.

The list in Example 5.4 is part of a discussion of differences between the past and the present: Dot is listing the types of retail establishments (*little stores* (line (a)), *little restaurants* (line (e))) that are no longer in her neighborhood. Dot's nostalgia for the old days, and her attitude toward change, are not only summarized at the end of the list (*Progress is ba:d* (line (j))): they are also conveyed through the description and evaluation of list items themselves. In lines (a) through (c), *the supermarkets* (line (c)) are portrayed metaphorically as antagonists who *knocked* the little stores *out of commission*. The first-mention of *little restaurants* is also evaluative. The repetition of *little* (from *little, uh stores*, line (a)) in *little restaurants* (line (e)) and the intonationally separate adjunct (*that you don't find today*) both prefigure the powerless position, and fate, of the restaurants. *That you don't find today* (line (f)) ties 'little restaurants' to the comparison underlying the list. The next-mention of 'little restaurants' is a full noun *little restaurants* whose generalization (*all the*) strengthens Dot's point by bringing even more 'little restaurants' into the scope of the criticism. Thus not only does Dot increase the generalizability of this example with *all*, but the explicit next-mention – repeating *little restaurants* from the first-mention – conveys that the fate of the restaurants is part of a repeated pattern, thus also contributing to the generalization.

Repetitive nouns in lists are sometimes alternatives not just to pronouns, but to ellipsis (Schiffrin 1994b). Although both provide cohesion, choosing repetitive nouns can make an evaluative difference. In Example 5.5, Frank has been recounting his jobs in a temporally structured list and expands upon his job for a dry cleaner:

Example 5.5
(a) I cleaned up
(b) and made **hangers** up for the-
(c) put the plastic on *the hangers*
(d) and the cardboard on *the hangers*
(e) and the paper around *the hangers* you put in your suit
     jackets.

The two main parts of Frank's job are general cleaning (line (a)) and preparing *hangers* (line (b)). Frank describes the latter task as a series of steps in which coverings are paired with *the hangers*. Frank's alternatives for this section of his list include both clause-final pronouns (e.g. *put the plastic on them*) and ellipsis of the prepositional phrase

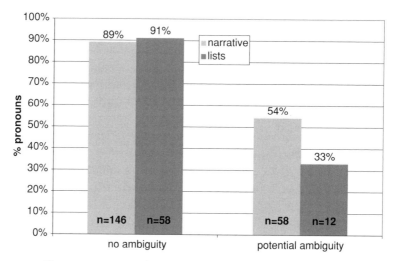

Figure 5.3   Potential ambiguity and next-mentions by genre

in which *the hangers* appear (*put the plastic [0], cardboard [0] and paper on the hangers*). Restating the prepositional phrase with a full noun as the destination of the coverings, however, not only establishes cohesion, but iconically helps to convey the cumulative repetitiveness of the task.

In sum, we have seen that recency favors next-mention pronouns in both narratives and lists. We have also seen that next-mention nouns after recent antecedents highlight the identity of a referent, thus re-establishing the connection between 'word' and 'world' at locations within a text where that connection makes a special contribution to the point of the text.

5.3.2   Potential ambiguity

Figure 5.3 shows that next-mention pronouns are less frequent when their referent is potentially ambiguous than when there is no potential for ambiguity.

Although the pattern of next-mentions is the same in narratives and lists, potential ambiguity is less frequent in lists than narratives. One reason for this might be that narratives disambiguate referents by actions (their predicates) but lists are often filled with stative predicates (e.g. pragmatic prototypes (Chapter 4)) with little semantic content.

Here we illustrate the important role of predicates for disambiguation with atypical cases in both narratives and lists. First is a narrative segment (Example 5.6) in which a predicate does not disambiguate a next-mention *he* (recall, also, *him* in Example 5.1 as either 'the doctor' or 'a young doctor'), and, second, is a list (Example 5.7) in which predicates do disambiguate next-mentions of *they*.

Example 5.6 is from a narrative jointly told by Henry and Zelda about their friend Louie Gelman (the topical referent) who was repeatedly misdiagnosed by several doctors; a family member finally diagnosed Louie Gelman's illness and he was rushed to the operating room. The unclear *he* appears in line (g):

Example 5.6

Henry:	(a)	Then he went to his cousin.
Zelda:	(b)	His nephew.
Henry:	(c)	His nephew.
	(d)	And she: – he called the same thing.
	(e)	Right away they put him right on the operating room.
Debby:	(f)	Wow!
→ Henry:	(g)	He said it would've been a little bit more, **he** could've strangled t'death.
	(h)	So doctors are- well they're not God either!

The narrative excerpted in Example 5.6 contains several self-initiated/completed and other-initiated/completed referrals. Like the repair in lines (a) to (c), most involve identification of 'who' did 'what.' Once Louie Gelman is correctly diagnosed and operated upon, however, the main characters involved in the action have been clarified. But far from clear is who contributes the devastating assessment of Louie Gelman's close brush with death: is it *Louie Gelman* (the topical referent), the *nephew* (a recent referent (*he* in line (d))), or the doctor (inferable from the recent *they* (line (e)))? General familiarity with medical complaint stories suggests that it is not a doctor – either one among those who initially erred or one among those who rushed Louie Gelman to surgery – who is criticizing the work of his/her colleagues in so dramatic a fashion. But ambiguity remains because the predicate is still applicable to more than one referent ('Louie Gelman' or 'nephew').

In contrast to the ambiguity in the narrative in Example 5.6, are next-mentions with *they* in a list (Example 5.7) in which predicates do disambiguate the referral. Zelda and I have been talking about the differences between daughters and sons. Zelda contrasts her daughter's insistence on buying clothes made by certain designers with her sons' nonchalance about what they wear. The excerpt in Example 5.7 shows how the referents of successive uses of *they* are differentiated by their predicates.

Example 5.7

(a)   Well I never- I never knew anything like this   [X2]
     with **the boys₁**.

(b)   If **they₁** got a nice pair of- well-   [X2]

(c)   wh- when my older son was growin' up,   [X2a]

(d)   it was sort of **the slim line pants₂**.   [X2a/a]

(e)   **They₂** weren't the wide legs.   [X2a/a]

Both uses of *they* are next-mentions that appear immediately after a nominal first-mention at a new hierarchical boundary: *they₁* (line (b)) is *the boys* [X2]; *they₂* (line (e)) is *the slim line pants*, two levels down at [X2a/a]. Since the antecedent of a pronoun in a list *can* be a higher level item in the hierarchy, the referent of *they* (line (e)) is not determined by either boundary or recency. Thus we can easily imagine an alternative after *pants₂* (line (d)), in which *they* is co-referential with the referent of [X2], e.g. *they₁ both really like those pants*. What differentiates the two referents of *they* (line (b)) from *they* (line (e)), then, is only the predicate *weren't the wide legs*.

In sum, word-to-world relationships can be re-established even when a next-mention pronoun has the potential of connecting with more than one antecedent. The great variety of predicates that appear in narratives – compared to the limited predicates used in most lists – creates different possible levels of ambiguity for pronouns. Although we have seen examples here in which ambiguity is *not* resolved in narrative, and *is* resolved in a list, this may be counter to the norm.

5.3.3   Topicality

Figure 5.4 shows that topicality makes less of a difference for next-mentions than the other constraints considered thus far, i.e. the

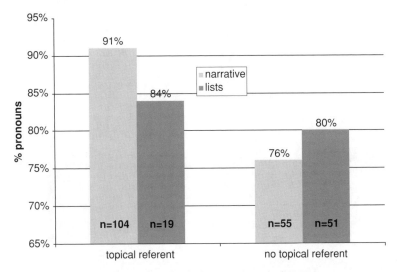

Figure 5.4 Topicality and next-mentions by genre

difference between the yes/no topicality columns is smaller for narratives and lists than for the other constraints.

Although it is not surprising to find that next-mentions in the two genres are similarly constrained by topicality, it *is* somewhat surprising to find so little difference between next-mention nouns and pronouns regardless of topicality. Since we already illustrated the role of topicality in distant next-mentions in Zelda's narrative about 'the doctor' and in the list about 'my mother's descendants' (Section 5.2), as well as a return to nominal next-mentions of a distant topical referent in Agnes' story and in lists (Section 5.3.1), I will not present additional examples here. However, we will return to topicality in Section 5.4, when we see how repeated next-mentions of a topical referent through full nouns in one discourse are used to remedy past ambiguities in others.

5.3.4 Boundaries

Figure 5.5 shows that boundaries have a different impact on next-mentions depending upon the genre. Whereas the presence or absence of boundaries has little effect on next-mentions in narratives, the presence of boundaries reduces the use of next-mention pronouns in lists.

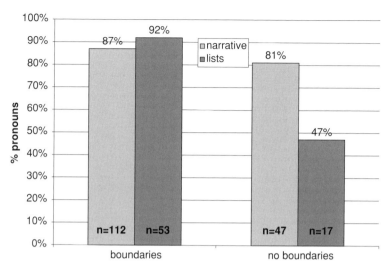

Figure 5.5 Boundaries and next-mentions by genre

There are several reasons for the genre difference in the bound-aries constraint. First, boundaries within narratives are less sharply delineated than in lists. In narratives, a descriptive clause may serve as both orientation and evaluation; a coda may begin within the resolution of the complicating action. Although some list-members *may* function at more than one level (such as when the name of a race-track, e.g. *Delaware*, is the same as the name of the state in which it is located (Schiffrin 1994b)), this is more the excep-tion than the rule. Second, the inner boundaries within a list differ structurally: lateral boundaries separate equal level categories, i.e. nodes at the same point on the tree; hierarchical boundaries separate different levels of categories, i.e. up or down the tree. It is only at lateral boundaries that we find next-mention pronouns. Thus there are reduced opportunities for pronouns after boundaries in lists than narratives.

Finally, my operational definition of boundaries combined inner boundaries (within the genre) with outer boundaries (between genre and surrounding discourse). By doing so, however, we lost the opportunity to examine whether the two different boundary types have a different impact on next-mentions. Examples of both narra-tives and lists whose textual worlds survive disruptions from changes in topic, participant and/or activity show that the referents previously active in those textual worlds may pick up exactly where they were left off.

In Example 5.8, Sally had been talking about her two different sisters, Pat (referent$_1$) and Nan (referent$_2$). Once she introduces and describes the two sisters (*my sister Pat* and *my sister Nan*), Sally tells a complaint story about Nan. Until Sally is interrupted by a friend, Nan was the only referent, appearing through three next-mention pronouns (*she*). Example 5.8 begins with the interruption by Jim:

Example 5.8

Jim:	(a)	Hey, is **Jody**$_3$ in here?
Sally:	(b)	Hello, baby doll.
Jim:	(c)	Hello.
Anne:	(d)	Who dat?
Jim:	(e)	Jody?
Sally:	(f)	No, **she**$_3$ just dropped some jeans off [and **she**$_3$ left.
Jim:	(g)	[Okay. Catch **her**$_3$ later.
Sally:	(h)	That's **Jody**$_3$'s husband.
	(i)	[The **girl**$_3$ that just- =
Anne:	(j)	[That's who was here.
→ Sally:	(k)	= And um, y'know **she**$_2$ married the same year. =
	(l)	**She**$_2$ was young.

Jim and Sally briefly discuss Jody, a new referent (referent$_3$), in line (a) and then refer to her with next-mention pronouns (lines (f) and (g)). But after Sally identifies Jim and Jody for Anne in lines (h) and (i) respectively, Sally continues (note *and um* as an important marker of this continuation) her narrative about her sister Nan with the same next-mention pronoun *she* that had preceded her interchange with Jim.

In Example 5.9, we see part of a list that serves as Frank's answer to Anne's question about his employment history. The list itself has a structure in which Frank mentions each job in temporal order, but then describes background conditions and tells stories about the job that recount why he left. In the segment in Example 5.9, Frank backtracks to describe his poor health and introduce (within

a mini-list of ailments in lines (c) to (h)) respiratory infections (as a
generic (line (d)), one of which eventually led to his being fired.

Example 5.9

  (a) I went to **a loom company**$_1$ that was cuttin' looms.

  (b) For about six months.

  (c) Well, see, I used to be a very sickly kid when I was younger.

  (d) I used to get **respiratory infection**$_2$,

  (e) ivy poison, poison ivy, I mean,

  (f) and I used to get all kinds of different things.

  (g) Worms. I had pin worms, and uh-

  (h) And like soon as one thing went over I had another thing.

  (i) Well, *the respiratory infection*$_2$ was the worst.

  (j) If you know anybody that has *a respiratory infection*$_2$ it's
very bad.

  (k) I used to come down with a hundred and four fever

  (l) and felt like I was gonna die, y'know, it was really bad.

  (m) All right, I was workin' for *them*$_1$ about six months.

Although space prevents detailed discussion of Example 5.9, notice
that despite the embedded mini-list ((c) to (h)), description and evaluation of his illnesses (repeated with full nouns (lines (i) to (j)), Frank
returns to his list and mention of the 'loom company' in line (m).
With the help of the discourse marker *all right*, and the predicate
was working, Frank returns to the textual world of his list of jobs
and uses *them* (line (m)) as a next mention of *a loom company*
(line (a)).

In sum, I have suggested in this section that inner boundaries
might impact next-mention pronouns within lists more than within
narratives. This could be due to several factors: the specification of
referents through full nouns is more critical to the structure of a list
than a narrative; boundaries are more sharply delineated in lists;
there are reduced opportunities for pronouns after boundaries in
lists than narratives. Outer boundaries between narratives/lists and
ongoing conversations may have a similar impact, i.e. not restrict
the use of next-mention pronouns.

5.3.5 Summary

In this section, we have combined quantitative analysis of constraints on next-mentions in different genres with descriptive and

analytical attention to typical and atypical referring sequences. In the next section, we use the tools developed thus far to analyze a single referring expression, *concentration camps*, in two atypical referring sequences, one established over time, space and person in public Discourse, the other resolving ambiguity from public Discourse in a text that defines the ambiguous term by highlighting its topicality through features of narrative (temporal sequence) and list (hierarchical structure).

5.4 A sequential problem and solution in public discourse

Our analyses thus far have focused on how constraints of recency, potential ambiguity, topicality and boundaries impact next-mentions of referents. The analysis in this section will address next-mention problems in a word-to-world relationship within a referring sequence that spanned over fifty years and involved users with little or no direct contact with one another. Although one site of the referring sequence is a text in its standard sense – a sequence of connected clauses with a beginning, middle and end – other sites are more diffuse. Thus I use the term 'D/discourse' here to evoke two different (but potentially overlapping) senses of the term 'discourse.' For some scholars, 'discourse' is the use of language or a level of language structure beyond the boundaries of the sentence. For other scholars, the scope of 'discourse' stretches beyond language itself to include "socially accepted associations among ways of using language, of thinking, valuing, acting and interacting, in the 'right' places and at the 'right' times with the 'right' objects" (Gee 1999: 17). It is this latter sense that is referenced by 'Discourse'.

The problematic referral is the term 'concentration camps'. This referring expression became a topic of public controversy when an exhibit entitled *America's Concentration Camps: Remembering the Japanese American Experience* opened at Ellis Island in 1998. The topic of the exhibit was the American internment of roughly 120,000 Japanese Americans during World War II (WWII). Although I had not seen the exhibit, and knew little more about it than what I just stated, I was called by Cable News Network (CNN) to offer a linguistic perspective on the use of *concentration camps* in the title. The CNN reporter told me that "some Jewish groups had been offended" by the use of the term, she wondered why, and thought that consulting a linguist might help explain the problem. By the time I had decided how to comment, the Jewish groups and the exhibit organizers had already reached a solution: an amendment to the sign announcing the exhibit and a footnote to the title in the exhibit brochure.

In this section, I discuss the problem created by the term *concentration camps* and its textual solution. Since *concentration camps* is a place (not person) referral that arose within public Discourse (not face-to-face linguistic discourse), I begin with a backward glance at place referrals in the type of discourse more familiar from other analyses in this book (Section 5.4.1). I then briefly review the historical context in which both Jews and Japanese-Americans were in concentration camps, outline the semantic, pragmatic and sequential sources of ambiguity underlining the development of *concentration camps* as a TYPE 4 (using the same referring expression for different referents, Chapter 2) problematic referral (Section 5.4.2).[7] Finally, I show how the textual solution to the problem combined recurrent nouns, with differentiating predicates, in a genre that blended narrative and list structure (Section 5.4.3).

5.4.1   Place referrals in face-to-face talk

When places are mentioned during face-to-face talk, their formulation often reflects a variety of factors, including ongoing topic, relevance of the place to topic, awareness of the actual physical location of self and other, and attention to recipient recognizability of place names (Schegloff 1972a). We can see these factors working together by briefly returning to Zelda's narrative about 'the doctor' in Example 5.1, specifically to her referrals to the two places in which the children of 'the doctor' had been tragically killed.

Notice, first, the simplicity of the reference to the location of the daughter's car accident:

(n)   His daughter was twenty, or twenty one
(o)   she went t'**California**.

California is a broad referral to place, evoking a large state on the West coast of the United States that has immediate recognizability (cf. other states such as South Dakota, Rhode Island) and a cluster of cultural associations as a place where people try to escape East coast problems (big cities, crime, cold winters) and seek a more restful life (cf. the song "California dreaming"). By saying *California* and nothing more, Zelda can presume that I am familiar with California, and perhaps some of its general attributes: she does not have to test its recognizability by prefacing it with *y'know*, using rising intonation, or mentioning qualities that would help me identity the place.

The concern is quite different with reference to the location of the son's accident:

Zelda: (r)   The following year, his son, who ha-was eighteen
             years old just graduating high school.
       (s)   [0] Was walking through **thee em . . . the fountain,**
             Logan Square Library?
       (t)   **y'know that fountain?**   bare footed, =
                          Z
Debby: (u)   Yeh.
Zelda: (v)   = and [0] stepped on a- a- a [bare wire.
Henry: (w)   [live wire.

Like the referral to *California*, the place name will locate the site of an action, here, where the son *was walking*. But here Zelda does not mention a broad location like state (Pennsylvania) or city (Philadelphia). The place initially mentioned, and then specified, is one site within the city with which we are both familiar and are located at the time of our conversation.

Referral to the place where the doctor's son was killed begins in a prepositional phrase at the end of the clause in line (s), a typical location for new and/or 'heavy' information (Chapter 3). Zelda self-initiates a repair (right at the beginning of the prepositional phrase) prior to the mention of *the fountain* with *thee em*, indicating a problem (with conceptual identity, lexical access, or recipient design) of the noun. After the initial unmodified definite noun *the fountain*, Zelda uses another place name *Logan Square Library* (s) as a postnominal modifier in a new intonation unit (*Logan Square Library?*) to specify which fountain she had in mind. This specificity is then re-connected with the 'fountain' and its familiarity re-checked through *y'know that fountain?* (line (t)). Notice that it is not until Zelda's extended modifications of *the fountain* that I

overtly acknowledge the referent (the phase of collaborative referrals that Clark and Wilkes-Gibbs (1992) call assert, rather than presuppose, acceptance). Once I do so (*yeh* line (u)), Zelda continues
the syntax of the clause: the recognitional work fits seamlessly into
the slot between the verb *was walking* and the adverb *barefooted*
(cf. discussion of long distance TYPE 1 repair, Chapter 2). Zelda
then goes on to describe what happened at the fountain that made
it so tragic.

The problem with the referral to be considered in this section –
concentration camps – parallels the two different referential
trajectories illustrated in Zelda's *California* and *the fountain*. For
one group of people, Jewish Americans, the term *concentration
camp* needed no D/discourse elaboration. Like Zelda's *California*,
it was immediately recognizable. For another group of people,
Japanese Americans, the same referring expression was a source
of difficulty (at various times and for different reasons) that had to
be resolved through dissection of the connections between the word
and the world. Like Zelda's *the fountain*, its reference had to be
cumulatively built, its identifying details emerging over time.

Obviously there are also differences between Zelda's place names
in a single narrative and the trajectories of *concentration camps* for
Jewish/Japanese Americans. Some of these differences stem from
concentration camps themselves: where were they? when were they
used? what happened there? who was imprisoned? why? Other
problems stem from the types of D/discourse in which *concentration camps* became problematic. Before turning to the analysis of
concentration camps, then, it is important to briefly describe the historical contexts in which concentration camps existed, the meaning
of the term itself, and how it became problematic (Section 5.4.2).
I then turn to how a definition of *concentration camps* in a text
blending properties of lists and narrative resolved the controversy
(Section 5.4.3).

5.4.2   *From World War II to collective narrative*

In this section, I briefly describe the D/discourse in which the term
concentration camps occurred. After providing an overview of the
social world in which 'concentration camps' existed, I describe
the semantic, pragmatic and sequential sources of ambiguity

underlying the appearance of *concentration camps* as a problematic referral.

During WWII, Nazi Germany undertook a systematic effort to kill all the Jews of Europe. This effort is commonly referred to as the Holocaust. The eventual extermination of 6,000,000 Jews was the last step in – and was facilitated by – their progressive dehumanization. This dehumanization built not only upon metaphor (e.g. portrayals in films, newspapers and speeches of Jews as vermin who had to be exterminated), as well as pseudo-scientific ideas of race and genetic purity (e.g. the Jewish gene pool was ruining the Aryan 'race'), but also upon a progressive isolation resulting from the incremental restriction of civil rights and removal of possessions and property. Although the isolation began with social and civil restrictions (e.g. segregation of Jewish children in schools, closing of Jewish businesses), it moved rapidly to physical restrictions (e.g. curfews, ghettoes) with harsh punishments (e.g. shooting) for real or imagined resistance, deportation (under brutal and inhumane conditions), labor camps and prison camps (in which inmates strong enough worked as slaves for the Nazi war effort; others were shot), and finally, concentration camps.

Nazi concentration camps were initially established as "protective custody quarters" (Broszat 1968: 405) to accommodate the growing number of citizens arrested for political opposition. By 1935, what counted as opposition were incidents as casual as "criticizing the regime over a drink, making light of the Nazi leadership, or grumbling over newly-instituted government policies" (Bartrop 2000: 4). Although Jews were often arrested for transgressing in ways such as those just noted, the 1935 Nuremberg Laws on Citizenship and Race legislated their victimization because of their Jewishness alone (Bartrop 2000: 7): marriage or sexual relationships between a Jew and a non-Jew were illegal; Jews were prohibited from participating in public life; Jews were no longer German citizens.

When WWII began in 1939, Jews were more actively persecuted: internal restrictions and punitive measures were supplemented by deportation to labor camps and concentration camps. By the end of the war, there were over 70 major concentration camps in over 15 countries in Nazi-occupied Europe (Bartrop 2000: 14–15). Whereas general conditions of intentional deprivation had led to many deaths in central European camps, inmates in the camps in occupied Poland were killed primarily in gas chambers. These camps became known as death camps or extermination camps. The efficiency of the Nazi effort was staggering. One third of the Jewish people in the world died in 4 years; in 1942 alone, 2,700,000 Jews were killed.

Japanese Americans also spent part of World War II in camps: in 1942, they were forced to evacuate their homes and live in camps established by a branch of the Federal government known as the War Relocation Authority (WRA). Although prior anti-immigration sentiment and prejudice against Japanese in the 1920s facilitated the action (Taylor 1999), the Japanese attack (December 7, 1941) on Pearl Harbor (the base of the United States Pacific Fleet) was its most immediate cause. Because the U.S. had been surprised by the attack, many worried that Japanese Americans had clandestinely helped the Japanese troops and were preparing for a Japanese assault on mainland U.S. (Smith 1995: 106).

A desire to protect America was expressed by many Americans of Japanese descent, but their patriotism sometimes clashed with worries about potential conflicts of interest and loyalty. In his wartime diary (quoted extensively in Smith 1995), for example, Charles Kikuchi clearly identified with America (e.g. *We are at war . . . we will all be called into the army right away*), but also worried about his father's display of a Buddha statue and his admiration of the Emperor. Similar dualities appeared on the community level. For example, the Japanese American Citizens League called upon its citizens not only to volunteer for the U.S. army and the American Red Cross, but also to work to eradicate subversive activities within their own community (Smith 1995: 98). Government and media discourse also reflected ambiguity. The journalist Walter Lippman for example, considered the "whole coast a war zone" and urged that Japanese Americans "prove a good reason for being there" (Smith 1995: 117). But other public discourse urged caution. President Roosevelt appealed for calm by juxtaposing American against Nazi ideology: "Remember the Nazi technique: 'Pit race against race, religion against religion, prejudice against prejudice. Divide and conquer'. We must not let that happen here." (Smith 1995: 100).

Despite calls for tolerance, further victories by the Japanese on the Pacific front intensified American fear: racist descriptions of

Japanese Americans appeared in newspapers (e.g. *viper, leopard*) along with public calls for their isolation. Thus began the process whereby the WRA forced roughly 120,000 Japanese Americans to leave their possessions, jobs and homes for several different kinds of places, some relatively temporary and some set up for a longer duration.

The centers to which Japanese Americans were sent did not have a single name. Appearing in both private journals and public media during WWII was a variety of terms for what seemed like the same type of camps: camps initially established by the WRA, for example, were called *evacuation centers, detention camps, internment camps,* and *concentration camps* (Daniels 1981, Drinnon 1987). But in other D/discourse, *concentration camps* was used only for camps in which "more interior police, more soldiers, tanks, far more limited movement in and out" (Smith 1995: 320) restricted the mobility of people identified as pro-Japan. Post WWII texts commented on the difference between American and Nazi camps. Although Uchida (1982: 147) used *concentration camps* when writing in her wartime journal, for example, she observes in later reflection that "the term is used not to imply any similarity to the Nazi death camps, but to indicate the true nature of the so-called 'relocation centers'."

Thus far, we have seen that camps in WWII varied in their degree of abuse toward their prisoners. Since 'degree of abuse' is a scalar phenomenon, the referring expressions for the camps can be represented along the following scale:

relocation<internment<forced labor<concentration<extermination

Like other scales that convey 'more or less' relationships (e.g. numerals, quantifiers), the terms on the right are stronger than, and semantically entail, the terms on the left: the qualities of extermination camps thus include those of concentration, forced labor, internment, and relocation centers. The terms on the left pragmatically implicate that the terms on the right do not hold: the qualities of 'relocation center' do not typically include those of 'internment,' 'forced labor,' 'concentration' and 'extermination' camps. And like all scalar implicatures, the inference may be explicitly cancelled. Just as one may say 'He didn't eat *some* cookies, he actually ate *all* the cookies,' so too, one may say 'It wasn't only a *concentration* camp, it was actually an *extermination* camp.'

Notice, however, that because some Nazi concentration camps had been used for mass extermination, the term *concentration camp* came to include not only the less abusive camps, but also the most abusive camp. We can see this in discourse such as book titles (e.g. *Inside the Concentration Camps: Eyewitness account of life in Hitler's Death Camps* (Aroneau 1996)) and dictionaries. *The Black-well Dictionary of Judiaca* (Cohn-Sherbok 1992: 95), for example, first defines *concentration camp* as "the prison camps established after the accession to power of the National Socialists in Germany in 1933." The entry then adds that "in six major camps . . . the mass extermination of millions of victims was carried out in specially constructed gas chambers." And rather than find a separate entry for 'extermination camps,' *The Blackwell Dictionary* instructs the user to "see 'concentration camps'." Although the change in 'world' led to the development of new 'words' (*death/extermination camp*), then, it also broadened the meaning of the old 'words' *concentration camp*.

These changes created three problems. First, the incremental scale can work only if *concentration camp* refers to a specific type of camp. If *concentration camp* serves as a cover term for all the other types of camps, it does not belong on the scale at all. Second, any single use of 'concentration camp' is potentially ambiguous between its narrow and broad meaning. As we saw in (5.2.3), what is predicated of (said about) a referral can disambiguate its referent (e.g. Zelda's *they* to evoke both her 'sons' and 'slim pants' (Example 5.7)) even if they are in close succession in a text. But if the predicate is potentially applicable to more than one referent (e.g. Zelda's *him* in the story about losing confidence in her doctor; Henry's *he* in the story about Louie Gelman's medical mishaps (Example 5.6)) the referent may remain unidentifiable. Although the title of the exhibit, *America's Concentration Camps*, mentioned the Japanese American Experience, it had no specifying predicate at all.

The third problem appears in sequential and user distribution in D/discourse. The narrow meaning of *concentration camp* was one of a cluster of terms for the camps in which Japanese Americans were interned *before* the atrocities committed by the Nazis became part of the broad meaning of *concentration camp*. Although the narrow meaning remained in the D/discourse of Japanese Americans

	Early WWII[8]	Mid WWII 1942- 45	Post WWII 1998
Jewish Americans	narrow 1939	narrow, broad	narrow, broad
Japanese Americans	narrow 1942	narrow	narrow

Figure 5.6 Meanings of *concentration camps* over time and by community

and Jewish Americans over time, the broad meaning may not have entered both groups' lexicons simultaneously (see Figure 5.6).

As Figure 5.6 suggests, concentration camps were not yet being used for mass murder – the far right of the scale – in the early years of WWII when Jews were first imprisoned in camps. It is unlikely that the extent of the atrocities taking place in the Nazi camps were fully known to Americans when internment of Japanese Americans began in 1942. Thus early WWII use of *concentration camps* to describe the Japanese American camps may not have had its more inclusive and horrific meanings. The D/discourse of WWII differed by 1998, the year of the exhibit. If intended in its specific sense, then *concentration camps* in 1998 can represent the American camps: it can serve as a remedy (a self-completion of an other-initiated referring problem) for the earlier terms (e.g. *detention center*) that underrepresented their abusive nature. But if understood in its general sense – as a cover term for a range of camps, including death camps – then it cannot.

In sum, the meaning of 'concentration camps' changed over time. By 1998, *concentration camps* had gained both a narrow and a broad meaning, the latter including 'extermination camps.' What the exhibit represented for Japanese Americans was in keeping with the narrow meaning of *concentration camp*. But for Jewish Americans, the use of the term *concentration camps* for the Japanese American experience ignored the intensification of the Jewish experience from deportation and internment to genocide. In the next section, we turn to the textual resolution of the 1998 conflict to see how *concentration camps* was framed in a way that ended up being accepted by two communities who had very different experiences in concentration camps in WWII.

5.4.3   Textual solution: the footnote

In this section, we draw upon earlier discussions of constraints and genre to see how the problematic referral *concentration camp* was publicly repaired in the footnote in the brochure to the exhibit on America's Concentration Camps. Earlier we noted differences between narratives and lists: whereas narratives group together referents whose actions are mutually consequential within a temporally organized sequence, lists group together entities whose relationship is based on co-membership in a conceptual category. We also found that (a) topical referents in both narratives and lists could be pronominalized despite textual boundaries, lack of recency and potentially ambiguous antecedents, and (b) repeated next-mentions of a topical referent as full nouns could reinstate the word-to-world connection. Here we will see that the topical referent 'concentration camps' in the footnote retains its word-to-world connection through repeated nouns. This constancy allows ellipsis (a reflection of topicality) as well as recurrent modification of the referent in a text whose details of time, place, person and goal instantiate an underlying list-like structure that dissects the components of 'concentration camp.'

I present the footnote as Example 5.10. Mentions of 'concentration camp' (the topical referent) are underlined. I have maintained the spacing between separate sections of the footnote on the brochure, but added parenthetical line references for ease of discussion.

Example 5.10

   THE FOOTNOTE

(a) A concentration camp is a place where people are imprisoned not because of any crimes they have committed, but simply because of who they are.

(b) Although many groups have been singled out for such persecution throughout history, the term "concentration camp" was first used at the turn of the century in the Spanish-American and Boer Wars.

(c) During World War II, America's concentration camps were clearly distinguishable from Nazi Germany's.

(d) Nazi camps were places of torture, barbarous medical experiments and summary executions; some were extermination centers with gas chambers.

(e) Six million Jews were slaughtered in the Holocaust.

(f) Many others, including Gypsies, Poles, Homosexuals and political dissidents were also victims of <u>Nazi concentration camps</u>.

(g) In recent years, <u>concentration camps</u> have existed in the former Soviet Union, Cambodia, and Bosnia.

(h) Despite the differences, <u>all [0]</u> had one thing in common: <u>the people in power</u> removed <u>a minority group</u> from <u>the general population</u> and <u>the rest of society</u> let it happen.

'Concentration camps' is defined in the footnote (Example 5.10) by combining conceptual parameters of existence and location (see Chapter 4) that appear through the pervasive use of 'be' as a main verb in the text and through aspectual forms (*have* past perfects) that show stativity and duration. Note, for example, the repetitive use of 'NP$_1$ were NP$_2$' predicate nominatives ((c), (d)) and the equative sentence (f).

Also establishing the definition is the combination of linear structure of narrative with descriptive hierarchical structure of lists. The organization of the footnote (Example 5.10) and the physical grouping of lines reflect the blending of the genres. The opening portion (lines (a), (b), (h)), separated by spaces, defines *concentration camps* by focusing generally on camps (note the type-identifiable *a concentration camp* (line (a)). The closing portion (line (h)) is also general: note the universal quantifier *all* and the use of inclusive referrals to victims (*people* (line (a), *the general population*). Within the inner portion of the footnote, the descriptions of 'camps' follows temporal and spatial parameters; the sections on the page are physically separated by 'time' and 'place,' thus showing their persistent existence despite differences in time and location.

The underlying hierarchical description of the footnote (in Figure 5.7 below) presents 'concentration camps' (the topical referent) as the top node through which a cluster of features (presented as prenominal modifiers and post-nominal predicates) combine to show that 'concentration camps' existed in different locations over time under the control of different countries.

The organization of the footnote and the physical grouping of lines reflect the blending of the genres. The opening portion (lines (a), (b)), separated by spaces, defines *concentration camps* by focusing generally on camps (note the type-identifiable *a concentration camp*

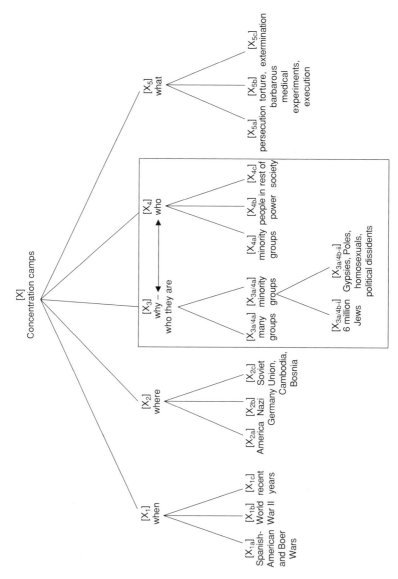

Figure 5.7 Definition of 'concentration camps'

(line (a)). The closing portion (line (h)) is also general: note the universal quantifier *all* and the use of inclusive referrals to victims (*people* (repeated from line (a)) and *the general population*). Within the inner portion of the footnote, the descriptions of 'camps' follows temporal and spatial parameters. Likewise, the sections on the page are physically separated by 'time' and 'place,' thus showing their persistent existence despite differences in time and place.

As noted above, the topical referent of the list is 'concentration camps.'[9] Its first-mention is as an indefinite NP that presents a type-identifiable entity; post-verbal information adds information about the referent in the typical 'heavy' sentence-final location. Although this is a common means of first-mentioning a referent in narratives and lists, it is not the typical format of the genre in which definitions usually appear, i.e. dictionaries, in which the term is first presented in a heading, followed by numerically ordered definitions (that do not repeat the term) and optional citations of how the term has been used. Nor is the sequence of mentions the typical NOUN FIRST/PRONOUN NEXT sequence: no pronouns at all appear for the topical referent (Section 5.3.3), even with recent antecedents (Section 5.3.1), with no potential ambiguity (Section 5.3.2), or within the same segment (no boundaries (Section 5.3.4)).

What we find instead are next-mention nouns of the topical referent (in lines (a), (c), (d), (f) and (g)) that serve evaluative functions similar to those in both narratives and lists (3.1), but also specific to the collective and public nature of the role of the genre in Discourse. The repeated nouns *camps* not only remind us that the specific identity of what is being evoked matters and iconically create continuity. They also allow modification of type (to be discussed below) and establish a cumulative set of properties through iconic repetition. Because they co-occur in conjunction with major time shifts, their repetition at each shift reinforces their similarity despite inner boundaries in the footnote, i.e. episodic differences in time, place and victim that define different historical periods. Other mentions of 'concentration camps' are quantified ellipses: *some* (line (d)), *all* (line (h)). By using only quantifiers. the underlying goal of the text is displayed to show differences and similarities among 'concentration camps.' Still another reinforcement of the topicality of 'concentration camps' is thematic role: 'concentration camps' is the sentence subject in all the clauses except line (f) (*victims of Nazi concentration camps*), where it nevertheless still has an agentive role.

Notice, however, that although 'concentration camps' repeatedly appears, it is not always treated as a referent. In fact, the first mention of 'concentration camp' focuses not on the referent at all, but on the words themselves: *the term "concentration camp" was first used at the turn of the century* in *the Spanish-American and Boer Wars* (line (b)). The first episode in the narrative is thus defined by referential practice. The contrast between the continuous existence of concentration camps (*throughout history*) and the inception of the term *concentration camps* is important: this distinction between long term existence (*throughout history*) and inchoate reference (*at the turn of the century*) embeds the dilemma to which the footnote (Example 5.10) is addressed in a backdrop of prior practice. By so doing, it provides a precedent for the existence of concentration camps in America (i.e. *America's concentration camps*) despite the lack of conventionalized reference to them as *concentration camps*.

The next episodes: *during World War II* (line (c)), *in recent years* (line (g)) help to differentiate types of 'concentration camps' by temporally grounding several factors that create two sub-nodes in the list structure: activity (*places of torture, barbarous medical experiments and summary executions* (line (d)): *what* [X5abc] in figure 5.7); place (*America* [X2a], *Nazi Germany* [X2b] (c); *former Soviet Union, Cambodia, Bosnia* (g) [X2c]: *where* in figure 5.7.

The differentiation of 'concentration camps' by country is an important part of the footnote, as is the use of the possessives *America's* and *Nazi Germany's* (line (c)). Possessives assert a possessor and possessee relationship between two nouns that can include a sub-component not only of 'own' but also 'control' (Heine 1997, Taylor 1996). Possessives also presuppose the existence of the possessee (Chapter 4). The repeated full noun *America's concentration camps* thus presupposes the existence of concentration camps under the control of America. By so doing, it settles the referential problem: what was called *concentration camps* did exist when they were set up in the 1940s and when the exhibit on the camps traveled to Ellis Island in 1998. The existence of 'America's concentration camps' is further reinforced by the repetition of the possessive in *Nazi Germany's* (line (c)): since it is uncontestable that Nazi Germany had concentration camps, the use of parallel forms solidifies the presupposition that America had concentration camps.

Despite the existential presupposition of both countries' 'camps,' the two sets of camps are *clearly distinguishable* (line (c)). However, no distinguishing characteristics are explicitly stated in the branching textual structures (cf. "Nazi Germany's camps were [details], but America's camps were [details]") often found in comparisons (Schiffrin 1987: 232–240). The focus, instead, is only on the *Nazi camps* (line (d)).

After listing three characteristic (nominalized) activities of the *Nazi camps – torture, barbarous medical experiments, and summary executions –* a subset (i.e. *some*) is identified as *extermination centers with gas chambers* (line (d)). Because of the recent referral to *extermination centers* (line (d)), and the bare quantifier (the 'zero' in *some* [0] (line (d)), we can infer that *extermination centers* are part of the general set of *concentration camps*. Thus the footnote again allows the more general meaning of *concentration camps* – that need not, however, apply to all camps. In fact, as we saw in line (d), it was *Nazi camps* that had the properties noted above. The inclusion of these details for only the Nazi camps cancels any implicatures that the American camps were similar to the Nazi camps.

Thus far, we have focused on 'concentration camps' as the topical referent. But there are also person referrals in the footnote. Within the inner portion of the footnote (lines (c) to (g)), the person referrals are mostly proper nouns (*Jews* (e), *Gypsies, Poles, Homosexuals*, line (f)) with one common noun (*political dissidents*, line (f)). Jews are noted separately in their own clause (line (f)), with their own modifier (*six million*), their own fate (*slaughtered*) and their own grammatical voice and sentence form: the use of the passive singles out this set of victims through textual contrast with the predicate nominatives and equative in the sequence. The others are included (as contained inferables through *also* (line (f)) in the set of *victims of Nazi concentration camps*. Notice that although groups of victims are mentioned, the victims themselves are mostly absent from the actions taken against them. For example, rather than say *Nazis tortured and exterminated Jews*, the footnote states that the *Nazi camps were places of torture* (d) and that *some were extermination centers* (line (d)). Actions are nominalized and the focus is on the places (the camps) as sites where completed actions took place.

The same sentences obfuscate or neglect the identities and roles of the perpetrators. Perpetrators are metonymically evoked through country names: we read of *America's concentration camps* and *Nazi Germany's* (line (c)), not of *camps run by Americans* or *Nazi Germans*. Likewise, concentration camps were in different countries (*former Soviet Union, Cambodia, and Bosnia*, line (c)) such that people were victims not of other people's actions, but of countries and *concentration camps* (lines (f) and (g)). Although this is consistent with the purpose and theme of the footnote – the definition of *concentration camps* – even the actions (e.g. 'imprison' (line (a)), 'single out' (line (b)) and 'slaughter' (line (e)) that had to be taken by specific people are devoid of people. Not only are the perpetrators' actions in the passive (a word order that de-emphasizes the agent by moving it out of subject position), but they are agent*less* passives: *people are imprisoned* [by whom?] (line (a)), *groups have been singled out* [by whom?] (line (b)), *six million Jews were slaughtered* [by whom?] (line (e)). Thus, despite the appearance of 'characters', emplotted roles that might be available from a more developed narrative structure are not highlighted.

The footnote (Example 5.10) closes by returning to the general level of description with which it began. Notice how the final section opens, with a space in the text and a preposed adverbial:

(h) Despite the differences, all had one thing in common: the people in power removed a minority group from the general population and the rest of society let it happen.

The preposed adverbial (*despite the differences*) works anaphorically and cataphorically in the text. It establishes a transition from what has just been reported (*the differences*) and thus old information, to what is about to be reported (*one thing in common*) and thus new information.

The new information about to be presented is the *one thing in common: the people in power* (i.e. the perpetrators) *removed a minority group* (i.e. the victims) *from the general population and the rest of society* (i.e. the bystanders) *let it happen*. The three roles in parentheses – perpetrators, victims, bystanders – are the very same roles that Hilberg (1992) has identified as central to the Holocaust. But the way the roles are evoked in the general summary sentence differs from earlier sentences. Whereas perpetrators and victims were either absent or indirectly mentioned in earlier sentences, here the text is explicit about who does what to whom. The two clauses conjoined by *and* both follow a subject-verb order (cf. the agentless passives above) that shows not only that somebody did something (cf. the nominalizations above), but to whom it was done. The closing part of the definition thus puts perpetrators in a thematic position as subject of the sentence – thereby highlighting the role of the Nazis and America.

In sum, the footnote about *concentration camps* (Example 5.10) did not mention the Jewish and Japanese American controversy. Rather than openly question – and then defend – the choice of the term *concentration camps* for the Japanese American experience during WWII, it presupposed that *concentration camps* controlled by *America* was the appropriate term for the places to which Japanese Americans were forcibly relocated and detained. This presupposition was reinforced by first separating material existence from referential practice and then reaffirmed through a narrative comparison (with an underlying hierarchical list) among different types of concentration camps. The comparison assumed the general meaning of *concentration camps*, thus including both the camps in which Japanese Americans were interned and the *extermination centers* in which *six million Jews* (and *many others*) were killed. But it also cancelled the more horrific interpretations that could then have been added onto *America's concentration camps* through both the comparison and the inclusion of details about the Nazi camps.

Recall, finally, that the footnote was designed to settle a controversy between Jewish and Japanese Americans. Because the footnote focused not on controversy, but on comparison *and* convergence, it was able to fulfill several functions for different audiences: it resolved a conflict for Jewish Americans and Japanese Americans who were party to the conflict; it created a partial parallel between the D/discourse of two peoples' different historical experiences for the general American public who saw the exhibit.

5.5   Conclusion

In this chapter, three different, but related, analyses have explored typical and atypical sequences of referring terms in narratives and lists from face-to-face talk and in a blended genre (a footnote with features of both narratives and lists) that resolved a public controversy in Discourse. By so doing, we have addressed – more explicitly than previous chapters – what can become a strategic balance between old/same/fixed and new/different/innovative. Whereas earlier chapters on referrals dealt mostly with problems that were repaired with new forms, this chapter dealt with how the sequential choice to continue an earlier form, or switch to a different form, is sensitive to many different levels of meaning.

As noted at the outset of this chapter, breaking discourse norms is a well known strategy of conveying a 'marked' meaning. The analyses in this chapter add to our understanding of the value of atypical, marked and dispreferred forms. [Sequential attention to nouns in sites that favor pronouns within the two genres allowed us to uncover the discursive value of deviations from a pattern.] Along with maintaining topicality and avoiding ambiguity, we also saw that emphasizing the word-to-world connection can have important consequences for narratives, not just personal narratives told during face-to-face talk, but also collective narratives that provide a continuous sense of 'who we are' based on 'where we have been' and 'what happened to us.'

The controversy over *concentration camps* also suggests some points about the collective nature of reference. Referring terms in collective stories of the past are embedded in linguistic, social, cultural, political and historical matrices of meaning. If we want to understand how these terms fit into the larger stories, then, we need to navigate the multiple matrices of meanings in which the terms are embedded. But the multiplicity of meanings has a consequence. Functionally based semantic analyses of sentence meaning often differentiate the topic (what the sentence is about, i.e. a referent) from the comment (what is being said about the topic). But the referring term *concentration camps* does not only point to a referent and tell us what a sentence is about. It also does some of the work that the rest of a sentence is presumed to do: it says 'something' about the referent. Thus, whatever other information is predicated about the referent takes its place alongside the already highly contextualized – and thus richly informative – background constructs of experience, people, or place.

A number of different textual worlds have thus been considered in this chapter. Narratives and lists provide different means of configuring and evaluating information. Collective narratives project skeletal features of these genres into a more abstract domain of representation that is widely distributed over time, place and person – a quite different sort of text. Despite their differences, one goal remains: all of these worlds must establish references that can take up a place in the discourse models that people use to navigate and understand what is being said and what it means for themselves and others. The next two chapters turn to the narrative construction of a textual world based on a 'real' world that has been difficult for those who were part of it to verbalize to show how re-framings and retellings can alter that textual world.

Notes

1. Corpus analyses provide valuable quantitative profiles of linguistic features across genres (Conrad and Biber 2001), but because of their tremendous breadth, they cannot always include depth afforded by close qualitative sequential analyses. See also Toole (1996).
2. For discussion of 'context' in different approaches to discourse analysis, see Schiffrin 1994a: Chapter 10.
3. My operationalization of recency ignores several important questions: Is there a difference between a recent noun phrase and a recent pronoun? Between human and non-human referents? Between prior referents that are subjects vs. other syntactic roles?
4. Exceptions are stories about 'I' and 'we,' or a co-present 'other' in multiparty interactions.
5. Mary's use of proper names without modifying kin terms (e.g. *my cousin*) suggests that she is primarily addressing Jane (her aunt) rather than Anne (the interviewer). Had Mary been addressing this list exclusively (or even primarily) to Anne, it is likely that the proper names would have been accompanied by kin terms (e.g. *my cousin*) as they often are in other texts in which family members are first-mentioned with names.
6. Also adding to this inference is that Agnes' father not only breaks his routine on Sunday to honor his commitment to his daughter (he finishes painting the basement): he also avoids arguing with his wife on Monday before dying that evening in his car on the way home from work.
7. Although I mention collective narratives in this chapter, I do not address the conflict over *concentration camps* in terms of story telling rights. But see general discussion in Chapter 6 and specific discussion in Schiffrin 2001b.

8. Experiences of persecution in the war differed for the two communities. Hence the 'starting dates' are different.

9. Notice two nodes for 'who,' One is part of 'why' and appeared in the more specific description of victims in the inner portion of the footnote (Example 5.10); the other is a separate higher level node that conveys more general identities in the closing portion.

6

Reframing experience

6.1 Introduction

Analyses in this book thus far have focused primarily on referring expressions: what problems arise as speakers try to use their words as links to the world? how is information status indicated? what happens when familiarity assumptions go awry? are there pragmatic solutions that help avoid problems? how are successive words connected within the different genres that provide textual worlds in which they reside? what happens when these problems are situated not only in everyday talk, but also in social, cultural, historical and ideological domains of Discourse?

This chapter and the next address some of these same questions. However, they do so not by analyzing referring expressions, but by analyzing how characters and actions are brought together in sequences of clauses that comprise a narrative. As noted in Chapter 1, evoking an entity through a referring expression and recounting an experience through a narrative share some common concerns. Both depend upon links between word and world, the building of sequences in which words connect, attention to recipient design, and an interplay among referential, social and expressive meanings. And just as referring expressions can be redone (sometimes, but not always, due to problems), so too, can narratives be replayed. All of these similarities allow the analyses in these two chapters to continue to address the tension between same and different, new and old, innovative and fixed – but in event sequences rather than referents.

In addition to continuing to address some similar questions, this chapter and the next also fill in some analytical gaps. Although our analyses of referrals paid a great deal of attention to referring expressions, not much attention was given to either the speaker or the speaker's relationship to what is said (variously called stance, footing, and positioning). And whereas 'familiarity' was central to some analyses of referring expressions, we have not even mentioned the more common uses of the term 'familiarity:' our familiarity with people both to whom, and about whom, we are speaking; our familiarity with experiences, such that how 'what happened' instantiates (or violates) a familiar schema so as to allow (or hinder) verbalization as a narrative.

The data through which we address these issues are narratives that contribute to memory culture about the Holocaust. We have already touched on Holocaust Discourse in Chapter 5, when we addressed the problematic referral to *concentration camps* in an exhibit on the Japanese American internment during World War II. In this chapter, and the next, I focus on how a single story (about a failed plan to escape, see Appendix 2) is retold by one speaker (a Holocaust survivor, Susan Beer) in four different oral history interviews.[1] Although the story recounts a single episode in Mrs. Beer's life, different parts of the episode were experienced in different ways: some through another's speech, some through anticipation of future action, and some through direct physical action itself. This chapter explores linguistic traces of these different experiential sources over time. Chapter 7 addresses the same story but by focusing on questions more familiar to narrative analysts: how does the structure of the story change? how does the evaluation of the experience change?

Since Mrs. Beer's four versions of her story reflect different facets of the self/other design of oral histories, I begin by describing this genre in a way that will serve as background for the analyses in both chapters (Section 6.2). After briefly discussing vicarious experience in narrative, and how different frameworks have deconstructed the self/language relationship (Section 6.3), I trace how different information sources are linguistically reflected and altered over time in the four versions of Mrs. Beer's story (Section 6.4). My conclusion considers the voicing and revoicing of others' experiences in terms of story telling rights and privileges (Section 6.5).

6.2 Holocaust discourse

In the early post WWII years, the death of 6,000,000 Jews was not frequently distinguished in academic, mass media, or private discourse from the general discourse of WWII (Dawidowicz 1981, Hertzberg 1996). Although Jewish survivors themselves were sometimes vocal about their experiences within their own communities, they maintained a relative silence in relation to the outside world (Greenspan 1999, 2001). By the 1990s, what came to be called the *Holocaust* had become a centralizing symbol for American Jews (Novick 1999) and a familiar topic in American Discourse (Schiffrin 2001c). Among the many social, political and cultural factors contributing to (and indicating) this transformation in collective memory were oral history projects. What had begun as a handful of projects in the late 1970s has grown to roughly 180 collections of tens of thousands of Holocaust testimonies/oral histories.

Like all oral histories, those told about the Holocaust serve different functions: they contribute to collective memory and public commemoration; they serve as historical documents that provide historical information about the Holocaust; they provide interactive opportunities for survivors to recount their past experiences. Each one of these functions contributes to the important symbolic role that the Holocaust has come to play in American Discourse.

Let us begin with the commemorative function of Holocaust oral histories. Edited segments and excerpts from oral histories are replayed in museums, on television, and in movies; they are also condensed, edited, and reproduced in both printed media (e.g. books and magazines), on interactive media (e.g. computerized learning centers) and on websites. Holocaust oral histories thus complement the many other material and symbolic resources (e.g. museums, monuments, memoirs, films, paintings, sculptures, fiction, poetry, drama) commemorating the Holocaust and add the voices of survivors to the multitude of others (e.g. historians, theologians, journalists, fiction writers, literary theorists) who also represent the Holocaust. Like other commemorative resources (Linenthal 1995, Young 1993), oral histories are (at least partially) designed for the audience(s) – including, of course, the general public – who will be learning from them (Blum 1991, Greenspan 1998, Kacandes 1994, Laub 1992, Mintz 2001).

Although public memorial of the Holocaust often embodies its sheer vastness, hearing one person tell about the changes and losses in his or her life personalizes the otherwise numbing horror of the Holocaust: subjective involvement in the details of individual lives is believed by a variety of people (e.g. Hammer 1998, Miller 1990, Strassfeld 1985) to offer a more accessible route toward understanding the devastating effects of the Holocaust upon individual, family, communal, and cultural life. Thus, the firm niche that the Holocaust has come to occupy within American collective memory is partially created one by one by one (Miller 1990) through the same kind of intersubjectivity between narrators and audience that pervades the telling of narratives of personal experience in general.

The second role of Holocaust oral histories is to provide first-person testimony for scholars. Although oral histories offer unique opportunities to focus upon personal experiences of everyday life, they can also address broader social, cultural and political inquiries. In this sense, their use in Holocaust studies is comparable to the Italian microhistory perspective developed in the 1970s (Iggers 1997: Chapter 9). This perspective draws from a wide range of disciplines – interpretive anthropology, Marxist social theory – to analyze both modern twentieth century history (for which oral histories are available) as well as earlier periods of history (for which other more conventional sources are relied upon). Microhistory does not substitute for the analysis of large scale social and political processes; nor does it completely reject the use of social-science methodology for investigating changes in those processes (see Bartaux 1981 for comparable points about the use of personal biography for studying society). Rather, by supplementing analyses of those processes with information about how they were experienced by everyday men and women, they add the perspective of those whose everyday lives might have helped set those processes into motion and those who felt the consequences of those processes. The wealth of detail offered by Holocaust oral histories can offer the same depth of insight for study of the Holocaust.

The two relatively public roles of oral histories discussed thus far – public commemoration, historical inquiry – are supplemented by a third, more private, role: oral histories can provide survivors with an empathetic milieu in which to tell their life stories.

Holocaust oral histories have sometimes enabled survivors to deal with "the psychological and emotional milieu of the struggle for survival, not only then but now" (Hartman 1996: 142) and to address a past whose memories had not yet found a language in which to be conveyed (Ballinger 1999, Eitinger 1998, LaCapra 2001). This redemptive view of 'talking' suggests that narrative might provide a pathway toward overcoming trauma. As Dominick LaCapra (2001: 90), a historian who has applied psychoanalytic theory to trauma, observes:

when the past becomes accessible to recall in memory, and when language functions to provide some measure of conscious control, critical distance, and perspective, one has begun the arduous process of working over and through the trauma.

Both observers and survivors, however, note that what had been experienced is not easily reconstructed or conveyed through language. Dori Laub (1998: 802), a psychiatrist who helped initiate one of the first Holocaust testimony projects, observes:

Because of the radical break between trauma and culture, victims often cannot find categories of thought or words to contain or give shape to their experience. That is, since neither culture nor past experience provides structures for formulating acts of massive destruction, survivors cannot articulate trauma even to themselves.

Laub's comments suggest that traditional narrative templates ("categories of thought") could not provide the discursive scaffolding through which survivors could call forth the language ("words") necessary for emplotting their catastrophic loss of community, friends, and family (see also Friedlander 1992). According to Lawrence Langer (1991), a literary scholar who has written extensively about Holocaust testimonies, stories about loss, suffering, atrocities and overwhelming death during the Holocaust are buried in different sites of personal memory (e.g. deep, anguished, humiliated) in which the Holocaust remains simultaneously part of – but separate from – one's current life world. Other observers address the limitations not of narrative schemas, but of language itself, noting the trope of silence pervading Holocaust literature (Horowitz 1997) or the turn to visual or physical media as alternative means through which to represent traumatic memories (Hirsch and Suleiman 2001). Thus the potential therapeutic outcome of narrativizing traumatic experience is not always realized. Survivors' oral histories reveal continuous struggles with 'what happened,' with how to convey what happened, and with how to integrate the self of past experience with the self of current existence.

I have suggested thus far in this section that Holocaust oral histories have three functions that contribute in different ways to memory culture and American Discourse: they complement other material and symbolic resources that commemorate the Holocaust; they provide data about 'what happened' for scholars engaged in Holocaust studies; they provide a venue in which survivors talk about their experiences. This blend of commemorative, scholarly and autobiographical functions creates complex participation frameworks that create identities that are both relatively concrete (e.g. interviewee, storyteller) and abstract (e.g. witness to a twentieth century tragedy). Participants thus balance the need to provide historical facts with the desire to create video clips that show and sound well on a screen, but still manage to respect the privacy of what can be a highly personal and painful story. Because oral history thus depends "on the shifting balance between the personal and the social, between biography and history" (Portelli 1997: 6), it is an inherently multivocalic genre (Portelli 1997: Chapter 2).

Multivocality arises in oral histories in relation not only to participant shifts in footings and goals, but also in relation to the means by which information is acquired and when it is done so (Schiffrin 2003). Although interviewees explicitly identify some information as retrospective knowledge (e.g. "what we didn't know then was that . . ." or "we only learned later that . . ."), other *ex post facto* information is seamlessly integrated into the overall texture of what is said. Included in the latter is the incorporation of English itself (a language that most survivors did not know during World War II), survivor myths (Wievorka 1994) and others' experiences that have become important emblems or icons of collective (rather than personal) experience (Allen and Montell 1981, Schiff et al. 2000).

Even more sweeping than the influx of *ex post facto* information is the non-chronological impact of time. The fluidity between past and present in Holocaust oral histories can be accompanied by a general teleological focus (common to all autobiography) in which past deeds end up being more goal directed in our stories than they were in our lives (Brockmeier 2001). Also reflected is a "double arrow of time" (Mishler, in press) that infiltrates not only the way we tell stories about what happened (i.e. narrative code), but also the arrangement of events into a plot, and how both event and plot are cognitively defined and located within memory (i.e. narrative competence). Although the double arrow of time is especially evident in turning points (pivotal transitions) within life stories (Mishler 1999), the overall process pervades narrative as an ever-widening context of later experiences provides gradual understandings of 'what happened' and leads to reconstruction of the meanings of past experiences. And as Linde (1993) reminds us, an underlying goal of life stories is the fitting together of experiences across time into an explanatory system in which the 'self' appears as a consistent and organized whole.

The incorporation of posterior information into autobiographical genres is thus not surprising. Non-linear time infiltrates our representations of events within memory, our arrangement of events into plots, our evaluation of events in relation to themes, and the ways we verbalize themes and plots within stories. What is surprising is the scholarly neglect of vicarious experience. In contrast to the analytical frameworks available for explaining how and why experiences from different times are integrated into such genres, there has been little attention to how experiences with different sources are incorporated into those very same genres. In the next section, I suggest some reasons for the neglect of vicarious experiences and how incorporating them into narrative analysis leads to the interrelated notions of positioning, footing and stance.

6.3 Language, experience and 'self'

The right to tell a story – whether it is a story about the past, present or future – is not always guaranteed to those who want to tell it (Tonkin 1992: Chapter 2). Gaining the right to use one's own voice to tell one's own story – and have it received in the manner for which it was intended – requires acknowledging the validity of individual cultures, peoples, and languages rather than automatically privileging those having more dominant positions in economies defined by materialistic, ideological or symbolic resources (Hymes 1981, 1996).[2]

An often tacit assumption in the struggle over story telling rights is that those who lived through an experience should be the ones to tell about it, or at least be given the first chance to do so. Donald Margulies portrays this conflict in his drama *Collected Stories* (1998). When a middle class WASP (White Anglo Saxon Protestant) is criticized by a fellow writer for trying to write in the 'voice' of a working class Jew, she then criticizes that same writer (who *is* a working class Jew) for having previously written in the 'voice' of a Black welfare mother. Likewise, in an article in the Washington Post (8/25/00, pp. C1-32), Phil McCombs criticized the writer Wolfgang Koeppen, whom he identified as "a well known German author, and a Gentile" for publishing what Koeppen claimed was a novel, that he entitled *Jakob Littner's notes from a hole in the ground*. The problem was that almost the entire text had appeared more than forty years earlier as a memoir *My Journey through the night: a document of racial hatred, eyewitness report* from Jakob Littner himself, a German Jew who had survived the war. In cases such as these, the borrowing voice is seen as inauthentic; the speaker, as acting in bad faith, perhaps seeking to exploit another's disadvantage by symbolically removing their authentic voice from the experience. But these uses of another's voice raise what is an even more fundamental problem: voicing the experience from the outside lacks the "stuff" – the subjectivity – of which experience is made.

The retelling of others' experience has been generally excluded from sociolinguistic studies of narrative since Labov's (1972b) seminal article on transforming experience into narrative syntax. Labov compared two narratives – one of vicarious experience, the other of personal experience – from the same speaker, a young African American boy. The differences between the two narratives were striking. The recounting of a television show had none of the syntactic complexity, artfulness, fluency and overall drama found in the same boy's narrative about his own experience. As Labov (1972b: 355) explains, it is "because the experience and emotions involved here form an important part of the speaker's biography" that he seems to partially relive his experience. The way he speaks is thus no longer as dependent on the need to monitor what he says for the reception of powerful (and potentially critical) others.

Labov's comparison between narratives of vicarious and personal experience played a key role in demonstrating the underlying linguistic competence of people who had been culturally, socially, and politically labeled (and stigmatized) as verbally deprived, thus providing just the kind of validation urged by Hymes. But it has had an unexpected analytical and theoretical impact on the study of narrative: what has ended up teaching us so much about the transformation of experience into narrative has been how a 'self' narrates bits and pieces of his/her own life, not the life of an 'other.' Thus narratives of vicarious experience have been excluded as grist for the analytical mill.

Vicarious experiences are harder to ignore in oral history life stories than in sociolinguistic interviews: the coherent reconstruction of one's own life can be augmented when the emotions, actions and experiences of one's own family and friends, especially those occurring during one's childhood (Premilovac 2002), or at pivotal turning points, are incorporated into a life story.[3] Yet we know little about how experiences of different types – being told something, thinking about something, engaging in collective actions or reactions, reading newspapers or books – are verbalized in stories of our lives. Nor do we know whether (or how) language will reflect the different sources of information that work their way into our stories.

If we want to deepen our understanding of the narratives told during oral histories and life stories, we need to examine the language through which we incorporate differently grounded pieces of our lives into a single narrative and the different facets of 'self' that are involved in doing so. We begin to do so by sketching some of the different frames (Goffman 1974) in which a 'self' and 'other' appear when telling a story (see Figure 6.1).

Personal narrative verbalizes 'what happened' to one person (a 'self') during an EXPERIENCE through a STORY WORLD in which the actions and reactions of a set of characters (often including 'self') move a plot forward. Moving outward from the STORY WORLD is a concrete site of situated INTERACTION in which the story is told by one person to another – yet another 'self' and 'other.' The interaction is simultaneously part of larger DISCOURSE (social practices, ideologies, and so on) that provides its own definitions (on a more ideological and often stratified level) of 'self' and 'other.' My main interest in this chapter is the relationship between the two

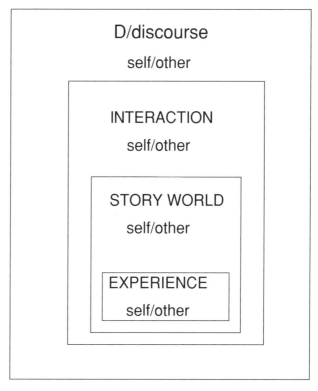

Figure 6.1 Frames of 'self'/'other' in narrative

inner frames: how 'self' in INTERACTION may become the teller of
a story that is built upon EXPERIENCE of an 'other,' while (possibly)
drawing upon resources from INTERACTION and DISCOURSE.

Analytical frameworks for addressing self, other, experience, and
language focus on different components of the overall process of
verbalizing 'events' as a story and its final product, i.e. the story.
Whereas *positioning* deconstructs speaker's identity projection in
relation to what is said, *footing* deconstructs the speaker's production format in relation to talk, and *stance* addresses the epistemic basis of the speaker/content relationship. After briefly reviewing these three constructs, I suggest connections among them that
facilitate the analysis of vicarious experience in the retellings of
Mrs. Beer's narrative from an oral history of the Holocaust (see
Appendix 2).

I begin with a version of positioning theory (Bamberg 1997, Korobov and Bamberg 2003, developed from Davies and Harré 1990) that differentiates three levels. Positioning Level 1(PL-1) concerns the presentation of referential meaning or denotational content. Positioning Level 2 (PL-2) situates the referential content in interaction: its concern is how referential content is interactively designed and received. Positioning Level 3 (PL-3) both motivates and builds upon PL-1 and PL-2 as the means by which participants project and develop identities: the way that we construct meanings (PL-1) within social interaction (PL-2) displays identities (PL-3) to which others can react with overt (or tacit) approval or disapproval.[4]

As we turn to Goffman's concept of footing, it is helpful to note that this (and related concepts of framing and participation framework) expanded upon his earlier perspective on the self (see brief review in Schiffrin, in press). Goffman's later work on the self (1974, 1981a) turned attention from analyses of self/other in social interaction to a deconstruction of 'self,' specifically, how we divide the labor underlying the production of an utterance. Nowhere does Goffman explicitly address the referential content of what is said (i.e. PL-1). In fact, his interest is quite the opposite: "ordinarily when an individual says something, he is not saying it as a bald statement of fact on his own behalf. He is recounting. He is running through a strip of already determined events for the engagement of his listeners" (Goffman 1974: 508).

Goffman (1974: 522) first introduced the terms principal, strategist, animator, and figure and only later defined 'footing' as "the alignment we take up to ourselves and the others present as expressed in the way we manage the production or reception of an utterance" (1981a: 128).What Goffman proposed in the later view of footing is the following: we author (design what is said), animate (present what another will hear), act as principal (commit to the meanings of what is said) and become a figure (a character in a textual world). Thus central to a textual world is not only the construction of a text (with its implicit referential meanings), but also the voicing (or in his earlier terms, emission) of that world through language, an implicit commitment to the information in that world, and (sometimes, but not always) a self-referential character in that world. What thus re-frames, re-keys and laminates that textual world at both sentence and textual levels (Goffman 1974,

Chapter 13) is the author's verbal production, the animator's presentation, the principal's proprietary rights and commitment to information (and its implications), and the figure's attributes, actions and relationships as linguistically portrayed in a text.[5]

Whereas positioning places the speaker in different (but interrelated) domains of linguistic (referential meaning) and social action (relating to others, projecting identity), and footing deconstructs the speaker's relationship to what is said, it is 'stance' that addresses the connection between the speaker and referential content. Here I will take 'stance' to be a combination of evidentiality (source of information), and epistemology (knowledge), that produces epistemicity (certainty of information (Kärkkäinen 2003)).[6] These terms are used differently by different authors: for example Kärkkäinen's epistemic stance is similar to what Mushin (2001) calls epistemological stance, i.e. the source of information and the type of knowledge that results from different sources (see also Strauss 2004 on cultural stance or 'standing' of information). Regardless of terminology, my interest is how (in reflection of Chafe's (1986) view) evidentials (whether grammaticalized in language or not) reflect a relationship between how one comes to know something (e.g. through senses (visual, auditory, tactile) or hypothesis), the type of knowledge (e.g. hearsay, induction, deduction) and the level of certainty resulting from both. An underlying assumption is that the more direct the information (e.g. first-hand physical or sensory experience) the more certain one is about its reliability and validity. I will speak of different levels of knowledge as *epistemicity*; and the expression of levels of certainty based on knowledge as *epistemic stance*.

Figure 6.2 relates positioning, footing and stance together in relation to the frames of action and interpretation in which 'self'/'other' are embedded (from Figure 6.1).

As Figure 6.2 suggests, stance requires a connection between two facets of 'self' and the 'real' world of referential meaning: the knowledge and evidence that allows commitment places the principal at PL-1; the expression of knowledge and evidence also places the author at PL-1. Thus PL-1 involves both principal and author. The active and interactive role of speaker establishes a link between animator and PL-2 (the interaction): the textual role as a self-referential character establishes a link between figure and PL-3 (the text). To put this another way, stance begins as a reflection of the speaker's

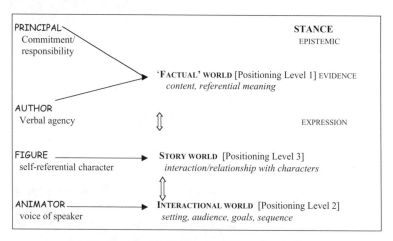

Figure 6.2   Positioning a 'self' and a stance

relationship (as *principal*) to experience. But it is also realized within texts in which an *author*, who is working at the 'real world' level, creates a *figure* who emerges in a text; both author and figure are interactively situated (by the work of an *animator*).

In this section, I have suggested that multi-vocalic oral histories and continuously constructed life stories arise not just from personal actions and interactions that make up 'first-hand' experience, but also from various kinds of vicarious experience. I have also suggested that three different constructs can be brought together to trace changes in the incorporation of different kinds of experience into narrative. Thus we are ready to turn to how different facets of experience are verbalized in four different versions of a single story told by one speaker.

6.4 'Self'/'other' experience in one story over time

The story that I focus upon here – Susan Beer's story about being captured by the Gestapo in 1944 Budapest – combines both 'self' and 'other' experience. I begin by presenting material preliminary to the analysis of footing changes in the four versions of the story (see Appendix 2). After summarizing Mrs. Beer's overall life story and the specific story to be analyzed (Section 6.4.1), I preview the footing changes (Section 6.4.2) and then analyze three aspects of the reframing of experience (Section 6.4.3).

6.4.1 Background to the story

The story to be analyzed is told by Susan Beer who, at the time
of the recounted events, was a young Jewish woman (Suzanna
Eisdorfer) from Slovakia living in Budapest, Hungary in 1944. Susan
Beer was the only child in an observant Jewish family; she grew up
in Topolcany, a small town in what was then Slovakia. Her father
was a doctor in the town. When the Germans seized control of
Slovakia, discrimination against Jews in Topolcany escalated: families had to give up their material possessions and their civil liberties;
Susan Beer's father was forbidden to practice medicine. As word of
deportations began to spread – and when Susan Beer herself received
an order to report for a transport to a labor camp – her parents
arranged for her to go illegally to Hungary, a country that was then
safer for Jews. Susan Beer's parents eventually escaped to Hungary
also and they all lived clandestinely with false identities.

When anti-Semitic measures in Hungary increased (with the rise
in power of Adolph Eichmann), Susan Beer's father learned of
an escape plan in which German soldiers would return Slovakian
nationals to a part of Slovakia freed by partisans. The plan turns
out to be a trap: the family is captured, imprisoned, and then sent
to Auschwitz. Despite the many hardships of Auschwitz, death
marches, near starvation and disease, Susan Beer and her parents
all survived. Susan Beer married a young man who had spent most
of the WWII years hiding with his family in the mountains. Mrs. Beer
and her husband emigrated to the United States; Mrs. Beer's parents
(because of restrictive immigration laws) emigrated to Canada.

Mrs. Beer spoke about her life in four oral history interviews.
Whereas two interviews were conducted in the relatively early days
of such projects (1982, 1984), two were conducted more than ten
years later (1995), one by the Shoah foundation, the other by the
United States Holocaust Memorial Museum. Since this is exactly
the period of time during which Holocaust discourse developed as
a more public genre, we may find that some of the changes in footing and stance arise as Mrs. Beer finds a template through which
language can fit her experience and a performative venue through
which her language can be fit to its audience.

The story that I analyze here (see Appendix 2) opens with Susan
Beer's father recounting the escape plan; it continues as the family
anticipates what will happen and then discovers that their rescuers

are really captors. The capture is a significant turning point in
Susan Beer's life story. Being captured and imprisoned ended the
family's period of relative success in avoiding active persecution by
the Nazis. It also began their transition to total immersion in the
Final Solution.

The capture story has three phases distinguishable by topic and
information source. In Phase I, THE PLAN, Mrs. Beer reports a plan
for the family to escape to an area of Slovakia controlled by partisans. Information is provided by Mrs. Beer's father, who recounts
(what he has heard from someone else) the following details about
the escape plan to the family: who will help, why, where, when, and
how. At the point that we hear this phase of the story, we assume
that the plan is not only necessary, but also plausible (it 'can' be
done) and credible (it is, in fact, a plan to rescue the family).

Since the information source in THE PLAN is complex, an analogy with the children's game "whispering down the lane" provides a helpful parallel. In the game, one child thinks of a message
and then whispers that message to another; that recipient whispers
what they heard to another, and so on "down the lane." The last
child to receive a message states publicly what she has heard. Typically, this utterance differs dramatically from the message that had
been whispered by the first child. Two features of THE PLAN resemble the actions in "whispering down the lane." First, the information is shrouded in secrecy. Second, the plan reported by Mrs. Beer
resembles what is verbalized by the last child who whispers "down
the lane": it is articulated by different voices and filtered through
different ears.

The information source underlying Phase II, ANTICIPATION, of
Mrs. Beer's story is quite different. Once the plan has been reported
to the family, it becomes part of family knowledge. In ANTICI-
PATION, Mrs. Beer projects the joint course of action entailed by
the plan. Thus here there is a discursive juncture between what has
become family knowledge (the plan) and the upcoming actions that
the family will soon undertake.

Neither THE PLAN nor ANTICIPATION give any indication that
the plan is actually a trap to capture the family. What happens in
THE CAPTURE is a complete surprise: Mrs. Beer and her parents,
along with 41 other people, are captured and sent to a Gestapo
prison. Underlying THE CAPTURE are two different sources of
information: the earlier phases of the story that detailed the plan

and its projected outcome; Mrs. Beer's own physical, visual and cognitive experience as described in Phase III (Schiffrin 2003).

The four versions of Mrs. Beer's narrative all tell 'what happened in 1944 in Budapest to Susan Beer and her family.' (See Appendix 2 for complete versions.) In the different phases of all four stories, however, there remain epistemic differences: reporting on multi-reported speech is not the same as anticipating a future course of action and engaging in action itself. Yet as each story is told again (in the second telling in 1984), again (in the third telling 1995a), and yet again (in the fourth telling, a month later in 1995), each narrative performance provides yet another information source: a reflexive source that provides templates of form, content and expression for later incarnations of itself.

Before discussing the language and footing changes that appear with the different versions of the story, however, it is important to be familiar with the overall textual characteristics of the four versions of the story. (For more detail see Chapter 7.) In the 1982 story, Phases I and II are presented in topic-centered stanza structures. Two event-clauses in THE PLAN build a topic of "escape." Between these two clauses is background information that supports the escape theme by showing the necessity of escape and establishing its credibility and plausibility of the plan. Time moves forward in THE PLAN only through the two event clauses. Since ANTICIPATION in the 1982 story is also largely descriptive, the structures of Phases I and II suggest that they serve as an orientation to the upcoming narrative action. THE CAPTURE in the 1982 story is strikingly different: it is a string of syntactically parallel event-clauses conjoined by *and*. What happens is portrayed as sudden and rapid: the group hardly has time to know what is going on. The structural split between Phases I/II and Phase III textually mirrors the split between expectation (freedom) and reality (capture). In subsequent versions of the capture story, the structural differences between the orienting phases (I, II) and the resolution phase (III) are leveled: all three phases are presented as event-based temporally ordered linear narratives.

6.4.2 Reframing experience in the story world

Let us turn, now, to the frames, footings, positions, and stances through which Mrs. Beer voiced and revoiced the varying experiences underlying her story. A summary of the frames within which footings are anchored, and the textual changes that reflect these changes, appears in Figure 6.3 by Phases (vertically) and year of the narrative (horizontally). For each Phase/version combination, there is an (unframed) 'outer world,' then a story world (with different levels of complexity) and a factual world of more direct experience. Within these frames are different footings that are taken by Mrs. Beer.

The outer world (cf. the life world that pervades all narrative) refers to the matrices of meanings that frame the telling of a Holocaust oral history narrative. This intentionally broad, heterogeneous and relatively unspecified world includes the physical (as well as social, cultural, political) situation in which the interview occurs, the symbolic role of the Holocaust in American culture, and general symbolic resources (including language) for memory culture that have developed since the time of the experience. The laminator footing appears when *post hoc* meanings explicitly infiltrate the narrative performance.

The interactional and story worlds are straightforward. The interactional world is the face-to-face interaction during which the story emerges on a local basis: turn by turn prior to the story; unit by unit (e.g. clause, intonation unit) within the story. The story world is the deictic center of the recounted experience. It includes the people (characters, including the self-referential figure) whose actions and interactions fit together to produce a sequence of activity recognizable as a story line or plot.

A distinction between an exterior and interior story world appears only in THE PLAN, where it reflects the "story within the story" structure described earlier. The interior story world in THE PLAN is minimal, simply because Mrs. Beer is recounting very little of her own experience. The exterior story world is Mrs. Beer's recounting of her father's activities (i.e. his experience), including how he comes up with a plan, reports the participants and speech activity of the speech event, and the content of the plan. Whatever really happened – the factual world – in THE PLAN is thus buried in the interior story world, i.e. what was actually told to Mrs. Beer's father by whoever revealed the escape plan to him.[7]

Since 'what happened' in Phases II and III was more directly experienced by Mrs. Beer than what happened in Phase I, I do

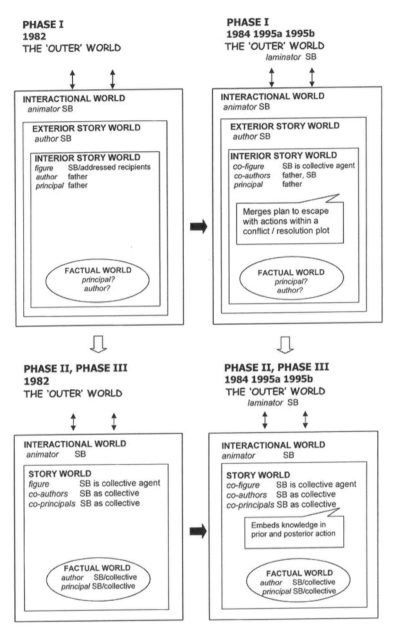

Figure 6.3 Reframing experience in the story world

not differentiate an exterior from interior world for these phases. Likewise, the factual world in these phases reflects quite different information sources: the information that provides for the factual world was not what Mrs. Beer's father was told (as in THE PLAN), but the activities in which Mrs. Beer and her family took part. Finally, the speech bubbles within the story world (1984, 1995a, 1995b) show the linguistic strategies through which changes in footing are displayed.

6.4.3 Language and footing

In this section, I discuss three key parts of the footing changes: the blurring of the exterior/interior story worlds in the father's plan (Section 6.4.3.1); a laminator from the 'outer' world about the credibility of the plan (Section 6.4.3.2); the expansion of co-figure, co-author and co-principal through a collective internal state (Section 6.4.3.3). We will see that initial stances (and hence footings and positionings) become more differentiated over time.

6.4.3.1 Father's plan

An analysis of the speech event 'making plans' and the content of the 'plans' reveals two different story worlds: an exterior story world in which Mrs. Beer tells about her father making plans; an interior story world in which Mrs. Beer's father reports and describes the plans. In post-1982 stories, the factual world recedes: Mrs. Beer elevates her father to a position of principal in the interior story world and joins her father as co-author. Both of these shifts blur the boundary between the interior and exterior social worlds, i.e. between recounting an 'other' and a 'self' experience.

We examine, first, how the main speech event ('making plans') is presented, i.e. the manner in which the plan is transmitted. In Example 6.1 we begin with the 1982 story. (In each of these extracts, event clauses are labeled E: numbers indicate sequence. Clauses whose event status is not clear are labeled E?)

Example 6.1

(1) E1 During the day my father made . . . or maybe not even a whole- just during the day . . . he made arrangements,

(2) someone told him of a German Wehrmacht . . .

Notice, first, that the goal of the speech event is presented as a completed act: *he made arrangements* (line (1)). As Hymes (1972b) points out in his etic SPEAKING grid of communicative components, the notion of 'goal' (through the mnemonic E as ends) can focus on either an intention (the initial point, something *to be* accomplished) or an outcome (the end point, something that *has been* accomplished). *He made arrangements* focuses on the outcome. In keeping with the non-linear structure of Phases I and II of the 1982 text (Chapter 7), Mrs. Beer then backtracks (in (2)) to provide the details of the arrangements. A speaker (*someone*) performs a speech act (*told*) to an addressee (*him*) and introduces a topic of talk (*a German Wehrmacht*) through which the content of the plan will unfold.

Notice that Mrs. Beer uses the indefinite noun phrase (*someone*) to report the source from which her father had learned of the plan, i.e. had been *told of a German Wehrmacht* (2). Although the source of the information is labeled with the informative noun *German Wehrmacht*, the quotative verb creates an opaque context that makes it impossible to know whether *Wehrmacht* is intended as referential (i.e. it 'exists') or attributive (i.e. it 'may exist' (see Chapter 2) and impossible to check on the veracity of what was said.

Subsequent versions alter the scenario in which Mrs. Beer's father learns of the plan and the transmittal chain through which the family receives the information. 'Making plans' becomes part of a temporally ordered quest, complete with a search for a way to accomplish a goal – the initial point, goal as intention – hence creating a miniplot in which a conflict (where can we get help?) is resolved (we can find help here). And as vague and ephemeral as the 1982 source of the plan was, the 1982 *someone* fades still further away in subsequent versions simply because speech event verbs shift from a verb of speech production to verbs of speech reception.

Example 6.2 shows how these shifts begin in the 1984 text:

Example 6.2
1984
(a) **E1** And uh my father went next day,
      in search of a way to get us back to Czechoslovakia.
(d) And we we were holding to any straw, I guess,
      because it was impossible for us to remain longer in
      Budapest.

(e)   **E2** And he came home, that he found such a way.
(f)   That there is a German Wehrmacht truck

The quest begins as the father went next day (line (a)) with a goal *in search of a way to get us back to Czechoslovakia* (line (a)). It is during the last part of the quest, when the father came home (line (e)) that the goal is accomplished and the plan is announced: *he found such a way* (line (e)). Although the making of the plans occupies a small conflict/resolution sequence, missing are several expected parts of the resolution: the speech event 'making plans' has no speaker, speech act verb, or recipient. The plan is thus embedded in the quest sequence with no information about its actual transmittal as a message from one person to another.

In the 1995a version (Example 6.3), Mrs. Beer begins the speech event through the perspective of its recipient (*he heard*), but then self-interrupts to backtrack to her father's quest (1.):

Example 6.3
1995a
   E2 he heard-
1.   **E1** he went among people some place,
2.   **E2** and he heard that there are some army personnel, with an army truck,

After the search *he went among people some place* (line 1.), the receipt of the plan (*he heard*) reappears, but with a crucial difference: *he heard* (line 2.) takes its sequential position within the quest. The plan is then described: it is framed (as in 1982) in terms of the Wehrmacht (translated from the German to *army personnel*) and their *army truck* as an indirectly reported message. Again, the speech event has no speaker or speech act verb – but it does have a recipient (*he heard* (line 2.)

In the 1995b version, Mrs. Beer's father again undertakes a quest complete with outset and goal:

Example 6.4
1995b
(A)   **E1** And my father went out to look for something for us to do,
(B)   you know, what would be the next step?
(C)   There weren't many options.

(D) **E2** And, as he went, he heard a story that today,
     I think your hair would stand up from disbelief,
(E) **E3** but he swallowed it.
(F) And the story was that there are some German Army
     Officers, or Army personnel, who are disillusioned with the
     army life

After evaluating the near-futility of the quest (lines (B), (C); see Section 6.4.3), the temporally preposed *as he went* (line (D)) embeds the speech event reporting the plan within the quest. Again, there is no source – only the father's reception of the information, labeled as *a story* (line (D)). The last step in the quest is the father's acceptance of the plan: *he swallowed it* (line (E)). The plan is then embedded as the content of *the story*, again, beginning with the Germans.

Comparison of the speech event 'making plans' shows that two 'facts' appear in all four versions. First is the anonymity of several key participants: we never learn who told Mrs. Beer's father about the plan or who was the actual originator of the plan. In fact, the versions over time show a gradual withering away of the sources of the plan as Mrs. Beer shifts focus to the father's quest for a plan and leaves her father as the only figure participating in the speech event. Second, Mrs. Beer's father accepts the arrangements. He does so not through a verb of speech production (e.g. 'and my father agreed'), but through verbs of speech reception: the father *found* (1984), *heard* (1995a, 1995b) or *swallowed* (1995b) the plan. These verbs move the father from a relatively active position (*found*) to a relatively passive position (*heard*) to one of gullibility (*swallowed* (Example 6.4)). Agency is thus reserved for the earlier part of THE PLAN, in which the father set out to find a way to save the family and to return them to their homeland.

The changes in construction of the 'speech event' (from 'X told Y that . . .' to 'Y heard that . . .') and its place in the story (alone or in a temporally ordered 'quest' sequence) are alterations in one phase of the transmission process: the transfer of information from an unknown source to Mrs. Beer's father. If we move to a still more interior part of the story world – what was reported and how it was done so – we find other changes that also diminish the narrative role of the unknown (supposed) rescuers.

The key parts of the plan presented to Mrs. Beer's father (i.e. the factual world in the interior story world) appear in Figure 6.4; on the left, I classify the content; within the figure are excerpts from the texts.

The various changes noted in Figure 6.4 suggest an increasing distance from the time, place and people of the actual events, i.e. the factual world. For example, rather than use the German word for the soldiers (*Wehrmacht*), Mrs. Beer shifts toward the English *army personnel*. Although detachment from the army remains as a motive, it shifts from dislike of a 'people' (*the Germans* (Example 6.1, 1982)) or an army-based identity (*being a Wehrmacht* (Example 6.2, 1984)) to disappointment with a facet of life (*being in the German army*). Likewise, a key motive for helping – a desire either for a change in one's one life or to help another – disappears in the 1995 versions. Thus the inner 'wants' of the supposed rescuers are unknown. Like the shift in modality in conveying the goal (in WHAT, from *will* to the less realis *would* (1995ab)), the partial loss of motivation reduces the certainty that the plan will actually be realized – simply because it provides no personal benefit for the rescuers. Although these shifts differ in their specific effects, together they reduce what we know about the 'facts' of the interior story world. Thus, if we assume that it is these facts to which a principal is committed, then their recasting challenges both their foundation and the strength of commitment that can be held by a principal.

When we examine the linguistic frames through which the facts are transmitted, we see further evidence of the winnowing away of the interior story world. It is well known that all acts of reporting speech are both appropriations of another's words and a transformation of the original act (Bakhtin 1981). The question here is what are the original acts and where, how (or if) we can locate them. Representations of the *someone* (who spoke for someone else, supposedly the Wehrmacht) to the father can be framed in different ways. For example, one could use direct quotation (e.g. *He said "I will help"*) or indirect quotation (e.g. *He said that he would help*). One could label what was said through a speech act verb (e.g. *He offered help*). Still another option is to shift perspective from the voice of the speaker to the ears of the hearer, again, through a range of devices: *I heard "We will help you," I heard that he would help, I heard him offer help*. Here there is no portrait of the author at all: the words are in the ear of the beholder.

	1982	1984	1995a	1995b
WHAT	will take group of Jews back	to get us back	would take us back	would take us back
TO WHERE	Slovakia	Czechoslovakia	Slovakia	Slovakia
FROM WHERE	park	park	park	park
WHO	German Wehrmacht	German Wehrmacht	army personnel	German army officers or army personnel
WHY				
DETACHMENT	sick and tired of the Germans	tired of being Wehrmacht	very disillusioned with being in G army	disillusioned with army life
DESIRE	want to return to civilian life	want to help us escape	-----	-----
HOW	for a fee	would cost money	for a fee	of course cost a lot of money

Figure 6.4 Back to Slovakia

What we find in post-1982 stories are indirect 'hearing' forms to replace the *someone* who *told* the father of a *German Wehrmacht* (1982). Notice that no offer of help is even mentioned. Rather, the means by which help will be realized H O W or W H O opens the details of the plan:

1984	he found such a way,	that there is a Wehrmacht truck
1995a	he heard	that there are some army personnel
1995b	he swallowed it	
	the story was	that there are some German Army officers

Mrs. Beer thus shifts from reporting a speaking source to a listening recipient, who hears through the syntactic screen of a complement clause (*that* S) about the existence (*there is/are*) of some people (or metonymically (1984), their truck). This shift situates the 'facts' of the plan far from the world in which those 'facts' were ostensibly transmitted by *someone* speaking for soldiers who were supposedly offering their help. This is thus another way in which the interior story world of 'facts' is gradually submerged within the exterior story world.

In sum, although the 'facts' that are presented in T H E   P L A N are consistent in the four versions, our knowledge of the 'facts' and the principal diminishes within the interior story world in which the plans are reported to Mrs. Beer's father. The shift from framing the speech event 'making plans' through a verb of speech production, to a verb of message reception, positions Mrs. Beer's father as the only character in the reported speech event. He thus adds to his authorship of the plan a role as principal: he is responsible for, and committed to, its content. As Mrs. Beer's father gains ascendancy in the interior story world, the experiences of more distant 'others' – especially the German soldiers – begin to fade. This is hardly surprising: Mrs. Beer's father is a familiar 'other' who appears repeatedly in Mrs. Beer's life and life story. Thus the interior (and factual) world is gradually submerged within the exterior story world.

6.4.3.2 Laminating doubt
The laminator footing appears when discursive strategies and *post hoc* meanings from interactional and outer worlds explicitly

infiltrate the narrative performance. Earlier we noted that the interactional world (of the animator) is the world of co-presence with an
interlocutor, in which setting, audience, goals and sequence frame
what is said. The outer (life) world refers to the matrices of meanings
that frame the telling of a Holocaust oral history narrative. What
develops in the post-1982 stories is a laminator footing that not
only comments upon the plan, but also conveys skepticism through
idioms, metaphor, formulaicity and meta-talk.

Observe, first, the integration of idioms within the father's quest
for a plan in the 1984 story.

Example 6.5
1984
(a)   E1 And uh my father went next day,
      in search of a way to get us back to Czechoslovakia.
(b)   Because some part of it was freed,
(c)   the partisans freed it.
(d)   And we- *we were holding to any straw*, I guess,
      because it was impossible for us to remain longer in
      Budapest.
(e)   E2 And he came home, that he found such a way.

Use of the idiomatic verb phrase 'hold on to any straw' conveys not
just desperation, but also naivety, and hence an implicit recognition
that the plan may have been more far fetched – less credible, less
plausible – than the family wanted to admit. However, there is more
to it than that. Like formulaicity in general, the use of idiomatic
phrases symbolically connects the sentiment being conveyed in the
world of the experience to a fuller range of intertextual meanings
that imbue the phrase with meaning. The invocation of other contexts, other texts, and other voices thus move the sentiment away
from an evaluation internal to the action toward an evaluation external to the action – a reshuffling of perceptions from the immediacy
of experience to the mediation of reflection (cf. Bamberg 1991).

Laminating voices proceed still further in the 1995 texts. In the
1995a text in Example 6.6, voices from outside the story world
appear twice in an evaluative space between two event clauses.
Between finding the plan and resolution of an obstacle is a meta-
linguistic rhetorical question – *Now why Slovakia?* (line 4.) – asked

by a reflective voice that is assessing the logic of the plan from the interactional world.

Example 6.6
1995a
3. and for a fee uh they would take us back to Slovakia.
4. *Now why Slovakia?*
5. Part of it, a very small portion of it in the mountain areas, was liberated by the partisans,
6. And so when you have no place else to go, you go over . . . y'know you think maybe you will be safe for a little short time yet.

The rhetorical question *why Slovakia?* is marked by *now* as the next move in the interaction (Schiffrin 1987: Chapter 8), not the story world. The deictic shifts in line 6. away from the personal collective *we* of the story world (*us* in line 3.) to the indefinite, general *you*, and to the general present tense establish this implicitly causal pair (i.e. '*when* X, Y') as a general truth about how the lack of choices (*no place else to go*) forces one to lower one's hopes for permanent safety to a refuge *for a little short time yet.*

A laminating voice between event clauses also appears in the 1995b text, again introduced by a marker (*y'know*, Schiffrin 1987: Chapter 9) that locates the question in the interaction in Example 6.7:

Example 6.7
1995b
(A) E1 And my father went out to look for something for us to do,
(B) y'know, what would be the next step?
(C) There weren't many options.
(D) E2 And, as he went, he heard a story that today, I think your hair would stand up from disbelief,
(E) E3 but he swallowed it.

The family's belief in the possibility of a plan is explicitly challenged from outside the story world by the rhetorical question *what would be the next step?* (line (B)), whose answer (*there weren't many options*, line (C)), restricts the range of potential rhetorical responses. As the father ventures on his search, he hears *a story*, a genre that can include the potential falsehood of fiction. The story is explicitly evaluated by the standards of *today* (line (D)): *I think your hair would stand up from disbelief.* In addition to the intrusion from outside the story world created by the idiomatic *your hair would stand up*, two contrasts depend upon a world more current than the story world. The invocation of *today* contrasts then and now; the mention of disbelief contrasts with the epistemic stance in the story world. Despite the emerging preposterousness of the plan, then, the father did more than believe the *story* (line (D)): *he swallowed it* (line (E)), a verb that metaphorically conveys gullibility.

The strategies illustrated thus far manipulate, and expose the permeability of, the boundaries between the story world, the interaction world and the outer world. This boundary is further exploited by the way information is voiced, not only from outside the story world, but with formulaic expressions that have imported *ex post facto* language as an evaluative frame for story world events.

Permeability of the boundary between story and story telling world also appears in the use of meta-talk. As we noted in Chapter 1, a meta-lingual function is one of Jakobson's (1960) six functions of language: it focuses on the code (the language), rather than other components of the speech situation (speaker, hearer, or message).[8] A change in meta-talk across the four versions of Mrs. Beer's capture story shows another means of reframing experience.

In each of the four versions, partisans are a key part of the plan. In the 1982 text (Example 6.8), Mrs. Beer uses a pragmatic prototype (anchored to the prior location *Slovakia*) to introduce the brand new referent *partisans*. But her hesitation before the new referent suggests a problem and she then attributes the word to her husband:

Example 6.8
1982
(4) and who for a certain amount they'll take a group of Jews back to Slovakia
(5) You know there was already uh . . . what my husband says "partisans,"
(6) so, a very small part of Slovakia was liberated.

Since she was not married (and had not yet met Adam Beer, the man she would marry), neither she nor her father could have heard the word "partisans" from Adam Beer himself. Thus the word was imported from the time of speaking back to the time of the experience.

Post-1982 versions continue to refer to 'partisans,' but the pragmatic prototype and meta-linguistic marker of its source disappear:

Example 6.9

1984

(a) E1 And uh my father went next day,
    in search of a way to get us back to Czechoslovakia.

(b) Because some part of it was freed,

(c) the partisans freed it.

1995a

4. Now why Slovakia?

5. Part of it, a very small portion of it in the mountain areas,
   was liberated by the partisans,

1995b

(H) and they would take us back to Slovakia.

(I) Now, part of Slovakia was liberated by partisans, very small
    part of it.

'Partisans' reappear in the same slot in the story (immediately after the mention of Slovakia) with the same role (tied to the liberation of Slovakia and plan to return). What shifts along with its source, however, is its specificity. Whereas 'partisans' are introduced as a type identifiable indefinite (Chapter 4) in 1982 (Example 6.8), they become a definite in later versions (see Example 6.9): *the partisans* (1984, 1995a), the generic *partisans* (1995b). This change in definiteness is accompanied by a shift from assumption to assertion: in 1982 (Example 6.8), we infer through clause order and *so* (*so, a very small part of Slovakia was liberated*) that the partisans liberated Slovakia; in post-1982 texts (Example 6.9), it is asserted that they liberated or freed part of Slovakia. Thus, when Mrs. Beer's husband fades as the meta-linguistic source of the term *partisans*, the epistemic status of 'partisans' also changes: because the 'partisans' are assumed to exist, and their actions are asserted, they are more firmly grounded in the story world.

Meta-talk does reappear in the post-1982 texts, but elsewhere in the narrative and with different roles. Rather than attribute a source to words, it has broader organizational and evaluative functions (Schiffrin 1980). Meta-linguistic clauses bracket a variety of segments that are parts of the plan: a reason in 1995a, a next action in

1995b, a destination 1995b. These meta-linguistic brackets have referential and evaluative importance because they add an overall systematicity (and hence, credibility) to the plan. Other meta-linguistic commentary voices a specific stance (of skepticism) that evaluates the plan: *he heard a story that today, I think your hair would stand up from disbelief* (1995b).

We have seen in this section that idioms, metaphor and formulaicity import ways of speaking that entered Mrs. Beer's repertoire well after the experience itself. Meta-talk also enters from the outer world, or the story telling world, to organize and evaluate the story world, laminating it with external commentary.

6.4.3.3 *What we knew*

In this section, we turn to the representation of internal states as collective reactions. Although what we think, know or feel is not directly accessible to another person, the turning point of the capture story combines choral constructed dialogue (Tannen 1989) with the representation of an internal state: in each version of THE CAPTURE, the group of people hoping to be saved realize through *we knew/felt* that they have been caught. By comparing successive versions of the enactment of collective knowledge, we see the emergence of Mrs. Beer as co-figure, co-author and co-principal. These footings are facilitated by a laminator footing that exploits intratextual connections with reports of prior sensory experience to animate and author a collective realization to which all can be committed (as principal). The same constellation of footings guarantees audience recognition of what happened to the group and its significance.

Before beginning, however, it is important to note some features of THE CAPTURE in the 1982 story. Whereas the 1982 PLAN and ANTICIPATION followed a stanza-based narrative structure (few event clauses, thematic development through description (Chapter 7)), THE CAPTURE comprises a sequence of syntactically parallel event clauses, as shown in Figure 6.5.

The sequential structure of the 1982 CAPTURE differs from that of the earlier phases in which the plan to escape is described and anticipated. Each of the parallel structures of the five E-clauses typifies the simple syntax of a paradigmatic narrative clause (Labov 1972b). The use of *and* to link the parallel structures further unites the sequence of events and highlights a series of spatially grounded

		conjunction	subject	verb	phrase
E3	(31)	and	we	came	into this little park
E4	(32)	and	the flashlight	lit	into our eyes
E4?	(33)	and	we	knew	that's it
E5	(34)	and	they	kicked [us]	into the truck
E6	(35)	and	they	took [us]	to the Gestapo headquarters in Buda

Figure 6.5 THE CAPTURE (1982)

experiential transitions. The transition begins with a change in physical space (*into the park*), continues with perceptual space (*into* our vision) and mental space (what *we knew*), and ends with another shift in physical space (*into the truck, to the Gestapo headquarters*). The progression of these transitions without interruption iconically creates a sense of rapidity: all this happened quickly, one thing after another. The radical shift in the 1982 text (from descriptive stanza structure) in THE PLAN and ANTICIPATION to a linear structure in THE CAPTURE is also evaluative: by replicating the contrast between what was expected and what actually occurred, the change in textual structure of the story world iconically represents the schematic violation of the life-world.

Post-1982 versions of THE CAPTURE differ in several crucial ways that shift the overall mood of the capture from rapid change (e.g. 'this happened so fast that we barely knew what was going on') to cumulative chaos (e.g. 'so many confusing things were going on at once that we barely knew what was happening'). The locus of evaluation in post-1982 stories also shifts: rather than depend upon a textual contrast between stanza and linear structure, it relies upon syntactic complexity, relationships between adjacent clauses, and abstract reflective voices that make explicit the information critical to grasping the significance of the experience.

The shifting locus of contrast is concentrated in 'we knew X.' Central to this shift is the internal and private foundation of mental activity and the difficulty of projecting its 'content' onto a collective plane. As we see below, what compensates for gaps in group epistemology are intratextual ties that invoke both intersubjectivity and veracity. Figure 6.6 presents the different versions of what 'we knew.'

What the group *knew* in the 1982 text (*that's it*) established the completion of a prior experience and a transition to something quite

1982
and we knew
that's it

1984
and we knew right away
that we were....
y'know it was uh- a scheme,
to get us, to get the money,

1995a
and we felt
well if it's supposed
to be a secret mission,
how could there be spotlights?

1995b
and we knew right away
when
there's a secret mission
you don't turn flood lights
on.

Figure 6.6 What we knew

different. Despite its indexicality (because of the demonstrative and the pronoun), *that's it* serves as a coda without telling us anything specific about what it was in that experience that provided closure. The post-1982 versions of what *we knew* replace the indexicality of the 1982 *that's it* with more complex relations of intratextuality that create representations of what the group *knew/felt*. By relying upon prior text, and inferences based upon and drawn from it, these representations clarify for the listener the disruption of the plans and the duplicitous intentions of the group's supposed rescuers.

In the 1984 text, a straightforward manifestation of intratextuality – repetition – pervades the capture story. Notice, first, that the predicates in each clause repeat *were*:

(r)		we	were coming
(s)		flashlights	were lit
(t)		we	were kicked
(u) we knew right away that	we	were . . .

The repetition of *were*, especially the passive *were* ((t), (u)), initially provides a syntactic frame for what the group *knew* in 'we knew X' (line (u)). Rather than continue the syntactic pattern (e.g. 'we were caught'), however, Mrs. Beer switches to a more global strategy that both draws upon, and provides, more information about the rupture of the plan.

1984 (u)   E4 we knew right away that we were . . .
     (v)   y'know it was uh- a scheme,
          to get us, *[Right]* to get the money,

After the self repair from *we were, y'know* to mark shared knowledge (Schiffrin 1987: Chapter 9) and a brief word search (*uh-*), Mrs. Beer redefines the plan as *a scheme* with two goals: *to get us, to get the money.* The term *scheme* is important: it lexicalizes the inferred disjunction between the anticipated plan and the actual plan, juxtaposing prior expectation against duplicity. This contrast reifies a crucial shift in perspective on the arrangements reported in earlier phases of the story: it incorporates the alternative teleological structure underlying the arrangements and anticipated actions. Thus a perspective that had not been arranged and previewed in earlier parts of the longer story is incorporated into the group's realization and simultaneously labeled for the audience.

Also intratextually based are the goals of the *scheme*. What the group now *knew* contrasts with two prior aspects of the plan: the father's goal and the 'fee.' The 1984 text opened with the father's goal: *And uh my father went next day, in search of a way to get us back to Czechoslovakia.* Whereas the father's goal is to *get us* home, the goal of the *scheme* is to *get us* (v). Earlier phases of the story also mentioned that a 'fee' was a requirement for the Wehrmacht's help: *and they want to help us escape on their truck and this would cost money.* Rather than use the *money* to help the group escape (h), the Wehrmacht want to *get the money* (v). Thus the *scheme* and the captors' goals both draw upon intratextually based contrasts: repetition and lexicalization reconfigure the prior *arrangements* as a *scheme* with very different goals than those presented in earlier parts of the story.

What 'we knew' in the 1995 texts becomes more complex both formally and functionally. Both 1995 versions draw upon

(1) performance features of constructed dialogue,
(2) repetition between constructed dialogue and prior text,
(3) syntactic, semantic and pragmatic features within the constructed dialogue, and
(4) repetition between constructed dialogue and posterior text.

The content of the constructed dialogue in 'we knew X' of the 1995 texts uses syntax, semantics and pragmatics to provide critical textual routes to the important evaluative contrast between expectation and actuality. Both texts use preposed clauses (conditional (1995a), temporal (1995b)) that provide 'given' information (Ward and Birner 2001) or 'topic' (Schiffrin 1991) to report information that is already common ground or intended to be treated as such. This information becomes a background against which 'new' information or a 'comment' is foregrounded.

Consistent with their informational role, both the *if* clause (1995a) and the *when* clause (1995b) present the group's *prior* understanding of the plan. Rather than reify what the plans are now known to have been (i.e. *a scheme* (1984)), the plan is firmly situated in the group's initial perspective through present tense stative predicates ((*it's supposed to be* (1995a) and *there's* (1995b)) and the noun phrase *a secret mission*. Yet evidence has been accruing (the shining lights) that this perspective cannot be sustained. Indeed, this conception of the plan is counter-factual: the proposition 'this is a secret mission' is one that Mrs. Beer (along with the others in *we*) do not then believe to be true. The counter-factuality of 'this is a secret mission' is established through sentence form and meaning, intratextual relations, and an assumption of shared knowledge. Consider, first, the typical connection inferable between the preposed and postposed clauses: a cause/result in the conditional 'if X, Y' (1995a) and temporal 'when X, Y' (1995b).[9] In a statement such as 'if/when there's a secret mission, people travel clandestinely,' for example, we would infer that a secret mission leads to, or results in, clandestine travel. Notice, however, the relationship between 'X' and 'Y' in the 1995 texts is quite the opposite: *And we felt well if it's supposed to be a secret mission, how could there be spotlights* (1995a, line (25)); *And we knew right away when there's a secret mission you don't turn flood lights on.* (1995b, line (AA)) is quite the opposite. In brief, Mrs. Beer states that a secret mission does *not* entail bright lights.

Contributing to the cancellation of the cause/result inference between 'secret mission' and 'lights' are linguistic form and meaning. Because existence of a secret mission has been posed as background information, whatever appears in the following clause is assessed in relation to that context. The following clause reveals doubt about the compatibility of the foregrounded 'shining lights' with the backgrounded 'secret mission.' The rhetorical question *how could there be spotlights?* (1995a) questions the possibility of lights. The declarative *you don't turn floodlights on* (1995b) negates the use of lights and gains generality through indefinite *you* and the present tense. Lexical repetition in the foregrounded clauses also contributes to the dismantling of the inference. Repetition of *spotlights* (1995a) and *floodlights* (1995b) recalls their appearance in the group's initial perception of their capture (*we see spotlights* (1995a, line (24.))), *there were big flood lights* (1995b, line (Z)). Repetition thus ties the cognitive grounding of the capture to the already presented perceptual evidence.

As important as language is for conveying counter-factuality, so too, is our knowledge of the world. Two internal relations are critical if a group of people is to rely upon secrecy as its form of existence:

> The first internal relation ... is the reciprocal confidence among its members. It is required to a particularly great extent, because the purpose of secrecy is above all, protection (Simmel, 1950: 345, italics in original).

Both confidence and protection are crucial to the relationship between the group and their supposed rescuers. Earlier parts of the story established that the family has confidence in the other 'members' of the secret society, i.e. the renegade German soldiers (Schiffrin 2003). It is precisely the need for protection that is so sharply violated by the sensory experience of the lights that *were lit* (1982), *aiming at us* (1995a) and *turning on us* (1995b). As Simmel (p. 345) points out, "of all protective measures, the most radical is to make oneself invisible." By publicly illuminating those – the hopeful escapees – who had so crucial a stake in invisibility, the lights shatter the presumption of solidarity between the escapees and their purported rescuers: far from sharing a secret, the potential escapees have been deceived and betrayed by their supposed rescuers. Thus, the group's prior perspective is dismantled in the 1995 texts. The increasing scope of the lights that targeted the group has reappeared in what they now know: perceptual experience has provided the warrant through which to infer the counter-factuality of 'this is a secret mission.'

The inference that the plan is null and void is further validated by repetition, negatives, and contrast in an affirm/deny/affirm sequence that asserts the duplicity underlying the rescue plan:

		1995a	1995b	
			(BB)	But we couldn't run away anymore,
AFFIRM	26.	well of course <u>we were taken,</u>	(CC)	<u>we were caught</u>
DENY	27.	you know *it was no mission,*	(DD)	And *it was no mission* of rescue.
AFFIRM	28.	*it was a mission* <u>to take us,</u>	(EE)	*It was a mission* <u>that we were caught</u> in

First, the capture is affirmed through concrete actions taken upon the group (*we were taken* (1995a, line (26.)), *we were caught* (1995b, line (CC)). Next, the validity of the prior schema is explicitly denied through negation (*it was no mission* (1995a, line (27.), 1995b, line

(DD)). Third, the true goals of the captors are reaffirmed (1995a, line (28.), 1995b, line (EE)). In both 1995 texts, the affirmations are locally cohesive through repetition (underlined above). The switch in polarity from denial to affirmation is also strengthened through repetition (italics above). The violation of expectation is thus conveyed not only inferentially as an internal evaluation: it is also concretized through a sequence that explicitly asserts the rupture of expectation.

The changes in 'we knew X' mark not only a shift in the role of collective knowledge in the capture story, locus of contrast and source of voicing, but also a shift in presumption of mutual knowledge. Those who hear the story – including not only the interviewer, but also the potentially broad and anonymous audience for the publicly accessible oral history – do not know at its outset how the plan will actually turn out. The capture in the post-1982 texts thus makes explicit the contradiction between the plans of the group (what was expected) and the plans of the captors (what actually occurred). This clarity positions the audience not only to grasp what happened, but also to understand the significance of the experience for Mrs. Beer and the group.

A cluster of actions after the *we knew* realization further establishes the authenticity of the group's change in epistemic status by grounding it in a world of physical experience:

1982	1984	1995a	1995b
			And they hit us,
And they kicked us,	and we were kicked	and they kicked us	kicked us into the truck,
		and beat us,	beat us up
		and that's how we ended up	
into the truck	into the truck	in the truck	

In sum, we have seen that what 'we knew' is a collective reaction from a collective figure (*we*) whose prior sensory experience warranted their joint commitment to a new realization. Adjacent text added external validity to reported knowledge. In the 1995 texts, the inference 'this is not a secret mission' relied not only upon linguistic form, meaning, and world knowledge about secret missions, but also a prior experience in the story world (*we see spotlights aiming at us* (1995a, line (24.)), *there were big floodlights turning on us* (1995b, line (Z))) and a cluster of posterior physical actions.

Although what we think, know or feel is not directly accessible to another person, then, the turning point in Mrs. Beer's capture story represents a collective internal state: the group of people hoping to be saved realize through *we knew/felt* that they are caught. Both prior text, and inferences based on world knowledge (about rescue and secrecy), combine to represent collective knowledge in the laminating voice of co-figure, co-author and co-principal. The footings guarantee audience recognition of what happened to the group and its significance: multiple sources of evidence come together in a stance that guarantees the veracity of being captured and clarifies for an audience their recognition of what happened.

6.4.4 Summary

In this section, we have analyzed how one speaker transformed experiences with varying sources into a narrative and how those sources were re-framed in successive retellings of the same story. Changes in the story suggest that Mrs. Beer became a co-figure, co-author, and co-principal. In her retelling of THE PLAN (a speech event) the factual world receded and the interior and exterior story worlds merged, reflecting a co-authorship between Mrs. Beer and her father, who had heard the plan and transmitted it to his daughter. The sensory experience underlying THE CAPTURE was reframed as evidence for collective knowledge, thus creating a co-commitment to the reliability of events and a co-principal. Collective knowledge was not only grounded in three sites of sensory experience (visual, cognitive, physical): it was also reaffirmed through a laminator's contrast between what the plan was supposed to be and what it turned out to be. Both changes allowed an outer world laminator to comment on the experience by initially conveying skepticism about the plan and then affirming the duplicity underlying the plan.

The overall trajectory of the changes suggests that each primary initial source of 'what happened' merged with Mrs. Beer's own experience with 'what happened,' including in the latter, Mrs. Beer's own experience of telling and retelling the story. Information with low reliability (THE PLAN recounted by her father) in the first telling became less credible in retellings, while information with high reliability (THE CAPTURE involving direct physical sensations) in the first telling became more credible in retellings. In other words, the successive re-authoring of *another's* experience intensified its questionable veracity, perhaps based on recurrent tellings of its *ex post facto* outcome. What happened became more and more open to doubt, just like the "whispering down the lane" game mentioned earlier. But retellings and successive re-animations intensified the *un*questionable veracity of one's *own* experience: the epistemic status of what happened became more and more certain as the experience and its retelling became repeatedly grounded in the subjectivity of the narrator's own life and its telling.

6.5 Conclusion: 'self', 'other', language and experience

In this chapter, we have analyzed how experience from different sources is framed and reframed in narrative. Given the inherent multivocality of oral histories, the incorporation of another's experience into oral history narratives should not be surprising and may indeed have a positive effect on memory culture. We are beginning to learn, for example, how iconic narratives (Schiff, Noy and Cohler 2001) and emblematic characters (Schiff and Noy (in press)) can be seamlessly incorporated into Holocaust narratives, especially if they help to consolidate and project idiosyncratic features of one's own experience into schemas that will be more familiar to a large and heterogeneous audience with little knowledge of the Holocaust.

As we observed at the outset of this chapter, however, Holocaust oral histories have a role not only in public memorial, but also in private lives and life stories. Here other questions about the value of incorporating 'other' experience into one's own story arises. Can collective or historical themes become ways of making sense of one's own life experience over time? Does the experience of another contribute to one's own sense-making, especially if one's own life includes experiences (e.g. catastrophes, genocide) that standard templates and schemas cannot easily accommodate? Does the distance of another's experience make it easier to recount than one's own experience? If so, could that lead more quickly toward the redemptive function of narrative hoped for by therapists? And could presenting the past as an author and animator firmly grounded in 'now' rather than 'then' ease (or exacerbate) the continuous struggles to integrate the self of past experience with the self of current existence?

Although there seem to be good reasons for including another's experience in one's own story, there are also risks. One risk is that the 'other' for whom the experience is primary may not welcome the use of their own experience in another's story (cf. conflict over *concentration camps* discussed in Chapter 5) or the way it is transformed for another's purpose or animated through another's style. Such dilemmas of rights, privileges and responsibilities appear throughout discourse from everyday 'speaking for another' (Schiffrin 1993) to community narratives and knowledge (Silverstein and Urban 1996, Roth 2002).

The importance of an authenticity that can derive only from direct experience has been expressed by Holocaust writers and scholars. Elie Wiesel (quoted in Marrus 1987: 2–3) has repeatedly stressed the limits to our efforts to understand the Holocaust: "Auschwitz defies imagination and perception; it submits only to memory. Between the dead and the rest of us there exists an abyss that no talent can comprehend." Langer (1991) argues that it is the voices of individual survivors who try to retell their experiences through the traditional tools of verbal narrative – and the failures of those forms to do so – that best capture the total chaos and disruption wrought upon individual lives by the Holocaust. And it is these same voices that have become so powerful a commemorative tool for those who want to learn not only about historical truth, but also about psychological truth. As Hartman (1996: 135) observes, "the conviction has grown that local knowledge, which speaks from inside a situation rather than from the outside in an objectifying manner, can provide a texture of truth that eludes those who adopt a prematurely unified voice."

In the next chapter, we analyze a set of changes in Susan Beer's capture story that illustrate not only the reframing of differently grounded experiences, but the restructuring and re-evaluation of experience. Both sets of changes will suggest that the telling of a story provides "local knowledge, which speaks from inside a situation" (Hartman 1996: 135) and that each telling then provides a subjective basis from which to represent what happened not just from "inside a situation," but also from inside *a story* whose underlying structure has become integrated into one's own narrative competence and whose telling has become part of one's own experience.

Notes

1. The Center for Advanced Holocaust Study (at the United States Holocaust Memorial Museum, Washington DC) and a Senior Faculty Research Fellowship (Georgetown University) provided material and symbolic support for research leading to the analyses in Chapters 6, 7 and 8. I am grateful to both. I also thank the Cleveland Alliance for Jewish Women, the USHMM and the Shoah Foundation for permission to cite excerpts from the 1984 and 1995 interviews with Susan Beer. I thank Bonnie Gurewitsch (Museum of Jewish Heritage, New York) for permission to use material from her 1982 interview with Susan Beer.

2. On institutional levels, politicians compete to establish their versions of the past so that they can use them as templates within which to enhance their chances of establishing their stories of, and for, the future. On more everyday and personal levels, teenagers establish elaborate metrics whereby they can decide who may tell what story during breaks between classes (Shuman 1986). Siblings struggle to gain the right to tell stories about daily events at the dinner table – stories for which parents may then supply the moral point (Blum-Kulka 1997, Ochs et al. 1991).

3. In this sense, life story narratives are similar to institutional narratives that can be retold by members of the institution whose arrival postdated the actual events.

4. As I understand Davies and Harré (1990), positioning is a discursive process at PL-3: "people are located in conversations as observably and subjectively coherent participants in jointly produced storylines" (1990: 37). Whatever alignments result are "actual relations jointly produced in the very act of conversing" (1990: 45).

5. The verbs frame, key and laminate are sometimes difficult to differentiate in Goffman (1974). Whereas re-keying maintains the same basic structure, but transforms its meaning, re-framing can alter both meaning and structure. Laminate can also transform meaning, but in a slightly different way: by adding another frame (e.g. from the outside, akin to another layer) through which the original can still be viewed. I build upon the slightly different sense of laminate in later analysis.

6. Although some authors include the linguistic marking of attachment or skepticism (as in Biber and Finegan's (1994) analyses of adverbial stance) or the display of an affective position toward an interlocutor or current topic (Wu 2004), the former can also be viewed as positioning (PL-1) and the latter as interpersonal alignment (included as a possibility within 'footing') or positioning (PL-2 and PL-3).

7. This is not to say that we learn nothing about the factual world – just that we do not know who bears responsibility for that information.

8. A wide range of meta-linguistic forms appears in ordinary sites of language use (e.g. meta-linguistic referents, meta-linguistic operators, and

meta-linguistic verbs), See Schiffrin 1980 for discussion of these groups and how they serve as both organizational and evaluative brackets in discourse.

9. In the conditional, the cause/result is semantically inferable; in the temporal, it is pragmatically inferable through a principle of informativeness.

Retelling a story

7.1 Introduction

In the previous chapter, we analyzed how four versions of a single story from one speaker reframed what were initially very different sources of experience into one story. Here we focus on structural and evaluative changes in the same story. To recapitulate the content: Susan Beer and her family (Jews from Slovakia) had escaped persecution at home in Budapest, Hungary. As anti-Semitic measures intensified there (with mass deportations to Auschwitz spreading from rural communities to cities), Mrs. Beer's father learned of an escape plan in which German soldiers would return Slovakian nationals to a part of Slovakia freed by partisans. The plan turns out to be a trap: the family is captured, imprisoned, and then sent to Auschwitz.

We begin by observing that all four versions of Mrs. Beer's story provide basically the same information, although the form in which they do so differs (Section 7.2). The main portion of the chapter analyzes the structural and evaluative changes from a stanza (theme-based) to linear (event-based) narrative. After analyzing changes in Phase 1, THE PLAN and Phase 2, ANTICIPATION (Section 7.3), and then Phase 3, THE CAPTURE (Section 7.4), my summary brings together the re-framing and retelling of Susan Beer's story (Section 7.5).

7.2 Overview of stability and change

In this section, I provide an overview of what stays the same in the four versions of Mrs. Beer's story (Section 7.2.1) and the structural changes (Section 7.2.2). Space prevents the presentation of the four versions in their entirety (but see Appendix 2 for the complete texts).

Initiation	Father makes arrangements to escape
Outset	Rabbi blesses the family
Caught-1	Perception: the lights shine
Caught-2	Cognitive: we knew [X]
Caught-3	Physical: kicked into truck
Closure	Group is taken to Gestapo headquarters

Figure 7.1 What happens

7.2.1 Stability in the four versions

Six events recur in Mrs. Beer's retellings, as listed in Figure 7.1. The recurrent events form two sets: those that frame the plan (Initiation, Outset, Closure), and those that reveal the violation of the expectations for escape (*Caught-1, 2, 3*).

Comparisons of the four versions of Mrs. Beer's story show that Initiation, Outset and Closure are more stable than the three Capture events. In addition to establishing a skeletal time line and plot, these three events also have broader functions within Mrs. Beer's life story. Initiation establishes a precondition for the family's escape from Budapest. But the fact that it is Mrs. Beer's *father* who makes the plan connects this event to an intertextual theme in her life story in which she recurrently positions her father as caregiver and provider. Outset is a formal closure to the family's stay in Budapest and a preface to their actual effort to escape. Like the father's Initiation, the Rabbi's blessing at the outset of their planned escape also evokes intertextual themes: religious faith (its loss and maintenance) and the web of reciprocity that provided concrete help for Mrs. Beer throughout her ordeals. The last recurrent event Closure begins a major transition in the family's life. Rather than manage to evade and escape the measures taken against them, they are caught in the machinery of the Final Solution: the truck ride to the Gestapo prison is followed by a train to Auschwitz. Thus Closure is both immediate *and* far-ranging: what closes are both the hopes of immediate respite and the family's ability to continue avoiding the Nazis. In contrast to the global functions, Caught *1, 2* and *3* work more locally within the capture story to disrupt the schema previously established by the plan to escape. They have a central evaluative role in the story: this is the vortex at which the 'point' of the story is concentrated.

7.2.2 Overview of structural changes

Before detailed analysis of how the six main events are retold, it is helpful to preview the overall changes in the stories. In the 1982 version, THE PLAN and ANTICIPATION are recounted in a stanza style (Gee 1989). In stanza-based narratives, the speaker recursively builds up a theme, whose links are based on form (e.g. parallelisms) and/or content (e.g. repetition, paraphrase). Between the recursive thematic development is information that comments upon, elaborates and provides a framework within which to understand the theme. THE PLAN and ANTICIPATION in the 1982 text contribute to a theme of escape. Between the first event (Initiation) and the second event (Outset) are lengthy descriptions and explanations that reinforce the escape plan by establishing its necessity, credibility and plausibility. The final phase, CAPTURE, in the 1982 text has a very different structure: the capture is recounted in a linear structure, identifiable through relationships of temporal juncture between events.

Post-1982 versions of all three phases are uniformly recounted in a linear structure. THE PLAN and ANTICIPATION recount events in temporal order. Lengthy descriptions and explanations that appeared in the 1982 text are condensed or removed. Thus the textual contrast between what was expected (freedom) and what actually occurred (capture) is no longer textually marked.

Two interrelated distinctions are relevant to analyzing and understanding the structural changes: event vs. non-event clause; dependent vs. independent clause. Consider, first, the traditional definition of independent clauses (subject/verb structures that are complete, bounded syntactic units) and dependent clauses (subject/verb structures attached to or embedded in another clause). In Labov's model, independent clauses with temporal juncture (i.e. textual order matches their inferred order of occurrence) are the basic unit of narrative: they are critical to the establishment of 'what happened when.' It is these independent clauses – with temporal juncture within the main story line – that I will call *event clauses* (abbreviated as E, with a number indicating place in the linear order, in transcripts); other independent clauses are non-event clauses.[1]

Non-event independent clauses (e.g. *it was late at night*) and dependent clauses (e.g. *when it was late at night, . . .*) can serve some of the same informational functions. Clauses that present information about time, cause, result and conditions, for example, are often evaluative: they can provide information (e.g. background occurrences, reasons, comparisons) that not only elaborates adjacent events (Labov 1972b), but also temporarily halts (or otherwise alters) the flow of narrative time. These sections (what Labov (1972b) calls "embedded orientations") suspend the action and build in the audience an anticipation for what will come next. But non-event independent clauses and dependent clauses can also have different functions. Whereas the position of dependent clauses (preposed or postposed to a main clause) can reflect different information statuses at both sentential and textual levels, non-event independent clauses can assert information that contributes to digressions or sub-stories.

We start with the distribution of event clauses (clauses with temporal juncture within the main story line) in the different phases of the four versions of Mrs. Beer's story. Figure 7.2 presents absolute and relative frequencies of event clauses and non-event independent clauses. Percentages of event clauses are out of all independent clauses in the phase of the story and the year.

Since event clauses provide the basic template of temporally ordered actions in the story, the numbers in Figure 7.2 tell us whether there is more or less narrative action over time. A glance at the totals shows, for example, that the 1995 versions have more event clauses than the 1984 version, with the fewest in the 1982 version. Yet there is also an important difference by phase: whereas event clauses in Phases I and II increase steadily from 1982 to 1995b, they diminish in Phase III. As we see in subsequent sections, the reasons for these changes differ: the increase over time in event clauses in THE PLAN reflects the absence of earlier digressions and sub-stories; the varying presence of event clauses in ANTICIPATION is related to a shift in information and boundaries; the relative decrease in event clauses in THE CAPTURE reflects the addition of external evaluation clauses.

Still another pattern in Figure 7.2 emerges from an examination of relative frequencies within each version, across the different phases. In the 1982 text, we see a striking imbalance in the percentage of event clauses in each phase: whereas 9% of the independent clauses were event clauses in THE PLAN, and 0% in ANTICIPATION, 80% of the independent clauses in THE CAPTURE were

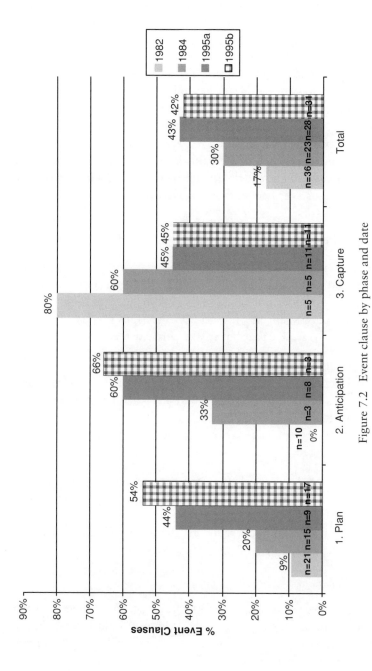

Figure 7.2 Event clause by phase and date

event clauses. Although increasing proportions of event clauses also appear over the phases in the 1984 text (20% ➔ 33% ➔ 60%), the proportions across phases level out in the 1995 texts: 44% ➔ 60% ➔ 45% (1995a); 54% ➔ 66% ➔ 45% (1995b). Thus, event clauses not only increase over time: they are also more evenly distributed among the different phases of the capture story.

In sum the overall structural change from stanza (1982) to linear (post-1982) narrative depends upon the presence of event clauses. We have seen a leveling over time across the different phases of Mrs. Beer's story: each phase gains a linear structure. In the next two sections, we examine the change from stanza to linear structure and the evaluative changes that accompany it.

7.3 Retelling 'the plan' and 'anticipation'

In this section, we discuss structural and evaluative changes in THE PLAN and ANTICIPATION together. Both phases combine to provide an orientation to THE CAPTURE. Also, a key part of the 1982 ANTICIPATION appears in post-1982 versions of THE PLAN. In Section 7.3.1, we see that linear structure emerges as

(1)   events are dissected into sub-events;
(2)   dependent clauses are dropped or changed to independent clauses that can be sequentially arranged to show temporal order;
(3)   descriptive passages with non-event clauses are dropped or re-ordered.

In Section 7.3.2, we see that linear structure is accompanied by an altered means of evaluation in which multiple voices (a laminator footing, Chapter 6) comment from the 'outer' world upon events. In Section 7.3.3, I turn to the reduction of information in the ANTICIPATION phase. Section 7.3.4 summarizes.

7.3.1 Events in 'the plan'

Two main events recur in THE PLAN; an accomplishment ('make plans'); a transmittal of information (both in **bold** below). In the 1982 text, Mrs. Beer begins with her father's *arrangements* in one event clause, shown in Example 7.1.

Example 7.1

1982

(1) **E1** During the day my father made . . . or maybe not even a
         whole- just during the day . . . he **made arrangements,**

(2)   **someone told him** of a German Wehrmacht . . .

Since to 'make' something is an accomplishment predicate, **E1** presumes the completion of an action. What follows this action is a
quotative (*someone told him*, line (2)) that frames the recounting of
the escape plan for which the father had arranged.

   In Example 7.2, from 1984, the father leaves home with a goal
(**E1** in line (a)) and then returns home having accomplished the goal
(**E2** in line (e)). Although **E1** and **E2** are separated by two additional
clauses (that describe reasons for going, Appendix 2), their relationship is established in several ways: the deictic opposition between
'go' and 'come,' the aspectual relation between inceptive 'search'
and completive 'find,' the repetition of *a way*, the anaphoric *such
a way* (line (e)) tying back to the initial search for *a way* (line (a)),
and ellipsis of *to get back to Czechoslovakia* (line (a)).

Example 7.2

1984

(a) **E1** And uh my father went next day,
         in search of a way to get us back to Czechoslovakia.

(e) **E2** And he came home, that he found such a way.

Notice that the focus on the outset (*went*) and the return (*came*),
however, overshadows the arrangements and the act of transmittal:
found such a way presents the accomplishment of 'making plans'
and, also, prefaces the details of those plans.

   In subsequent versions, the communicative act between Mrs.
Beer's father and whoever informed him of the plans is presented
prior to the completion of the arrangements. By prefacing the
arrangements with temporally prior events, Beer thus 'unpacks' the
accomplishment to include other events that describe the process of
reaching towards completion.

   In Example 7.3, from the 1995a text, Mrs. Beer begins with her
father's discovery of the plan (*he heard*), but then self-interrupts to
backtrack to the more preliminary action of going out *among people
some place* (**E1** in line 1.):

Example 7.3
1995a

    E2 he heard-

1.   **E1** he went among people some place,
2.   **E2** and he **heard** that there are some army personnel, with an army truck,
15. **E3** And he **made arrangements** that that evening [continues]

Although Beer's father hears the plan (**E2**, line 2.), it is not until after the plan has been detailed (see the 13 clauses between lines 2. and 15. in Appendix 2) and evaluated in a mini-narrative that the arrangements are completed: *and he made arrangements* (**E3**, line 15.). Thus the arrangements are not completed until 14 lines after their initiation.

    In Example 7.4 from the 1995b version, Mrs. Beer's father again undertakes a quest complete with outset and goal:

Example 7.4
1995b

(A)   **E1** And my father went out to look for something for us to do,

(B)   y'know, what would be the next step?

(C)   There weren't many options.

(D)   **E2** And, as he went, he **heard** a story that today,
          I think your hair would stand up from disbelief,

(E)   **E3** but he **swallowed** it.

Three event clauses appear in Example 7.4: inception (*went out*, line (A)), discovery (*heard*, line (D)) and acceptance (*swallowed it*, line (E)). Thus the *Initiation* of THE PLAN – making the arrangements – is broken down into three interrelated events.

    As we turn from the arrangements to the plan itself, we see that included in each version of THE PLAN are details of the mission. In Example 7.5 from the 1982 text, the details occupy no independent clauses at all. Rather, all clauses are appended to *a German Wehrmacht* (line (2)):

Example 7.5
1982

(2)   someone told him of a German Wehrmacht . . .

(3) I don't know how many, were sick and tired of the Germans, who want to return to civilian life

(4) and who for a certain amount they'll take a group of Jews back to Slovakia.

After introducing the Wehrmacht, Beer pauses, and then parenthetically qualifies her knowledge of *how many* Wehrmacht *were sick and tired of the Germans* (line (3)). This affective state ('be sick and tired of') provides a reason for the Wehrmacht's participation in the mission. Mrs. Beer then presents 3 critical pieces of information about the plan. The way she does so, however, does not assign them the status (through either syntax or intonation) of separate idea units. Rather, the information is presented by conjoining two relative clauses (whose head noun remains *a German Wehrmacht*) that describe what the Wehrmacht want, what they require, and what the mission will accomplish.

In Example 7.6 the 1984 text, similar information appears, but in two independent clauses:

Example 7.6
1984
(e) **E2** And he came home, that he found such a way.
(f)   That there is a German Wehrmacht truck
(g)   and some German Wehrmacht, who are tired of being Wehrmacht,
(h)   and they want to help us escape on their truck.
(i)   And this would cost money,

Mrs. Beer introduces the information about the plan (beginning with the German Wehrmacht and their truck) as the complement of *found such a way* (line (e), i.e. *to get us back to Czechoslovakia*, inferable through line (a)). As in 1982, the physical state 'be tired of' appears as a relative clause (line (g)). The Wehrmacht's goal (line (h)), however, is presented as an independent clause with the more agentive subject pronoun *they* rather than the relative pronoun *who* (cf. 1982). Likewise, the fee is introduced in its own separate clause (line (i)).

In Example 7.7 from 1995a, we again find the Wehrmacht (i.e. *army personnel*) and their *truck* opening the plans (line 2.).

Example 7.7

1995a

2.   **E2** and he heard that there are some army personnel, with an
     army truck, who are getting to be very disillusioned with
     being in the German army,

3.   and for a fee uh they would take us back to Slovakia.

The reason for the Wehrmacht's interest in the mission still appears
in a relative clause. But the affective state (*are sick and tired* (1982),
are tired (1984)) has become an inceptive: *getting to be very disillusioned*. By adding a starting point to a state, the underlying reason
for the mission begins to resemble an event. The fee still appears in
a prepositional phrase (line 3). The goal of the mission, however,
appears in its own clause.

   Example 7.8, the 1995b version of the plan, has the most elaborate configuration of independent clauses. The section opens as the
plans are grouped together and labeled generically as *the story* (line
(F)):

Example 7.8

1995b

(F)   And the story was that there are some German Army
      Officers, or Army personnel, who are disillusioned with the
      army life
(G)   and they have their German army truck
(H)   and they would take us back to Slovakia.
(I)   Now, part of Slovakia was liberated by partisans, very small
      part of it.
(J)   And that was where we were going to go.
(K)   Of course, it cost a lot of money

In keeping with the textual label of story – which entails a beginning, middle and end – the characters are introduced (*some German
Army officers, or Army personnel* (line (F)) and briefly described
(*disillusioned with the army life* (line (F)). Their ownership of a
truck appears as an independent clause (*they have their German
army truck* (line (G)) whose sequential location licenses the inference
that this is what enables the mission (*and they would take us back
to Slovakia* (line (H)). After briefly leaving this mini-story world
(with *now* (Schiffrin 1987: Chapter 8)) to explain why Slovakia is a

feasible destination (line (I)), Mrs. Beer uses a mini-coda (*and that was where we were going to go* (line (J))) to link Slovakia with the impending actualization of the plan. The fee (line (K)) follows the coda, also in its own clause.

We have seen, thus far, two changes in the event structure of THE PLAN: what had initially been represented as the father's accomplishment becomes a process; dependent clauses reporting the Wehrmacht's expected actions become independent clauses. Additional changes are the development of temporal order in the cousin's sub-story and a complication in the plot (the fee) that adds an event (the recruitment of participants in the plan).

Consider, first, how a change in event structure stems from the story roles of Mrs. Beer's cousin. In all four versions of Mrs. Beer's capture story, the cousin has two roles: the loss of her family helps explain her willingness to join the supposed rescue plan; it also highlights the dangerous situation that necessitates the family's participation in the plan. Both of these story roles emerge in a short sub-story in which dependent clauses partially shift to independent clauses and begin to appear in temporal order. The following notation helps us see these changes. T (for time) indicates temporal order in the cousin's sub-story. When T is embedded in the story world in which the arrangements are made, **T** is bolded. If the reference time is outside (either before or after) the story world, I do not bold T. When T is prior to the story world, i.e. within the cousin's sub-story, I italicize *T* and include numerical subscripts. The lower the number, the earlier the reference time: *T1, T2* moves time forward; *T2, T1* moves time backward.

In Example 7.9, from the 1982 text, we see one independent clause (*the countryside was already taken*) and numerous dependent (temporal, causal, relative, complement) clauses. This clausal configuration contributes to an interplay among different reference times, as well as multi-directional movements within the time line of the cousin's sub-story:

Example 7.9
  1982

  (12)   and by the time he made these arrangements   **E1 T**
         which was in June,
         they- the countryside was already taken.   *T1*

(13)   Because my cousin said   *T3*
       the reason she wanted to actually uh . . .   *T2*
       she let herself be talked into going with us,   *T2*
       the one who's now in Switzerland,   *T*
       because her family was already gone.   *T1*

The cousin's sub-story in 1982 (Example 7.9) serves as an explanation for why she joined the mission The initial motivating event
(*T1*) is first presented in general terms (*the countryside was already
taken* (line (12)) and then paraphrased in more specific terms (*her
family was already gone* (line (13)) at the close of the sub-story. After
the earliest occurrence (the general taking of *the countryside (T1)*),
the text jumps to the most recent occurrence, the cousin's report of
her reason for participating in the plan (*T3*), retracts to the temporally prior reason itself (*T2*), includes an occurrence completely
outside of the story world (*the one who's now in Switzerland* (T)),
and then retracts again to the earliest occurrence, the specific loss of
her family (T1).

  Although temporal reference also shifts backward in the 1984
version (Example 7.10) of the cousin's sub-story, the time line itself
is linear:

Example 7.10
  1984

(j)   E3 So he got my cousin,   **E3 T**
         the- the ones whose sister I took the name,   T
(k)   and by then her parents
         and everyone else was taken to camp already,   *T1*
(l)   so she was the only . . . survivor in her family,   *T2*

The segment in Example 7.10 also opens with a story world event
(*he got my cousin* (j)) and includes descriptive information about
the cousin that is outside of the story world itself. The regression
of time begins with an independent clause at *T1* and proceeds to
another independent clause at *T2*. The fate of Mrs. Beer's cousin's
parents (specific) *and everyone else* (general) is combined into one
structure (line (k)) that is the first event within the cousin's sub-story.
The loss of the cousin's family results in (note *so*) in her status as
the only . . . survivor in her family (line (l), *T2*).

The linear structures of both 1995 texts parallel that of the 1984 text. In the 1995a text, Mrs. Beer follows a story world event (Example 7.11, line 10.) with a description of her cousin that includes the cousin's loss (*T1*). This loss is separated into two clauses: first, her specific loss (line 11.) and, next, the general loss (line 12.). The consequence of the loss (*T2*) – the cousin's solitary status as *the only one* (line 13.) – appears in an independent clause.

Example 7.11
1995a

10.	**E4** so we got my cousin	**E4**	**T**
	who lived in Budapest by then too, hiding,		T
11.	because already her family was taken from this small town,		*T1*
12.	all the families were taken,		*T1*
13	so she was the only one,		*T2*

In (1995b), the story world event is in line (N), the specific loss in line (P), the general loss in line (Q) and the consequence of the loss in line (R) (see Example 7.12):

Example 7.12
1995b

(N)	**E6** He got forty four people in all,	**E6**	**T**
(O)	among them was my cousin, the one that I slept in her house when I first escaped.		T
(P)	And her family by then was already taken away		*T1*
(Q)	because from small towns they took families earlier		*T1*
(R)	and she knew she was the only one left.		*T2*

Thus, what began as an interplay among different reference times in the 1982 text (Example 7.9) becomes, in subsequent versions, a single shift back to the sub-story world and a temporally ordered linear sequence of independent clauses within that world.

The shift toward an event-based structure also appears as a complication in the plans – the need to pay a fee – comes to play a more critical role in the plot. In the 1982 text, Mrs. Beer's cousin, the additional participants in the plan, and the fee are completely unrelated. Mrs. Beer's cousin enters the 1982 text in THE PLAN in relation to the timing of the arrangements (*by the time he made these arrangements* in Example 7.9, line (12)). Additional participants do not appear in the 1982 text until THE ANTICIPATION, when they are listed as an elaboration of a *we* in a thematic event clause that is part of the stanza structure.

The fee in the 1982 text (Example 7.13) is buried syntactically and functionally within a description of the Wehrmacht (line (3)):

Example 7.13
1982
(2)   someone told him of a German Wehrmacht . . .
(3)   I don't know how many were sick and tired of the Germans, who want to return to civilian life.
(4)   And who for a certain amount they'll take a group of Jews back to Slovakia.
(5)   You know there was already uh . . . what my husband says "partisans,"
(6)   so, a very small part of Slovakia was liberated.

The fee (a *certain amount*, line (4)) is in a preposed prepositional phrase that prefaces the central goal of the mission *they'll take a group of Jews back to Slovakia* (line (4)). Both are part of a description of *a German Wehrmacht* (line (2)). They appear together in a relative clause (in line (4)) that is conjoined to a prior relative clause (in line (3)) in a structure that clearly embeds the information:

'Head NP [Wh $_{rel}$ [clause] + Wh $_{rel}$ [[prepositional phrase] clause].'

Another indicator of the subordinate role of *a certain amount* is that what follows the relative clause is information establishing the plausibility of the plan. The fee is not mentioned again.

In subsequent texts, the fee becomes more prominent both formally (as an independent clause) and functionally (it becomes an obstacle to the escape plan). Mrs. Beer's cousin (and her sub-story) is linked to the fee, as are the people who join the family in the plan.

We see the fee appearing in an independent clause in 1984 (Example 7.14):

Example 7.14
1984
(i)   And this would cost money,
          and he wanted to help others with this escape.
(j)   E3 So he got my cousin, [sub-story]
(m)   and 'participants' [list of participants is in Appendix 2,
          see also Chapter 8]

The cousin is introduced after the fee with *so* (Example 7.14, line
(j)), thus marking the father's action (*he got*) as a consequence of *cost*
and wanting *to help*. After the cousin's sub-story, Mrs. Beer opens
a list of the other people who became part of the purported escape
(lines (m) and (n)) with *and* (line (m)) and ellipsis of the previous
subject/predicate *he got* from line (j).

The same structure, as presented below, reappears in the 1995
texts:

Obstacle: *fee*
Solution: *so*   [E] *he/we got*   *my cousin*
                                         [sub-story]
                                         some (other) friends/people

              and
                                         [list of types of people]

In Example 7.15 (1995a), Mrs. Beer first introduces the fee as
a preposed prepositional phrase (line 3.), but then, after descriptive and evaluative details elaborating the plan, returns to the fee
(line 8.) and its solution, the latter beginning in line 10. and continuing (after the cousin's sub-story) in line 14.

Example 7.15
  1995a
    3.   and for a fee uh they would take us back to Slovakia.
    8.   first of all we didn't have enough money to pay these
           people by ourselves,[2]
   10.   E4 so we got my cousin [sub-story]
   14.   and uh some other people, ['participants' in list,
           Appendix 2, Chapter 8]

In Example 7.16 (1995b), the fee, obstacle and solution appear in
a four part sequence (lines (K) to (N)) that follows the plans (con-
cluded in line (J)):

Example 7.16

1995b

(J)   And that was where we were going to.

(K)   E4? Of course, it cost a lot of money

(L)   E4   and my father didn't have it,

(M)   E5   so he tried to organize some more into coming with us,

(N)   E6   He got forty four people in all,

(O)   Among them was my cousin, [sub-story]

(S)   And [for list, see Chapter 8]

The fee is the initiating action of a brief temporal sequence, in which each clause appears in parallel form. The fee is introduced (*it cost a lot of money*, line (K)), its high cost (whose obviousness is marked with *of course*) creates an obstacle (*he didn't have it*: E4, line (L)), for which a solution is attempted (*so he tried to organize some more into coming with us*; E5, line (M)), and then achieved (*He got forty four people in all*; E6, line (N)). Mrs. Beer's cousin line (O)) is here presented as part of the group (*among them*; line (O)) comprising the solution. The list of people recruited for the mission then continues with *and*, and ellipsis of *he got* (line (N)) in *and some friends* line (S)).

Notice, also, that the difference between the insertion and structure of the list in the 1982 text (Example 7.13), and the post-1982 texts (Examples 7.14, 7.15 and 7.16), epitomizes the shift from stanza to event-based mode of narrative. As we will see in Section 7.3.3, the members of the 1982 list are linked by repetition of existential *there* sentences. The stativity of this predicate makes sense. The list of participants have a descriptive role in the 1982 story: the group is introduced in ANTICIPATION, along with temporal and spatial information, as Mrs. Beer anticipates what will happen when the plan is carried out. It has no relation to Mrs. Beer's cousin, to the fee or to the obstacle that it poses. In the post-1982 texts, however, other participants in the plan are brought together with Mrs. Beer's cousin and all appear as part of the expansion of an event clause (*he/we got*). This event clause is part of a chain of events recounting how the family gathered together their resources to facilitate the accomplishment of the plan. Whereas repetition of *there* sentences in 1982 links the participants together descriptively (Section 7.3.3), then, ellipsis links the participants together as part of an event that is integrated into the conflict-resolution plot of the narrative.[3]

In this section, we have seen several ways that the event structure of Mrs. Beer's story increased in complexity and length over time: expansion of the father's arrangements from accomplishment to process, transformation of the Wehrmacht's expected actions from dependent to independent clauses, the emergence of temporal juncture and independent clauses within the cousin's sub-story, elaboration of the fee into an obstacle–solution sequence, integration of the cousin into the obstacle–solution sequence, and incorporation of the cousin and other participants in the plan into a list headed by an event clause with an action verb. All of these changes were anchored to characters in Mrs. Beer's story: her father (who found the plan, resolved the obstacle, recruited the participants), the Wehrmacht (who will carry out the plan), the cousin and other participants (who will be aided by the plan). Along with the changing structural configuration of THE PLAN, and the altered positions of the characters to whom it is anchored, is a reduction in the role of one ancillary character, the Rabbi. As we see in (7.3.2), the father's plan with the Rabbi comes to occupy a less evaluative, and more transitional role, in Mrs. Beer's capture story.

In sum, three interrelated structural changes – a shift from dependent to independent clauses, the addition of event clauses, the appearance of temporal juncture – work both separately and together to move the 1982 stanza structure to a linear structure. These changes account for the overall increase in event clauses in THE PLAN over time initially observed in Figure 7.2. As we see in the next section, an outcome of the increased length and complexity of event sequences provides an opportunity for changes in evaluation.

7.3.2 Evaluation in 'the plan'

The emergence of a linear structure in THE PLAN of Mrs. Beer's capture story works in tandem with the development of alternative means of evaluation. In the 1982 stanza-based narrative, event clauses (comprising only 9% of the total independent clauses in THE PLAN (7.3.1)) reported transitional events that contributed to the theme of 'escape.' Although these event clauses developed a nascent

story of 'what happened,' they did so alongside descriptions and
explanations that not only supported (and evaluated) the 'escape'
theme, but also competed for attention through a wealth of detail
that both predated the initiation, and postdated, the outcome of the
story. As we see in this section, evaluation in post-1982 texts depends
upon forms that suspend the narrative action reported in the event
clauses by expanding the range of voices, devices and strategies that
enter Mrs. Beer's story from sources outside the story world.

Recall that the chronicle in which Mrs. Beer's capture story is
embedded is one of increasing danger and the narrowing of options
for safety. Mrs. Beer's father had just been caught with two identification cards (one true, one false) and had escaped from the police by
trickery. The family hurriedly leaves their apartment and finds temporary refuge with a Rabbi, although as Mrs. Beer states *we never
knew* (1995b), *will we be kicked out or y'know, invited in* (1995a).
The plan to return to Slovakia is the next step in an ever dwindling
series of hopes for safety. Not surprisingly, then, Mrs. Beer evaluates
that plan not only in terms of its credibility (can it be believed?) and
plausibility (is it likely to work?), but also its necessity: this plan is
what we need to survive.

One way that necessity is established throughout the four versions
is description of the cousin's loss of her family. Mrs. Beer's cousin
joins the group because her family from the countryside *was taken
to camp already* (1984): she was the only remaining member. In
addition to motivating the cousin's participation in the plan, it also
highlights the danger of death spreading across Hungary and the
perils faced by Mrs. Beer's family and by Jews in general. It thus
serves to establish the necessity of escape.

Although the cousin's loss reappears in all four versions, other
means of establishing necessity are more varied. Consider, for example, the mention of Budapest. In 1982 (Example 7.17), four clauses
follow the description of the arrangements with a description of
Budapest:

Example 7.17
1982
(7)   And you know Budapest was just hell of a city,
(8)   y'know there was no escaping anymore any place.
(9)   They were just loaded with Germans
(10)   and catching- they wanted to catch everyone.

Two clauses (lines (7) and (8)) use stative predicates to portray a situation within the story world. Whereas the former uses *hell* as an intensifier (a term also used by Mrs. Beer to describe Auschwitz), the latter intensifies the situation through negation (*no escaping*), comparison (*anymore*) and rhythmic repetition (*anymore any place*) of the universal quantifier *any* + time/place. The lack of escape portrayed in Example 7.17 line (8) is elaborated by the overwhelming presence of the captors (*loaded with Germans*, line (9)) whose goal (*they wanted to catch everyone*, line (10)) is as exhaustive as the family's inability to escape *anymore any place* (line (8)). Because they appear after the plans, these descriptive/evaluative clauses provide for them an *ex post facto* justification.

Although conditions in Budapest also appear in the 1984 text (see Example 7.18), they do so in a different location and through a different strategy. First, notice the location. Whereas the four clauses in the 1982 Budapest evaluation followed a single event clause in which the arrangements had already been completed, the 1984 Budapest evaluation (in Example 7.18, line (d), shorter than the 1982 text (Example 7.18)) intervenes between two event clauses that appear as part of the shift to an event-based narrative structure:

Example 7.18
1984
(a) **E1** And uh my father went next day,
        in search of a way to get us back to Czechoslovakia.
(b)   Because some part of it was freed,
(c)   the partisans freed it.
(d)   And we- we were holding to any straw, I guess,
          because it was impossible for us to remain longer in
          Budapest.
(e) **E2** And he came home, that he found such a way.

The evaluation of Budapest (line (d)) intervenes between an event clause that sends the father on his search for plans (**E1**, line (a)) and an event clause that returns the father home with the plans (**E2**, line (e)). Thus the location shift – facilitated by the increase in event clauses – is accompanied by a strategy shift: the use of descriptive information to suspend the narrative action.

Another aspect of the shift in strategy should also be noted. Both descriptions of Budapest depend on contrast: *there was no escaping anymore any place* (1982, Example 7.17, line (8)); *it was impossible for us to remain longer in Budapest* (line (d)). The 1984 contrast, however, is not embedded in a set of descriptive clauses that characterize the city (1982). Rather, it is marked (by *because*) as a justification for the family's desperation: *we were holding to any straw* (Example 7.18, line (d)). As we noted in Chapter 6, use of the idiomatic verb phrase 'hold on to any straw' is an important evaluative change that implicates desperation and reshuffles perceptions from the immediacy of experience to the distance of reflection.

Budapest does not appear at all in the 1995 texts. But the evaluative shifts just noted – to suspension of action and external evaluation – proceed still further in the 1995 texts. In the 1995a text, for example, voices from outside the story world appear twice in the evaluative space between event clauses. Between finding the plan (*he heard that there are some army personnel* (**E2**, line, 2.) and resolution of the obstacle (*so we got my cousin* (**E4**, line 10.) is a metalinguistic rhetorical question – *Now why Slovakia?* (line 4.) – asked by a reflective voice that is assessing the logic of the plan. Another abstract reflection follows the answer to the rhetorical question (see Example 7.19):

Example 7.19
1995a
6.   And so when you have no place else to go
      you go over . . . y'know you think maybe you will be safe for
      a little short time yet.

This expression of desperation provides for the necessity not only of participating in the plan, but also of believing that it is both credible and plausible. Since the family has little choice but to be part of the plans, they are willing to proceed despite the obstacle hindering their participation, i.e. *we didn't have enough money to pay these people by ourselves* (line 8.).

External evaluative voices between event clauses also appear in Example 7.20 from the 1995b text:

Example 7.20
 1995b
 (A)   **E1** And my father went out to look for something for us to
            do,
 (B)   y'know, what would be the next step?

(C)   There weren't many options.

(D)   **E2** And, as he went, he heard a story that today,
      I think your hair would stand up from disbelief,

(E)   **E3** but he swallowed it.

The family's belief in the possibility of a plan is explicitly challenged from outside the story world by the rhetorical question *what
would be the next step?* (line (B)), whose answer (*there weren't many
options* line (C)), restricts the range of potential rhetorical responses.
As the father ventures on his search (note the temporal clause *as he
went* (line (D)) is another means of suspending the action), he hears
a story. As we observed in Chapter 6, a *story* is a genre that can
include the potential falsehood of fiction – a reading reinforced by
Mrs. Beer's epistemic stance on the *story* through *I think your hair
would stand up from disbelief* (line (D)) and the response of her
father (*he swallowed it* line (E)) as gullible.

Notice, also, the effect of the placement of these evaluative clauses
between event clauses. Because evaluation precedes the details of
the plan, it presents an overt challenge to its credibility and plausibility. This adds poignancy to the family's willingness to try the
plan – even though the plan seems unrealistic, they must try it anyway – and thus provides an indirect indicator of their desperation.

The overall changes in evaluation reviewed thus far show a movement to external evaluation. The embedding of information between
event clauses in THE PLAN of Mrs. Beer's post-1982 texts manip-
ulates, and exposes the permeability of, the boundary between the
story world and the story telling world (also manipulated through
meta-talk, Chapter 6). Even syntactic modifications of, or additions
to, sentence structure begin to function as external evaluation. For
example, relative clauses appear in all four versions of THE PLAN.
For the most part, they provide descriptive information about characters (e.g. the Wehrmacht, Mrs. Beer's cousin, the Rabbi) that not
only motivates features of the plan, but also integrates these characters into different times and places, including (but not limited to)
Mrs. Beer's broader life story. Example 7.21 lists the relative clauses
describing Mrs. Beer's cousin:

Example 7.21

1982   (13)   because my cousin said [. . .] the one who's now in
                Switzerland

1984   (j)   so he got my cousin, the- the one whose sister I took
                the name,
1995a   10.   so we got my cousin who lived in Budapest by then
                too, hiding
1995b   (O)   among them was my cousin,
                the one that I slept in her house when I first escaped.

Each relative clause about the cousin reports different information:
the cousin's current location (1982), a relationship to someone
whose prior act helped save Mrs. Beer's life (1984), the story world
circumstance (1995a), a prior act that helped save Mrs. Beer's life
(1995b). Thus each relative clause embeds the cousin within parts
of Mrs. Beer's life story and shows her salience in Mrs. Beer's life.

In 1995b (Example 7.22), however, a relative clause also modifies
the text itself, specifically, the father's plan as generically labeled as
a story:

Example 7.22
1995b
(D)   And, as he went, he heard a story
       that today, I think your hair would stand up from disbelief,
(E)   but he swallowed it.

Like the relative clauses modifying characters, the relative clause in
line (D) also situates its head noun in a different time and place.
But what it describes is a meta-linguistic construct (*a story*), what it
conveys is doubt in the veracity of the information conveyed through
that construct, and how it conveys such doubt is through formulaic
and figurative language. These three levels of abstraction are a sharp
contrast with the concrete details about characters whose actions
and reactions impinge directly on the story world and life world.

In sum, the structural re-configuration of narrative structure in
THE PLAN allows evaluation through suspension of the action. Yet
this means of evaluation also expands the range of voices and the
variety of devices that they exploit from outside of the story world.

Analysis of the next two phases in Mrs. Beer's capture story
reveals parallel changes in structure, voicing, and function, thus
showing that the changes in THE PLAN have set up a textual frame
to be maintained throughout the remainder of the capture story.

7.3.3 Changes in 'anticipation'

In ANTICIPATION, Mrs. Beer outlines how the plan to escape to Slovakia will be initiated by reporting three types of information: what the group will do (meet), where (park) and when (night). The stanza structure again disappears: post-1982 versions of ANTIC-IPATION remove descriptive information by subordinating time expressions to events; shift the descriptive structure of an existential-based list of participants from ANTICIPATION to the event-based list in THE PLAN; use an event clause to provide closure to the anticipated plans.

Let us begin with temporal information. Time reference in the 1982 text was highlighted through a separate clause. In subsequent versions, time is integrated with place and action. Compare the openings of the four versions of ANTICIPATION in Example 7.23:

Example 7.23
1982
   (22)   But anyway, so **it was at night,**
   (23)   we were supposed to meet in a park,
1984
   (o)   and uh we were supposed to meet, **at sundown,** in a little park,
1995a
   15.   And he made arrangements that **that evening,**
   16.   uh we will meet in this little park,
1995b
   (V)   And we were supposed to meet the Germans
         with their truck at this little park **at night.**

Because time in the 1982 text appeared in its own clause *it was at night* (line (22)), it has a scene-setting function. In subsequent texts, both time and place appear as phrases within a clause that reports the anticipatory action 'meet.' The condensation of reference time to a postposed prepositional phrase (*at sundown*: 1984 (line (o), *at night*: 1995b, line (V)), or a preposed noun (*that evening*: 1995a (line 15.), allows the clause to focus on the pseudo-event *we were supposed to meet*, rather than time itself.

Changes in the closure of ANTICIPATION (see Example 7.24) are functionally parallel to changes in its opening: both focus on action or event. In the 1982 text, the Rabbi does provide a blessing, but also provided is a synopsis of the Rabbi's fate (the hope that he will be able to follow the same escape plan and his eventual safety despite the failure of that hope). In each post-1982 text, the Rabbi appears in only one event clause – the Rabbi blesses the family – that moves from the hypothetical world of anticipatory actions (and thus pseudo-events) back to the concrete story world of physical actions (and event clauses):

Example 7.24
1984
(r)   E4 And the Rabbi gave us . . . his blessing.
1995a
21.   E6 So this Rabbi where we stayed blessed us,
1995b
(W)   E7 And the Rabbi where we stayed blessed us
(X)   E8 and we left.

Like the Rabbi's provision of a blessing in ANTICIPATION of the 1982 text, the blessing in ANTICIPATION of subsequent texts provides both a formal and ritual transition for the family: they will leave the relative (but temporary) safety of his home to begin their supposed escape to their home country. The placement of this blessing, and the transition for which it provides, is thus a concrete counterpart to the anticipation of action that opened ANTICIPATION. As such, it also provides an event-based closure to ANTICIPATION, comparable in textual function to the (pseudo) event-based opening.

Whereas opening and closing clauses of ANTICIPATION are similar across the post-1982 texts, intervening material is different, as shown in Example 7.25

Example 7.25
1982
(23)   we were supposed to meet in a park,
(24)   we were about forty four people,
(25)   there were some from my hometown who lived in Budapest who were included,
(26)   there was an old woman and her son,
(27)   there was a couple and a child and the woman was pregnant.
(28)   and there was a couple from my town with a child and the woman was pregnant.

(29)   So there were two children and two pregnant women among
       them.

1984

(p)   and we will be going back to Slovakia.

1995a

15.   E5 And he made arrangements that that evening,
16.   uh we will meet in this little park,
17.   the army personnel will be there with their truck,
18.   and they will take us,
19.   we'll pay them,
20.   and that's it.

1995b

(V)   And we were supposed to meet the Germans
       with their truck at this little park at night.

In Example 7.25, the 1982 text continues the stanza structure of
ANTICIPATION: the *we* of the pseudo event (*we were supposed to
meet*) is described in a list built upon stative (non temporally sequential) predicates that report the composition of the group (see Chapter
8). The 1984 and 1995b versions are brief anticipatory summaries.
Whereas the 1984 text anticipates the goal of the mission (line (p)),
the line from the 1995b text actually doubles as the opening line: it
packs all the anticipatory information into one sentence, beginning
with the action (*and we were supposed to meet*) and continuing
with whom (*the Germans*) they will meet, what will be there (*their
truck*), where (*at this little park*), and when (*at night*).

The length of the 1995a text in Example 7.25 is in sharp contrast
to the brevity of the 1984 and 1995b texts: Mrs. Beer recounts the
future plans as a mini-narrative. Reported in ANTICIPATION are
not just time, place, and one inceptive action (lines 15. and 16.),
but also a sequence of pseudo-events that previews the entire plan
in temporal order (lines 17. to 19.), including the resolution to the
financial obstacle (*we'll pay them*, line 19.). The mini-story then
closes with an indexical turning point *and that's it* (line 20.), as
well as a more detailed closure from the Rabbi. This expansion
of material replicates an expansion in THE PLAN in which Mrs.
Beer presents the plans through a sequence of events complete with
complication (fee) and resolution (a group of participants). Thus
the emergence of this mini-story in ANTICIPATION parallels the
increasing complexity in THE PLAN in the same version.

In sum, ANTICIPATION outlines how the plan will be initiated. Presented in Example 7.25 in all four versions is what the group will do to initiate the plan, where, and when. The post-1982 versions all shift from the stanza mode of the 1982 text toward an event-based linear structure. The shifts involve the subordination of temporal and physical information to information about anticipatory action, the movement or reduction of descriptive/evaluative information, and the use of an event clause as a closing boundary and as a complementary bracket to the action-based opening of ANTICIPATION.

7.3.4 Summary of changes in 'the plan' and 'anticipation'

In this section, we found two overall changes in THE PLAN and ANTICIPATION. One change expanded the event structure of THE PLAN, leading away from the stanza-based organization of the 1982 text to a more linear event-based organization of subsequent texts. The second change was a gradual shift toward external evaluation of the credibility, plausibility and necessity of the plan. The main change in ANTICIPATION was its shifting role as a transitional phase. Presented in all four versions is what the group will do to initiate the plan, where, and when. The shifts subordinate temporal and physical information to information about anticipatory action, move or reduce descriptive/evaluative information, and use an event clause as a closing boundary and as a complementary bracket to the action-based opening of THE PLAN.

7.4 Retelling 'the capture'

In THE CAPTURE, Mrs. Beer recounts how the plan to escape to Slovakia – a plan that had appeared credible, plausible and necessary – turns out to be something quite different, and intentionally so, by those who had initially formulated it. The unraveling of the arrangements and, hence, recognition of the captors' deception, creates a shift from hope to despair. In concrete physical terms, the failure of the plan precedes a transition in place and circumstance very different than that for which the family had planned and hoped. The family's hope for partial control over their life, through a return to their liberated homeland, is transformed to a complete loss of personal and collective agency, first, when they are transported in a truck to a Gestapo prison and, later, when they are taken from prison to the train that will transport them to Auschwitz.

The transformation from potential freedom to imprisonment in THE CAPTURE of the 1982 text appeared through a linear sequence of event clauses whose structural shift from earlier phases mirrored the schematic violation characterizing the supposed plan of rescuers with the actual plan of the captors.

		conjunction	subject	verb	phrase
E3	(31)	and	we	came	into this little park
E4	(32)	and	the flashlight	lit	into our eyes
E4?	(33)	and	we	knew	that's it
E5	(34)	and	they	kicked [us]	into the truck
E6	(35)	and	they	took [us]	to the Gestapo headquarters in Buda

The sequential structure of the 1982 CAPTURE differed from the earlier thematically organized phases and their stanza structure, creating a sense of rapidity: all this happened quickly, one thing after another. Since this linear sequence was an abrupt shift from the 1982 stanza structure of THE PLAN and ANTICIPATION, it created a textual contrast that replicated the rupture in the group's expectations of what was to happen.

Although the violation of expectations is again recounted in a sequence of event clauses in the post-1982 texts, interrelated changes alter the interpretation of that violation. The primary change is a range of linguistic strategies that externally evaluate the disjunction between expectation and actuality. Because this evaluation builds upon strategies used in earlier phases of these texts, THE CAPTURE continues – rather than alters – the style of the earlier phases. The evaluative additions also mark a shift in presumption of mutual knowledge. It is important to recall that Mrs. Beer's audience – including not only the interviewer, but also the potentially broad and anonymous audience for the publicly-accessible oral history – do not know at the outset of the story how the plan actually turned out. Mrs. Beer's additions to the event sequence in the post-1982 texts make explicit the contradiction between the plans of the group (what was expected) and the plans of the captors (what actually occurred), thus positioning the audience not only to grasp what happened, but also to understand the significance of the experience for Mrs. Beer and her family.

We see in this section that event structure varies in three ways that impact evaluation across the different versions of THE CAPTURE: the unpacking of an event, adjustments of stativity and activity, addition of semantically/pragmatically compatible events.

The first clause of THE CAPTURE (see Example 7.26) illustrates the unpacking of an event. The 1982 text is the only version in which the group enters the park in an event clause:

Example 7.26
1982
(31)   E3 we came into this little park
(32)   E4 and the flashlight lit into our eyes
1984
(r)   and uh we were coming to that park
(s)   E5 and as soon as we approached that truck flashlights were
        lit into our eyes
1995a
24.   and uh so uh as we were getting closer to the park at night,
        E8 we see spotlights, aiming at us.
1995b
(Y)   and as we were approaching the park
(Z)   E9 there were big flood lights turning on us.

In the post-1982 texts, Mrs. Beer unpacks the meeting in the park in ways similar to her unpacking of her father's arrangements in THE PLAN. Yet she does not do so by creating more event clauses – quite the opposite. What Mrs. Beer does is alternate between progressive verbs and dependent clauses to delay the actual entry to the park: a progressive and a temporal clause in the 1984 text, a temporal clause with a progressive verb in the 1995 texts. These clauses bring the group to the place where they are about to meet. Rather than actually 'meet' (an accomplishment verb) in the park, however, the group engages in actions that are logically necessary to, and should lead up to, the anticipated meeting, thus suspending the action that is supposed to lead to the group's meeting with their rescuers.

Notice that this strategy alters not only the event structure, but also the way we interpret what happened (a referential consequence) and our understanding of how the plan is dismantled (an evaluative consequence). On the referential side, we cannot be sure when the group was actually captured: before or during their entrance to the park? On the evaluative side, the use of dependent clauses briefly suspends the narrative action: the lights will appear as the group is working to achieve the first part of their anticipated goal (i.e. meeting in the park, cf. ANTICIPATION), rather than actually fulfilling that goal. By overlapping entry to the park with perceptual evidence for the capture, Mrs. Beer portrays the captors as ready to confront the group as soon as possible, thus not only highlighting their efficiency and preparedness, but also intensifying their zeal for their mission.

The next two clauses – shining of the lights, 'we knew' – illustrate a fluctuation in event structure based upon the distinction between stativity and activity. The *aktionsarten* of verbs plays a major role in determining the status of clauses in a narrative. Event clauses generally have verbs that have a starting and/or ending point and that convey an activity, accomplishment, or achievement. However, the event status of clauses with stative verbs is not always clear: when presented in a sequence of event clauses, a durative event may be interpreted as having a speaker-centered starting point whose inception nevertheless preceded the story character's awareness of it. Blurring the otherwise clear distinction between actions that have a clear forward motion (event clauses) and those that do not (non-event clauses) provides a resource through which narrators can convey an altered sense of time and action, and thus a means of portraying and evaluating chaotic and disruptive circumstances.

Adjustments of stativity/activity appear in two locations in THE CAPTURE: the perceptual evidence of capture (*Capture 1*, the turning on of the lights) and the reflective realization of capture (*Capture 2*, what 'we knew'). Let us start with the turning on of the lights in Example 7.27:

Example 7.27

1982	(32)	E4	and the flashlight lit into our eyes
1984	(s)	E5	flashlights were lit into our eyes,
1995a	24.	E8	we see spotlights, aiming at us.
1995b	(Z)	E9	there were big flood lights turning on us.

Along with structural variation through an aspectual shift, we find lexical differences in the description of the 'lights' that work along with stativity for evaluative effect.

Notice, first, the lexical differences: *flashlight(s)* (1982, 1984), *spotlights* (1995a), *floodlights* (1995b). The change from ordinary hand held lights that illuminate a relatively small area, to those specifically designed to cover a broader area, increases the degree to which the group can feel "trapped" and intensifies the seriousness of the captors' intent. In the 1995 texts, the locus of experience is less metonymic: when *spotlights* are *aiming at us* (1995a) or *turning on us* (1995b), the lights are directed not to a part of us (*our eyes*), but to our total beings (*us*).

These lexical changes work along with grammatical and aspectual shifts to have evaluative effects. In the 1982 text, *the flashlight lit* continues prior canonical narrative syntax: *flashlight* appears as the subject of the relatively punctual action *lit* (1982). When clause structure shifts to the passive – *flashlights were lit into our eyes* (1984) – the contour of what happened can be interpreted as more durative. Two grammatical features add duration: the use of historical present in *we see*, and the progressive *aiming* (Schiffrin 1981). In *there were big flood lights turning on us* (1995b), lights are, again, directed *on us*; duration is conveyed through the existential predicate *there were*. By creating a partial overlap with adjacently presented occurrences (entry into the park), these shifts to stativity add to the confusing sensations and chaos that accompany being trapped.

Another move along the stativity/activity continuum appears in the turning point and its temporal relationship with other occurrences. The quotative verbs 'know' and 'feel' are both stative verbs. Although their sequential placement provides them with an implicit starting point, adding the adverbial *right away* in Example 7.25, (1984, 1995b) provides a sudden onset to the starting point, thus adding an aspectual feature of inceptiveness that shifts 'know' toward the activity end of the continuum.

Example 7.28

1982	(32)	and the flashlight lit into our eyes
	(33)	and we knew
1984	(t)	and we were kicked into the truck,
	(u)	we knew right away

1995a	24.	we see spotlights, aiming at us.
	25.	And we felt
1995b	(Z)	there were big flood lights turning on us.
	(AA)	we knew right away

Also contributing to the activity/stativity difference above is the inherently internal and private foundation of mental activities such as 'know' and 'feel,' as well as the subjectivity of what is known/felt. These qualities play a prominent mediating role between the world and how that world is represented through language. Just as we cannot know what Mrs. Beer knew/felt when she saw the lights, neither can Mrs. Beer know what the others knew/felt when they saw the lights. Nor can we know *when* Mrs. Beer or the others actually underwent the transformation in knowledge/feeling that revealed the plan to be something so different than what they had expected. Hence it is not surprising that not only is the starting point of what *we knew/felt* differently specified, but so, too, is its sequential placement within the four texts. In 1982, for example, *we knew* follows *the flashlight lit* and precedes being *kicked into the truck*; in 1984, both the lights and being kicked precede what *we knew*. In the 1995 texts, what we felt/knew occurs while the lights are aiming/turning on the group and prior to being kicked into the truck. Thus the inherent opacity of mental states allows fluidity in the temporal contour of what the group knew/felt and when they did so.

The third change in event structure in THE CAPTURE arises from the addition of semantically/ pragmatically compatible events to the action by which the group is taken into the truck, see Example 7.29:

Example 7.29
1982
| (34) | **E5** | And they kicked us into the truck, |

1984
| (t) | **E6** | and we were kicked into the truck, |

1995a
29.	**E10**	and they kicked us
30.	**E10?**	and beat us
31.		and that's how we ended up in the truck

1995b
| (FF) | **E11** | and they hit us, |

(GG)   **E12** kicked us into the truck
(HH)   **E13** beat us up

The only consistently reported action in Example 7.29 is 'kick,' varying by grammatical voice: active (1982, 1995a, 1995b) and passive
(1984). Also consistent is that the group ends up in the truck (specified in 1995a (line 31.)) when the locative phrase *into the truck* does
not appear in the event clause). The 1995 texts add further force to
the actions of the captors through *beat us (up)* (1995a, 1995b) and
hit (1995b).

   Thus far, we have discussed three changes in event structure
across the different versions of THE CAPTURE: the unpacking of an
event (entry to the park); a continuum between stativity and activity (lights, what we 'knew'); addition of semantically/pragmatically
events similar to 'kick.' However, Example 7.30 shows that once
the group has been captured and is in the truck, variation in event
structure disappears:

Example 7.30

1982   (35)   **E6**   and they took us straight to the Gestapo
                       headquarters in Buda
1984   (w)   **E7**   and they took us straight to the Gestapo
                       headquarters
1995a 32.   **E11** and they sped the truck into the Gestapo
                       headquarters up in the Buda?
        33.   It was in the part of Budapest that's Buda.
1995b (II)   **E14** and sped to the Gestapo headquarters to Buda.

Mrs. Beer consistently details the destination of the truck: she always
mentions *Gestapo headquarters*; in all but one version (1984), she
adds that the headquarters are in *Buda*. But it is not only detail
that is consistent: this is the only information in THE CAPTURE
that is consistently presented as an event clause. Thus the repeated
descriptive clarity of the truck's destination parallels its consistent
appearance as an event clause.

   Variation in this final clause of THE CAPTURE is lexical. Differences in the motion verb implicate slightly different qualities
of the captors: whereas *took us straight* (1982, 1984) suggests a
goal-orientation, *sped* (1995a, 1995b) adds urgency associated with

those who are disregarding (or controlling) legal and social convention. Consistent inclusion of the location to which the group was taken, and the consistent appearance of an event clause, clearly marks Mrs. Beer's capture story as an explanatory narrative: one of its main functions is to explain how changes in circumstances (place, experience, and so on) come about. Thus the plans that Mrs. Beer's father had so carefully orchestrated – plans that were supposed to return the family to their liberated homeland – end up taking them directly into the heart of the danger from which they had been hoping to escape.

In sum, although all versions of THE CAPTURE follow a linear structure, their adoption of a structure differs because of variability in the appearance of event clauses. Except for the trip to the Gestapo headquarters – the last clause of THE CAPTURE that had intertextual meanings – we found variability in the event clause status of each occurrence: entry to the park, shining of lights, the turning point, the force used to get the group into the truck. This variability involved syntactic changes that traditionally have evaluative effects.

7.5 Conclusion: re-framing and retelling

When Susan Beer told her story about being captured in Budapest in four different oral history interviews over a thirteen year period, she reframed the sources of her experience, reconfigured events, reordered them in text, and re-evaluated what happened. Although I have analyzed these changes in different chapters, and used different analytical perspectives to do so, the changes come together to reflect different overall functions of oral history narratives.

Several types of narratives appear in oral histories (Schiffrin 2000). *Illustrative narratives* elaborate a particular instance of a more general experience, e.g. what it was like to be separated from parents or to be trapped in a barn. *Explanatory narratives* provide sequences of temporally and causally linked events that explain a transition from one time, place, situation or state of mind to another. A third type is *performative narratives*: these stories (which can have either explanatory or illustrative roles) bear traces of being oft-told stories, designed for a broad audience; they are full of performance features and evaluative devices that enhance their point. Whereas explanatory, illustrative and performative narratives are all bounded units, comprised (largely) of adjacent clauses, *intertextual narratives* are non-contiguous units that emerge across a set of discourse segments that are linked in some way, for example, by characters (e.g. mother and daughter) or type of episode (e.g. close calls).

All four versions of Mrs. Beer's capture story explained how the family was duped and caught in Budapest. One might paraphrase this general explanatory function as "how a trap led from hiding in Budapest to imprisonment in Auschwitz." The trap and its outcome places the capture story within a broader intertextual narrative about "how difficult it was to protect ourselves." The expanded event structure, and external evaluative voices of the post-1982 event based narratives, also suggest a move towards performativity: "this story is so important and reportable a part of my life story that I am telling it in a way that will guarantee general recognition of its importance."

These multiple functions can be elucidated by bringing together the different aspects of change whose analysis was separated into Chapters 6 and 7. We can begin to see the connection between the two means of 'redoing' a story – reframing and retelling – by going a bit further in the quote from Goffman (1974: 508, my emphasis) presented in Chapter 6:

ordinarily when an individual says something, he is not saying it as a bald statement of fact on his own behalf. He is recounting. He is running through a strip of already determined events for the engagement of his listeners. *And this is likely to mean that he must take them back into the information state – the horizon – he had at the time of the episode but no longer has.*

What is critical about the last sentence of the quote (for my purposes) is that the shift in information state entails a shift back not just to the epistemic beginning of the experience, but also to the temporal starting point.

Temporal/epistemic shifts have an important consequence: "*any presentation of a strip of experience falls flat if some sort of suspense cannot be maintained*" (Goffman 1974: 506, emphasis in original). We can thus suggest that a story that moves progressively forward, from its temporal/epistemic starting point to its closing point, might very well intensify suspense, not only through overt evaluative devices but through linearization itself. (Imagine, for example, if Mrs. Beer's story had opened with an abstract such as "We were captured by people pretending to be disenchanted German soldiers who we thought would take us home but who were really working for the Gestapo.") If progression from a temporal/epistemic starting point is itself an *evaluative* device that creates suspense, then re-authoring the story as a canonical (linear event-based plot-driven) narrative is recipient-designed in more than one sense: not only is it easier for an audience to reconstruct what happened when events are presented in order, but it is easier for an audience to appreciate what happened – to get its significance – when the audience is symbolically seated along with the speaker-as-figure in the story. Thus the retelling of the capture story clarifies its role as an explanatory narrative that is part of a broader intertextual theme: it also enhances its performativity for the general audience for whom it is designed.

Of course there is more to the retelling of narrative than replicating temporal order within the narrative itself. There is also the issue of temporality across successive retelling: the first story is differently positioned than the second story, and so on. Thus each retold narrative is *itself* a next-event, a replaying of experience that is discursively constructed by an evolving set of differently layered components of 'self' that combine and recombine numerous experiences, *including the experience of having told the story*. And this suggests that each successive narrative is as much *meta*-narrative as narrative: because it incorporates parts of earlier stories (structure, lexis, evaluation), it is not only about an experience, but also 'about' prior narratives. Perhaps the incorporation and reframing of one's own prior narrative as an experience – drawing on both narrative competence and narrative code (Chapter 1) – is the most important experiential source of all for a retold narrative.

Notes

1. Not all independent clauses are event clauses: some have stative predicates that do not move the action forward (although they may reveal the narrator's realization of a new state that may dramatically alter the course of action). Other clauses represent events – indeed, some of them in temporal order – but are nonetheless not part of the main story line (i.e. the main set of circumstances being recounted): they may report a set of events that (taken together) form a mini-narrative that preceded the time of the story world events.

2. Note cohesion with prior text through co-reference: *these people* (line 8.) evoke a referent (earlier evoked through *some army personnel* (line 2.)) that has remained accessible despite intervening text.

3. This submersion of characters, and merging of the plan to escape, within a conflict/resolution plot change also reveals Mrs. Beer's co-authorship within the interior story world (cf. Chapter 6).

Who did what (again)?

8.1 Introduction

In this book, we have been analyzing referrals and narratives that have recurred in 'second-positions' of varying types and scope, from an article prefacing a noun (e.g. *the- the*) to a story told in 1982, 1984 and 1995. Although we have approached these recurrences from numerous directions, we have not yet brought them together by examining recurrent referrals within recurrent narratives. It is the goal of this chapter to do so.

In keeping with the general concerns of innovative vs. fixed, old vs. new and same vs. new running throughout this book, I return to stories that I have already discussed elsewhere and say something new about them. First is Susan Beer's capture story (analyzed in Chapters 6 and 7): here we examine Mrs. Beer's referrals to eight referents in relation to their actions and integration into the story (Section 8.2). Second is a narrative from a sociolinguistic interview that I first analyzed more than twenty years ago (Schiffrin 1984a, see Appendix 3). The story was told by Jack Cohen (a middle aged man from Philadelphia) about a childhood experience with a friend (Joey Bishop) who later became a well known comedian. In the story, Joey played a funny melody during a formal school performance with Jack of an elegy (a poem/song of sorrow or mourning). Immediately after telling what happened, Jack retold the complicating action and evaluation. In my 1984 analysis, I analyzed general features of the story: here I add attention to the referrals and the retelling (Section 8.3).

The two stories are different in many ways. Not only do they differ in key (sad vs. funny), but they are situated in different social interactions (oral history interview vs. sociolinguistic interview) and oriented toward different types of recipients (general public vs. wife, nephew and student (me)). And, of course, their retellings are differently distributed over time (years vs. seconds apart). Yet they share two crucial features: they are both about duplicity; they both build a collective *we* central to the story. Thus together they offer an opportunity not only to compare the retellings of different stories to one another, but more generally, to address how referring expressions function in textual worlds of characters and actions, as well as social worlds of people and interactions (Section 8.4).

8.2 'Who did what' in the retold capture story

In this section, we examine the eight referents in Susan Beer's capture story.[1] Our analyses of Mrs. Beer's capture story focused almost completely on linguistic changes in events. But just as the construction of footing and the representation of events in stories changed over time, so, too, did referrals. There were eight referents in the capture story: two family members ('father' (Section 8.2.1), 'cousin' (Section 8.2.2)); 'rescuers/captors' who figured in the plan to help/capture the family (Section 8.2.3); a protector of the family ('Rabbi' (Section 8.2.4)); two collectives, the 'family' and the 'group' who joined in the mission (Section 8.2.5). Each analysis examines how referrals to the referents are integrated with other aspects of narrative structure, evaluation and footing.

8.2.1 Father

Since the plan to escape from Budapest was transmitted to Susan Beer by her father, it is not surprising that 'father' is important in the capture story and is the topical referent (Chapter 4) in its initial phase (THE PLAN). As is typical of referrals to family members, 'father' is introduced in each version of the story with a possessive, *my father.* And as is common with next-mentions, 'father' is typically evoked as *he* in all versions of the story (cf. the use of pronouns for another kin term ('mother') in Schiffrin 2002).

Other regularities familiar from our discussion of genre constraints (Chapter 4) also appear in referrals to 'father.' In the 1982 text, for example, there is an interlude between the interviewer and

Mrs. Beer (not included in the transcript in Appendix 2). We saw similar digressions from the ongoing topic in Chapter 4, in which a pronoun picked up the topical referent after the digression. Here we see an equally common option: Mrs. Beer uses the full noun *my father* to reinstate the referent. The Interviewer's prompt *so you made the arrangements* to renew Mrs. Beer's story mentions not 'father', but Mrs. Beer herself. By using *my father*, then, Mrs. Beer not only renews the topical referent, and continues to highlight her father's role as principal (and originator) of the plan, but also other-initiates and other-completes the problematic referral *you*,

Another constraint that impacts next-mentions of 'father' is possible ambiguity. *My father* was used when the Rabbi was a potentially ambiguous recent referral: *and this Rabbi gave us a mishebeirach and they had a certain signal in Hebrew lettering with my father* (1982, lines (14) and (15)); *So this rabbi where we stayed blessed us, and my father even gave him in Hebrew uh that there will be a signal* (1995a, lines 18. and 19. (see Appendix 2)). Likewise, when 'father' was orchestrating an important part of THE PLAN, gathering together the group of people who would join the family (see Section 8.2.5) and help cover the fee required for the escape, he reappears as a full noun: *So my father didn't want to . . . didn't have enough money to pay these people by ourselves* (1995a line 5.); *it cost a lot of money and my father didn't have it* (1995b, lines (J) and (L)). Thus when ambiguity, plot development and evaluation required clarity about exactly who was responsible for an activity, the full NP *my father* was used instead of the pronoun *he*.

8.2.2 Cousin

Susan Beer's 'cousin' appears briefly in the capture story: in all versions, her first-mention is *my cousin* and next-mentions are *she*. Her minimal appearance, however, should not undermine her importance in the story, albeit in two very different ways across the different versions. In the 1982 text, the description of the fate of the cousin's family (*her family was already gone* (line (13)) *because the countryside was already taken* (line (12))) had an important evaluative role: the taking of the cousin's family intensified the need for others to escape. In post-1982 texts, 'cousin' enters the narratives in relation to a newly developed subplot: the need to pay the purported rescuers. The information about the cousin's family's fate remains, but it is truncated and presented in linear order (Chapter 7). The first appearance of the 'cousin' in post-1982 texts (see Example 8.1), is in the list of people, whose 'gathering together' through an event clause (*he got* (*he* = 'father')) provides a solution to the problem of paying and therefore facilitates the plan:

Example 8.1
1984
(i)   And this would cost money,
        and he wanted to help others with this escape.
(j)   So he got **my cousin** [the sub-story about family]
(m)   and some other friends [list continues]

The mention of the 'cousin' as the first member of the list recurs in the 1995 texts (as we see again in Section 8.2.5). Thus even though her role in the story changes significantly, the NOUN FIRST/PRONOUN NEXT referrals to the 'cousin' remain the same. And perhaps reflecting her membership in the family, she never becomes completely incorporated into the general group 'we' (Section 8.2.5).

8.2.3 Rescuers/captors

In contrast to the specific referents 'father' and 'cousin,' the 'rescuers/captors' is a vague identity category with different members who change over the course of the story. In all four versions of THE PLAN, the purported rescuers are portrayed as soldiers. What changes is the language of the referrals themselves. In the 1982 and 1984 mentions of the 'rescuers/captors', both German (*Wehrmacht* (1982), *Wehrmacht truck* (1984)) and English (*the city was loaded with Germans* (1982), *German Wehrmacht* (1984)) are used.[2] But in the 1995 texts, we find only English: *army personnel* (as both first-mention in THE PLAN and next-mention in ANTICIPATION) and *army truck* (1995a); *German army officers* or *army personnel*, *German army truck* (both in THE PLAN) and *the Germans* (in ANTICIPATION). The repetition of detail in next-mentions of the 1995 texts reiterates the supposed identity of the supposed rescuers. The shift from German to English has a similar function, but on a broader scale: it clarifies the referents for a general audience (see also 8.2.4).

Also part of the general set of 'rescuers' are the 'partisans' waiting for the family in Slovakia. In each version, 'partisans' are tightly tied to the plan to return to Slovakia: they repeatedly appear immediately after the mention of Slovakia. Likewise, the referring expression *partisans* appears in all four versions, but the attribution of that term to Mrs. Beer's husband *what my husband says "partisans"* disappears in post-1982 texts (Chapter 6). Also shifting is the specificity of 'partisans.' Whereas 'partisans' was introduced as an indefinite (in an existential *there* construction 1982), it becomes a definite in later versions – hence treated as a more accessible and familiar part of the rescue schema.

Once the PLAN and ANTICIPATION phases end, the 'rescuers' (both German soldiers and partisans in Slovakia) no longer have explicit roles in the story. The family is captured and sent to a Gestapo prison, but it is never completely clear who is responsible. This lack of clarity is reflected in the recurrent uses of *they* in THE CAPTURE portion of the story: it is always *they* who took the group to prison and *they* who hit, beat or kicked, the group into the truck (except for the agentless passive in 1984 *we were kicked*). Thus we never really learn the identity of the actual captors: we do not know who orchestrated the trap and who captured the group. Whereas the specific identity of the purported rescuers in THE PLAN had helped to establish its credibility and plausibility, then, the inability to be precise about who it was that had tricked the family, and was taking them to prison, was part of the overall confusion swirling around the capture.

8.2.4 Rabbi

The role of the 'Rabbi' (he is a protector) is diametrically opposed to the role of the 'rescuers/captors' (they are the enemy). Since their roles are so different, it is not surprising that the 'Rabbi' is very differently integrated into the capture story than 'rescuers/captors.' The 'Rabbi's' provision of a blessing, his role in helping the family, and his prior relationship with the father (who had helped a family member of the Rabbi), connects to several intertextual themes: the family's religious beliefs, practices and values; the close calls they endure; the web of reciprocity established by the father with his patients and friends. This role is reflected in referrals to the 'Rabbi.'

The first-mention of the 'Rabbi' in all versions of the capture story suggest familiarity – *this Rabbi* (1982, 1995a)), *the Rabbi* (1984, 1995b) – and, indeed, the 'Rabbi' is not a completely new referent. The CAPTURE story was part of a chronicle of events and the 'Rabbi' had been a topical referent in the prior segment of the chronicle: he had provided refuge for the family when Mrs. Beer's father had been caught with false identification papers and the family had to flee its hiding place. Thus the use of *this* and *the* noted above are cataphoric (Chapter 3): they hark back to the prior salience of the 'Rabbi' in the longer chronicle.

Like the cousin's story, the Rabbi's role in the capture story also diminishes. The 1982 details of the father's plan to help the Rabbi follow the same path to freedom is greatly reduced or disappears in later versions. Yet a trace of the 'Rabbi's' prior role prevails in a relative clause (*where we stayed* (1995a, 1995b)) that indicates his provision of help for the family. Inclusion of this information also establishes the transitional role of blessing as the family sets out for the park.

Despite different textual integration of the Rabbi and the Wehrmacht, what is said about both characters changes from one language, Hebrew (or German Section 8.2.3) to another (English). Just as *Wehrmacht* became *German soldiers* in post-1982 versions, so too, the Rabbi's *misheberaich* (Hebrew for a Jewish blessing for healing the sick) became a *blessing*. Not only did these changes from German and Hebrew make the referents clearer to a broad audience, but also they show Mrs. Beer (as author and animator) linguistically accommodating to her audience and displaying herself more through her current identity (an American speaking English) than her earlier identity (a Slovakian who speaks several languages).

8.2.5 *We: family, group*

Analyses of the re-framing and retelling of the capture story have already observed the importance of a collective *we* in the structure, evaluation and footing underlying the story. Yet there are actually two different constellations of *we* in all four versions of the story: a 'family' *we* (Beer and her parents); a 'group' *we* who embarks on the plan to escape.

The means of transitioning between the two referents of *we* is typical of uses of one referring expression for more than one referent (as observed for multiple referrals of *they* (Chapter 4) and other pronouns (Chapter 5)). Apart from the explicit assertion of the composition of the group *we* (1982), it is information in the text and predicates (attributes, actions) that allows us to infer who the plural pronoun 'contains.'[3]

Let us first look at Example 8.2 and examine how and why the 1982 text explicitly presents the identity of the 'group' *we*.

Example 8.2
1982
(22)   But anyway, so it was at night,
(23)   **we** were supposed to meet in a park,
(24)   **we** were about forty four people,
(25)   there were some from my hometown who lived in Budapest who were included,
(26)   there was an old woman and her son,
(27)   there was a couple and a child and the woman was pregnant
(28)   and there was a couple from my town with a child and the woman was pregnant.
(29)   So there were two children and two pregnant women among them.
(30)   E3 And we came into this little park.

Mrs. Beer begins to anticipate what will happen with a scene setting temporal clause (line (22)) and then continues with the expected action (line (23)). Consistent with the stanza narrative structure (in which event or event-like clauses are embellished through descriptions), *we* in line (23) is expanded in an equative sentence to *forty four people*.

Members of this group are then detailed in a THERE IS list (Chapters 4, 5) in which recurrences of *there is* preface each new member. The list indicates different character types who were *supposed to meet in a park* (line (23)). In addition to having the referential function of specifying the members of the group *we*, the details of the collection itself are evaluative. Included are people who are familiar (line (25)), elderly (line (26)), and families (lines (26) to (28)). Pregnancy is mentioned twice: we learn that a woman *was pregnant* (lines (27) (28)); the summary of the list (prefaced by *so*) sums the number of *children* (two) and *pregnant women* (two (line (29)).

In post-1982 stories, the list of people who plan to escape with Mrs. Beer and her family is differently incorporated into the narratives. Rather than appear in a stative list (introduced by *there is*) and as part of the background information about the plan, the post-1982 versions integrate the list of people into the plot of the story: the group of people provides the solution to a problem (the need for money). In keeping with this change, the list introducer becomes an event clause *he/we got*. Notice that when the group is amassed by the family (*we got* 1995a), there is a clear distinction between the family *we* (pre-list) and the group *we* (post-list). And even though the 'cousin' is not part of the 'family' *we*, her special status in the 'group' is recurrently indicated by her position as the first member of the list.

Thus far, we have noted different means of introducing the group *we* and integrating it into the story. Also changing are two other features:

(1)   the place of the total *forty four*: this switches from initiating (1982, 1995b) to closing the list (1995a);
(2)   the level of detail for the group *we*: the 1982 and 1984 lists have the most detail, the 1995b list, the least.

What remains in the least detailed list is the summary number *forty four*, the *cousin, friends,* and *pregnant women* with *children*. The importance of pregnant women and children is suggested by their introduction (with *there were*, the only explicit introducer of list-members in any of the *he/we got* prefaced lists) and the use of *even*, that implicates the unexpectedness of their inclusion.

8.2.6 Summary

In this section, we have examined eight referents in the four versions of Mrs. Beer's capture story. In addition to showing that referring patterns for the referents reflect already familiar constraints (Chapter 5), we have also observed a familiar alteration of the NOUN FIRST/PRONOUN NEXT sequence: next-mention nouns at locations in the story critical to its point.

When we examined referrals across the different versions of the capture story, however, we saw that although the NOUN FIRST/PRONOUN NEXT sequence reappeared over time for both 'father' and 'cousin,' other referrals changed along with the changing plot line, evaluation, and story structure. Recall, for example, that the disappearance of the subplot about the 'Rabbi' (the father's plan to help him escape (1982)) was part of an overall change from stanza to linear structure. Although the 'Rabbi' still had a transitional role in the story (blessing the family at the outset of their supposed rescue) the loss of the subplot meant *the/this Rabbi* ((1982), (1984)) was too minimal as a first mention. The relative clause *where we stayed* (1995a, 1995b) then reminded us of the 'Rabbi's' prior role in the story and established his qualifications as someone who could send the family out towards what was supposed to be their rescue.

The textual differentiation of the family *we* from the group *we* was also affected by the change from stanza to linear structure. In the 1982 text, *we* was first-mentioned in a pseudo event clause (*we were supposed to meet* (line (23))) and then explicitly equated with the forty-four people (*we were about forty four people* (line (23))) who were gathered together to be part of the rescue. The role of the group *we* shifted, however, when the story structure became more linear. As the fee became an obstacle, with the gathering together of people its solution, the group was no longer explicitly introduced. Rather it was implicitly differentiated from the family *we* (as when *we got* prefaced the list (1995a)) or clarified through its sequential relationship with the list: pre-list *we* is the 'family'; post-list *we* is the whole 'group.' The relative consistency of the group *we* membership, and the steady presence of *pregnant women* and *children* (intensified in 1995b), not only revealed a continuous collective over time: it also had the evaluative function of displaying the cruelty of the captors, whose list of to-be-prisoners includes the familiar, the old, the young, and the vulnerable.

Finally, we also saw a change that reflected an altered view of potential recipients: the change from Hebrew (the 'Rabbi's' *mishe-beraich*) and German (*Wehrmacht*) to English in the 1995 versions. Mrs. Beer's shift to the language of her recipients is not surprising: she had been living in the United States for almost forty years at the time of the first interview and, no doubt, expected that an interview in the United States, in English, would be heard by English speaking audiences. Thus, although we found changes in Mrs. Beer's versions of her story in plot structure, events and audience design, we also found overall consistency in the ways in which referrals reflected closeness of prior mentions, topicality, and evaluative meanings.

In the next section, we turn to the referrals in the retelling of a very different story. As we examine the referrals in Jack's story about a childhood prank, keep in mind how referrals (their introduction, form, distribution and repair) may be related to the role of the characters in the story, their actions in the story, their relationship to the narrator, and the situated interaction in which the stories appear.

8.3 'Who did what' in the retold prank story

In this section, we analyze referrals and events in a replayed story that recounts the narrator's funny incident with a childhood friend (Joey) when they were children: the friend (who later became a well known comedian, known as Joey Bishop) played a funny melody during a formal school performance of an elegy (a poem/song of sorrow or mourning). The storyteller is Jack (a middle aged man from Philadelphia) and the story is told to me (the sociolinguistic interviewer), Freda (Jack's wife) and Rob (Jack's nephew). Jack replays the complicating action and evaluation immediately after having finished it.

Jack's prank story is very different in many ways from Susan Beer's capture story: it is funny, not tragic; it is told to an audience of three people, including two family members, not intended for a large, anonymous, heterogeneous audience; its retelling is immediate, not distant. Yet, like Susan Beer's story, the situation recounted by Jack ends with a surprise based on someone else having duped the narrator, as well as a group of co-present characters in the story who become a collective *we*. Thus both stories set up and dismantle expectations for the audience by starting from a temporal and epistemic starting point set by the narrator as figure in the story.

Like discussion of Susan Beer's story (where we reviewed other parts of her life story to contextualize the capture), we will also need to provide some additional information about Jack, especially his interaction prior to the story with Freda, Rob and me. I discuss the story by segments, starting with pre-story talk (Section 8.3.1), telling the story (Section 8.3.2) and then retelling what happened (Section 8.3.3). The complete version (minus one section, to be noted) is in Appendix 3. My quotes of lines in this chapter conform to the line arrangement in the Appendix. Lines in pre-story talk are numbered; lines in the story entry are lettered (lower case); lines in the story itself are lettered (upper case). A summarizing comparison of the referrals completes the analysis in Section 8.3.4.

8.3.1 Pre-story talk: what y'call dry humor

Jack's childhood friendship with Joey is part of his identity construction during our sociolinguistic interviews. Jack grew up in a working class Philadelphia neighborhood. One of his friends, then known as *Joey Gottlieb*, became a well known comedian in the United States who adapted the stage name *Joey Bishop*: he had a television show in the 1960s, and through his later membership in a well known group of entertainers (mostly singers, known as the Rat Pack), he appeared in several movies. Four features of Jack's discourse reveal the important of his relationship with Joey: how Jack refers to Joey; how Jack refers to himself with Joey; Jack's epistemic stance towards Joey; Jack's affective stance towards Joey. Each of these features appears prior to the story and within the story.

Let us begin by noting that Jack often uses Joey's name as a means of reference – but which name? There are stages in life where people may rightfully change their names: most typically, women may change their surnames when they marry. The taking on of a new name with a new career is not as common, relatively limited, for example, to entry into some religious orders. When one's career is in show business, however, a name that is hard to pronounce, not catchy enough, too long, or too ethnic is routinely changed from one's 'real' name to one's 'stage name.' Although most people who become familiar with that person only through their fame may know only their stage name, those from an earlier phase of life may know both names. Thus knowing someone's real name can convey an epistemic stance: *I had knowledge of this person before he became known to you as something else.*

Jack evokes his epistemic stance towards Joey repeatedly throughout his references to him. In Example 8.3, as Jack was fumbling while pinning a microphone on himself at the outset of our first interview, Jack commented to Freda *He'd be ashamed of me, wouldn't he?* with *he* a referring expression for Joey Bishop:

Example 8.3
Jack:
(a)   He'd be ashamed of me, wouldn't he?
(b)   Uh G- uh . . . Bishop.
(c)   I was gonna say Gottlieb.
(d)   Bishop would've been ashamed of me.

Jack's *he* (in (a)) is a first-mention that I can not interpret: it is the beginning of our interview and no male referents had been introduced. Thus *he* is a premature definite.

Jack begins to backtrack to a name (*uh G-* in line (b)), a referring expression higher in familiarity with implications of constancy regardless of context (cf. Chapter 1; see also Downing 1996, Mulkern 1996). But Jack not only self-interrupts (*uh G-*): he also comments on his own false start after his *uh* . . . prefaces the stage name *Bishop*. Through the meta-linguistic *I was gonna say* (line (c)), Jack laminates his role as author in relation to what has just been animated. Since we do not typically backtrack to comment on what we have just repaired (cf. Goffman 1981b), Jack's comments on his misnaming highlight the presence of the repairable and heighten its relevance in the conversation. After presenting both stage name and real name, Jack then returns to his initial point (*Bishop would've been ashamed of me* (d)) in a repetitive structure (similar to a long distance TYPE 1 repair, Chapter 2) but with a counterfactual shift backward in time.

Other referrals to Joey also appear before Jack's story about the prank. For example, Rob had asked Jack if he knew Jack Klugman (another Philadelphian who became a comedian). Jack and Freda both answer by noting that Jack had lived in a different neighborhood (Example 8.4 below is from Appendix 3; line numbers correspond with the longer transcript in the appendix).

Example 8.4
Jack:
(4)   Klugman was from Porter Street.
(5)   I knew uh . . . y' know . . . Joey Gottlieb.

(6)   Uh Joey Bishop to you.
(7)   That's who I knew.
(8)   But I didn't know Klugman. I knew of him.

After showing familiarity with Klugman by providing the street name (*Klugman was from Porter Street* in line (4)), Jack specifies who he did know out of the co-constructed and emergent category of 'famous comedians who I might have known as a kid.' In keeping with his display of familiarity, Jack again uses Joey's earlier name *I knew uh . . . y' know . . . Joey Gottlieb* (line (5)) and again differentiates who he *knew* (his epistemic stance) from the way in which his hearers would know that same person (*Joey Bishop to you*, line (6)).

As we continue to talk about the two comedians, Jack begins to praise Klugman and to contrast him with Bishop. In Example 8.5, Jack's prior epistemic stance is supplemented with an affective stance:

Example 8.5
Jack:
(19)   Well I'll tell y', Klugman has much more talent,
(20)   I hate to admit this but he has much more talent than uh . . .
        <u>my</u> boyfriend.
(21)   Gottlieb. I mean bo- Joey Bishop.

Jack draws attention to his stance about *Klugman* with a meta-linguistic preface of an announcement; *I'll tell y'* (line (19)). He then uses another meta-linguistic strategy known as a response-controlling *but*-preface (e.g. phrases like *This is none of my business, but . . ., I don't want you to think I'm a bigot, but . . .* (Baker (1975)). Jack's *I hate to admit this but* (line (20)) glosses what is about to be said, as well as potential responses to it, in two ways. The main verb *hate* indicates a reluctance (as principal) to put into words (as author) an upcoming proposition. The speech act verb *admit* shows that what he is about to say (as animator) has negative connotations (i.e. we usually admit that we're guilty, not that we're innocent). Thus Jack's meta-linguistic bracket provides an advantage noted by Goffman (1974: 521):

Anyone who identifies himself with the standards against which the culprit is being judged (and is found wanting) can't himself be all bad – and isn't, and

in the very degree that he himself feelingly believes he is. A self-deprecator
is, in a measure, just that, and in just that measure is not the self that is
deprecated.

Having thus glossed his upcoming comment – as one that challenges
only a portion of his moral self – Jack can go on to criticize Joey.

Still another way that Jack laminates his criticism of Joey Bishop
is to use a referring expression for Joey Bishop that states their relationship – _my_ boyfriend (line (20)) – not only lexically (_boyfriend_)
but through stress on the possessive pronoun _my_. Highlighting his
level of intimacy with Joey not only permits the criticism (because
it shows Jack's access to special knowledge), but it also buffers
its impact on their relationship: 'Saying something negative about
someone does not mean that we do not remain close.' Jack then
retraces his relationship with Joey back to its epistemic starting
point yet again, through a right dislocated noun phrase that specifies
identity through the already familiar 'real name' _Gottlieb_, and then
again, through the recipient-designed clarification to 'stage name' _I
mean bo- Joey Bishop_ (line (21)).

In Example 8.6, Rob and Freda expand upon Jack's criticism of
Joey – but without the same face-saving reluctance shown by Jack:

Example 8.6
Rob: 23) I think so too.   Joey Bishop stands up there,. . . . he's- he's =
                         Z   Z
Jack: 24)   Sure.   Well: =
Rob: 25) = always with the straight face,
                                         Z
Jack: 26)   = Well he has what y'call dry
             humor.[4]
Freda: 27) That's his-   [That's his humor.
                         Z
Jack: 28)   = A quick wit. [It's supposed to be wit.

Criticism of someone who is close can be a subtle way of show-
casing the solidarity of their relationship. Like sociable argument
(another speech activity in which verbal negativity displays solidarity (Schiffrin 1984b)), both criticism and disagreement can show that
a relationship is strong enough to withstand what might for others
be interpreted as real criticism or antagonism. Jack, Freda and Rob
all agreed that Joey Bishop has dry wit. But this joint criticism results

in Jack losing some status that he had been gaining from having a famous friend: after all, if others can criticize Joey Bishop, then how can *Jack's* ability to criticize Joey provide evidence of their close friendship?

Joint criticism resembles sociable argument in another sense: surface forms of agreement can be competitive. Within this conversational style, one may thus continue the patter by intensifying one's criticism or providing more evidence for one's point of view. Either route establishes continued agreement with the point, but can also challenge one's 'ownership' of the point, or in Goffman's (1974) terms (Chapter 6), one's role as author and principal. Thus, in Example 8.7, after Freda says that *Bishop is no actor* (line (32)), Jack adds more criticism of Joey based on evidence not only from 'now,' but also from 'then.'

Example 8.7

Rob: 29) Jack Klugman gets excited, . . . [he's a good actor.
Jack: 30)   [Different types of uh:
          Oh I think so. Yeh.
Freda: 31) Yes. Yes. He's a fine:- a good actor,
          32) Where eh Bishop is no actor.
Jack: 33) Bishop is limited. Bishop is a good contact man.
          34) He al:ways knew who to go see.
          35) Even as a kid. When we were kids, he knew what to do.
          36) He was a real: . . . he was very ambitious, but lacked talent.
          37) He really didn't have too much.
          38) But he had guts! hhhHe had- and he had dedication.
          39) I will say that.

Once Jack retreats to an earlier information state – his childhood knowledge of Jack – he is able to draw upon a much vaster foundation of information from which to voice criticisms. Thus after evoking (along with Freda) Joey's name from the current life world (*Bishop* (line (33)), Jack not only explicitly locates Joey *as a kid*, but also positions himself right there, together with Joey, as children together (*when we were kids* line (35)). By joining Joey in the earlier world, Jack is providing himself with a direct source of knowledge through shared experience. Indeed, what follows (see Appendix 3) is testimony from other childhood friends about Joey's shortcomings and more criticisms from Jack.

We have seen thus far that Jack makes a claim about Joey's humor not only from his own adult (current life world status) perspective, but from his own childhood perspective of Joey Gottlieb, as well as the perspective of their friends. But running through the interaction is competitive agreement about Joey's value as a comedian. Despite the levity and humor of the story, and recipients' laughter that will evaluate the interaction between characters within the story, then, there are slightly darker underpinnings of competition framing the telling of the story. At stake in the conversational interaction prior to the story is the right to make a provocative claim about a friend, to recognize his faults, and remain secure enough in his friendship to do so.

8.3.2 First telling: I realized he did have dry wit

In this section, we see how Jack's story re-confirms his expertise about Joey: the plot reveals Joey's humor; the complicating action firmly implants Jack within a public display of Joey's humor; the evaluation provides public acknowledgement of Joey's humor and evidence for Jack's insider knowledge. Thus Jack is not only a figure in the enactment of humor, but also an omniscient author who 'realizes' and 'knows' even back then, as a child, that Joey had exactly the quality (dry wit/humor) that Jack, Freda and Rob had agreed upon. The same four features of Jack's discourse noted before – referrals to Joey, joint referrals of Jack and Joey, Jack's epistemic and affective stance towards Joey – reappear within the story.

We begin Example 8.8 with how Jack gains a turn in the interaction for a story about Joey's humor.

Example 8.8

Jack: 55) Mike Feldman would say   "Go to work y' bum! =
                                         Z
Freda: 56)   That's unusual for- =
Jack: 57) = You'll never-
Freda: 58) = a young fellow he was what? Sixteen, seventeen years
           old-, to have a nervous stomach. =
                                         Z

Jack: 59)   = You'll never be
        in show business. Go to work." =
Freda: 60) That's unusual.
Jack: 61)   = He used t say: . . .
Freda: (a) They were Bar Mitzvahed together. Him and uh . . . Joey.
Debby: (b) Really?
Jack: (c) We went to school together.
        (d) We were in the same hh room together.
        (e) We used to hooky together!
        (f) He played the piano, I played the violin in the assembly.
        (g) hh We used to jazz it up.
Debby: (h) Did you go to Southern?   Southern High, yeh.
                                   Z
Jack: (i)   Southern High. Yeh.
        (j) Y' know that teacher that came over to me, over at uh . . .
        (k) She used to be- take care of all the entertaining, =
Freda: (l) Yes I do.
Rob: (m) Lamberton?
Jack: (n)   = and musical things, y' know.
        (o) She used to raise holy hell with both of [us!
Freda: (p)   [Oh I bet she's
        had a lot of kids at-
        (q) that passed through her, [that . . . became- . . . Became
        all kinds of things! =
Jack: (r)   [Oh::! But she re<u>mem</u>bered me!
        =
Freda: (s) = hhhh[hhhhhhhhhhhhhhhhhhhh   I guess your mother
        knew of: =
Jack: (t) = [She used to say to me, to Joey Bishop   ["Don't =
                                   Z
Freda: (u)   = all these . . .
        . . .dif[ferent =
Jack: (v) = you [play the piano, when he plays elegies!" =
                                   Z
Freda: (w)   [that became...   different things! =
Jack: (x) = One day-   [He and I:
              Z
Freda: (y)   = Different things like [jail: birds, and eh comedians!

In Example 8.8 above, Jack has just finished telling us that Joey had a nervous stomach. Freda's evaluation of Joey's condition (lines (56) and (58)) is interspersed with Jack's conclusion of a story (lines (55), (57), (59) and (61)) about how another friend had also criticized Joey. When Freda begins to assert evidence of Jack's closeness with Joey (line (a)), Jack provides his own list of joint activities with Joey (lines (c) to (g)) that demonstrates their close relationship. Not only are they continuously presented as a pair through *we* (lines (c), (d), (e) (h)) or *he* and *I* (g)), but the list builds a relationship in which the two are increasingly engaged together. Jack starts with an activity that could encompass many people (*went to school together*, line (c)), narrows down to one engaging a smaller set of members (*were in the same hh room together*, line (d)) and then to those who broke rules together (*used to hooky* (skip school) *together*, line (e)), played particular instruments together (*piano, violin*, line (f)) and, while doing so, *used to jazz it up* (line (g)). Included in that list is a violation of one set of school rules – playing *hooky* – and mention of the joint activity (*he played the piano, I played the violin*, line (f)) that will be the site of the prank. Notice also that *jazz it up* has a metaphorical extension of innovation and excitement based on the improvisational basis of jazz as a musical form.

Although the last activities of Jack's list prefigures what will become funny in the story, Jack cannot yet open his story. One reason is that Freda has opened a byplay with me when she asks about my mother (*I guess your mother knew of all these differen- that became different things!* lines (s), (u) and (w)). Another reason is that Rob and I react referentially to utterances designed as 'tickets' to a story opening (Schiffrin 1984a: 318–323): after Jack has listed his joint activities with Joey, I ask *Did you go to Southern?* (line (h)); after Jack has introduced the teacher without mentioning the school, Rob asks *Lamberton?* (line (m)). Thus Jack's efforts to create a familiar context (lines (h) to (p)) in which to anchor the past experience are treated more for their referential value than their interactional value.

What Jack *has* accomplished, however, is the presentation of his relationship with Joey as a close friendship and the introduction of a character that can ground his story in a familiar context. By mentioning a recently seen former high school teacher through a variant of the pragmatic prototype: *Y'know that teacher that came over to me, over at uh* . . . (line (j)), and identifying her role at the school in terms relevant to his previous list of activities with Jack (*She used to be- take care of all the entertaining, and musical things, y'know*, lines (k) and (n)), Jack brings his past relationship with Joey into the present. Once the teacher has been mentioned, Jack anchors the sub-theme of 'trouble' (preshadowed through 'hooky' and 'jazz it up') to the teacher's recurrent interactions with both Jack and Joey: *She used to raise holy hell* (i.e. scold, get angry with) *with both of us!* (line (o)).

Finally, in addition to narrowing down the broad activities shared with Joey to a specific activity with implications of mischief, and bringing the past into the present by introducing a character from the past who remembered him and his activities with Joey, Jack uses constructed dialogue to prefigure the plot line of the story. In *she used to say to me, to Joey Bishop, "Don't you play the piano, when he plays elegies!"* (lines (t) and (v)), Jack issues a warning from an authority figure (the teacher) almost begging to be broken. This warning brings the two main characters together not only as recipients of the warning, but also through its form and content. Notice, also, that this is the only time (in the entire excerpt, see Appendix 3) when the stage name *Joey Bishop* is presented without repair (no mention of *Gottlieb*) and as the full (first name + last name) stage name. This mode of referral suggests that the warning – and how it plays out through action – will be relevant to Joey's status in his adult role as a comedian known as Joey Bishop.

Given Jack's build up towards a story, it is not surprising that what he next presents (Example 8.9) is a standard story opening that identifies a specific time, participants and activity (z):

Example 8.9

Jack: (x) = One day-   [He and I:

                     z

       (y)   = [Different things like [jail: birds, and

Freda: eh comedians![5] And...

                        z

                    One day he and

Jack: (z) I were [supposed to play elegies,

Freda: (aa)   [How m- long has your

mother been teaching?

Debby: (bb) Well she hasn't been teaching that long. =

Freda: (cc) Oh. [Cause:-   [That's very h- very =

Debby: (dd) =   [But she keeps in touch with some of [them.

Freda: (ee) = interesting to look back!

Despite Jack's opening line, the story still does not begin. Freda pursues a source of common ground different from the 'teacher' whose coincidental sighting had helped to set off Jack's incipient story: she continues to build upon the act of 'remembering past students' to ask how long my mother (who was then a teacher) has been teaching (line (aa)). It is not until this byplay winds down that Jack resumes his bid for a story space (line (A)) and is successful, see Example 8.10.

Example 8.10

Jack: (A) Y'know one day, she- we- I was supposed to play elegy on the violin.

         (B) D' you remember then?

Freda: (C) Oh, yes!   [Oh, that's the =

                              Z

Jack: (D)   All kids would [play that. =

Freda: (E) = first! [My! My!

Jack: (F)   [So he was supposed to accompany me.

         (G) On the piano.

         (H) So she had to teach him the chords.

         (I) He only hit certain chords while I'm playin' elegy.

         (J) So, everything is set fine,

         (K) I get up,

         (L) and I start to play elegy,

         (M) and he's givin' me the chords.

         (N) And in a chord, he goes daa da da da daa, da daa!

         (O) Well the whole: audience broke up!

         (P) Because they don't wanna hear that elegy y' know!

         (Q) And we: . . .

         (R) y' know then I knew, he had the-

         (S) I realized he did have dry wit. =

Freda: (T) That- hhh

Jack: (U) = He knew how to get the-

(V) he knew the whole audience'd laugh so he must've
     had something to him
(W) Even this teacher, this one that- she laughed. =
Freda: (X) Even the teachers, huh?
Jack: (Y) She couldn't help it!

Jack's story opening replays the temporal setting (*one day*) and
schema (*supposed to play elegy on the violin*) portrayed in his earlier unfulfilled bid for the floor (line (z)). In addition to adding
y'know (a marker that can either display or create shared knowledge
(Schiffrin 1987: 268–290)), Jack re-formulates the referrals in subject position to reflect the altered position of the opening bid for the
story.

A comparison between Jack's two bids for the story shows its
sensitivity to position:

FIRST BID   SECOND BID
One day-   Y'know one day,
he and I: (x)   she- we- I (A)
one day he and I were [supposed   was supposed to play elegy on
to play elegies (z)   the violin. (A)
                                   D' you remember then? (B)

Jack's first bid had followed the teacher's warning to both Jack and
Joey, in which both boys appeared in the quotative frame: *She used
to say to me, to Joey Bishop* (line (t)) and in the quoted warning
itself: *you play the piano* and *he plays elegies* (line (v)). Thus the
opening referrals in the premature bid for the floor continue the
two recent referents: *he and I:* (line (x)) and then again *he and I* (line
(z)). Once the story opening is re-positioned, well past the teacher's
warning, the opening referral is up for grabs and indeed, we see
two false starts: *she- we- I was supposed to play elegy on the violin*
(line (A)). Note that each option provides a different link to adjacent
discourse, any of which are possible. Jack's initial *she* continues the
prior thematic (subject) role of the teacher (from lines (k), (o), (r)
and (t)). The next try *we* reflects both anaphoric and cataphoric
concerns: *we* combines those to whom the warning had been issued
with the upcoming joint topical referents of the story. Finally, Jack
adopts the first person *I*, the most familiar referent possible and
most continuously accessible focus. *I was supposed to play elegy on*

the violin thus anchors the schematic activity to the *I* of his own figure.

Once Jack acquires an extended floor in which to tell a story, he situates the occasion as a typical activity (*All kids would play that* (line (D)) and sets up the basic routine: he would *play elegy on the violin* (line (A)); Joey is *supposed to accompany* him (line (F)) *on the piano* (line (G)) by only hitting *certain chords* (line (I)) during Jack's violin playing. Jack's description of what is expected establishes a basic schema: Jack will play a familiar piece on the violin; Joey will learn and play particular piano chords to accompany Jack.

We noted earlier that Jack's story about Joey's prank set up expectations that are then dismantled by someone other than the narrator – someone with ulterior motives and goals who alters the course of events. The story thus begins with the temporal and epistemic starting point of Jack *qua* character in the story, and includes expectations about what will happen through a fusion between the narrator/author's voice and a character's voice. As we see in a moment, much of the first telling of the story establishes what is expected (lines (F) to (I)), even though the expectations had actually already been presented when Jack had been trying to gain the floor.

The first statement of the rule in Jack's story had been from the teacher, whose immediacy in the life world had been used to gain the floor for the story world. It was right after 'teacher' had been introduced that her relevance for the upcoming was established. Although we saw this section earlier, it was interspersed with a contribution from Rob and a conversation between me and Freda. In Example 8.11 it is on its own, along with the redone abstract once Jack has the floor:

Example 8.11

- Y' know that teacher that came over to me, over at uh . . . she used to be- take care of all the entertaining, and musical things, y' know. (lines (i), (k), (n))
- She used to raise holy hell with both of us! (line (o))
- She used t'say to me, to Joey Bishop, "Don't you play the piano, when he plays elegies!" (line (t) and (v))
- One day- he and I: one day he and I were supposed to play elegies. (line (z))
- Y'know one day, she- we- I was supposed to play elegy on the violin. (line (A))

When the musical expectations were presented after Jack had finally gained a turn, they joined with their previous presentation to delay (and create suspense for) the high point of the story: during a recital that is supposed to present somber music (the schema), Joey plays a light-hearted tune (the violation).

Once the expectations have been presented (and their violation prefigured), Jack's event clauses provide more concrete details about what is supposed to happen at the recital. In Example 8.12 he reports what is supposed to happen:

Example 8.12
(H) So she had to teach him the chords.
(I)   He only hit certain chords while I'm playin' elegy.

After the teacher's instructive role is established (H) in relation to the expected outcome (I), there is a transitional clause (J).

Example 8.12
(J) So, everything is set fine,

The plan unfolds in Example 8.13 with verbs that are preparatory (*get up*) and inceptive (*start*), followed by a continuous action through the progressive (*givin' me the chords*):

Example 8.13
(K) I get up,
(L)   and I start to play elegy,
(M) and he's givin' me the chords.

Extending the action replicates for the listener the experience of the recital from both Jack's perspective and that of the audience: we can watch him get up, hear him start to play, and watch and listen to Joey's provision of the chords.

What happens next breaks the musical norms: instead of continuing the melancholy, somber, formal composition, Joey plays a cartoon jingle (which Jack sings).[6] The music also breaks the rhythm of the story. In contrast to the slow pace of the set up (preparing, beginning, listening), the next action is quick and performed *as* music:

(N)   And in a chord, he goes {fast rhythm}

Notice that story content is mirrored in story form: whereas Jack's anticipation of the violation is slow and durative, the climax is fast and punctive.

Recall that, in addition to providing a means for recapitulating past experience, temporal ordering also provides a discourse strategy through which the speaker organizes information about the past for social and/or expressive purposes (Chapter 7). Indeed, the matching of clauses to events is a way of transforming past events into the narrator's perspective, and seating the audience in the narrator's temporal and epistemic position. This co-construction of perspective is also indicated by Jack's use of the historical present tense in most of the complicating action clauses, a tense whose transformative effects are made possible by temporal juncture between narrative clauses (Schifffin 1981; see also comments in Chapter 1).

An internal evaluation (*Well the whole: audience broke up* (line (O)) switches tense (from historical present to preterit) to move out of the action-oriented story world. Notice that the metaphorical verb *broke up* not only conveys a loss of control, but also the 'breaking up' of the schema: the unified expectation of norms has disintegrated. In Example 8.14, Jack's explanation for this audience reaction also mocks the initial validity of the schema: *Because they don't wanna hear that elegy y' know!* (line (P)):

Example 8.14

Jack: (O) Well the whole: audience broke up
         (P) Because they don't wanna hear that elegy y' know!
         (Q) And we: . . =
Freda: (R) That-hhhhhhhhhh
Jack: (S) = y'know then I knew, he had the-
         (T) I realized he did have dry wit.
         (U) He knew how to get the- he knew the whole audience'd laugh
         (V) so he must've had something to him.
         (W) Even this teacher, this one that- she laughed. =
Freda: (X) Even the teachers, huh?
Jack: (Y) She couldn't help it!

The abandoned *and we:* . . . is put off until the retelling (and a change in footing). What Jack does instead is clarify the role of his story in the prior interaction by beginning to present his own knowledge as an inference (note the dual temporal and inferential readings of *then* (Schiffrin 1991)) warranted by the events in the story: *y'know then I knew, he had the-* (line (S)). As Jack continues, he shifts from events to three different states of knowing: what he himself knew (line (S)), what he himself realized (*I realized he did have dry wit* (line (T)) and what Joey knew (*He knew how to get the- he knew the whole audience'd laugh* (line (U)). Like his earlier admission: *I hate to admit this but* (line (20)) in the interactional world, which presupposed the truth of its complement (that Joey was not as funny as Jack Klugman), Jack's realization in the story world also presupposes the truth of its complement: framing *he did have dry wit* through the verb 'realize' marks its incontestability. Finally, these multiple assertions of knowledge warrant Jack's restated conclusion (conveyed explicitly through *so* and *must*) that *So he must've had something to him* (line (V)).

In sum, we have seen in this section how Jack's story established an epistemic stance within a childhood experience in which privileged knowledge enabled him to support an affective stance towards Joey Bishop's humor. As we see in the next section, these events are immediately replayed, but with slightly different temporal contours and participation statuses that create different possibilities for evaluation.

8.3.3 The second telling: even the teacher admitted it

In this section, we compare the events, referrals and evaluation of Jack's replay with those of the first telling. As we see in Example 8.14, Jack moves fluidly from the evaluation of the performance (lines (W) and (Y)) back to the ongoing performance itself (line (Z)).

Example 8.15

Jack:	(W)	Even this teacher, this one that- she laughed. =
Freda:	(X)	Even the teachers, huh?
Jack:	(Y)	She couldn't help it!
	(Z)	And I'm playin' {melody},
	(AA)	and I'm playin', y' know =

                                          Z
Freda: (BB)   hh Oh [God!

Jack: (CC)   = [And he goes, . . .
         (DD) he gives me the chord,
         (EE) and I'm not- re- re- for the next phrase.
         (FF) I know the musical phrase,.
         (GG) I'm ready to go
         (HH) and he goes, . . .
         (II) he gives me another chord,
         (JJ) and then he goes,
         (KK) at the end of the chord he goes daa da da da daa, da
               daa!
         (LL) Real fast and quiet.
         (MM) That was f- I had to laugh myself hhh
Freda: (NN) That'sz cute!
Jack: (OO) Well we made a hit that day.
         (PP) Even the teacher admitted it.
         (QQ) She says, "Well it was- y' shouldn't do it! But it was
               nice."
         (RR) What's she gonna say?
Freda: (SS) Second grade? Third grade, I guess? I couldn't
               see you-
                         Z
Jack: (TT)   Oh: it was- no! It was about the seventh
               grade. Or the eighth grade.
Freda: (UU) I think by the seventh or the eighth grade, you'd
               have played somethin'   better than that!
Jack: (VV) Well elegy's a tough number to play! . . .
         (WW) And I was squeakin' away on that violin hh =
Freda: (XX) Well it-
Jack: (YY) = And he was- we were laughin' that day, all day I
               remember.
Debby: (ZZ) You still play the violin?

Figure 8.1 compares the complicating action of the first and second tellings. As we see in Figure 8.1, Jack retells what happens
not only by replaying the recital itself, but also by expanding each
constituent activity. Jack's own playing increases from *start to play*
(line (L)) to *playing* (lines (Z) and (AA)), as does his preparation: he
knows the music (line (FF)) and is *ready* (line (GG)). Joey's playing
also expands: he gives Jack *the chord* (line (DD)) and then *another*

First telling

(J) So, every thing is set fine,
(K) I get up,

(L) and I start to play elegy,

(M) and he's givin' me the chords.

(N) And in a chord, he goes [sings]

Second telling

(Z) And I'm playin' /melody/,
(AA) and I'm playin', y' know=
(CC) And he goes,...
(DD) he gives me the chord,
(EE) and I'm not- re- re- for the next phrase.
(FF) I know the musical phrase,
(GG) I'm ready to go
(HH) and he goes, ..
(II) he gives me another chord
(JJ) and then he goes,
(KK) at the end of the chord he goes [sings]
(LL) Real fast and quiet.

Figure 8.1 Complicating action in first and second tellings

chord (line (II)). Further duration is added through two false starts of the climactic action: *and he goes* (lines (CC) and (HH)) that tease the audience into expecting to hear the punchline, and then force them to wait still longer for it. Even when Jack finally gets to Joey's grand finale: *and then he goes* (line (JJ)), he still backtracks to more precisely place that finale *at the end of the chord* (line (KK)). The alternation of stative and active clauses extends the action: we are listening through constituent actions – successive phases and chords – and kept waiting until the end of the chord for what we already know will happen.

Although the changes just discussed blend structure and evaluation, we can also compare the more explicit evaluation clauses across the two versions, as in Figure 8.2. Although both versions evaluate Joey's action as funny, the locus of the evaluation shifts. Whereas the evaluators in the first version were the audience (lines (O) and (P)), Jack (lines (S) to (V)) and the teacher (lines (W) and (Y)), the evaluative role in the second version falls primarily to the teacher (lines (PP) to (RR)). Not only is the teacher the one who *admits* the success of the music (line (PP)), but she also presents a counterpoint to her earlier warning (*She used t'say to me, to Joey Bishop, "Don't you play the piano, when he plays elegies!"* lines (t) and (v)), as well as juxtaposing her praise against an admonition: *"y' shouldn't do it! But it was nice"* (line (QQ)).

Also similar in both telling and retelling is the teacher's stance. In both versions, the teacher's evaluation positions her as relatively powerless. But notice that the dimension of power differs. The powerlessness of the teacher first appears as a kind of flooding out (Goffman 1963) in an affective domain (*She couldn't help it!* (line (Y)). This reaction resembles Jack's own involuntary reaction, in which he switches from an external evaluation of the act as funny (*That was f-*) to an internal evaluation that centers upon himself: *I had to laugh myself hhh* (line (MM)) along with actual laughter that performs the humor. In contrast to the teacher's initial role as one who can speak with the moral authority needed for an invective (*"Don't you play the piano, when he plays elegies!"* (lines (t) and (v))), her next move appears as a collapse of verbal authority: *What's she gonna say?* (line (RR)).

Finally, although Jack was one of the key evaluators of Joey's humor in the first telling, he is realigned in the second telling not as

First telling	Second telling
(O) Well the whole: audience broke up!	
(P) Because they don't wanna hear that elegy y' know!	(MM) That was f- I had to laugh myself hhh
	(OO) Well we made a hit that day.
(Q) And we: ..=	
(S) = y'know then I knew, he had the-	
(T) I realized he did have dry wit.	
(U) He knew how to get the-	
he knew the whole audience'd laugh	
so he must've had something to him	
(V)	
(W) Even this teacher, this one that- she laughed.	(PP) Even the teacher admitted it.
	(QQ) She says, 'Well it was- y' shouldn't do it!
	But it was nice."
Freda: (X) Even the teachers, huh?	
(Y) She couldn't help it!	(RR) What's she gonna say?
	(WW) And I was squeakin' away on that violin hh
	(YY) And he was-
	we were laughin' that day,
	all day I remember.

Figure 8.2 Evaluation in first and second tellings

someone who appreciated Joey's joke as an observer – but relished it as a participant: *Well we made a hit that day* (line (OO)), *we were laughin' that day, all day I remember* (line (YY)). Thus the humor of Joey's prank is appreciated from the inside, as a co-participant and co-principal in its execution and effect. In his second telling, then, Jack tells not just a narrative, but a meta-narrative in which he was co-author and co-principal of his friend's plan to amuse the school audience.

8.3.4 Summary

In prior sections, I discussed Jack's story by segments, focusing on both referents and events, i.e. examining referrals to the characters and their role in the story (what they do, how, when and why). Although we have noted, in passing, referrals to Joey, joint referrals of Jack and Joey, and Jack's epistemic and affective stance towards Joey, we can more systematically compare the referrals to get a clearer view of their role in the story.

Let us start with Joey Bishop. We saw in pre-story talk that Jack's referrals to his childhood friend veered back and forth between real name and stage name, often juxtaposing one against the other to reveal both his epistemic and affective stance. Once Joey became a referent, he was – not surprisingly – next-mentioned as *he* or through zero anaphora. As Jack moved toward the story world in which Joey's friend *as* Joey Bishop is relevant to the point of the story, however, Jack used the full stage name *Joey Bishop* only once: when prefacing a quote stating the rule that would later be broken.

What is celebrated through Joey's prank is not only his ability to be funny (and Jack's privileged access to awareness of Joey's skill), but the friendship between Jack and Joey. This appears before the story (through the recurrent list of activities of the *we*), lessens in the first telling of the story (substituted by *he* and *I*) and then reappears in the retelling when Jack joins Joey as co-author and co-principal of humor. It also appears through a close balance between the frequency of referrals to self (as *I* or *me*, 12 in the two tellings) and reference to Joey (as *he*, 13 times in the two tellings).[7]

Although Jack and Joey shared the main role in the story, the supporting role was certainly played by 'the teacher'. Not only did she speak as the voice of authority – the one whose veneer of power was shattered by the humor of the incident – but she provided the bridge between conversation and story (*Y'know that teacher that came over to me* (line (j))). Because Jack could call upon a recent sighting of the teacher (with Freda present), he was able to anchor the incident to her. How helpful it was when she could not only present the rule to be broken (*She used to say to me, to Joey Bishop "Don't you play the piano when he plays elegies!* (lines (t) and (v)), but also appreciate the violation (*Even this teacher, this one that- she laughed* (line (W))) and endorse Joey Bishop's humor in a way that could support Jack's own assessment of his friend's humor. It is hardly surprising, then, that 'the teacher' is reinstated as *this teacher* (line (W)) or *the teacher* (line (PP)) each time she re-enters the story world. In contrast to Joey, whose name indexes both his fame and his familiarity and is thus crucial to his story role, it is the institutional identity of the teacher *as teacher* that is foundational to her role in the story.

8.4 Conclusion

In this chapter, I have been discussing various features of Jack Cohen's and Susan Beer's narratives: what is reported, who does what, and what happens when the story is retold. As we noted initially, both stories report the disruption of a plan and the immersion of the narrator in a *we*. Yet it is also obvious that they are profoundly different: the goals, the audience, the setting – and of course the experience and its consequences – differ tremendously, as we discuss in Chapter 9. The linguistic similarities summarized below are thus all the more startling.

First, both stories set up expectations in similar ways. Whereas Mrs. Beer used her father's voice to report THE PLAN about what was supposed to happen, Jack used the teacher's voice to state a central rule that established an expectation about who would play what instrument. Both narrators also anticipated the expected course of action (e.g. 'we were supposed to do X') and used transitional clauses (the Rabbi's 'Outset' in the capture story, the initial chords in the prank story) to move from expectation to actuality.

Second is a cluster of structural similarities. Jack's expanded event structure was reminiscent of Mrs. Beer's expansion of her father's plans in the PLAN and ANTICIPATION phases of her story, as well as the increasingly durative entry of the group into the park (e.g. through the progressive *coming to, getting closer to, approaching*). Likewise, Jack presented a group of preparatory clauses that unpacked events and alternated with repeated fragments of clauses in which Joey (*he goes* . . .) began to provide a chord. This arrangement resulted in an overall increase in event clauses that added duration, and joined with a prepositional phrase (*at the end of a chord*), to suspend the action.

Third is the replication of story content by story form. Although this appeared only in Mrs. Beer's first (1982) version of her story, it is worth noting: both the PLAN and its ANTICIPATION were largely descriptive (only a few event clauses with interspersed descriptions), and the CAPTURE was a rapid series of event clauses. In both of Jack's versions (and especially in the retelling), anticipation of the violation is slow and durative, with the climax fast and punctive.

Fourth, the shift from action to cognition in Jack's story is reminiscent of the turning point in post-1982 versions of Mrs. Beer's story, in which the group *we* presented the inferential basis for concluding that the plan to escape had really been a trap. The enactment of knowledge, buttressed by reflections (that drew upon prior events) and logic-in-use (e.g. conditionals, epistemic uses of modals), in both stories showed that participants had little choice but to realize that what they had expected was quite different from what they were experiencing. And just as the actions of others in Mrs. Beer's story (the captors who kicked, hit and beat the group) confirmed the group's supposition about the real goal of the mission, so too, the impact of Joey's action was reinforced through others' concrete actions: not only did Jack laugh, but so did the audience and the teacher.

Of course the altered state of knowledge, and the actions that reified it, had very different consequences in the two stories. Mrs. Beer's group realization meant a fate whose possibility had been underlying the prior portions of her life story (cf. Brockmeier (2001) on the teleological orientation of life stories) and whose actualization had countless effects on the rest of her life. The impact of Jack's realization was more local and limited in scope: by confirming that he had the grounds from which to speak with authority about Joey Bishop's humor, it contributed to Jack's status (however fleeting) in the interaction.

Finally, just as Mrs. Beer became a co-author and co-principal of her father's plan to help the family escape, so too, Jack became a co-author and co-principal (through playing and replaying the melody, making a hit) of his friend's plan to amuse the audience gathered together to hear the elegy. Although Jack was one of the key evaluators of Joey's humor in the first telling, he was realigned in the second telling not as someone who appreciated Joey's joke as an observer, but who relished it as a participant: *Well we made a hit that day* (line (OO)), *we were laughin' that day, all day I remember* (line (YY)). Thus the humor of Joey's prank is appreciated from the inside, as a co-participant and co-principal in its execution and effect.

Whereas the features of the stories just discussed concerned the violation of a schema, the collective *we* was more pertinent to the evaluation of what happened. Notice that evaluation – by definition – provides a link between the subjectivity underlying the 'facts' ('what do these events mean to *me*?', 'what is the point of the story in which these events are embedded?') and how that subjectivity both reflects (and creates) ongoing interactional concerns, as well as broader domains of Discourse. Once we remember (and slightly reformat) the traditional distinction between inclusive and exclusive *we*, it will seem very obvious that the pronoun *we* can play a crucial role in evaluation.

We combines the self-reference of *I* with another referent in one of two ways: *we* can be either inclusive or exclusive. In the former case, *we* includes the addressee, i.e. the person who could be indexed by the second person pronoun *you*. In the latter case, *we* excludes the addressee, conveying instead the inclusion of a non-present person as referent (or collection of 'others') who could otherwise be conveyed by third person pronouns (*he, she, they*). All referrals have a potential of dual indexicality: to give (intentionally) information about a referent and give off (unintentionally) information about the speaker. But *we* is always dually indexical: not only is the 'self' always evoked, but so too, are other referents (a co-present addressee, non-present others, or both) with whom the *I* acts and is aligned.

When we tell a story about specific people with whom we shared an experience, our referrals display characters that reveal complex attributes, take specific actions, and form social relationships with other characters within the changing spatial, temporal and epistemic parameters of a story world. If those characters join us as a *we* – as co-agents within the story world – what is produced is a projection of the speaker as both figure (character in the story) and animator (who is authoring what happened to self). Thus the speaker emerges in a textual world, occupied by people, situated in a place and developing a shared information state over time, and within another site of social action and interaction: a concrete social world that forms its own microcosmic and fleeting world.

This duality – the embedding of people from the 'real' world in both a world of representation and a world of social action – gives references like *we* an important role in creating a bridge between the story world and the social world. Although we often think of narrative as being about an individual – one who reconstructs the past for self-aggrandizement – we do not often think of narrative as supporting what Goffman (1971b) has called a 'with.' Yet like our physical and verbal displays of togetherness (our 'tie signs' (Goffman, 1971b)) in the real world, our symbolic displays of togetherness in story worlds can tell others a great deal about the people with whom we feel (or want to feel) a sense of solidarity. Referrals are thus excellent ways to discover the textual emergence of a 'with' that can reflect the life world existence of (or desire for) that same 'with.'

The immersion of self in a collective appears in many stories through both joint actions and referrals. In my analysis (Schiffrin 2000) of the life story of Ilse Kahane, another Holocaust survivor, for example, I found that Mrs. Kahane repeatedly used informative nouns (*my friends, we four, we five*) for a set of friends, rather than the pronoun *they*, even in cases where *they* was sequentially expected and the referral to the whole group was redundant or inaccurate. Her referrals meshed with her use of direct quotes – a performative form of constructed dialogue that creates a sense of verisimilitude – to show her relationship with the four women with whom she survived the Holocaust as one based on long-lasting solidarity and interdependence.

Susan Beer's referrals to her father, and Jack's referrals to Joey Bishop, also project a 'with' from the story world onto an interactional plane. Mrs. Beer's meshing of two voices (merging as co-author and co-principal of the plan in its retellings) display the closeness of father and daughter, thus continuing a major intertextual theme throughout her life story: her father was responsible for many of the lessons of her childhood; his role as a physician placed him at the center of a network of people who provide help for the family. And Jack's recurrent mentions of *he* and *I* (in close succession and equal frequency), that eventually merged with the *we* of joint production of humor in his retelling, joined his other carefully managed repairs and referrals (i.e. using Joey's real name *and* stage name) to project the relevance of reported events within the story world for an interactional world of people and social actions. Although the relationship between Susan Beer and her father clearly differed in many ways to Jack's relationship with Joey, the two narrators thus incorporated part of another's experience into their stories, each in ways that created not only story worlds, but also worlds in which their individual pasts of 'there and then' could make sense in their ongoing construction of 'here and now.'

In sum, just as reference plays a pivotal role in portraying the characters about whom a speaker is talking in a textual world, so too, does it have a role in constructing the 'character' of the speaker him/herself in the interactional world. We can return to the communicative properties of referrals (Chapter 1) to understand why they initiate a process whereby we see others in multiple domains. Referrals allow us to connect language to an external world of people, places and things that is typically assumed to exist independently of each particular mention in language. The linguistic job of a referral is thus to set up a word-to-world connection: a referring expression evokes an entity from the world, an external link to a part of the world that it denotes. Once a word-to-world connection is established by a speaker for a hearer, and an entity has been evoked through language, it is an object of attention within a text that is situated in an interaction. But we do not stop there: our hearers expect something *to be said about* the entity to which they are attending and we oblige.

Given all the different domains in which what we say has an impact, and is interpreted by 'other' as a basis for a next contribution, it is hardly surprising that a referent can have more than one thing *said about it* at a time: it can evoke a character that takes action, has attributes, and interacts with other characters *and* help display speaker identity and adjust speaker/hearer relationships. And given that we tell and retell narratives throughout our lives, at different times, in different places, and to different people – but have a limited number of referring expressions available through our lexicons – it should hardly be surprising that the 'same' referring expression is pressed into service in multiple ways, including simultaneously connecting story to situation, as well as story teller to person.

Notes

1. To recap what happened: Susan Beer was the only child in an observant Jewish family; she grew up in a small town in Slovakia. When the Germans seized control of Slovakia, discrimination against Jews in Topolcany escalated. After Susan received an order to report for a transport to a labor camp, her parents arranged for her to go illegally to Hungary, a country that was then safer for Jews. Susan Beer's parents eventually escaped to Hungary also and they all lived clandestinely with false identities until they were captured, imprisoned, and then sent to Auschwitz.
2. The *Wehrmacht* was the name of the German armed forces from 1935 to 1945. Although all soldiers in the Wehrmacht had to swear loyalty to Hitler, former Wehrmacht members claimed that the Wehrmacht just did its duty out of a sense of loyalty and honor, but was not part of the systematic murder carried out by the Nazis, did not commit any war crimes, and were abused by the Nazis, too. Because of contradictory evidence, the debate continues.
3. The shift from the 1982 explicit identification of the 'group' *we*, to inference of its members, is related to the changing narrative structure (from stanza to linear) and plot development (the incorporation of a conflict/resolution mini-plot) in post-1982 texts (Chapter 7).
4. Dry wit/humor is the use of subtle juxtapositions of word meaning and performance style whose humor is appreciated only by recognition of a 'mismatch' between the words and their mode (or context) of presentation.
5. This comment suggests that Jack was once imprisoned. Nothing about this was mentioned elsewhere in our interviews and I never asked.
6. What Joey played was a tune from a cartoon, a snappy, fast-paced jingle whose words ("Shave and a haircut, two bits!") are familiar to Americans growing up in the 1940s to 1970s (e.g. it sometimes appeared at the end of televised cartoons). It is not part of a longer score.

7. I counted all tokens of *he* (*him*) and *I* (*me*) in the two tellings. When one of these pronouns was in a TYPE 2 repair (referent and referring expression changed), I counted only the repaired-to form (not the repairable). When these pronouns were in a TYPE 1 repair (repetition of the referring expression), I only counted it once.

9

Redoing and replaying

9.1 Introduction

We began this book with a collection of examples illustrating what could be innovative, new, and different in language as opposed to fixed, old, and the same. After suggesting that an expanded and extended version of variation analysis could help us understand two different arenas of language use in which these oppositions appear – reference and narrative – we analyzed variation within both arenas by focusing on what happens when either recurs in 'second position.' Each recurrence was different in some way from the first, if only because it was the second 'doing' of something that had already appeared in discourse. Sometimes the same concept or meaning reappeared in other words. Other times, the same word reappeared in different texts, in constellations of different words. Sites of second position varied by type and distance, ranging from a word repeated immediately after its completion to a life story narrative told more than ten years apart. My review in this concluding chapter of redoing referrals (Section 9.2) and replaying narratives (Section 9.3) addresses several topics and themes that crosscut both areas of research. I close with general comments about how the analyses are related to several key constructs drawn from different approaches to discourse (Section 9.4).

9.2 Redoing referrals

Referrals are communicative attempts by a speaker to evoke a referent (the idea a speaker has of something in the world) through a referring expression. Accomplishing a referral requires interactive coordination between speaker production and hearer interpretation.

Both production and interpretation depend upon general pragmatic principles of quantity and relevance that work in synchrony with information accrued during prior text/context and developed within emergent and co-constructed interactive sequences. Thus what a speaker produces is intended to be interpreted by another person within a discourse that is cumulatively and jointly constructed during an ongoing interaction. The referring expression used by the speaker (ideally) allows a hearer to recognize the speaker's intention: to identify a referent sufficiently similar to what the speaker intends so that each can then say (and understand) something about that referent. Because I view localized and interactive construction of referrals as actions that are directed outward toward both the world and other persons, I use a verb of action 'do' (*redoing*) to describe recurrent referrals, regardless of whether those referrals recur as the target of a repair (Chapters 2, 3, 4) or because they have already been evoked earlier in a sequence (Chapters 5, 8).

When a referral is introduced into the discourse (if it has not yet been explicitly mentioned), recipient recognition of the referent draws more upon knowledge of the world than if a referral is already in place in the discourse. First-mentions of a referent, however, are rarely brand new and may even be eased into a discourse through a pragmatic prototype (THERE IS, THEY HAVE, Chapter 4) that provides both an abstract conceptual link to a mental model and a concrete link to a prior text. When a referral is a next-mention, speakers and recipients need to attend to and use information not only about the world, but also about a prior text in which several referents may actually compete for attention (through recency, semantic similarity, topicality or co-presence in a textual segment, Chapter 5).

Referrals can become problematic and be redone for a variety of reasons. In Chapters 2, 3 and 4, I tried to identify some of those reasons by looking at what part of the referral is repaired (conceptual (referent) or linguistic (referring expression)), what kind of referring expression is repaired (noun or pronoun), where the repair begins (at the article, at the noun), how the repair proceeds (what is the outcome? is other material also changed or added?), and where the referral occurs (with what kind of noun? in what position in the sentence? the text? and the turn?). These are not all 'constraints' in the classic variationist sense, but they are all factors that may help us explain the 'why' of a second-position referral that can be characterized as a repair.

In Chapter 2, we analyzed problems that arose at various points in the process of connecting a referring expression with a referent (the external perspective) and making successive referrals to the same referent (the internal perspective). Chapter 2 suggested two different outcomes for both referring expression and referent: a speaker (who self-initiated a repair) could continue referring expression and referent (e.g. *he- he*), change referring expression and referent (e.g. *he- they*), change referring expression but continue referent (e.g. *he- the boy*), or continue referring expression but change referent (e.g. *they₁- they₂*). By examining examples of each type in discourse, we built up an understanding of how such problems and their solutions worked.

A quantitative comparison at the end of Chapter 2 showed that pronouns were involved in slightly more repairs than nouns. Repairs with pronouns were more likely to be in subject position, regardless of whether the pronoun was the problem (*he- my friend*) or the solution (*my friend- he*) or whether the referent changed or continued. Thus the problem with pronouns seemed to concern the speaker's sense of what a hearer would be able to identify – and/or be familiar with – in a form and sentence position associated with old information.

Problems with pronouns, especially in sentence positions in which familiarity is favored and expected, should not be altogether surprising. Although all pronouns are shifters (Jakobson's (1957) term for deictics), the source of their 'shifting' can include not only objective (and subjective) proximity (or distance) in a physical world of participants, times and places, but also in a textual world. For example, we saw how pronouns in narratives and lists were disambiguated by sentence predicates and/or adjacent text, especially when text-level constraints conflicted with one another (Chapter 5). And we also saw an example (*Then there was a few went to public school when they- when we were younger, growin' up, the ones that went to Catholic school, we hh we used to fight them all the time* (Chapter 2)) in which different syntactic parsings, and intonational segmentation of adjacent talk, led to different resolutions of the referent of *we*.

Our exploration of the dual indexicality of the pronoun *we* highlighted how the proximal (close to me) distal (distant from me) axis resonated in both text and social life (see Helmbrecht (2002) for analysis of its grammatical complexity and prominence from a typological perspective). *We* served as a resource for conveying collectives in a textual world that could also establish a position in the interactional world and in broader worlds of Discourse (Chapter 8). The open 'reach' of pronouns can also allow the traditional definiteness of pronouns to drift toward indefiniteness. We saw in Chapter 4, for example, a variety of ways in which *they* extended its reach from a third person plural pronoun to a vague entity inferable from a prior place mention (as in *Here at Saint Monica's which is downtown, **they** have a commercial course*) or a pronoun with no antecedent at all (as in *And uh, every once in a while we'd stop and get a soda, y'know, or something like that. And then- **they**- **they** always had these little ice cream parlors around, which they don't have today*).

Returning to Chapter 2: when we combined syntactic position with interactional units, pronouns did not figure quite so prominently. What did matter was that one type of repair, in which both referring expression and referent continued (e.g. *he- he, a big- big difference*), patterned differently than the others. It was only in these TYPE 1 repairs that nouns *or* pronouns were clustered at the start of both syntactic and interactional units (sentences and turns respectively). I suggested that the presence of these repairs in multiple sites of initiation could provide planning time for the rest of the sentence and turn.

Chapter 3 continued the micro-focus on parts of a referral, again using both extensive analyses of individual cases and examination of quantitative trends to profile types of repair – this time, a problem type defined by location in the noun phrase, i.e. articles that precede the noun. Again, we examined the possibility of change (switching to a different article) and continuation (repeating the same article) in a range of environments.

Analysis of the article switches suggested that although some switches reflected a functional convergence between *the* and *a*, others reflected deictic shifts in information state, epistemic changes, porous levels of inclusiveness, or the peripheral (vs. core) status of a referent within a conceptual category. Article shifts that maintained (in)definiteness reflected the replacement of a referral in an ongoing sentence, text and/or interaction. Thus, article switches seemed to reflect not just miscalculations of information status, but also trouble finding the 'fit' between word and world that would also fit comfortably within a text.

All the quantitative comparisons in the book assumed that some aspect of the environment (of the referent, of a clause) impinged upon its means of expression. Analytical selections of environments (or constraints) thus also impinge upon our interpretation of 'why.' Chapter 3, however, also relied upon a slightly different use of quantitative comparisons than Chapter 2. In Chapter 3, the quantitative analyses of article repetitions in sentence and text positions incorporated insights from both markedness theory and conversation analysis, both of which depend upon implicit assumptions about the pairing of forms with meanings and/or contexts. Both perspectives expect exceptions in form–meaning correspondences, the former from a linguistic paradigm or pattern, the latter from an interactional norm. Both also expect that exceptions will be formally marked in some way. If the information status conveyed by an article is inappropriate to its position in a sentence, text, or turn, for example, its repair may be a formal mark of that trouble.

As shown through analysis of the placement of article repetitions in sentence and text, however, sentence or text location did not seem problematic: distributions of both *a- a* and *the- the* nouns generally conformed to the typical positioning of indefinites and definites in sentences, of noun weight (in relation to position), and of order of mention (first-mention, next-mention) in text. What the article repetitions seemed to reflect, instead, was the very local problem of verbalizing a noun. Since the cut-off and repeated articles, and the nouns that they prefaced, were already appropriately placed within their sentences (in initial or final positions) and texts (as first- or next-mentions), it seems that speakers can coordinate information status, sentence and text prior to the verbalization of a noun.

The local nature of the article problem makes sense in relation to Levelt's (1983) suggestion that speakers self-interrupt when self-monitoring identifies a problem. If a speaker anticipates a problem with the upcoming noun, a logical place to interrupt is right before that noun, i.e. at the article. One type of noun raised more red flags than others: nouns evoking animate abstract roles or collections of

people (i.e. Sacks' 1992 [1966] membership categories). Since articles are forward looking, interrupting them prior to the noun might
offer preparation time for the noun itself, much as the problematic
referrals in Chapter 2 (in which referent and referring expression
continued) might offer preparation time for the sentence and turn.
Thus perhaps references to membership categories require complex
conceptual work or are difficult to label with the right word.

Chapter 4 explored problems that began in some of the same ways
as other repairs: self-interruption of an article or noun, In contrast to
the other repairs, however, the solutions did not rephrase the noun,
but switched the noun to sentence and/or text. Analysis of both
initiation and completion of these repairs suggested problems in
information status: the speaker had initially assumed more recipient
familiarity with a referent than was warranted.

In the first part of Chapter 4, we saw that referring expressions from different positions on an assumed familiarity scale were
resolved in the same ways: a problematic referral was re-framed
from noun to sentence and/or text providing easily accessible information to which the cut-off referral could be anchored. In the next
section of Chapter 4, I suggested that what served as a reactive
strategy for resolving problems could also serve as a proactive strategy for referrals. We examined *there is* and *they have* as variants
of this strategy, grouped together as a pragmatic prototype based
upon conceptual and linguistic connections among existence, location and possession. We saw how two parts of the prototype – *there*,
they; the post copular NP – could anchor the referent into a knowledge base presumably shared by both speaker and hearer. We also
explored how the two variants of the prototype could be deployed as
resources in text for differentiating evaluative foci and/or structural
segments.

The grouping together of two semantically different clauses –
there is, they have – in Chapter 4 expanded the locus of variability
from variants that (primarily) maintained the same referential meaning to those with more abstract semantic and pragmatic similarities. The analysis of next-mention referrals in two different genres
(Chapter 5) moved the locus of variability in still other directions.
First, the focus on next-mention referrals moved the site of 'redoing'
from a position immediately adjacent to a referral (within the noun
phrase that displayed trouble) to a more distant site that could be

trouble free: the next-mention of a referral within a text. Second, because the two genres (narratives, lists) establish strikingly different textual worlds, they offered the opportunity to consider both genre-specific and genre-varying constraints. Third, the focus on different genres had a bearing on text level variation. We spoke of narratives and lists as discrete genres, with a narrative as a linear recounting of events grouped together as one experience, and a list as a hierarchically constructed description of set members. But we also noted that there were similarities between them and that features of each could combine to produce blended genres.

Chapter 5 grouped together three different analyses of the NOUN FIRST/PRONOUN NEXT sequence to examine the same constraints (recency, possible ambiguity, topicality, structural boundaries) on next-mention referrals in the genres. The first analysis provided an in-depth view of the referring sequences (in one narrative and one list) that illustrated the constraints and how they might impact the use of next-mention nouns or pronouns. We then examined how the four constraints correlated with nouns vs. pronouns as next-mentions. A key part of this analysis explored reasons for the *atypical* sequences, thus continuing the assumption of markedness/preference theories that an exception to the pattern occurs for a reason. Thus this part of Chapter 5 dealt with how the sequential choice to next-mention a referent with a lexically informative noun, rather than a pronoun, was sensitive to many different types and levels of meaning.

Further social and expressive subtleties of reference appeared in Chapter 8, when we examined the referrals in two very different kinds of stories: Susan Beer's story from Holocaust oral history interviews; Jack Cohen's story about his friend's childhood prank. In Chapter 8, we were able to explore the strategic value of proper names and intentional repairs of those names, as well as how the form and content of referrals (including a collective *we* in narrative evaluations) could reflect the integration of a character into a narrative plot or the embedding of a narrative within a longer life story on an ongoing interaction.

Returning to Chapter 5 on referring sequences, the third analysis in this chapter turned our attention to a more public form of Discourse in which a place referral (not a person referral) had become controversial. Here we analyzed the developing ambiguity of the term *concentration camps* over time within the communal experiences (and memory culture) of two groups of people. We saw that a text combining features of narrative and list, that relied partially upon recurrences of the noun, achieved a compromise in the struggle for ownership of a referring expression.

In sum, the analyses of referrals – the relationship between referring expressions and referents – relied upon very similar constructs that have been instrumental in the development of more socially constituted views of language: speaker, hearer, context. Our analyses of referrals thus drew from approaches that have already helped us understand how we use language in everyday life: pragmatics, discourse analysis, and a broadly construed variation analysis that systematically analyzes what is same and what is different in specific sites of language use.

9.3   Narratives

[Narrative is a form of discourse through which we reconstruct and represent past experience both for ourselves and for others] Not surprisingly, it is one of the most analyzed, and best understood, genres of spoken language. My analyses of narratives (Chapters 5, 6, 7 and 8) depended partially on what has become the 'standard' sociolinguistic view of narrative, stemming from Labov's (1972b) code-based approach. And many of the narratives (all in Chapter 5 and one in Chapter 8) were typical of those amenable to the Labovian approach: narratives from sociolinguistic interviews that recounted a funny, scary, or unusual experience.

In addition to drawing upon the code-based approach associated with Labov, and analyzing the narratives found during sociolinguistic interviews, however, the analyses in Chapters 6 and 7 turned to some different issues and to a different sort of narrative, both stemming largely from the topic, purpose and setting. Analyses of Mrs. Beer's narrative from oral history interviews raised several issues not necessarily pertinent to the more 'everyday experience' narrative told during sociolinguistic interviews. Holocaust narratives can challenge narrative competence if the teller is still struggling to verbalize an experience that was traumatic (Chapter 6). Complicating the struggle is that the need to tell is set amid a cluster of other expectations arising from oral history interviews: to situate a narrative in global levels of public Discourse and memory culture, as well as more local levels of interaction (e.g. as a response to a question or other prompt from an interviewer); to manage a narrative that might be serving multiple functions (i.e. it might become part of a historical record and/or a museum collection); to tailor a narrative to a wide range of audiences whose reception and interpretation cannot be anticipated.

Retelling a narrative highlights the relevance of all of these considerations not just for the analyst, but for the storyteller him/herself. Presumably, once one has already told a story, one has the competence to tell it again, having already filled in its template with characters and events, actions and reactions, problem and resolution. But what about changes in context and audience? Even if a narrative is 'rewound' and replayed immediately after its first telling (as in Jack's story about Joey Bishop), the audience is differently positioned: it is hearing the story from a different information state (e.g. Freda, Rob and I knew exactly how Joey Bishop had made the audience laugh). Thus the context is one in which the audience waits not in suspense, but in anticipation. When an experience is funny (as was Jack's), it does not seem surprising that a narrator might want to keep the audience waiting, savoring together the knowledge of what is to come. Thus immediate replays have an evaluative function in and of themselves: by conveying 'this is important enough for me to want to tell it – and for you to hear it – all over again,' they create involvement through joint appreciation of a now-familiar experience.

Replaying a narrative about trauma and hardships to a series of different audiences, over a period of years, raises a number of different issues. Once the audience changes, the retelling cannot depend on the audience already knowing the story: thus the evaluative effect of 'sharing' achieved by replaying the story is not relevant. Nor does the narrator have to slightly alter nuances of events to maintain interest. And the distance between first and later tellings makes it more difficult – one would think – to replicate details. Despite these differences between immediate and later replays of narrative, Chapter 8 found surprising similarities between the retold stories that we examined.

Before turning to comparisons of the retellings between Susan Beer's and Jack Cohen's stories from Chapter 8, however, let us back up for a moment to review the analyses (in Chapters 6 and 7) of the narrative told and retold by Susan Beer in four different oral history interviews. Oral histories have not been addressed as data sources for linguists: yet, they provide not only a wealth of linguistic data, but also the opportunity to examine the 'writing' of official history (since they contribute to the study of history), as well as the multi-vocality and multi-functionality of discourse in both private and public domains. They also offer new opportunities for interdisciplinary research, e.g. between linguists and psychologists (interested in memory), linguists and historians (interested in how texts help shape understandings of past events). And they add new forms of narratives to the narrative types already identified (see collection in Bamberg 1997) and raise numerous questions that more light-hearted personal anecdotes might not raise: the boundaries between personal, vicarious and collective experiences; the effect of long term changes in affect and emotion; the impact of memory on the retelling of things long past.

We suggested in Chapter 6 that vicarious experience might play a greater role in stories of the Holocaust (and other oral histories) than in other narratives. We thus examined how the 'ownership' of an experience was reflected in Mrs. Beer's narrative over time. We did so by combining three different frameworks that deconstruct the relationship among self, other, language and experience – positioning, stance and footing. The analysis focused on a story that had several different sources of information: a set of plans presented by the narrator's father to the narrator; anticipation by the narrator and her family of what would happen; physical experience that revealed the plans to be something very different from what had been anticipated.

Careful analysis of a variety of details (e.g. the representation of a speech event, the use of meta-talk, the organization of a list in the story) showed how information from different sources was framed and re-framed. We saw that as an initial source of information began to disappear in the text, more doubt about credibility crept into the text. In contrast, a first hand experience in which the narrator was involved (and bore the brunt of physical action) became more concretized through multiple expressions of validity. I suggested that integrating the experience of another can help make sense of one's own life, especially if it includes experiences (e.g.

catastrophes, genocide) that standard templates and schemas cannot easily accommodate.

Chapter 7 analyzed a set of changes in the same story, focusing not on the re-framing of differently grounded experiences, but on their restructuring and re-evaluation. The first telling followed a stanza mode of organization based on descriptive information that supported a theme. Later tellings relied upon a linear, event-based narrative structure, full of performance and evaluative features. When we compared these changes to those in Jack's funny anecdote about Joey Bishop (Chapter 8), it was surprising to find a cluster of parallels between them in structure, footing, and evaluation. This was surprising not only because the narratives were so differently situated, about different topics, and part of very different modes of discourse and Discourse, but also because one was replayed for a co-present audience seconds after its initial telling and the other appeared years apart for completely different audiences (including both the co-present face-to-face interviewer and the anticipated public audience).

Here we can only explore both repercussions and reasons for these similarities. As we discussed in Chapter 6, Holocaust narratives (and oral histories) are inherently multi-vocalic genres that are mediated by the passage of time, the change in language, and the acculturation and assimilation of the survivor into a new culture and society, along with changing roles of the Holocaust in memory culture. Susan Beer's narrative was pivotal to her World War II experience: what happened to her and others transformed her life in countless ways. The narrative from my sociolinguistic interview with Jack Cohen was about a childhood friendship that may very well have contributed to his current array of identities, but without the sort of long lasting impact on himself, his family, and his community as living through a war in which Jews were the target of genocide. The social, cultural and historical impact of Susan Beer's story makes it a contribution to Holocaust discourse. Although Jack tells a story about Joey Bishop (who himself performed on a public stage and contributed to public Discourse) it is not likely to reach a very broad audience. Nor would it have many repercussions in the larger cultural, social and ideological world of Discourse if it did. But not only are the repercussions of the Holocaust vast, but so too are its representations through testimonies, narratives, life stories and oral histories.

Searching for linguistic patterns across different contexts (whether defined narrowly or broadly) is a basic *modus operandi* of sociolinguistics and discourse analysis. Yet sometimes the contexts themselves are so different – and seem to exert so pervasive an influence on what occurs 'inside' the context – that it is hard to know whether what seems to be the same 'inside' really *is* the same. Recognizing that cultural frames of speaking, acting and being have a potent role in interpretation of even the smallest detail of life is a basic assumption of anthropological research: can a behavior that seems to be the 'same' in more than one culture really be 'the same' if frameworks of speaking, acting, and being so differently contextualize and lend meaning to that behavior? The same questions drive interactional sociolinguistic research that investigates contextualization cues (Gumperz 1982) and meta-messages. Overlapping speech, for example, can convey interruption and rudeness for some people, but friendly overlap and involvement for others (Tannen 1984). So what seems the same on the surface may be interpreted very differently below the surface.

We need to apply the same caution to comparing narratives as different as Susan Beer's and Jack Cohen's. Added to this caution is an extra caveat stemming from the array of past and present questions (social, cultural, political, ideological) that continue to haunt the historical place of the Holocaust in contemporary life. Berel Lang (2002), a philosopher who has written extensively on history, ethics, art, and memory, calls some of these questions "mischievous," and what makes them so is that:

> the answers invited by them misrepresent important facets of the Holocaust. It is not only that the questions cited are 'leading' questions, but that the directions in which they 'lead' are specious, both from the standpoint of the person asking the question and in the representation conveyed (p. 15).

The specious questions mentioned by Lang tap into extensive worry about the loss of collective memory and distortion of history for political ends, especially in the face of recent anti-Semitism (Rosenbaum 2004), the misuse (Marrus 1991) or denial (Lipstadt 1994) of the Holocaust, detraction from its historical uniqueness (Marrus

1988), or inappropriate incorporation of memory into a national ethos (Flanzbaum 1999, Novick 1999).

Such worries are exacerbated by language, e.g. the use of the term *concentration camps* to convey the internment camps in which Japanese Americans were held (Chapter 5) or extensions of the term *Holocaust* (Schiffrin 2001b) as in the phrase *Holocaust on a plate* used by People for the Ethical Treatment of Animals as a description of a chicken dinner (Chapter 1). Such uses of language not only threaten the collective memory of American Jews by extending (or trivializing) a tragedy that threatened the existence of all Jews: they also feed into what seems to have become cultural, social and political struggles to compare one group's ability to claim a privileged status of 'victim' to another's (Rosenbaum 1996).

As linguists, we can learn a great deal by analyzing narratives of various forms and contents, while realizing and respecting the differences in experience and their myriad meanings for both speaker and audience. Talking about casual everyday experiences by no means presents the same verbal, social, cultural or emotional challenge as talking about experiences of trauma, catastrophe, and destruction. And if we find equivalent forms and strategies used in retelling both types of narrative, we need not assume that the similarity implies the same emotional weight or social significance. Just as the recurrence of form across cultures or styles can have very different meanings, so too, can the recurrence of a narrative device convey very different things. With these cautionary caveats in mind, I suggest two general reasons why changes in Jack's story were similar to changes in Mrs. Beer's story: the underlying schema; the development of a meta-narrative.

Consider, first, that narrating a deception invokes a particular schema that raises questions of 'who knew what, when, where and how?' Both stories retold the violation of a schema that proceeded by deception: one deception was cruel and nefarious; the other, innocent and playful. To narrate deception from the point of view of the figure who is him/herself duped requires going back to the temporal and epistemic starting point: 'this is why I expected X to happen.' By establishing a set of expectations that the audience will share, not only can the disruption be understood for what it was, but the narrator can save face and not seem like an easy 'mark' who should have known better (hence, the incorporation of skepticism in post-1982 versions of Mrs. Beer's story). Avoiding the impression of naivety and gullibility also helps account for the immersion of Susan Beer in a collective *we* ('I wasn't the only one who was fooled') and Jack Cohen as a co-participant with Joey Bishop (*we made a hit that day*). The explanation of how the main character came to share the knowledge of deception (*we knew*, *I realized*, etc.) further embeds the audience in the epistemological world of the story figure and aligns it with the affective reaction of the storyteller.

Consider, next, that a retold narrative is not only a narrative, but also a meta-narrative: by incorporating parts of earlier stories (structure, lexis, evaluation), a retold narrative is not only about an experience, but also about prior narratives. Both narrative competence and performance have roles in the formation of meta-narrative. On the competence side, the terms schema and template both suggest an abstract set of rules that are activated when a narrative is formulated and verbalized. Whereas a schema is a structured set of general expectations about what usually happens (e.g. who is present, during an event, in a place), a template is like a blueprint that has to be filled in with specific characters and events, actions and reactions, a problem and a resolution. Thus a schema can be (re)instantiated; a template can (re)concretize abstract possibilities. On the performance side, we find not abstract cognitive structures, but evaluative devices that (re)highlight the point of the story for an audience. Such devices bring out what is important through contrasts, constructed dialogue, expressive phonology, and numerous other means of drawing the audience's attention to certain parts of the story, hence leading the audience to infer what is important about the story.

Notice that retold narrative is a *replaying* of narrative (not a *redoing*, cf. referrals). What I want to capture by *play* is not the whimsical sense of games, but a sense of 'play' that recalls the scripted sense(s) in which we not only activate a story from our narrative competence, but also deploy dramatic devices during a narrative performance to help convey the point of the story to an audience. 'Play' also evokes Searle's (1969) distinction between constitutive and regulative rules, in which the paradigm example of constitutive rules is a game. Searle points out that when we play chess, for example, the rules actually *create* the game: the rules are not norms that govern (regulate) something that already exists *a priori*. To suggest an analogy: just as the rules of chess are 'in play' when one castles a King, or says *check mate*, so too, the schema and the template are both 'in play' when one tells a narrative. Recall, also, that the term *replay* also captures the performance side of narrative. Here what is evoked by 'play' is the dramatization of a script. *Play* is thus especially pertinent for retelling a story since the first telling of a story (the story that has activated the template through details) has become a basis – somewhat like the script of a play – from which to add expression, innovate, and embellish what is in the script for an audience.

In sum, just as the analyses of redone referrals demanded attention to speaker, hearer and context, so too, did the analyses of replayed narratives. Both referrals and narratives depend upon links between words and world, the building of sequences in which words connect, and the interplay among referential, social and expressive meanings. In the conclusion in the next section (9.4), I bring together some overall constructs underlying all of the analyses as a way of returning to the oppositions between innovative/fixed, old/new and same/different and the paradigms through which we have tried to understand them.

9.4   Social and linguistic 'turns'

We noted initially in this book that although language serves several functions (often simultaneously), many linguists focus only on its referential function. Also noted was that many 'alternative' perspectives in linguistics developed (at least partially) as a way to avoid privileging the referential function of language or to account for features or qualities of language that did not fit the structural paradigm often adopted by linguists who assumed its theoretical centrality.

Perhaps it seems odd, then, that roughly half of the analyses in this book focused on reference, with the remainder focusing on narratives that represent what happened. Analyses of both reference and narrative (or, in their more practice-oriented guise, referrals and stories), however, all took a social turn that incorporated speaker, hearer and context into underlying theory and methodology. But social turns in Linguistics abut linguistic turns in the social sciences and humanities. Whereas linguists have moved steadily toward contextualizing language in domains of social and cultural life, including both abstract (e.g. ideology) and concrete domains (e.g. actions), and macro-level structures (e.g. means of production that reinforce hegemony) and micro-level structures (e.g. turns at talk), sociologists, anthropologists, literary scholars and philosophers in our postmodern era have moved in the opposite direction to locate society, culture, literature, and thought in the exigencies of language. Since the social turn in linguistics is more familiar to me, and has pervaded this volume, I use this as a seque to discussion of three constructs (indexicality, sequentiality, intertextuality) that not only help theorize my study of variation in reference and narrative, but also help mitigate the hyper-relativity of the postmodern linguistic turn.

The social turn in the study of 'what we are talking about' (reference) and 'what happened' (narrative) is what led us to explore a variety of problems and propose explanations for a variety of concrete phenomena: how we conceptualize and lexicalize a referent; begin a sentence and/or a turn at talk; address known and unknown audiences; gauge and re-gauge familiarity; incorporate and alter information from different sources in a story; adjust stativity and activity of clauses. It has also led to somewhat surprising junctures, e.g. between grammar and turn exchange; existence, location and possession; narrative competence and performance.[1]

What joined the different topics was 'second position', defined broadly in terms of sequence and delimited by what occurs 'first.' Second position included repeats of cut-off parts of a noun (Chapters 2, 3), paraphrases of an incipient noun as a descriptive clause (Chapter 4), switching between different variants of a pragmatic prototype within a text (Chapter 4); referring expressions that continued a referent from earlier D/discourse (Chapter 5), and retelling a story (Chapters 6, 7, 8). What recurred can be described as repairing, repeating, paraphrasing, altering, re-framing, restructuring, redoing and replaying, each reflecting different degrees of 'sameness' as well as different aspects of the 'item' being redone. The distance between first and second position also varied from the closeness of one constituent within one utterance to the distance of different times, people, and situations.

Yet everything that was found in second position can be defined as syntagmatic variation: each option that filled a second position

had a degree of 'fit' with what had preceded. We saw that variation in the 'fit' stemmed from the ways in which options maintained
(or altered) the link between word and world; how they fit into the
textual sequences in which words connected and the interactional
sequences in which turns were taken and actions were realized;
through complex interplays among referential, social and expressive meanings. Of course once a second position was filled, it also
opened a slot for what could come next, thus anticipating – in the
sense of delimiting upcoming options – what could follow.

Most slots are self-perpetuating at some level of social organization: conversations, relationships, encounters, occasions and situations recur, if not immediately, then perhaps at some later time
and other place. What is said and done in the slots created at different social organizational levels is *restricted* (by prior slots from
the same level) and *restrictive* (by delimiting similar slots that can
follow). Yet, what is in a slot also builds upon prior opportunities,
and by so doing, provides further opportunities. Of course the more
distance between slots, the harder it is to restrict options, and perhaps the easier it is to allow opportunity. During talk-in-interaction,
however, the difference between schemas and their realizations provides a division of productive and interpretive labor: we can parcel
out restrictions to "a limited set of basic reinterpretation schema"
and allocate opportunities for our ability to realize schemas "in an
infinite number of ways" (Goffman 1981c: 68).

A metalogue from Bateson (1972: 32, a dialogue about dialogue
in imagined response to his daughter) comments on our inability to
recognize the basic schemas in the midst of our ongoing realizations
of them:

D: What did you mean by a conversation having an outline? Has this conversation had an outline?
F: Oh, surely, yes. But we cannot see it yet because the conversation isn't
finished. You cannot ever see it when you're in the middle of it. Because if
you could see it, you would be predictable – like the machine. And I would
be predictable – and the two of us together would be predictable.

Bateson's metalogue suggests that the schemas in which slots reside,
and through which their realizations make sense, are more easily
identified once those slots are been filled. Thus we are reminded
that the regularity of a product can be masked by the fluidity of the

process through which it has emerged. Or to put it another way, focusing on an ongoing process can obfuscate the underlying order of its product.

What results in discourse is an emergent structure that is not only locally based, but also dependent upon social interaction. As we know from both Goffman's work and linguistic pragmatics, speakers' utterances give information intentionally (they realize communicative goals) and *un*intentionally (they express information). Since "most concrete messages combine linguistic and expressive components" (Goffman 1963: 16), utterances are built upon a fundamental division of informational labor with "the proportion of each differing widely from message to message."

The varying distribution of information within and across messages has a consequence for interlocutors. Recipients of messages are faced with a set of strikingly different choices depending upon which aspect of information (e.g. given or given off, literal or implicated) they focus upon to construct a response: they can draw upon either (or both) as the basis from which to infer meaning and design their own utterances. By assigning the 'other' a role in directing the course of an interaction as potentially potent as that of the 'self,' what happens in interaction can thus be the result of a fundamental differentiation of participant stances toward information: what I intend on a linguistic level may not be the message you infer on an expressive level. This differentiation of responsibility, however, is reallocated again and again: once I reply to you, I have the same opportunity to manage the direction of interaction – and hence, the discourse structure – by selecting what facet of your utterance will be the basis of my response.

Not only does this give each utterance, and each participant, a role in creating discourse, but it also exerts its own restraint: choosing which facet of an utterance as the basis for response *shifts* from one person to the next. Although there may be a cost to being in a situated role of respondent, then, there is also a benefit: the onus of restriction (within limits of course) will fall to the 'other' in his/her role as next-speaker in the next turn at talk. And since we recurrently trade participatory roles during interactions (i.e. we take turns speaking and acting), we each have a chance at being the 'you' for whom communicative intentions and actions are designed and an 'I' who is involved in the design process.

Thus far I have suggested that discourse structure unfolds through the organization of participation and the management of information. Here I will explore how three different constructs that are associated with different ways of thinking about and working on language – indexicality, sequentiality, intertextuality – can play important roles in balancing what is innovative (or fixed), new (or old), and different (or same) in second position. I will suggest that it is a compilation of these three constructs that can help us learn how order within a product emerges from fluidity within a process and contribute to our understanding of how what we know, say and do emerges within texts that are co-constructed during interactions.

We begin with indexicality. We have been speaking throughout this book of language representing (or sometimes displaying, evoking, or constructing) referents and experience. But there are numerous ways in which language can take on such work. As summarized concisely by Scollon and Scollon (2003: 24), "a sign can resemble the object (icon), it can point to or be attached to the object (index), or it can be only arbitrarily or conventionally associated with the object (symbol)."[2]

Within the fields of semantics and pragmatics, indexicality retains its 'pointing to' role and is thus most frequently associated with deixis: the ways in which language grammaticalizes features (typically, person, time and place) of the context of an utterance. The meanings of pronouns, tense, and demonstratives, for example, cannot be established apart from a consideration of how the utterances in which the words are used are situated in the world. Thus language has an indexical function when it points to features of the context (including, for example, identity (DeFina, Schiffrin and Bamberg (in press) Ochs 1993)) in which an utterance is situated.

Complications arise, however. Traditionally, what has differentiated deixis from anaphora is the particular world to which they point: the world to which deictics anchor an utterance has usually been defined as external to talk (a non-linguistic world called 'context'), whereas the world to which anaphors anchor an utterance has usually been defined as internal to talk (a linguistic world called 'text'). Still there are complications. Although the distinction between deixis and anaphora might seem clear in principle, particular expressions can be used in ways that are difficult to identify as purely deictic or purely anaphoric: in some cases, the expressions seem to be indexical in both of these ways; in other cases, it is difficult to decide whether an expression is indexing only one domain (text or context) or both domains. Not only pronouns, but temporal expressions (Schiffrin 1990, 1991) and discourse markers (Schiffrin 1987) can be simultaneously deictic and anaphoric (cf. Lyons 1977: 667–8 on pure and impure deixis). Thus it is sometimes analytically difficult to maintain the distinction between deixis and anaphora.

Studies of referrals in this book drew upon indexicality in several ways. Together they suggest that contiguity can help recipients identify referents. Early in this volume, I differentiated external and internal perspectives on reference: first-mentions of a referent establish a connection between words and the world; next-mentions depend on word-to-word connections within a text. But both first-*and* next-mentions draw upon both modes of indexicality noted by the Scollons, simply because they point to contiguous material. First-mentions, for example, can be inferentially connected to prior information in a text or grounded in *there is* and *they have* structures that establish space and/or person connections with contiguous text. Second-mentions point back to first-mentions (or at least to the referent evoked by the first-mention). Here contiguity combines with other textual factors. Although pronouns are preferred next-mentions, they are favored not only by recency (cf. contiguity), but also by a lack of ambiguity, the absence of structural boundaries, and topicality.

Repairs in which an in-progress word is either repeated, or replaced by another word (or set of words), illustrate other aspects of contiguity. Repairs of first-mentions proceed by adding to the common ground in which the referent is situated, thus building upon contiguity (or closeness) of knowledge. The mechanical aspects of repair also highlight contiguity. Since the site of interruption is usually the site of the problem, both within the same sentence constituent, the repair is based on temporal and structural contiguity. Like the other sites of indexicality noted above, contiguity between self-initiation and self-completion might help the recipient's goal of interpreting a referral and identifying a referent. Although the first part of a repair does not provide lexical information about the second part, remaining in the same constituent allows structural continuity that may facilitate interpretation of the information in the utterance.

The discussion thus far has suggested that indexicality can be stretched to cover different goals of pointing and sites of contiguity. Sacks (1973, Lecture 4: 11–12) suggests that prior-position (the utterance most contiguous to the current utterance) is the default location to which a current utterance points:

> There is one generic place where you need not include information as to which utterance you're intended to relate an utterance to . . . and that is if you are in Next Position to an utterance. Which is to say that for adjacently placed utterances, where a next intends to relate to a last, no other means than positioning are necessary in order to locate which utterance you're intending to deal with.

In their collection *Rethinking sequentiality*, Fetzer and Meierkord (2002: 8) establish that although sequentiality is "the central conversational-analytic concept par excellence," it is also important to analyses of speech acts, implicatures, dialogue grammar, mental representations and processes. The wide ranging relevance of sequentiality is anticipated in ethnomethodology (Garfinkel 1967, 1974), the perspective from which CA itself developed.

Ethnomethodology is concerned with the "ordinary arrangement of a set of located practices . . . a member's knowledge of his ordinary affairs, of his own organized enterprises, where that knowledge is treated by us as part of the same setting that it also makes orderable" (Garfinkel 1974: 17). The knowledge that ethnomethodologists seek to uncover, then, is neither decontextualized nor autonomous. Rather, whatever sense of order emerges is displayed through ongoing activity that provides a practical basis, and a sense of intersubjectivity, through which to sustain further activity. Social action is thus critical to the creation of knowledge: one's own actions produce and reproduce the knowledge through which individual conduct and social circumstance are intelligible.

The link between knowledge and action has an important bearing on the conversation analytic study of language. Although language is the medium through which common-sense categories of knowledge are constituted, the meaning and use of a particular term (and thus the boundaries of a category) are nevertheless negotiable. The relationship between words and objects is as much a matter of the world of social relations and activities in which words are used, as of the world of objects that is being evoked. Put another way, the meaning of a particular utterance (including the sense of words) is indexical to a specific context and purpose. It is this contextualization of language that provides its entry into the mutually constitutive relationship between action and knowledge: speakers produce utterances assuming that hearers can make sense out of them by the same kind of practical reasoning and methodic contextualizing operations that they apply to social conduct in general. And it is because actors succeed in using the sequential progression of interaction to display their understandings of its events and rules that the shared world that has been jointly achieved is publicly available for analysis (Taylor and Cameron 1987: 104).

The goals and beliefs that I have just described continue to influence conversation analysis. Each utterance in a sequence is shaped by the actions and knowledge enabled through the immediately prior utterance and the accrual of actions and knowledge from past utterances. Each utterance also provides a context for the next utterance. In Heritage's (1984: 242) terms, "the significance of any speaker's communicative action is doubly contextual in being both *context-shaped* and *context-renewing*." This notion of context as being both retrospective and prospective can be seen as yet another way that meanings are continually adjusted and sequentially emergent.

Conversation analysis is wed to data "that anyone else can go and see whether what was said is so" (Sacks 1984: 26). Although it can thus show in explicit (and often exquisite) detail how meanings are grounded in (and implicated by) prior utterances, it cannot (nor does it seek to) ground current words in past utterances. Yet the general notion that utterances are both retrospective and prospective also underlies the development of meanings, actions and knowledge across non-contiguous utterances, texts, and interactions, including those differentiated by time, place and person. As suggested by linguists such as Becker (1984, 1988) and Tannen (1989), all interactions are made up of prior texts that we draw upon in new ways: "both the meanings of individual words . . . and the combinations in which we put them are given to us by previous speakers, traces of whose voices and contexts cling inevitably to them" (Tannen 1989: 100).

The notion of intertextuality drawn upon by both Becker and Tannen has a long and rich history in literary studies. Kristeva (1980), for example, pointed out that texts have not only a horizontal axis that connects author to recipient, but also a vertical axis that connects a text to other texts. As Fairclough (1992: 84) explains:

Intertextuality is basically the property texts have of being full of snatches of other texts, which may be explicitly demarcated or merged in, and which the text may assimilate, contradict, ironically echo, and so forth. In terms of production, an intertextual perspective stresses the historicity of texts: how they always constitute additions to existing 'chains of speech communication' (Bakhtin 1986: 94) consisting of prior texts to which they respond.

Notice that just as an utterance can draw upon previous utterances from distant prior texts, so too, can it provide material for future utterances (and/or texts) by a recipient at a later time or place. The interchange between different interlocutors (the horizontal axis) is thus crucial, as stated by Bakhtin (1986: 68):

The fact is that when the listener perceives and understands the [language meaning] of speech, he simultaneously takes an active, responsive attitude toward it . . . Any understanding is imbued with response and necessarily elicits it in one form or another: the listener becomes the speaker.

Bakhtin's view is strikingly reminiscent of our earlier point about how information is managed through alternation of participant roles, as well as the shared sense of meanings, actions and knowledge that are grounded in the sequential organization of talk-in-interaction. The difference, of course, is the deictic center of information and participation: the listeners and speakers who draw upon intertextual connections with prior texts need not be co-present. And of course this reduces the potential for evidence of shared meanings. Prior position in a sequence can always provide a resource for proximal indexicality simply because of its contiguity. However, the deictic displacement of distal intertextuality means that we cannot be sure that our listeners can draw their interpretations from the same prior texts (cf. Hamilton 1996 on intratextuality). Nor can we know if alternative interpretations of what we said were based upon prior texts with which we ourselves were unfamiliar.

The analyses in this volume found resources for shared (or divergent) interpretations both locally in face-to-face talk and more globally in past texts. On the more local level, for example, we saw that Jack Cohen could not open his narrative without attending to the various informational needs, and interactional byplays, of his potential addressees (Chapter 8).[3] Jack's story itself, however, was less locally bound: it was filled with performative and evaluative details that harked back to an earlier part of the interaction and to the voicing of still-earlier speech from non-present interlocutors (childhood friends, a teacher at school). On a still more distal plane, we might note that the description used by Jack for his action with Joey – We used to jazz it up – forecasts the means by which Jack's retelling 'jazzes up' the story with innovative details, performance and evaluation. Thus the form and content of his retelling mirrors the musical innovation in the story world, transferring the practices from one performance realm to another. And because this transfer indexes the musical world, it also establishes interdiscursivity (a type of intertextuality suggested by Fairclough 1992) that draws upon prior practices, rather than texts per se.

Our discussions of Holocaust discourse depended explicitly on intertextuality. Mrs. Beer's retellings clearly incorporated others' texts, both prior to the experience (e.g. the plans brought to the family by her father) and posterior to the experience (e.g. the use of English idioms, her husband's term partisans). The recurrence of lexis, structure and evaluation in Mrs. Beer's retellings – separated by years and told to widely different audiences – are intertexual connections that suggest the mingling together of different texts within the narrative template that was honed over time as a means of reconstructing her past. My notion of meta-narrative thus extends the narrative unit itself into an intertextual (or interdiscursive) unit: the narrative not only incorporates part of prior narratives, it is also about those prior narratives.[4]

Another facet of Holocaust discourse – the controversy over the term 'concentration camps' – centered on an intertextual conflict: the ability of one group to use a term that had been a central part of the memory culture of another. The footnote to the exhibit on America's Concentration Camps created a melding together of prior texts about concentration camps that was designed not only to appease those who had been privy to the conflict, but also those who knew nothing about the controversy.

We have been focusing thus far on a cluster of constructs that have become part of the social turn in Linguistics. As mentioned earlier, this social turn abuts a linguistic turn urged by poststructural and postmodern scholars. Although I cannot pretend to do justice to this rich and complex body of thought, it is worth mentioning it if only to be so pompous as to suggest a partial corrective to what seems to be one of its weaknesses.

The linguistic turn is basically the adoption of a postmodernist perspective on language (Rorty 1967). Stemming from de Saussure's separation of signifier from signified (and apparently ignoring the crucial role of convention in re-connecting these two aspects of the sign), the postmodern perspective was developed through Derrida's claim that language was an "infinite play of significations" (quoted in Evans 1999: 82) and Barthes' claim that History was "a parade of signifiers masquerading as a collection of facts" (quoted in Evans 1999: 81). Postmodernism thus shifts what is a well known and accepted assumption – meaning can be relative to context – to a level of hyper-relativity: meaning is indeterminate and ever changing.

Perhaps the social turn in Linguistics can help zero in upon the constraints on what seems to be indeterminacy and endlessly changing meanings. Socially constituted linguistic perspectives have had much to say about the same aspects of language that postmodernists have addressed. Indeed, the wide range of approaches that combine to characterize contemporary linguistic discourse analysis (cf. Schiffrin 1994a) all provide different means of exploring the complex interdependence between what 'is' context and what is 'in' context (e.g. text). Likewise, privileging functional (as well as, or even instead of, structural) models of language permits what Hymes 1974a: 9 (see also Hymes 1984b) describes as the:

primacy of speech to code, function to structure, context to message, the appropriate to the arbitrary or simply possible; but the interrelations always essential, so that one cannot only generalize the particularities, but also particularize the generalities.

It is the balance between text/context, structure/ function, and particular/general that not only allows us to make sense of theoretical constructs such as indexicality, sequentiality, and intertextuality, but also to use them to help identify the sites from which contested, negotiated and congruent meanings arise.

In contrast to the theoretical hyper-relativism of postmodern approaches, linguistic approaches to discourse drawn upon in this volume offer a situated relativism that not only imbues methodology and theory, but also motivates analysis of crucial interfaces between language and 'reality.' This enables them to address questions that arise within that interface: how are representations of people, and what happens to them, immersed within texts? how are texts immersed within their contexts? how do contexts both inform, and restrict, the vast (but not infinite) web of potential interpretations and meanings? how do the interrelated constructs of indexicality, sequentiality and intertextuality help to both expand (and delimit) the range of potential meanings within and across utterances? As we continue to search for answers to questions such as these, we will learn more about how we continuously cast what we know, say and do 'in other words' or in the same words surrounded by 'other words.' And perhaps such analyses will bring us closer to understanding how and why we seem to need to balance what is innovative and fixed, old and new, and same and different not only in our references and narratives, but also in our lives.

Notes

1. Certainly this social turn could be further explored. For example, in addition to noting a fundamental interactional division of labor between self- and other-repair (and preference for the former), one could examine repair from a micro-analytic perspective of footing and participation framework (e.g. the roles of animator vs. author or principal in repair), as well as from a more macro-analytic perspective of how repairs are oriented toward (and index the properties of) situations as different as radio broadcasts (Goffman 1981b), court rooms (Philips 1992) and classrooms (MacBeth 2004). Likewise, we could examine how a narrative is re-shaped as it is told for different purposes, in different situations, and/or by different people, or how footings are embedded in different situations (Matoesian 1999) or grammaticalized in different languages (Irvine 1996, Levinson 1988).
2. Whereas the Scollons build upon both the pointing and contiguous aspects of indexicality in their study of geosemiotics, a great deal of anthropological and linguistic research on social identity (e.g. Ochs 1993) and interaction (Gumperz 1982) has built more upon the 'pointing' qualities of indexicality.

3. Following Hamilton (1996), we might call these traces of past speech *intra* textual rather than intertextual.

4. My analysis of thematically connected narratives within a single oral history as an intertextual narrative is another extension of the text-to-text connection (Schiffrin 2000).

Appendix 1

Transcription conventions for data excerpts (adapted from Schiffrin 1987, Tannen 1989)

.	period indicates sentence-final falling intonation
,	comma indicates clause-final intonation ("more to come")
!	exclamation mark indicates exclamatory intonation
?	question mark indicates final rise, as in a yes-no question
...	three dots in transcripts indicate pause of $\frac{1}{2}$ second or more
´	accent indicates primary stress
STRESS	underlining indicates emphatic stress
[	brackets show overlapping speech.
Z	zig-zag shows no perceptible inter-turn pause
:	colon following vowel indicates elongated vowel sound
::	extra colon indicates longer elongation
-	hyphen indicates glottal stop: sound abruptly cut off
" "	quotation marks highlight dialogue
( )	parentheses indicate 'parenthetical' intonation: lower amplitude and pitch plus flattened intonation contour
hhh	indicates laughter (number of hs indicates duration by second)
=	equal sign at right of line indicates segment to be continued after another's turn; equal sign at left of line indicates continuation of prior segment after another's turn
/?/	indicates inaudible utterance
{ }	brackets indicate comment on what is said

Appendix 2

Four Versions of Susan Beer's capture story

Event clauses are labeled E; numbers indicate sequence. Clauses whose event status is not clear are E? Different line markers are used for each version of the story.

1982

I The Plan

(1)   E1 During the day my father made . . . or maybe not even a whole- just during the day . . . he made arrangements,

(2)   someone told him of a German Wehrmacht . . .

(3)   I don't know how many, were sick and tired of the Germans, who want to return to civilian life

(4)   and who for a certain amount they'll take a group of Jews back to Slovakia

(5)   You know there was already uh . . . what my husband says "partisans",

(6)   so, a very small part of Slovakia was liberated.

(7)   And you know Budapest was just hell of a city,

(8)   y'know there was no escaping anymore any place.

(9)   They were just loaded with Germans

(10)   and catching- they wanted to catch everyone

[Interviewer asks a question not directly pertinent to the story. This section could not be transcribed. However, after Mrs. Beer answers, the Interviewer states: *So you made the arrangements* . . .]

(11)   E1 My father made these arrangements,

(12)   and by the time he made these arrangements which was in June, they- the countryside was already taken.

(13)   Because my cousin said the reason she wanted to actually
            uh . . . she let herself be talked into going with us, the one
            who's now in Switzerland, because her family was already
            gone.
(14)   E2   And this Rabbi gave us a mishebeirach
(15)   and they had a certain signal in Hebrew lettering with my
            father,
(16)   if we get saved there, he would send him the paper, he
            could go the same way too. And what happened was that
            the Germans took this paper
(17)   and we were terrified,
(18)   that the Rabbi would misinterpret that we are safe and
            would take that way.
(19)   But thank God he somehow got to Switzerland
(20)   and he was among the few that went to Switzerland.
(21)   Y'know I think there was one load full of people who were
            able to go.

II   Anticipation

(22)   But anyway, so it was at night,
(23)   we were supposed to meet in a park,
(24)   we were about forty four people,
(25)   there were some from my hometown who lived in
            Budapest who were included,
(26)   there was an old woman and her son,
(27)   there was a couple and a child and the woman was pregnant
(28)   and there was a couple from my town with a child and
            the woman was pregnant.
(29)   So there were two children and two pregnant women
            among them.
(30)   E3   And we came into this little park

III   The Capture

(31)   E3   And we came into this little park
(32)   E4   and the flashlight lit into our eyes
(33)   E4?   and we knew that's it.
(34)   E5   And they kicked us into the truck, you know like the army
             trucks, on two sides there were benches

(35)   **E6** and they took us straight to the Gestapo headquarters in
            Buda, the other side of Budapest.

1984

I   The Plan

(a)   **E1** And uh my father went next day, in search of a way to get
            us back to Czechoslovakia.
(b)   Because some part of it was freed,
(c)   the partisans freed it.
(d)   And we- we were holding to any straw, I guess, because it
            was impossible for us to remain longer in Budapest.
(e)   **E2** And he came home, that he found such a way.
(f)   That there is a German Wehrmacht truck
(g)   and some German Wehrmacht, who are tired of being
            Wehrmacht,
(h)   and they want to help us escape on their truck.
(i)   And this would cost money, and he wanted to help others
            /umhmm/ with this escape.
(j)   **E3** So he got my cousin, the- the one whose sister I took the
            name,
(k)   and by then her parents and everyone else was taken to
            camp already,
(l)   so she was the only . . . survivor in her family,
(m)   and some other friends, and people from our home town,
(n)   there were eight children, and a couple pregnant women,

II   Anticipation

(o)   And uh we were supposed to meet, at sundown, in a little
            park,
(p)   and, we will be going back to Slovakia.

III   The Capture

(r)   **E4** And the rabbi gave us . . . his blessing, and uh we were
            coming to that park,
(s)   **E5** and as soon as we approached that truck flashlights were
            lit into our eyes,

(t)   E6   and we were kicked into the truck,
(u)   E6?   and we knew right away that we were . . .
(v)   y'know it was uh- a scheme, to get <u>us,</u>   to get the
             money,=
Interviewer: Right
(w)   E7   = and they took us straight to the Gestapo Headquar-
             ters.

1995a

I   The Plan

        Meanwhile my father didn't want to take this privilege,
        and besides this was no solution
        E2 he heard-
1.   E1 he went among people some place,
2.   E2 and he heard that there are some army personnel, with
        an army truck, who are getting to be very disillusioned
        with being in the German army,
3.   and for a fee uh they would <u>take us back</u> to Slovakia.
4.   Now why Slovakia?
5.   Part of it, a very small portion of it in the mountain areas,
        was liberated by the partisans,
6.   And so when you have no place else to go, you go over . . .
        y'know you think maybe you will be safe for a little short
        time yet.
7.   E3 So my father didn't want to . . .
8.   E3 first of all we didn't have enough money to pay <u>these people</u>
        by ourselves,
9.   first of all we didn't have enough money to pay these
        people by ourselves
10.   E4 so we got my cousin who lived in Budapest by then too,
        hiding,
11.   because already her family was taken from this small
        town,
12.   all the families were taken,
13.   so she was the only one,
14.   and uh some other people,
        some people from my hometown, who were refugees in
        Budapest, was a husband wife and child,

some pregnant- couple of pregnant women,
all in all about forty four people.

II   Anticipation

15.	E5	And he made arrangements that that evening,
16.		uh we will meet in this little park,
17.		the army personnel will be there with their truck,
18.		and they will take us,
19.		we'll pay them,
20.		and that's it.
21.	E6	So this rabbi where we stayed blessed us, closure,
22.	E7	and my father even gave him in Hebrew uh that there will be a signal,
23.		if we make it, then maybe he could follow us.

III   The Capture

24.		And uh so uh as we were getting closer to the park at night,
	E8	we see spotlights, aiming at us.
25.	E8?	And we felt well if it's supposed to be a secret mission, how could there be spotlights,
26.	E9	well of course we were taken,
27.		you know it was no mission,
28.		it was a mission to take us,
29.	E10	and they kicked us
30.	E10?	and beat us,
31.		and that's how we ended up in the truck,
32.	E11	and they sped the truck into the Gestapo headquarters up in the Buda?,
33.		it was in the part of Budapest that's Buda,

1995b

I   The Plan

(A)	E1	And my father went out to look for something for us to do,

(B)   y'know, what would be the next step?

(C)   There weren't many options.

(D)   E2   And, as he went, he heard a story that today, I think your
             hair would stand up from disbelief,

(E)   E3   but he swallowed it.

(F)   And the story was that there are some German Army
             Officers, or Army personnel, who are disillusioned with
             the army life

(G)   and they have their German army truck

(H)   and they would take us back to Slovakia.

(I)   Now, part of Slovakia was liberated by partisans, very
             small part of it.

(J)   And that was where we were going to go.

(K)   E4?   Of course, it cost a lot of money

(L)   E4   and my father didn't have it,

(M)   E5   so he tried to organize some more into coming with us.

(N)   E6   He got forty four people in all,

(O)   among them was my cousin,
             the one that I slept in her house when I first escaped.

(P)   And her family by then was already taken away

(Q)   because from small towns they took families earlier

(R)   and she knew she was the only one left.

(S)   And some friends,

(T)   and there were even two women who were pregnant and
             had young children,

(U)   there was all kind of people.

II   Anticipation

(V)   And we were supposed to meet the Germans with their
             truck at this little park at night.

(W)   E7   And the Rabbi where we stayed blessed us

(X)   E8   and we left.

III   The Capture

(Y)   And as we were approaching the park

(Z)   E9   there were big flood lights turning on us.

(AA) **E9?** And we knew right away when there's a secret mission
             <u>you</u> don't turn flood lights on.
(BB) **E10?** But we couldn't run away anymore,
(CC) **E10?** we were caught
(DD)   And it was no mission of rescue.
(EE)   It was a mission that we were caught in,
(FF) **E11** And they hit us,
(GG) **E12** kicked us into the truck,
(HH) **E13** beat us up,
(II)   **E14** and sped to the Gestapo headquarters to Buda,

Appendix 3

Jack Cohen's narrative about Joey Bishop's childhood prank

Lines in pre-story talk are numbered; lines in the story entry are lettered (lower case); lines in the story itself are lettered (upper case). I use zig-zag Z to show no perceptible inter-turn pause; and {brackets} to indicate comment on what is said.

Jack:	(1)	I didn't know Jack Klugman.
Freda:	(2)	Well he didn't actually know Jack.
	(3)	He came from further s: eh eh closer to town.
Jack:	(4)	Klugman was from Porter Street.
	(5)	I knew uh . . . y' know . . . Joey Gottlieb.
	(6)	Uh Joey Bishop to you.
	(7)	That's who I knew.
	(8)	But I didn't [know Klugman. I knew of him.
Rob:	(9)	[Oh. I thought you-
Debby:	(10)	Who's Klugman?
Freda:	(11)	Jack Klugman. The comedian.
Jack:	(12)	But uh . . .
Debby:	(13)	Oh yeh. [I didn't know his name.
Freda:	(14)	[Y' know the other half of [the odd couple?
Jack:	(15)	[The one uh:

what d' they call him, thee   the odd couple.
                       Z

Debby:	(16)	Oh, sure.
	(17)	The other odd one hh.

             Z

Freda:	(18)	The other half.
Jack:	(19)	Well I'll tell y', Klugman has much more talent,
	(20)	I hate to admit this but he has much more talent than uh . . <u>my</u> boyfriend.
	(21)	Gottlieb. [I mean bo- Joey Bishop.

                   Z

Rob:	(22)	Yeh. [I think so too. Who? Oh. Joey Bishop?
	(23)	I think so too. Joey Bishop stands up there, . . . he's- he's =

       Z   Z

Jack:	(24)	Sure. Well:
Rob:	(25)	= always with the straight face,

            Z

Jack:	(26)	Well he has what y'call dry humor.

Freda: (27)   That's his-   [That's his humor.
Jack: (28)   = A quick wit. [It's supposed to be wit.
Rob: (29)   Jack Klugman gets excited, . . . [he's a good actor.
Jack: (30)   [Different types of uh: Oh I think
                 so. Yeh.
Freda: (31)   Yes. Yes. He's a fine:- a good actor,
         (32)   Where eh Bishop is no actor.
Jack: (33)   Bishop is limited. Bishop is good contact man.
         (34)   He al:ways knew who to go see.
         (35)   Even as a kid. When we were kids, he knew what to do.
         (36)   He was a real: . . . he was very ambitious, but lacked talent.
         (37)   He really didn't have too much.
         (38)   But he had guts! hhh He had- and he had dedication.
         (39)   I will say that.
{Omitted: interaction where Jack asks Freda to hold his glass of water; joking
follows}
Jack: (40)   And uh: I was just uh: we had a friend in our group uh: named
                 Duffberg.
         (41)   A much more talented- now if he-
                                          Z
Freda: (42)   He had more talent. The only
                 thing is:
         (43)   we have learned, that he wasn't really talented, he was crazy!
Jack: (44)   Well, whatever it was:,   He had more talent in fact, =
                                          Z
Freda: (45)   Huh? Huh? Right?!
Jack: (46)   = Joey used to say to him, "I wish I had what you have."
                 {story about Duffberg's humor not included}
Jack: (47)   An- and Joey used to say, "If I had his talent, I'd know what to do
                 with it."
         (48)   Always used to say that.
         (49)   And he never did have any talent, but still he made it!
Freda: (50)   No: he's no dope.
Jack: (51)   He's nervous. Always nervous, though.
         (52)   He used to drink a lot of- I used to tell him milk is good for your
                 stomach.
         (53)   It's good for a nervous stomach.
         (54)   And he'd drink hhh he'd hh an-
         (55)   Mike Feldman would say   "Go to work y' bum! =
                                          Z
Freda: (56)   That's unusual for- =
Jack: (57)   = [You'll never-
Freda: (58)   = [a young fellow he was what? Sixteen, seventeen years old, to
                 have a nervous stomach. =
                                          Z
Jack: (59)   = You'll never be in show business. Go
                 to work." =
Freda: (60)   That's unusual.
Jack: (61)   = He used t say: . . .
Freda: (a)   They were Bar Mitzvahed together. Him and uh Joey.
Debby: (b)   Really?
Jack: (c)   We went to school together.
         (d)   We were in the same hh room together.
         (e)   We used to hooky together!
         (f)   He played the piano, I played the violin in the assembly.

```
         (g)  hh We used to jazz it up.
Debby:   (h)  Did you go to Southern?                    Southern High, yeh.
                         Z
Jack:    (i)               Southern High. Yeh.
         (j)  Y' know that teacher that came over to me, over at uh . . .
         (k)  She used to be- take care of all the entertaining, =
Freda:   (l)  Yes I do.
Rob:     (m)  Lamberton?
Jack:    (n)            = and musical things, y' know.
         (o)  She used to raise holy hell with both of [us!
Freda:   (p)                                         [Oh I bet she's had a lot of
              kids at- that passed through her,
         (q)  [that . . . became- . . . became all =
Jack:    (r)            [Oh::! But she remembered me! =
Freda:   (s)  = kinds of things!hhhh[hhhhhhhhhhhhhh I guess your mother
              knew of: =
Jack:    (t)                        [She used to say to me, to Joey Bishop =
                                                              Z
Freda:   (u)                                                  = all these =
Jack:    (v)  =    [Don't you [play the piano, when he plays elegies!"
                                              Z
Freda:   (w)  =. . . diff[erent- [that became              different
              things!
Jack:    (x)  = One day-                      [He and I:
                         Z
Freda:   (y)            = [Different things like [jail: birds, and eh comedians!
              And. .
              Z
Jack:    (z)        One day he and I were [supposed to play elegies,
Freda:   (aa)                             [How m- long has your mother been
                                          teaching?
Debby:   (bb) Well she hasn't been teaching that long. =
Freda:   (cc) Oh. [Cause:-                          [That's very h- very =
Debby:   (dd)  = [But she keeps in touch with some of [them.
Freda:   (ee)  = interesting to look back!
Jack:    (A)  Y'know one day, she- we- I was supposed to play elegy on the
              violin.
         (B)  D' you remember then?
Freda:   (C)  Oh, yes!                    [Oh, that's the =
                         Z
Jack:    (D)             All kids would [play that. =
Freda:   (E)  = first! [My! My!
Jack:    (F)          [So he was supposed to accompany me.
         (G)  On the piano.
         (H)  So she had to teach him the chords.
         (I)  He only hit certain chords while I'm playin' elegy.
         (J)  So, everything is set fine,
         (K)  I get up,
         (L)  and I start to play elegy,
         (M)  and he's givin' me the chords.
         (N)  And in a chord, he goes daa da da da daa, da daa!
Jack:    (O)  Well the whole: audience broke up!
         (P)  Because they don't wanna hear that elegy y' know!
         (Q)  And we:. . . =
Freda:   (R)  That-hhhhhhhhhh
```

Jack: (S)   = y' know then I knew, he had the-
         (T)   I realized he did have dry wit. =
Jack: (U)   He knew how to get the- he knew the whole audience'd laugh
         (V)   so he must've had something to him
         (W)   Even this teacher, this one that- she laughed. =
Freda: (X)   Even the teachers, huh?
Jack: (Y)   She couldn't help it!
         (Z)   And I'm playin' /melody/,
         (AA)   and I'm playin', y' know =
                                            z
Freda: (BB)   hh Oh [God!
Jack: (CC)   = [And he goes, . . .
         (DD)   he gives me the chord,
         (EE)   and I'm not- re- re- for the next phrase.
         (FF)   I know the musical phrase,
         (GG)   I'm ready to go
         (HH)   and he goes, . . .
         (II)   he gives me another chord,
         (JJ)   and then he goes,
         (KK)   at the end of the chord he goes daa da da da daa, da daa!
         (LL)   Real fast and quiet.
         (MM)   That was f- I had to laugh myself hhh
Freda: (NN)   That's cute!
Jack: (OO)   Well we made a hit that day.
         (PP)   Even the teacher admitted it.
         (QQ)   She says, "Well it was- y' shouldn't <u>do</u> it! But it was nice."
         (RR)   What's she gonna say?
Freda: (SS)   Second grade? Third grade, I guess? I couldn't see you-
                                                        z
Jack: (TT)   Oh: it was-
                no! It was about the seventh grade. Or the eighth grade.
Freda: (UU)   I think by the seventh or the eighth grade, you'd have played
                somethin' better than that!
Jack: (VV)   Well elegy's a tough number to play! . . .
         (WW)   And I was squeakin' away on that violin hh =
Freda: (XX)   Well it-
Jack: (YY)   = and he was- we were laughin' that day, all day I remember.
Debby: (ZZ)   You still play the violin?

References

Abbott, B. (1993). A pragmatic account of the definiteness effect in existential sentences. *Journal of Pragmatics* 191, 39–56.

Abu-Akel, A. (1999). Episodic boundaries in conversational narratives. *Discourse Studies* 1:4, 437–453.

Aitchison, J. (1987). *Words in the mind: an introduction to the mental lexicon*. Oxford and New York: Blackwell.

Allen, B., and Montell, L. (eds.). (1981). *From memory to history*. Nashville, Tennessee: The American Association for State and Local History.

Aniya, S. (1992). semantics and the syntax of the existential there-construction. *Linguistic Analysis* 22 (3–4) 154–184.

Ariel, M. (1990). *Accessing noun-phrase antecedents*. London: Routledge.

Arnold, J., Fagnano, M., and Tanenhaus, M. (2003). Disfluencies signal thee, um, new information. *Journal of Psycholinguistic Research* 32/1, 25–36.

Arnold, J. E., Wasow, T., Losongco, T., and Ginstrom, R. (2000). Heaviness vs. newness: the effects of structural complexity and discourse status on constituent ordering. *Language* 76(1), 28–55.

Aroneau, E. (1996). *Inside the concentration camps: eyewitness accounts of life in Hitler's Death Camps*. Translated by Thomas Whiseen Westport CT: Praeger.

Austin, J. (1962). *How to do things with words*. Cambridge, MA: Harvard University Press.

Baker, C. (1975). "This is just a first approximation, but...". *Papers from the Eleventh Regional Meeting, Chicago Linguistic Society*. Chicago: Linguistics Department, University of Chicago.

Bakhtin, M. (1981). *The dialogic imagination*. Translated by M. Holquist and C. Emerson; M. Holquist (ed.). Austin: University of Texas Press.

Bakhtin, M. (1986). *Speech genres and other late essays*. Translated by V. W. McGee, M. Holquist and C. Emerson (eds.). Austin: University of Texas Press.

Ballinger, P. (1999). The culture of survivors: post-traumatic stress disorder and traumatic memory. *History and Memory* 11/2, 99–132.

Bamberg, M. (1987). *The acquisition of narratives: learning to use language.* New York: Mouton de Gruyter.

Bamberg, M. (1991). Narrative activity as perspective taking: the role of emotionals, negations, and voice in the construction of the story realm. *Journal of Cognitive Psychotherapy* 54, 275–290.

Bamberg, M. (1997). Positioning between structure and performance. *Journal of Narrative and Life History* 7, 335–342.

Barsalou, L. (1983). Ad-hoc categories. *Memory and Cognition*, 11, 211–227.

Bartaux, D. (1981). *Biography and society.* Beverly Hills, CA: Sage Publications.

Bartlett, F. (1932). *Remembering: a study in experimental and social psychology.* Cambridge: Cambridge University Press.

Bartrop, P. (2000). *Surviving the camps: unity in adversity during the Holocaust.* Lanham, MD: University Press of America.

Bateson, G. (1972). Metalogue: why do things have outlines? In G. Bateson. *Steps to an ecology of mind.* pp. 27–32. New York: Random House.

Bauman, R. (1986). *Story, performance and event.* Cambridge: Cambridge University Press.

Becker, A. L. (1984). Biography of a sentence: a Burmese proverb. In E. Bruner (ed.), *Text, play and story: the construction and reconstruction of self and society.* pp.135–155. American Ethnological Society.

Becker, A. L. (1988). Language in particular: a lecture. In D. Tannen (ed.), *Linguistics in Context.* pp.17–35. Norwood, NJ: Ablex Publishing.

Bell, A. (2001) Back in style: reworking audience design. In P. Eckert, and J. Rickford (eds.), *Style and sociolinguistic variation.* pp. 139–169. Cambridge: Cambridge University Press.

Bell, A., Jurafsky, D., Fosler-Lussier, E., Girand, C., Gregory, M., and Gildea, D. (2003). Effects of disfluencies, predictability, and utterance position on word form variation in English conversation. *Journal of the Acoustical Society of America* 113/2, 1001–1024.

Biber, D. and Finegan, E. (1994) *Sociolinguistic perspectives on register.* New York: Oxford University Press.

Blackwell, S. (2003) *Implicatures in Discourse.* Philadelphia: John Benjamins.

Blommaert, J. (2001). Investigating narrative inequality: African asylum seekers' stories in Belgium. *Discourse & Society* 12 (4), 413–450.

Bredart, S. (1991). Word interruption in self-repairing. *Journal of Psycholinguistic Research* 20/2, 123–138.

Brennan, S., and Schober, M. (2001). How listeners compensate for disfluencies in spontaneous speech. *Journal of Memory and Language* 44/2, 274–296.

Britain, D. (1992). Linguistic change in intonation: the use of high rising terminals in New Zealand English, *Linguistic Variation and Change* 4, 77–104.

Biber, D. (1988). *Variation across speaking and writing.* Cambridge: Cambridge University Press.

Bilmes, J. (1988). The concept of preference in conversation analysis. *Language in Society* 172, 161–82.

Blum, L. (1991). Tellers and listeners. In P. Hayes (ed.), *Lessons and legacies.* pp. 316–328. Evanston: Northwestern University Press.

Blum-Kulka, S. (1997). *Dinner talk: cultural patterns of locality and socialization in family discourse.* Mahwah, NJ: Lawrence Erlbaum.

Bolinger, D. (1997). *Meaning and form.* London: Longman.

Brinton, L. (1996). *Pragmatic markers in English: grammaticalization and discourse functions.* New York: Mouton de Gruyter.

Britton, B., and Pellegrini, A. (1990). *Narrative thought and narrative language.* Hillsdale, NJ: Lawrence Erlbaum.

Brockmeier, J. (2001). From the end to the beginning: narrative, identity and the reconstruction of the self. In Brockman and Carbaugh (eds.), *Narrative and Identity.* pp. 283–298. Philadelphia: John Benjamins.

Brockmeier, J., and Carbaugh, D. (2001). *Narrative and identity: studies in autobiography, self, and culture.* Amsterdam; Philadelphia, PA: John Benjamins.

Broszat, M. (1968). The concentration camps, 1933–1945. In H. Krausnick, H. Buchheim, M. Broszat, and H-A. Jacobsen (eds.), *Anatomy of the SS State.* p. 403. London: Collins.

Brown, G. (1995). *Speakers, listeners and communication.* Cambridge: Cambridge University Press.

Brugman, C. (1988). The syntax and semantics of HAVE and its complements. Unpublished doctoral dissertation, University of California at Berkeley.

Bruner, J. (1986). *Actual minds, possible worlds.* Cambridge, MA: Harvard University Press.

Bruner, J. (1987). Life as narrative. *Social Research* 54, 11–31.

Bruner, J. (1990). Autobiography as self. In *Acts of meaning.* pp. 99–138. Cambridge, MA: Harvard University Press.

Bruner, J. (2001). Self-making and world-making. In J. Brockmeier and D. Carbaugh (eds.), *Narrative and identity: studies in autobiography, self and culture.* pp. 25–37. Philadelphia: John Benjamins.

Butterworth, B. (1981). Speech errors: old data in search of new theories. *Linguistics* 19/7–8, 627–662.

Chafe, W. (1976). Givenness, contrastiveness, definiteness, subjects, topics, and point of view. In C. Li and S. Thompson (eds.), *Subject and topic.* pp. 25–56. New York: Academic Press.

Chafe, W. (ed.) (1980a). *The pear stories: cognitive, cultural and linguistic aspects of narrative production.* Norwood, NJ: Ablex.

Chafe, W. (1980b). The deployment of consciousness in the production of a narrative. In W. Chafe (ed.), *The pear stories: cognitive, cultural and linguistic aspects of narrative production.* pp. 9–50. Norwood, NJ: Ablex.

Chafe, W. (1986). Beyond Bartlett: Narratives and remembering. *Poetics* 15, 139–151.

Chafe, W. (1987). Cognitive constraints on information flow. In R. Tomlin (ed.), *Coherence and grounding in discourse.* Amsterdam: John Benjamins.

Chafe, W. (1990). Some things that narratives tell us about the mind. In B. Britton and A. Pellegrini (eds.), *Narrative thought and narrative language.* pp. 79–98. Hillsdale, NJ: Lawrence Erlbaum.

Chafe, W. (1991). Prosodic and functional units of language. In J. Edwards and M. Lampert (eds.), *Talking data: transcription and coding in discourse research.* Hillsdale, NJ: Lawrence Erlbaum.

Chafe, W. (1994). *Discourse, consciousness and time.* Chicago: University of Chicago Press.

Chafe, W. (1998). Things we can learn from repeated tellings of the same experience. *Narrative Inquiry* 8, 269–285.

Chambers, J. K., Trudgill, P., and Schilling-Estes, N. (2002). *The handbook of language variation and change.* Malden MA: Blackwell.

Clancy, P. (1980). Referential choice in English and Japanese narrative discourse. In W. Chafe (ed.), *The pear stories: cognitive, cultural and linguistic aspects of narrative production.* pp. 127–202. Norwood, NJ: Ablex Publishers.

Clark, E. (1978). Locationals: A study of existential, locative and possessive sentences. In J. Greenberg (Ed.), *Universals of human language* (vol. 4). *Syntax* (pp. 85–126). Stanford, CA: Stanford University Press.

Clark, H. and Fox Tree, J. E. (2002). Using uh and um in spontaneous speaking. *Cognition* 84, 73–111.

Clark, H., and Haviland, J. (1977). Comprehension and the given-new contract. In R. Freedle (ed.), *Discourse production and comprehension.* pp. 1–40. Norwood, NJ: Ablex Publishers.

Clark, H., and Marshall, C. (1992). Definite reference and mutual knowledge. In H. Clark, *Arenas of language use.* pp. 9–59. Chicago: University of Chicago Press.

Clark, H., Schreuder, R., and Buttrick, S. (1992). Common ground and the understanding of demonstrative reference. In H. Clark, *Arenas of language use.* pp. 78–99. Chicago: University of Chicago Press.

Clark, H. and Schober, M. (1992). Understanding by addressees and overhearers. In Clark, H. (ed.), *Arenas of language use.* pp. 176–197. Chicago: University Press.

Clark, H., and Wilkes-Gibbs, D. (1992). Referring as a collaborative process. Reprinted in H. Clark, *Arenas of language use.* pp. 107–143. Chicago: University of Chicago Press.

Cohn-Sherbock, D. (1992). *The Blackwell dictionary of Judaica.* Oxford: Blackwell.

Collins, P. (2001). Some discourse functions of existential sentences in English. In C. Allen (ed.), *Proceedings of the Australian Linguistics Society*. pp. 1–6.

Conrad, S., and Biber, D. (2001). *Variation in English: multi-dimensional studies*. London: Longman.

Cornish, F. (1999). *Anaphora, discourse, and understanding: evidence from English and French*. Oxford and New York: Clarendon Press.

Coupland, N. (1983). Patterns of encounter management: further arguments for discourse variables. *Language in Society* 12, 459–476.

Daniels, R. (1981). *Concentration Camps, North America*. Malabar, FA: R. E. Krieger.

Davies, B. and Harré, R. (1990). Positioning: the social construction of selves. *Journal for the Theory of Social Behaviour* 20: 43–63.

Dawidowicz, L. (1981). *The Holocaust and the historians*. Cambridge, MA: Harvard University Press.

DeConcini, B. (1990). *Narrative remembering*. Lanham, MD: University Press of America.

De Fina, A., Bamberg, M., and Schiffrin, D. (in press). *Discourse and identity*. Cambridge: Cambridge University Press.

Dell, G. S., and Reich, P. A. (1981). Stages in sentence production: An analysis of speech error data. *Journal of Verbal Learning & Verbal Behavior* 20, 611–629.

Dines, E. (1980). Variation in discourse: "And stuff like that". *Language in Society* 9 (1), 13–33.

Donnellan, K. S. (1966). Reference and definite descriptions. *Philosophical Review* 75, 281–304.

Donnellan, K. (1978). Speaker reference, descriptions, and anaphora. In P. Cole (ed.), *Pragmatics (Syntax and Semantics 9)*. pp. 47–68. New York: Academic Press.

Drinnon, R. (1987). *Keeper of concentration camps*. Berkeley: University of California Press.

Downing, P. (1996). Proper names as a referential option in English Conversation, in B. Fox (Ed.) *Studies in Anaphora*. pp. 95–143. Philadelphia/Amsterdam: John Benjamin.

DuBois, J. (1980). Beyond definiteness: the trace of identity in discourse. In W. Chafe (ed.), *The pear stories: cognitive, cultural and linguistic aspects of narrative production*. pp. 203–274. Norwood NJ: Ablex.

DuBois, J. (1987). The discourse basis of ergativity. *Language* 63, 805–55.

DuBois, S., and Sankoff, D. (2001) in D. Schiffrin, D. Tannen, and H. Hamilton, Handbook of discourse analysis. pp. 282–303. Oxford: Basil Blackwell.

Eckert, P., and Rickford, J. (2001). *Style and sociolinguistic variation*. Cambridge: Cambridge University Press.

Edelsky, C. (1981). Who's got the floor? *Language in Society*. 10, 383–421.

Egbert, M. (1996). Context-sensitivity in conversation: eye gaze and the German repair initiator "bitte?". *Language in Society* 25 (4), 587–612.

Eitinger, L. (1998). Holocaust survivors in past and present. In B. and A. Peck (eds.), *The known, the unknown, the disputed and the re-examined.* pp. 767–784. Bloomington, IN: Indiana University Press.

Ellis, J., and Boadi, L. A. (1969). "'To be' in Twi". In J. W. M. Verhaar, (ed.), *The verb "be" and its synonyms: philosophical and grammatical studies*, part 4. pp. 1–70. Dordrecht: Reidel.

Epstein, R. (2001). The definite article, accessibility, and the construction of discourse referents. *Cognitive linguistics* 12:4, 333–378.

Erdmann, P. (1976). *There sentences in English.* Munich: Tuduv.

Ervin-Tripp, S. (1976). Is Sybil there? The structure of American English directives. *Language in Society* 5, 25–66.

Evans, R. (1999). *In defense of history.* New York: W. W. Norton and Company.

Fairclough, N. (1992) *Discourse and social change.* Cambridge: Polity Press.

Fasold, R. (1990). *Sociolinguistics of language.* Oxford: Blackwell.

Ferrera, K. (1994). *Therapeutic ways with words.* New York: Oxford University Press.

Fetzer, A., and Meierkord, C. (2002) *Rethinking sequentiality.* Philadelphia: John Benjamins.

Fillmore, C. (1975). The case for case. In E. Bach and R. Harns (eds), *Universals in linguistic theory.* pp. 1–88. New York: Holt.

Firbas, J. (1964) On defining the theme in functional sentence analysis. In *Travaux linguistiques de Prague* (vol. 1). pp. 267–280. Tuscaloosa: University of Alabama Press.

Fitzmaurice, S. (2004) Subjectivity, intersubjectivity and the historical construction of interlocutor stance. *Discourse Studies* 6 (4), 427–448.

Flanzbaum, H. (1999). *The Americanization of the Holocaust.* Baltimore, MD: The Johns Hopkins Press.

Fleischman, S. (1990). *Tense and narrativity.* Austin: University of Texas Press.

Ford, C. (1993). Grammar in interaction: adverbial clauses in American English conversation. Cambridge: Cambridge University Press.

Ford, C., and Fox, B. (1996) Interactional motivations for reference formulation. In B. Fox (Ed.) *Studies in anaphora.* pp. 146–166. Philadelphia/Amsterdam: John Benjamins.

Fox, B. (1987). *Discourse structure and anaphora.* Cambridge: Cambridge University Press.

Fox, B., and Jasperson, R. (1995). A syntactic exploration of repair in conversation. In P. Davis (ed.), *Descriptive and theoretical modes in the alternative linguistics.* pp. 77–134. Philadelphia: John Benjamins.

Fox, B., Hayashi, M., and Jasperson, R. (1996). Resources and repair: a cross-linguistic study of syntax and repair. In E. Ochs, E. Schegloff, and S. Thompson, (eds.) *Interaction and grammar*. pp. 185–237. Cambridge: Cambridge University Press.

Fox, B., and Thompson, S. (1990). A discourse explanation of the grammar of relative clauses in English conversation. *Language* 66/2, 297–316.

Fox Tree, J. E., and Clark, H. (1997). Pronouncing "the" as "thee" to signal problems in speaking. *Cognition* 62 (2), 151–167.

Freeze, R. (1992). Existentials and other locatives. *Language* 68/3, 553–595.

Fretheim, T., and Gundel. J (1996). *Reference and referent accessibility*. Philadelphia: John Benjamins.

Friedlander, S. (1992). Trauma, transference and "working through" in writing the history of the Shoah. *History and Memory* 4/1: 39–55.

Fromkin, V. (1973). Slips of the tongue. *Scientific American* 229/6, 110–117.

Fromkin, V. (1980). *Errors in linguistic performance*. New York: Academic Press.

Garfinkel, H. (1967). Studies in Ethnomethodology. Englewood Cliffs, NJ: Prentice Hall.

Garfinkel, H. (1974). On the origins of the term "ethnomethodology". In R. Turner (ed.), *Ethnomethodology*. pp. 13–18. Harmondsworth: Penguin.

Garnham, A., Shillcock, R., Brown, G., Mill, A., and Cutler, A. (1981). Slips of the tongue in the London-Lund corpus of spontaneous conversation. *Linguistics* 19/7–8, 805–817.

Gee, J. P. (1989). Two styles of narrative construction and their linguistic and educational implications. *Discourse Processes* 12, 287–307.

Gee, J. P. (1999). *An introduction to discourse analysis*. London: Routledge.

Gee, J. P, and Michaels, S. (1989). Discourse styles: variations across speakers, situations, and tasks. *Discourse Processes* 12/3, 263–266.

Geluykens, R. (1994). *The pragmatics of discourse anaphora in English: evidence from conversational repair*. Berlin: Mouton de Gruyter.

Givón, T. (1979). *On understanding grammar*. New York: Academic Press.

Givón, T. (1983b). *Topic continuity in discourse: a quantitative cross-linguistic study*. Typological studies in language series (vol. 3). Amsterdam: John Benjamins.

Givón, T. (1989). *Mind, code, and context: Essays in pragmatics*. Hillsdale, NJ: Lawrence Erlbaum Associates.

Goffman, E. (1963). *Behavior in public places*. New York: Free Press.

Goffman, E. (1971a). Supportive interchanges, in *Relations in Public*, pp. 62–94. New York: Basic Books.

Goffman, E. (1971b). Remedial interchanges, in *Relations in Public*. pp. 95–187. New York: Basic Books.

Goffman, E. (1974). *Frame analysis*. New York: Harper and Row.

Goffman, E. (1981a). Footing. In *Forms of talk*. pp. 124–159. Philadelphia: University of Pennsylvania Press.

Goffman, E. (1981b). Radio talk. In *Forms of talk*. pp. 197–330. Philadelphia: University of Pennsylvania Press.

Goffman, E. (1981c). Replies and responses. In *Forms of talk*. pp. 5–77. Philadelphia: University of Pennsylvania Press.

Goodwin, C. (1981). *Conversational organization: interaction between speakers and hearers*. New York: Academic Press.

Goodwin, C. (1986). Audience diversity, participation and interpretation. *Text* 6, 283–316.

Green, G. (1989). *Pragmatics and natural language understanding*. Hillsdale, NJ: Lawrence Erlbaum Associates.

Greenspan, H. (1998). *On listening to Holocaust survivors*. Westport CN: Praeger.

Greenspan, H. (1999). Imagining survivors: Testimony and the rise of Holocaust consciousness. In H. Flanzbaum (ed.), *The Americanization of the Holocaust*. pp. 45–67. Baltimore, MD: The Johns Hopkins Press.

Greenspan, H. (2001). The awakening of memory. Monna and Otto Weinmann Lecture Series. Washington DC: United States Holocaust Memorial Museum.

Grice, H. P. (1975). Logic and conversation. In P. Cole and J. Morgan (eds.), *Speech acts syntax and semantics* (vol. 3). pp. 41–58. New York: Academic Press.

Grosz, B. J. 1981. Focusing and description in natural language dialogues. In A. K. Joshi, B. L. Webber and I. A. Sag (eds.), *Elements of discourse understanding*. pp. 84–105. Cambridge: Cambridge University Press.

Grosz, Barbara J., Joshi, Aravind K., and Weinstein, S. (1995). Centering: a framework for modeling the local coherence of discourse. *Computational Linguistics* 21:2, 203–225.

Gumperz, J. (1982). *Discourse strategies*. Cambridge: Cambridge University Press.

Gundel, J., Hedberg, N., and Zacharski, R. (1993). Cognitive status and the form of referring expressions in discourse. *Language* 69/2, 274–307.

Halliday, M. (1967) Notes on transitivity and theme in English. Parts 1 and 2. *Journal of Linguistics* 3: 37–81, 199–244.

Hamilton, H. (1996) Intratextuality, intertextuality and the construction of identity as patient in Alzheimer's Disease. *Text* 16/1, 61–90.

Hammer, R. (1998). Commemorations and the Holocaust. In P. Hayes (ed.), *Lessons and legacies: teaching the Holocaust in a changing world*. pp. 175–191. Evanston, IL: Northwestern University Press.

Hannay, M. (1985). *English existentials in functional grammar*. Dordrecht: Foris Publications.

Hartman, G. (1996). *The longest shadow: in the aftermath of the Holocaust*. Bloomington: University of Indiana Press.

Hawkins, J. A. (1978). *Definiteness and indefiniteness: a study in reference and grammaticality prediction.* London: Croom Helm; Atlantic Highlands NJ: Humanities Press.

Hayashi, M. (2004). Discourse within a sentence. *Language in Society* 33 (3), 343–376.

He, A. W. (1996). Narrative processes and institutional activities: recipient guided storytelling in academic counseling encounters. *Pragmatics* 6/s, 205–216.

Heath, S. (1982). What no bedtime story means: narrative skills at home and school. *Language in Society* 11, 49–76.

Heath, S. (1983). *Ways with words: language, life, and work in communities and classrooms.* Cambridge: Cambridge University Press.

Heeman, P. A., and Hirst, G. (1995). Collaborating on referring expressions. *Computational linguistics* 21:3, 351–382.

Heine, B. (1997) *Possession: cognitive sources, forces, and grammaticalization.* Cambridge: Cambridge University Press.

Helmbrecht, J. (2002) Grammar and function of *we*. In A. Duszak (ed.), *Us and others.* pp. 31–50. Philadelphia: John Benjamins.

Heritage, J. (1984). *Garfinkel and ethomethodology.* Oxford: Basil Blackwell.

Hertzberg, A. (1996). The first encounters: survivors and Americans in the late 1940s. Washington D.C: The United States Holocaust Research Institute.

Hilberg, R. (1992). *Perpetrators, victims, bystanders.* New York: Harper Collins.

Hirsch, M., and Suleiman, S. R. (2001). Material memory: Holocaust testimony in post-Holocaust art. In J. Epstein and L. Lefkovitz (eds.), *Shaping losses: cultural memory and the Holocaust.* pp. 87–104. Chicago and Urbana: University of Illinois Press.

Hopper, R. (1992). Speech errors and the poetics of conversation. *Text and Performance Quarterly* 12/2, 113–124.

Horowitz, S. (1997). *Voicing the void.* Albany, NY: State University of New York Press.

Horvath, B. (1987). Text in conversation: variability in story-telling texts. In K. Denning S. Inkelas, F. McNair-Knox and J. Rickford (eds.), *Variation in language: NWAV-XV at Stanford.* pp. 212–223. Stanford, CA: Stanford University Linguistics Department.

Houston, A. (1989). The English gerund: syntactic change and discourse function. In R. Fasold and D. Schiffrin (eds.), *Language change and variation.* pp. 173–196. Philadelphia: John Benjamins.

Huang, Y. (1994). *The syntax and pragmatics of anaphora.* Cambridge: Cambridge University Press.

Hurford, J. and Heasley, B. (1983). *Semantics: A coursebook.* Cambridge: Cambridge University Press.

Hymes, D. (1974a). Toward ethnographies of communication. In *Foundations in sociolinguistics: an ethnographic approach*. pp. 3–28. Philadelphia: University of Pennsylvania Press.

Hymes, D. (1974b). Why linguistics needs the sociologist. In *Foundations in sociolinguistics: an ethnographic approach*. pp. 69–82. Philadelphia: University of Pennsylvania Press.

Hymes, D. (1981). *"In vain I tried to tell you."* Philadelphia: University of Pennsylvania Press.

Hymes, D. (1985). Language, memory and selective performance: Cultee's "Salmon Myth" as twice told to Boas, *Journal of American Folklore* 98, 391–434.

Hymes, D. (1996). *Ethnography, linguistics, narrative inequality.* London: Taylor and Francis Ltd.

Iggers, G. (1997). *Historiography in the twentieth century.* Hanover: Wesleyan University Press.

Irvine, J. (1996). Shadow conversations. In M. Silverstein and G. Urban (Eds.) *Natural Histories of Discourse.* pp. 131–159. Chicago: University of Chicago Press.

Jakobson, R. (1971 [1957]). Shifters, verbal categories and the Russian verb, in *Selected Writings of Roman Jakobson.* (vol. 2). The Hague: Mouton.

Jakobson, R. (1960). Closing statement: linguistics and poetics. In T. Sebeok (ed.), *Style in language.* pp. 350–377. Cambridge, MA: MIT Press.

Jasperson, R. 2003. Some linguistic aspects of closure cut-off. In *The language of turn and sequence.* pp. 257–286. Cambridge: Cambridge University Press.

Jefferson, G. (1972). Side sequences. In D. Sudnow (ed.), *Studies in social interaction.* pp. 294–338. New York: Free Press.

Jefferson, G. (1974). Error corrections an interactional resource. *Language in Society* 3: 181–199.

Jefferson, G. (1978). Sequential aspects of storytelling in conversation. In J. Schenkein (ed.), *Studies in the organization of conversational interaction.* pp. 219–248. New York: Free Press.

Johnstone, B. (1980). *Stories, community and place: narratives from middle America.* Bloomington: University of Indiana Press.

Johnstone, B. (1994). *Perspectives on repetition: interdisciplinary perspectives*, vol. 1. Norwood, NJ: Ablex Publishers.

Kacandes, I. (1994). "You who live safe in your warm houses": Your role in the production of Holocaust testimony. In D. Lorenz and G. Weinberger (eds.), *Insiders and outsiders: Jewish and Gentile culture in Germany and Austria.* pp. 189–213. Detroit: Wayne State University Press.

Kaltenbock, G. (2003). On the syntactic and semantic status of anticipatory it. *English language and linguistics* 7:2, 235–255.

Kärkkäinen, E. (2003). *Epistemic stance in English conversation*. Philadelphia PA: John Benjamins.

Kartunnen, L. (1976). Discourse referents. In J. D. McCawley (ed.), *Syntax and Semantics: notes from the Linguistic Underground*. pp. 363–394. New York: Academic Press.

Kirschenblatt-Gimblett, B. (1974). The concept and varieties of narrative performance in east European Jewish culture. In R. Bauman and J. Sherzer (eds.), *Explorations in the ethnography of speaking*. pp. 283–308. Cambridge: Cambridge University Press.

Korobov, N. & Bamberg, M. (2003). Between childhood and adolescence: multiple positioning in 10 year olds. *American Association of Applied Linguistics Panel*, Washington D.C.

Kristeva, J. (1986). Word, dialogue, and the novel. In T. Moi (ed.), *The Kristeva reader*. pp. 35–61. New York: Columbia University Press.

Kronfeld, A. (1990). *Reference and computation*. Cambridge: Cambridge University Press.

Labov, W., and Waletzky, J. (1967). Narrative analysis. In J. Helm (ed.), *Essays on the verbal and visual arts*. pp. 12–44. Seattle: University of Washington Press.

Labov, W. (1972a). The isolation of contextual styles. In *Sociolinguistic patterns*. pp. 70–109. Philadelphia: University of Pennsylvania Press.

Labov, W. (1972b). The transformation of experience in narrative syntax. In *Language in the inner city*. pp. 354–396. Philadelphia: University of Pennsylvania Press.

Labov, W. (1973). The boundaries of words and their meanings. In C-J. Bailey and R. Shuy (Eds.) *New Ways of Analyzing Variation in English*. pp. 340–373. Washington: Georgetown University Press.

Labov, W. (1978). Where does the linguistic variable stop?: A reply to Beatriz Lavandera. *Working Papers in Sociolinguistics, 44*. Austin, TX: Southwest Educational Development Laboratory.

Labov, W. (1997). Some further steps in narrative analysis. *Journal of Narrative and Life History* 7, 395–415.

LaCapra, D. (2001). *Writing history, writing trauma*. Baltimore, Maryland: Johns Hopkins University Press.

Lakoff, G. (1987). *Women, fire and dangerous things*. Chicago: University of Chicago Press.

Lambrecht, K. (1990). *Information structure and sentence form*. Cambridge: Cambridge University Press.

Lang, B. (2002). Uncovering certain mischievous questions about the Holocaust. Monna and Otto Weinmann Lecture Series. United States Holocaust Memorial Museum, Washington D.C.

Langer, L. (1991). *Holocaust testimonies*. New Haven: Yale University Press.

Laub, D. (1992). Bearing witness: of the vicissitudes of listening. In S. Felman and D. Laub (eds.), *Testimony*. pp. 75–104. New York: Routledge.

Laub, D., and Allard, M. (1998). History, memory and truth: Defining the place of the survivor. In B. and A. Peck (eds.), *The known, the unknown, the disputed and the re-examined*. pp. 799–813. Bloomington, IN: Indiana University Press.

Lavandera, B. (1978). Where does the sociolinguistic variable stop? *Language in Society* 7, 171–183.

Leech, G. (1983). *Principles of pragmatics*. London: Longman.

Lefebvre, C. (1989). Some problems in determining syntactic variables: The case of WH questions in Montreal French. In R. Fasold, and D. Schiffrin, D. (eds), *Language Change and Variation*. pp. 351–366. Philadelphia: John Benjamins.

Levelt, W. (1983). Monitoring and self-repair in speech. *Cognition* 14/1, 41–104.

Levelt, W. (1999). Models of word production. *Trends in Cognitive Sciences* 6/27, 223–232.

Levelt, W., Roelofs, A., and Meyer, A. (1999). A theory of lexical access in speech production. *Behavioral and Brain Sciences* 22/1, 1–38.

Levinson, S. (1983). *Pragmatics*. Cambridge: Cambridge University Press.

Levinson, S. (1988) Putting Linguistics on a proper footing. In P. Drew and A. Wootton (Eds.) *Erving Goffman: an interdisciplinary appreciation*. pp. 161–227. Oxford: Polity Press.

Levinson, S (2000). *Presumptive meanings*. Cambridge, MA: MIT Press.

Linde, C. (1993). *Life stories*. Oxford: Oxford University Press.

Linenthal, E. (1995). *Preserving memory*. New York: Penguin Books.

Linenthal, E. (2001) *The unfinished bombing: Oklahoma City in American memory*. Oxford: Oxford University Press.

Lipstadt, D. (1994). *Denying the Holocaust*. New York: The Free Press.

Luborsky, M. (1987). Analysis of multiple life history narratives. *Ethos* 15/4, 366–381.

Lyons, J. (1967). A note on possessive, existential and locative sentences. *Foundations of Language* 3, 390–396.

Lyons, J. (1977). *Semantics*. Cambridge: Cambridge University Press.

Macaulay, R. (2002). Discourse variation. In J. K. Chambers, P. Trudgill and N. Schilling-Estes (eds.) *The handbook of language variation and change*. Oxford: Basil Blackwell.

Mandler, J. (1984). *Stories, scripts, and scenes: aspects of a schema theory*. Hillsdale, NJ: Erlbaum.

Margulies, D. (1998). *Collected stories: A play*. New York: Theatre Communications Group.

Marrus, M. (1987). *The Holocaust in history*. London: Penguin.

Marrus, M. (1988). *The Holocaust in history*. London: George Weidenfeld and Nicolson Limited.

Marrus, M. (1991). The use and misuse of the Holocaust. In P. Hayes (ed.), *Lessons and Legacies*. pp. 106–119. Evanston: Northwestern University Press.

Matoesian, G. (1999). The grammaticalization of participant roles in the constitution of expert identity. *Language in Society* 28: 4.

Meechan, M, and Foley, M. (1994). On resolving disagreement: linguistic theory and variation – "There's bridges." *Linguistic Variation and Change* 6 (1), 63–86.

Mey, J. (2001). *Pragmatics*. Oxford: Basil Blackwell.

Michaels, S., and Collins, J. (1984). Oral discourse styles: Classroom interaction and the acquisition of literacy. In D. Tannen (ed.), *Coherence in spoken and written discourse*. pp. 219–244. Norwood, NJ: Ablex.

Miller, J. (1990). *One, by one, by one*. New York: Simon and Schuster.

Milsark, G. (1977). Towards an explanation of certain peculiarities of the existential construction in English. *Linguistic Analysis*, 3 1–31.

Mishler, E. (1999). *Storyline: craftartists' narratives of identity*. Cambridge, MA: Harvard.

Mishler, E. (In press). Narrative and identity: the double arrow of time. In D. Schiffrin, A. De Fina, and M. Bamberg (eds.), *Discourse and identity*. Cambridge: Cambridge University Press.

Mintz, A. (2001). *Popular culture and the shaping of Holocaust memory in America* Seattle: University of Washington Press.

Moerman, M. (1988). *Ethnography and conversation analysis*. Philadelphia: University of Pennsylvania Press.

Morris, C. (1938). Foundations of the theory of signs. In O. Neurath, R. Carnap, and C. Morris (eds.), *International encyclopedia of unified science*. pp. 77–138. Chicago: University of Chicago Press.

Mulkern, A. (1996). The game of the name. In T. Fretheim and J. Gundel (eds.) *Reference and referent*. pp. 263–289. Amsterdam/Philadelphia: John Benjamins.

Mushin, I. (2001). *Evidentiality and epistemological stance*. Philadelphia: John Benjamins.

Myhill, J. (1988). A quantitative study of future tense marking in Spanish. In K. Ferrara et al. (eds.), *Linguistic change and contact*. pp. 263–272. Austin: The University of Texas Linguistics Department.

Nelson, K. (ed.) (1989). *Narratives from the crib*. Cambridge, MA: Harvard University Press.

Nicolle, S. (1988). "Be going to" and "will": a monosemous account. *English Language and Linguistics* 2, 223–243.

Nooteboom, S. (1980). Speaking and unspeaking: detection and correction of phonological and lexical errors in spontaneous speech. In V. Fromkin (ed.) *Errors in Linguistic performance*. pp. 87–95. NY: Academic Press

Norrick, N. (1997). Retelling stories in spontaneous conversation. *Discourse Processes* 25, 75–97.

Norrick, N. (1998). Retelling again. *Narrative Inquiry* 8, 373–378.

Norrick, N. (2000). *Conversational narrative*. Philadelphia: John Benjamins.

Novick, P. (1999). *The Holocaust in American life*. New York: Houghton Mifflin.

Ochs, E. (1985). Clarification and culture. In D. Schiffrin (ed.), *Meaning, form and use: linguistic applications*. pp. 325–341. Washington, DC: Georgetown University Press.

Ochs, E. (1993). Indexing gender. In A. Duranti and C. Goodwin (eds.), *Rethinking context*. pp. 335–358. Cambridge: Cambridge University Press.

Ochs, E. and Capps, L. (2001). *Living narrative*. Cambridge MA: Harvard University Press.

Ochs, E., Schegloff, E., and Thompson, S. (1996). *Interaction and Grammar*. Cambridge: Cambridge University Press.

Ochs, E., Taylor, C., Rudolph, D., and Smith, R. (1991). Storytelling as a theory-building activity. *Discourse Processes* 151, 37–72.

Ochs, E., and Capps, L. (2001). *Living narrative: Creating lives in everyday storytelling*. Cambridge, MA: Harvard University Press.

Pan, Y. (2000). *Politeness in Chinese face-to-face interaction*. Stamford, CT: Ablex Publishers.

Philips, S. (1992). The routinization of repair in courtroom discourse. In A. Duranti and C. Goodwin (eds.), *Rethinking context: language as an interactive phenomenon*. pp. 311–322. Cambridge: Cambridge University Press.

Polanyi, L. (1978). False Starts Can Be True. In *Proceedings of Fourth Annual Meeting of Berkeley Linguistics Society*. pp. 628–639. University of California, Berkeley, CA.

Polanyi, L. (1981) Telling the same story twice. *Text* 1: 4, 315–336.

Polkinghorne, D. (1988). *Narrative knowing and the human sciences*. Albany, NY: SUNY Press.

Polkinghorne, D. (1991). Narrative and self-concept. *Journal of Narrative and Life History* (1): 135–153.

Pomerantz, A. (1984). Agreeing and disagreeing with assessments: Some features of preferred/dispreferred turn shapes. In J. Atkinson and J. Heritage (eds.), *Structures of Social Action: Studies in Conversation Analysis*. pp. 57–101. Cambridge: Cambridge University Press.

Portelli, A. (1997). *The Battle of Valle Giulia: Oral history and the art of dialogue*. Madison, WI: University of Wisconsin Press.

Premilovac, A. (2002). The Discursive Construction of Memory in Holocaust Survivor Testimonies. M.S. Thesis. Washington D.C: Georgetown University Department of Linguistics.

Prince, E. (1981). Toward a taxonomy of given-new information. In P. Cole (ed.), *Radical pragmatics*. pp. 223–256. New York: Academic Press.

Prince, E. (1992) The ZPG letter: subjects, definiteness, and information-status In Thompson, S. and W. Mann, W., eds. *Discourse description: diverse analyses of a fund raising text.* pp. 295–325. Philadelphia: John Benjamins.

Rando, E., and Napoli, D. J. (1978). Definites and *there* sentences. *Language 54/2:* 300–313.

Reaser, J. (2003). A Quantitative approach to (sub)registers: the case of 'Sports Announcer Talk' *Discourse Studies 5* (3), 303–322.

Roberts, L. (1993). *How reference works: explanatory models for indexicals, descriptions and opacity.* Albany: State University of New York Press.

Romaine, S. (1981). On the problem of syntactic variation: a reply to B. Lavandera and W. Labov. *Working Papers in Sociolinguistics 82.* Austin, TX: Southwest Educational Development Laboratory.

Rorty, R. (1967). *The linguistic turn.* Chicago: University of Chicago Press.

Rosch, E. (1973). Natural categories. *Cognitive Psychology 4,* 328–350.

Rosch, E. (1978). Principles of categorization. In E. Rosch and B. Lloyd (eds.), *Cognition and categorization.* pp. 27–48. Hillsdale, NJ: Laurence Erlbaum.

Rosen, H. (1988). The autobiographical impulse. In D. Tannen (ed.), *Linguistics in context.* pp. 69–88. Norwood, NJ: Ablex.

Rosenbaum, A. (1996). *Is the Holocaust unique?* Boulder, Colorado: Westview Press.

Rosenbaum, R. (2004). *Those who forget the past: the question of anti-Semitism.* New York: Random House.

Roth, A. (2002). Social epistomology in broadcast news interviews. *Language in Society* 31 (3), pp. 355–382.

Sacks, H. (1973). Lecture notes. School of Social Sciences, University of California at Irvine.

Sacks, H. (1984). Notes on methodology. In J. M. Atkinson and J. Heritage (eds.), In J. Atkinson and J. Heritage (eds), *Structures of social action: studies in conversation analysis.* pp. 21–27. Cambridge: Cambridge University Press.

Sacks, H. 1992[1966]. The baby cried: the mommy picked it up. In H. Sacks *Lectures on conversation.* pp. 236–266. Cambridge MA: Blackwell.

Sacks, H., and Schegloff, E. (1979). Two preferences in the organization of reference to persons in conversation and their interaction. In G. Psathas (ed.), *Everyday language: studies in ethnomethodology.* pp. 15–21. New York: Irvington.

Sankoff, D. (1988). Sociolinguistics and syntactic variation. In F. Newmeyer (ed.), *Linguistics: the Cambridge survey.* pp. 140–61. Cambridge: Cambridge University Press.

Sankoff, D., and Thibault, P. (1981). Weak complementarity: tense and aspect in Montreal French. In B. Johns and D. Strong (eds), *Syntactic change*. Natural Language Studies (vol. 26). Ann Arbor: University of Michigan.

Schegloff, E. (1972a). Notes on a conversational practice: formulating place. In D. Sundow (ed.), *Studies in social interaction*. pp. 75–119. New York: Free Press.

Schegloff, E. (1979). The relevance of repair to syntax for conversation. In T. Givón (ed.), *Syntax and semantics 12: Discourse and syntax*. pp. 261–288. New York: Academic Press.

Schegloff. E. (1987). Recycled Turn Beginnings, in G. Button and J. R. E. Lee (eds.), *Talk and Social Organization* Clevedon, England: Multilingual Matters. pp. 70–85. Clevedon, England: Multilingual Matters, Ltd.

Schegloff, E. (1992). Repair after next turn: The last structurally provided defense of intersubjectivity in conversation. *American Journal of Sociology* 97: 5, 1295–1345.

Schegloff, E., G. Jefferson, and H. Sacks (1977). The preference for self-correction in the organization of repair in conversation. *Language* 53, 361–382.

Schiff, B., Noy, C. and B. Cohler 2001. "Collected Stories in the Life Narratives of Holocaust Survivors". 11:1, 159–194.

Schiff, B., and Noy, C. (In press). Making it personal: Shared meanings in the narratives of Holocaust survivors. In D. Schiffrin, A. De Fina and M. Bamberg (eds.), *Discourse and identity*. Cambridge: University Press.

Schiffrin, D. (1977). Opening encounters. *American Sociological Review* 424, 671–691.

Schiffrin, D. (1980). Meta-talk: Organizational and evaluative brackets in discourse. *Sociological Inquiry* 50 (3/4), 199–236.

Schiffrin, D. (1981). Tense variation in narrative. *Language* 57/1, 45–62.

Schiffrin, D. (1984a). How a story says what it means and does. *Text* 44, 313–346.

Schiffrin, D. (1984b). Jewish argument as sociability. *Language in Society* 13 (3), pp. 311–335.

Schiffrin, D. (1985). Multiple constraints on discourse options: a quantitative analysis of causal sequences. *Discourse Processes* 8 (3), 281–303.

Schiffrin, D. (1986). Turn-initial variation: structure and function in conversation. In D. Sankoff (ed.), *Diversity and diachrony*. pp. 367–380. Philadelphia: John Benjamins.

Schiffrin, D. (1987). *Discourse Markers*. Cambridge: Cambridge University Press.

Schiffrin, D. (1990). Between text and context: Deixis, anaphora and the meaning of *then*. *Text* 103: 245–70.

Schiffrin, D. (1991). Conditionals as topics in discourse. *Linguistics* 30/1, 165–197.

Schiffrin, D. (1992). Anaphoric *then*: Aspectual, textual and epistemic meaning. *Linguistics* 30: 4, 753–792.

Schiffrin, D. (1993). "Speaking for another" in sociolinguistic interviews. In D. Tannen (ed.) *Framing in discourse.* pp. 231–59. Oxford: Oxford University Press.

Schiffrin, D. (1994a). *Approaches to discourse.* Oxford: Basil Blackwell.

Schiffrin, D. (1994b). Making a list. *Discourse Processes* 17/3, 377–405.

Schiffrin, D. (1996). Narrative as self portrait: the sociolinguistic construction of identity. *Language in Society* 25/2, 167–203.

Schiffrin, D. (2000). Mother/daughter discourse in a Holocaust oral history. *Narrative Inquiry* 10/1, 1–44.

Schiffrin, D. (2001a). Discourse markers: language meaning and context In D. Schiffrin, D. Tannen, and H. Hamilton (eds.), *Handbook of discourse analysis.* pp. 54–75. Oxford: Blackwell.

Schiffrin, D. (2001b). Language, experience and history: "What happened" in World War II. *Journal of Sociolinguistics* 5/3, 323–352.

Schiffrin, D. (2001c). Language and public memorial: "America's concentration camps." *Discourse and Society* 12: 505–534.

Schiffrin, D. (2002). Mother and friends in a Holocaust life story. *Language in Society* 31/3, 309–354.

Schiffrin, D. (2003). Linguistics and history: The narrative connection. In D. Tannen and J. Alatis (eds.), *Discourse and beyond.* pp. 35–60. Washington D.C.: Georgetown University Press.

Schiffrin, D. (in press). From linguistic reference to social identity. In A. De Fina, M. Bamberg, and D. Schiffrin (eds.), *Discourse and identity.* Cambridge: Cambridge University Press.

Scollon, R., and S. W. Scollon (2003). *Discourses in place.* London: Routledge.

Searle, J. (1969). *Speech Acts.* Cambridge: University Press.

Sherzer, J. (1981). Tellings, retellings and tellings within tellings: The structuring and organization of narrative in Kuna Indian discourse. In R. Bauman and J. Sherzer (eds.), *Case studies in the ethnography of speaking.* pp. 249–273. Austin: Southwest Educational Development Laboratory.

Shuman, A. (1986). *Storytelling rights: Uses of oral and written texts by urban adolescents.* New York: Cambridge University Press.

Silverstein, M., and Urban, G. (1996). *Natural histories of discourse.* Chicago: University Press.

Simmel, G. (1950[1908]). *The Sociology of Georg Simmel.* Translated by K. Wolff (ed.). New York: MacMillan.

Smith, P. (1995). *Democracy on trial: the Japanese American evacuation and relocation in World War II.* New York: Simon & Schuster.

Smith, S. W., and Jucker, A. H. (1998). Interactive aspects of reference assignment in conversations. *Pragmatics and cognition* 6:1–2, 153–187.

Strassfeld, M. (1985). *The Jewish holidays.* New York: Harper and Row.

Strauss, C. (2004). Cultural standing in expression of opinion. *Language in Society* 33: 2, 161–194.

Swerts, M. (1998). Filled pauses as markers of discourse structure, *Journal of Pragmatics* 30, 486–496

Tannen, D. (1980). A Comparative analysis of oral narrative strategies: Athenian Greek and American English. In W. Chafe (ed.), *The pear stories: cognitive, cultural and linguistic aspects of narrative production.* pp. 51–88. Norwood NJ: Ablex Publishers.

Tannen, D. (1982). Oral and literate strategies in spoken and written narratives. *Language* 58, 1–21.

Tannen, D. (1984). *Conversational style.* Norwood NJ: Ablex Publishers.

Tannen, D. (1989). Talking voices: repetition, dialogue, and imagery in conversational discourse. Cambridge: Cambridge University Press.

Tannen, D. (1990). *You just don't understand.* New York: Morrow.

Taylor, J. (1989) *Linguistic categorization.* Oxford: Clarendon Press.

Taylor J. (1996) *Possessives in English: an exploration in cognitive grammar.* Oxford: Clarendon Press.

Taylor, R. (1999). The internment of Americans of Japanese ancestry, in R. Brooks (ed.) *When sorry isn't enough: the controversy over apologies and reparations for human injustice.* pp. 165–168. New York: University Press.

Taylor, T. (1984). Editing rules and understanding: the case against sentence-based syntax. *Language and Communication* 4/2, 105–127.

Taylor, T., and Cameron, D. (1987). *Analyzing conversation.* Pergamon Press.

Tonkin, E. (1992). *Narrating our past: the social construction of oral history.* Cambridge: Cambridge University Press.

Toole, J. (1996). The effect of genre on referential choice. In T. Fretheim and J. Gundel (eds.), *Reference and referent accessibility.* pp. 263–289. Philadelphia: John Benjamins.

Trudgill, P. (1974). *The social differentiation of English in Norwich.* Cambridge: Cambridge University Press.

Walker, M., Joshi, A., and Prince, E. (1998). *Centering theory in discourse.* Oxford: Clarendon Press.

Ward, G. and Birner, B. (1995). Definiteness and the English existential. *Language* 71, 722–742.

Ward, G., and Birner, B. (2001). Discourse and information structure. In D. Schiffrin, H. Hamilton, and D. Tannen (eds), *Handbook of discourse analysis.* pp. 119–137. Oxford: Blackwell.

Webb, K. (1977) An evolutionary aspect of social structure and a verb "have". *American Anthropologist* March 79 (1), 42–49.

Wertsch, J. (1998). *Mind as action.* Oxford: University Press.

Wieviorka, A. (1994). On testimony. In G. Hartman (ed.), *Holocaust remembrance.* pp. 23–32. Oxford: Basil Blackwell.

Wolfson, N. (1976). Speech events and natural speech: some implications for sociolinguistic methodology. *Language in Society* 5: 189–209.

Wolfson, N. (1978). A feature of performed narrative: The conversational historical present. *Language in Society* 7, 215–237.

Wolfson, N. (1979). The conversational historical present alternation. *Language* 55, 168–182.

Wortham, S. (2001). *Narratives in action.* New York: Teachers' College Press.

Wu, R-J. (2004). *Stance in talk: a conversation analysis of Mandarin final particles.* Amsterdam: John Benjamins.

Young, J. (1988). *Writing and rewriting the Holocaust.* Bloomington: Indiana University Press.

Young, J. (1993). *The texture of memory.* New Haven: Yale University Press.

Ziv, Y. (1982). Another look at definites in existentials. *Journal of Linguistics* 18, 73–88.

Index